Anonymous

Proceedings of the first meeting of the Holstein-Friesian Association of America

Anonymous

Proceedings of the first meeting of the Holstein-Friesian Association of America

ISBN/EAN: 9783743329638

Manufactured in Europe, USA, Canada, Australia, Japa

Cover: Foto ©ninafisch / pixelio.de

Manufactured and distributed by brebook publishing software (www.brebook.com)

Anonymous

Proceedings of the first meeting of the Holstein-Friesian Association of America

PROCEEDINGS OF

THE FIRST MEETING

OF THE

HOLSTEIN - FRIESIAN ASSOCIATION

OF AMERICA.

HELD AT BUFFALO, NEW YORK,

MAY 26, 1885.

ALSO, THE

BY-LAWS OF THE ASSOCIATION,

REPORT OF FIRST MEETING OF THE BOARD OF OFFICERS,

RULES REGULATING THE ADVANCED REGISTRY, AND A
LIST OF MEMBERS OF THE ASSOCIATION.

IOWA CITY, IOWA:
1885.

OFFICERS OF THE

Holstein-Friesian Association of America.

FOR 1885-6.

President,	THERON G. YEOMANS,	Walworth, N. Y.
First Vice-President,	F. W. PATTERSON, M.D., .	Locheam, Md.
Second Vice-President,	W. M. SINGERLY, .	Philadelphia, Penn.
Third Vice-President,	GEO. F. JACKSON,	Minneapolis, Minn.
Fourth Vice-President,	F. C. STEVENS,	. Attica, N. Y.
Treasurer,	W. C. BRAYTON,	Syracuse, N. Y.

Directors for Two Years.

GERRIT S. MILLER,	Peterboro, N. Y.
C. W. HORR,	Wellington, Ohio.
C. R. PAYNE,	Hamilton, N. Y.

Directors for One Year.

WING R. SMITH,	Syracuse, N. Y.
W. G. POWELL,	Springboro, Penn.
E. M. WASHBURN,	Lenox Furnace, Mass.

Superintendent of Advanced Registry,

S. HOXIE,   Whitestown, N. Y.

Secretary and Editor,

THOMAS B. WALES, JR.,   Iowa City, Iowa,

FIRST MEETING

OF THE

HOLSTEIN-FRIESIAN ASSOCIATION

OF AMERICA,

AT BUFFALO, N. Y., MAY 26, 1885.

The members of the Holstein Breeders' Association of America, and of the Dutch-Friesian Herd-Book Association of America, met together at the Genesee Hotel, Buffalo, New York, at two o'clock P. M., May 26th, 1885, to act upon the following report of the joint committee of the two associations in regard to a union:

REPORT OF COMMITTEE.

At a meeting of the joint committee of the Holstein Breeders' Association of America and the Dutch-Friesian Herd-Book Association of America, held at the Genesee, Buffalo, New York, April 16th, 1885, the following resolutions for the consolidation of the two associations were adopted unanimously by the said committees:

Resolved, That a new association shall be formed, to be called the "Holstein-Friesian Association of America;"

That the officers shall consist of one President, a First, Second, Third and Fourth Vice-Presidents, one Secretary and Editor, and six Directors, and such other officers and directors as may be provided for by the By-Laws of the association;

That in other particulars the features of the charters of the two previous associations, so far as they are similar, be incorporated in the charter of the new association;

That where there are differences between the charters of the two previous associations, we leave it to the discretion of the Committee on Legislation to adjust them;

That the obtaining of the necessary charter and legislation shall be put into the hands of a committee of four, consisting of two gentlemen belonging to the Holstein Association and two belonging to the Dutch-Friesian Association, with the instruction that they bring about this result within six weeks from

Tuesday last, and, if in so doing, they meet with legal obstacles, they be fully authorized to vary from the regulations so as to overcome those obstacles; that the committee shall consist of T. G. Yeomans, Dr. F. W. Patterson, Thomas B. Wales, Jr., and S. Hoxie;

That the same committee be instructed to recommend By-Laws, Rules and Regulations that they may deem necessary for the adoption of the new association, at the meeting to be held six weeks from Tuesday last;

That the present registration go on until after this last named meeting and the election of the officers of the new association, and cease then;

That each association turn over all funds, properties, archives and effects that remain in their possession after paying all indebtedness of their association, and that if legislation is necessary in order to enable the association to do so that the committee above referred to have the power to perfect such legislation;

That the expenses of this committee shall be paid out of the general fund;

That the new association establish a thorough system of advance registration;

That the two associations agree that no imported animals be received for registration that were shipped from Holland on or after March 18th, 1885, excepting by the payment of the fees required by the Holstein Association;

That the offspring of cattle registered in either of the present Herd-Books shall be entitled to pedigree registration in the Herd-Books of the Holstein-Friesian Association;

That our committee be instructed to procure the charter in the names of all the officers of the two present associations and of all other members of said two associations;

That we, the undersigned, pledge ourselves to use our influence with the associations to which we severally belong to procure the organization of the new association on the plan embodied in the foregoing.

[Signed]
GEORGE M. EMRICK, M.D.
WILLIAM BROWN SMITH.
T. G. YEOMANS.
M. L. SWEET.
THOMAS B. WALES, JR.
F. W. PATTERSON, M.D.
C. W. HORR.
E. R. PHILLIPS.
F. C. STEVENS.
CORNELIUS BALDWIN.
WATKINS G. POWELL.
S. HOXIE.
GEORGE F. JACKSON.
C. R. PAYNE.

PROCEEDINGS.

Mr. T. G. YEOMANS: Gentlemen, for the purpose of organizing and perfecting the union of the two societies, I will nominate for temporary Chairman, Dr. F. W. Patterson.

The motion was carried.

Dr. F. W. PATTERSON, on taking the chair, spoke as follows: Gentlemen of the society of Holstein-Friesian Breeders — I thank you for the high honor you confer upon me to-day, and I congratulate you as breeders of thoroughbred cattle, that for the first time all the interests that are vested in these cattle are to-day one. We have come together mutually, feeling for each other that respect which we have learned in years past. It is not necessary for me now to make any address to you. The object we have before us, as I understand it, is to perfect the consolidation which has been agreed upon through committees appointed by the individual associations. The joint committee met in due form and entered into an agreement. I understand the committees are ready to report. Then we will know formally as soon as they have reported that the report of the joint committee, or the action of the joint committee is ratified, and we will be ready to proceed to business.

In order to expedite proceedings, it will be best for the Secretaries to be appointed.

Mr. Thos. B. Wales, Jr., and Mr. S. Hoxie were duly elected Temporary Secretaries.

Dr. F. W. PATTERSON: Gentlemen, in order that we may act consistently, it is perhaps well for us to know in our collective capacity, the result of the action of the two associations. Of course we all know from individuals, what has been done, yet formally I would like the report of the two committees from the two associations to be made now to this body as as a whole, and to that end I will call first upon the Holstein Association, or the chairman of the committee, or Secretary, or President, to report what action has been taken to-day upon the report of the conference committee.

Mr. T. G. YEOMANS: Mr. Chairman, the action of the Holstein committee in the session this forenoon was to ratify wholly the proceedings of the joint committee and the recommendations. I thought a committee had been appointed to advise your association, and to notify the President of your association, transmitting the reports.

Dr. F. W. PATTERSON: Is the committee appointed by the Dutch-Friesian Association ready to report?

Mr. IRWIN LANGWORTHY: Mr. Chairman, in behalf of the Dutch-Friesian Association, I offer the following resolution, which was offered by Mr. E. R. Phillips, of Michigan:

Resolved, That we adopt the basis of union proposed by the joint committee of the Holstein Association, and the Dutch-Friesian Herd-Book Association; that we approve of the action of the committee as to uniting the membership of both associations; and that we accept and adopt that charter so far as it is possible for us to do in our capacity as a separate organization.

Dr. F. W. PATTERSON: I see it is very plain the two associations have ratified, so far as in their power, the action of the two associations, or of the joint committee. That committee put before the legislature of New York a charter to be passed for the organization of the new Holstein-Friesian Association. The resolutions have ratified that. I would like to have that charter read in order that we may intelligently know how to proceed in the future.

The Secretary read to the meeting the charter:

CHAPTER 333.

AN ACT TO INCORPORATE THE HOLSTEIN-FRIESIAN ASSOCIATION OF AMERICA.

PASSED May 25, 1885; three-fifths being present.

The People of the State of New York, represented in Senate and Assembly, do enact as follows:

SECTION 1. Theron G. Yeomans, William M. Singerly, William C. Brayton, Thomas B. Wales, Jr., Gerrit S. Miller, Frederick C. Stevens, Wing R. Smith, J. D. Guthrie, Frederick L. Houghton, Francis W. Patterson, Wayne Macveagh, G. M. Emrick, George F. Jackson, H. H. Hatch, William H. Hemmingway, Daniel D. Durnall, Irwin Langworthy, John B. Tuckerman, Charles R. Payne, Robert Burch, E. R. Phillips, Solomon Hoxie, and all other members of the present "Holstein Breeders' Association of America," and "The Dutch-Friesian Herd-Book Association of America," and all other persons at any time hereafter duly associated as provided by the By-Laws with, or succeeding them, under and for the purposes of this charter and act of incorporation, are hereby organized and constituted a body corporate and are a corporation under and by the name of the "Holstein-Friesian Associa'ion of America," for the purpose of improving the breed of Holstein-Friesian cattle; ascertaining, preserving and disseminating, as provided by its By-Laws, all useful information and facts as to their pedigrees and desirable qualities, and the distinguishing characteristics of the best specimens, and preparing, publishing and supplying all necessary volumes of the Holstein-Friesian Herd-Book; and generally for promoting and securing the best interests of the importers, breeders and owners of said cattle, and thereby the public generally; and for the purposes and to attain the objects aforesaid, said corporation is hereby given all necessary power, authority and rights, including the powers, and subject to the liabilities prescribed by title three, chapter eighteen, part one of the Revised Statutes.

SEC. 2. The officers of said association shall be a President and four Vice-Presidents, to be designated as first, second, third and fourth, one Secretary and Editor, six Directors, and such other officers as may be provided for by the By-Laws of this association; and said officers shall respectively perform the duties imposed upon them by the By-Laws. Said officers shall be elected by ballot from and by its members at its first meeting, and thereafter at its annual meeting to be held on the third Wednesday of March, of each and every year, in the city of Buffalo, at its place of business, or other convenient time or place fixed by the By-Laws and duly designated by the Secretary in his notice by mail to members of such meeting.

SEC. 3. Said corporation shall issue its certificate of membership signed by its President and Secretary and sealed with its corporate seal, to each of its lawful members, which certificate shall not be transferable, and shall be evidence of membership, and shall entitle its owner, while a member in good standing, to vote personally, or by proxy, at its meetings, and to all the privileges and advantages of such membership. But said corporation may cancel any certificate and forfeit and terminate any membership, and all rights and privileges arising therefrom, for his willful disobedience or evasion of its By-Laws, or other rules and regulations, and for any wrongs committed by him against said corporation or its property, interest or rights; which forfeiture and eviction shall be cumulative to any other legal remedy said corporation may have against such evicted member.

SEC. 4. Said corporation may hold such other meetings, in addition to said annual meeting, and said annual meetings may be held at such other places than Buffalo, as provided by its By-Laws.

SEC. 5. The By-Laws of said corporation shall be made and adopted by a majority of its members voting personally, or by proxy, at the first regular meeting held under the provisions of this act. Said By-Laws may be altered, amended or repealed at any annual meeting by a like vote of its members.

SEC. 6. At the first regular meeting of said corporation, its members shall agree upon and adopt its corporate seal.

SEC. 7. All property, rights and interests of said "Holstein Breeders' Association of America," and "The Dutch-Friesian Herd-Book Association of America," of every name or nature, shall, by virtue of this act, vest in and become the property of this corporation.

SEC. 8. No debts or pecuniary obligations shall be incurred by this corporation except duly authorized by a previous two-thirds vote of all its members.

SEC. 9. Upon the organization of this association and election of its officers in pursuance of this act, the associations formed under chapters four hundred and forty-seven of the laws of eighteen hundred and eighty, and two hundred and seven of the laws of eighteen hundred and eighty-two, shall cease to exist.

SEC. 10. This act shall take effect immediately.

STATE OF NEW YORK,
OFFICE OF THE SECRETARY OF STATE, } ss.:

I have compared the preceding with the original law on file in this office, and do hereby certify that the same is a correct transcript therefrom and of the whole of said original law.

JOSEPH B. CARR,
Secretary of State.

Dr. F. W. PATTERSON: Gentlemen of the association, upon reading this last section, "upon the organization of this association and election of its officers in pursuance of this act, the associations formed under chapter 447 of the laws of 1880 and 207 of the laws of 1882 shall cease to exist," in order to complete the ratification of the action of this committee and form a new association, the first business in hand is the election of officers, and on the election of officers depends and hinges all our future proceedings. Therefore, the chair is ready to entertain the question of the election of officers.

Mr. J. D. GUTHRIE: First comes the question of the charter.

Dr. F. W. PATTERSON: The election of officers ratifies the charter in so many words.

A motion was made and carried that a committee of five from each former association be appointed for the nomination of officers.

The chair appointed the following committee: W. B. Smith, G. S. Miller, F. C. Stevens, C. W. Horr, H. E. Boardman, S. Burchard, G. F. Jackson, W. I. Phillips, Irwin Langworthy, and Mr. Wheeler.

An informal recess was taken until the report of the committee should be presented, and the meeting was afterwards called to order by the chairman.

Dr. F. W. PATTERSON: It has been suggested that we have some business to transact now. It can be gone through with without the committee. As soon as the committee on nominations report, the question of voting will be moved.

A motion was made to appoint a committee of five to examine proxies.

Mr. J. W. STILLWELL: Before that motion is acted upon, I desire to say a few words. There is a question in the minds of a great many of us here at this meeting to-day whether any proxies can be used at this meeting or not — whether a proxy is valid that has been given for an organization that does not exist. A good many of us think the officers of this association should be elected by the members of the association that are here.

Mr. W. M. SINGERLY: The proxies were given in contemplation of this new association coming into existence.

A Member: I happen to know that some of the proxies given in the Holstein Breeders' Association were intended by those who have them not only to cover the meeting of the Holstein Association, but also the combined meeting of the new association.

Mr. W. G. POWELL: The charter provides for that, I think.

Secretary reads: "The By-Laws of said corporation shall be made and adopted by a majority of its members voting personally, or by proxy, at the first regular meeting held under the provisions of this act. Said By-Laws may be altered, amended or repealed at any annual meeting by like vote of its members."

A Member: Does not that refer to the first meeting after this has been adopted — and this constitution has been adopted — by the association? If I mistake not, it does.

Mr. J. D. GUTHRIE: The same question might arise whether anybody had the right or not. According to the argument produced by the gentleman, it is no organization. The proxies given were intended to cover that point, and if my proxy has no right to vote on this question, then I have not.

The Chairman: The Secretary will call the roll and the gentlemen can report their proxies.

Mr. ISAAC C. OTIS: It seems to me we can perfect no organization according to your decision until this committee report. When this committee have reported, we have accepted the charter. We cannot act under that charter until it is accepted.

The Chairman: The election of officers makes the acceptance or completes the organization. We have informally ratified the whole thing. Now, to complete the legal organization, we are to elect officers. Then comes the question how we are to elect officers and who are to vote for officers.

Mr. ISAAC C. OTIS: We cannot do anything until we have elected officers.

A Member: This is for the purpose of gathering in the proxies so that when the time comes we can decide on them.

The respective Secretaries called the rolls of the former associations, showing to be present in person, sixty-six members, and by attorney, one hundred and fifty-five; in all, two hundred and twenty-one members.

A motion was made that a committee of three be appointed to examine the proxies, and the chairman appointed as such committee, Messrs. Lamb, Singerly, and Wheeler.

Mr. S. HOXIE: I wish to refer to the matter of membership of the two Associations. According to our former rules we received honorary members to all the privileges of the association, except voting. As I understand it the Holstein Association received honorary members, and gave them the privilege of voting. Now, why ought not our honorary members have the privilege of voting in this new association, so as not to have two classes of members? If the honorary members of the Holstein Association have all the rights and privileges of the whole association, our honorary members should have as a matter of equity and justice.

Mr. J. D. GUTHRIE: I think under the new association we ought to make no rules permitting that privilege. If the honorary members have been voting in our association, they have not been voting in this.

Dr. E. LEWIS STURTEVANT: I am an honorary member, and I do not think an honorary member would desire to vote. He is not the owner of these cattle, and I do not think he has any justifiable right to vote. I think it would better satisfy the honorary members not to have the privilege of voting, if there is any question about it.

Mr. C. W. HORR: I think it is a matter of legal construction. Our charter stipulates who have the right to organize. It is for our chairman to construe that as to whether that includes or excludes honorary members, and any gentleman may appeal from his judgment.

The Chairman: My own opinion is this, judging from the course pursued in the Dutch-Friesian Association, where it was stipulated, that a man, though he is a member, could not vote unless he is the owner of cattle, that they ought not to vote. Honorary members are ordinarily men who are noted for their taste and knowledge, and the advantage they have been to cattle breeders, and most of them are not owners of cattle. I should therefore decide that no man, though he may be an honorary member of either association, can vote at this preliminary organization, unless he is the owner of cattle. If any one desires to appeal from the decision, I will put the question.

Mr. S. HOXIE: I certainly do not want any appeal. I simply wanted it discussed and decided.

The report of the Committee on Nominations was announced.

Mr. SMITH: Mr. Chairman, your Committee on Nominations have had considerable on hand and have tried to consider all sides, the different localities, etc., and they finally arrived at the conclusion which our Secretary will be kind enough to read.

The Secretary read as follows:

"Your Committee on Nominations respectfully present the following names, for officers of the Holstein-Friesian Association:

President,	T. G. YEOMANS.
First Vice-President,	Dr. F. W. PATTERSON.
Second Vice-President,	W. M. SINGERLY.
Third Vice-President,	GEORGE F. JACKSON.
Fourth Vice-President,	F. C. STEVENS.

FOR DIRECTORS.

G. S. MILLER, two years.	WING R. SMITH, one year.
C. W. HORR, two years.	M. L. SWEET, one year.
C. R. PAYNE, two years.	E. M. WASHBURN, one year.
For Secretary and Editor,	THOMAS B. WALES, Jr.
For Treasurer,	W. C. BRAYTON."

The report was accepted.

A motion was made that the chairman be instructed to cast the ballot of the association for Mr. T. G. Yeomans for President.

The motion was carried.

Dr. F. W. PATTERSON: Gentlemen of the association, I have the pleasure to announce the vote of this association for President is unanimously for Mr. T. G. Yeomans. I therefore declare Mr. T. G. Yeomans President of this permanent organization. I have the honor to introduce to you Mr. T. G. Yeomans, President of the Holstein-Friesian Association.

Mr. T. G. YEOMANS: Gentlemen, I thank you sincerely for this expression of your confidence; it is more gratifying to me as signalizing the cementing of the two organizations into one association. I had the pleasure of serving only for a few days — only for a day, I might say, because since my election to the Presidency of the Holstein Association I had no opportunity of serving until to-day. But it is a greater pleasure since the interests of these joint associations have seemed to be so harmoniously united. The action of your joint committee several weeks since at this place gave me the assurance, as I trust it did all others who attended upon the meetings of that committee, that this joint organization would be accomplished harmoniously. The fact that it has been accomplished in this very agreeable and harmonious manner gives the greatest assurance that the result will be successful and prosperity will attend our efforts for the attainment of the objects of the association. I am fully satisfied that every interest of every member of both associations will be promoted by this union. I am unable to see how any individual member of either association can feel otherwise than friendly to the union which is about to be consummated here to-day.

I think most of us who have given much attention to the breed of cattle which this organization is intended to promote and propagate have felt a growing interest in that breed of cattle; I believe that most of us have been surprised in finding the development of those animals in production, not only of milk, but of butter. It has been long conceded by all parties that had any knowledge of this breed of cattle that they were great milkers. It is beginning to be understood that they are the greatest of all butter-makers. There can be no question on this point, I think, on the part of those who have investigated that part of the subject thoroughly.

I will not occupy your attention by any further remarks. I will await your pleasure in regard to the further proceedings of this organization.

Mr. ELON G. FAY: I now move that the President of the association be instructed to cast the vote of this meeting for the balance of the ticket reported by the committee.

On motion, Mr. Thomas B. Wales, Jr., and Mr. S. Hoxie were appointed tellers.

Mr. E. G. FAY: I renew my motion that the President cast the vote for the other officers.

An amendment was proposed that the tellers be instructed to take the votes by ballot from individuals.

Mr. W. R. SMITH: I think this is a bad precedent to establish — not that I have any special objection to the ticket; I may have and I may not. I have several proxies on which I have been instructed to vote in certain ways. I think we ought to vote for each individual officer.

Mr. J. W. STILLWELL: I cannot see why there should be any objection now to the President or some individual casting the ballot for this whole ticket. I must acknowledge that I do not see what we have come here for and have our proxies for, if there is nobody that can be put in nomination except by the five men who bring in a ticket which we must swallow whether we want to or not.

Mr. W. R. SMITH: The By-Laws specify the way in which the vote shall be cast.

Dr. F. W. PATTERSON: The report of the committee is not conclusive. Any gentleman of the association has the privilege of nominating a candidate for any of the officers to be elected. (The amendment proposed by Mr. W. R. Smith was carried, and then the preceding motion as amended was adopted.)

The President: The chair is of opinion we cannot proceed to ballot until the Committee on Proxies have reported.

Mr. EDGAR HUIDEKOPER: I move the President cast a ballot for Mr. F. W. Patterson as First Vice-President of this association.

Adopted, and Dr. F. W. Patterson declared elected First Vice-President.

Mr. ISAAC C. OTIS: I move the President cast the vote of the association for Mr. W. M. Singerly for Second Vice-President.

Mr. W. R. SMITH: Mr. President, Mr. Singerly knows very well that I shall vote for him with the greatest pleasure, so I think this is a good opportunity to explain my position. I want to say right here that I do not think it is a good idea to proceed in this manner. Some of us are doing simply what we voted we would not do. This is not giving a member an opportunity to vote against any one that may be nominated. We may be in favor of all the ticket and we may not. This is establishing a precedent which I think is bad. I am compelled to call for the ayes and noes on that question.

A Member: As long as we have only one name suggested, I do not see the necessity of quibbling over this nonsense. It seems to me a mere quibble to occupy the valuable time of this whole meeting in this way. If anybody wishes to nominate some one else, let them name them.

Further discussion was here suspended to receive the report of the Committee on Proxies.

The report showed one hundred and fifty-six proxies in the list accepted by the committee.

The President: On consultation with the chairman of the committee, I will say that the Committee on Proxies are not yet prepared to report. They have not got their report in form.

The report of the Committee on Proxies was received and corrected.

The President: I will say to the members of the association, that whilst the Committee upon Nominations have presented their report in full, it does not preclude any individual member or any number from presenting the names of other candidates for any of the offices. It is entirely proper before proceeding to ballot, for any member to propose any name for any one of the offices, either substitute it for the name presented or placing it in opposition to the other.

Mr. EDGAR HUIDEKOPER: It is very unpleasant to make a nomination in opposition to a report handed in. Now, take this course, for instance, take a list of directors, if any one wishes to nominate any one man, or two men, or any number of men on the Board of Directors outside of that list as handed in by the committee, he has the privilege of nominating any name as a Director simply. The three men who obtain the highest number of votes among all the nominees, should be the men to hold the office for the two years. The next three should hold the position as Directors for one year. That obviates the unpleasantness of nominating a man in opposition to any particular name.

The President: The suggestion is a good one, but under the report of the committee, they report these specific names, and it would change that somewhat, but if you were taking one at a time of course, the highest on each ballot would receive the nomination.

Mr. J. W. STILLWELL: I think the officers should be divided between the two associations also, and that they should be equally distributed geographically. I do not think it is proper, just or fair, although the proxies of the people of the west and southwest are principally held by eastern men. You may go and do the same thing that was done at Chicago, and leave the west out entirely, which made us feel very sore. We had no representative on the Board of the Holstein Breeders' Association; and by a scratch we have got one man now in the central part of the state. I think it would be nothing more than just and right that these officers should be scattered along from Iowa to Massachusetts, and from Tennessee to Michigan or Wisconsin.

Mr. ISAAC C. OTIS: While it may be proper and right to do that, it would be rather impracticable if they wanted to call a meeting of the Board of Directors to get them together from Iowa and Massachusetts, and Tennessee and Michigan. While, if they were located in some locality nearer together, they might be got together.

Mr. C. W. HORR: In order to follow out the suggestion, I will put in nomination a worthy brother of the Holstein-Friesian Association, Thomas M. Spofford, of Pulaski, Tennessee. I think the south is deserving a worthy representative. They have a large interest in that section of the country, and I think it is no more than right, as he is a young man full of vim and ability and a good breeder. I hope he will be one of the Directors for two years.

Mr. T. M. SPOFFORD: Permit me to thank my friend for his kindly expressed opinion of me, but I appreciate fully the weight of the remarks that Mr. Otis has just made, my long distance from this state, which would render it almost impossible to discharge the duties of the office. I must therefore decline the nomination, with many thanks for the zeal of my friend.

Mr. GERRIT S. MILLER: As a member of the nominating committee, I will say that we considered in regard to localities, and if Mr. Stillwell or anybody interested will examine it, he will see that we represent Iowa, Michigan, Illinois, New York, Massachusetts, and Minnesota.

Mr. J. W. STILLWELL: I fail to see where there is any man nominated from the south.

Mr. GERRIT S. MILLER: Our First Vice-President is from Maryland.

Mr. EDGAR HUIDEKOPER: I will nominate Mr. J. D. Guthrie for Director.

The President: Properly if you are taking them in the order in which they are presented by the committee, we are acting in reference to Vice-President at present.

A Member: Is not all this out of order? Haven't we passed a resolution to confer the right upon the chair to appoint a committee to make nominations? Now, that resolution has been passed; the chair acted accordingly. The nominations have been made. Now, unless that resolution and that vote are rescinded, can they go on and make other nominations? It seems to me that must be rescinded first.

The President: The chair is of opinion the committee having made nominations does not preclude any individual from making nominations. They have presented the nominations they thought would be acceptable to the association, but it does not preclude the association from changing that in any manner they see fit.

Mr. F. C. STEVENS: Taking you on your own statement, I think my friend, Mr. Hill, is in order. You said that he could make nominations for any office that he sees fit, and he has made a nomination for Director, and you ruled him out on the ground that we are now considering the question of Vice-President.

The President: I think you will see that a fair construction of my expression would be that as we come to the nominees for the different offices, that is in the order of the time; but I do not think it will be in order to take some one from the bottom of the list.

Mr. S. HOXIE: It seems to me we have mixed two methods of election together. There are two forms for the election of officers, one by a nominating committee and another by individual nominations. The method of procedure in individual nominations is first to take an informal ballot. Then the men are put in nomination, and you take your formal ballot. Now, it seems to me you are mixing it up, and it is going to take a great deal of valuable time, and perhaps not result in a satisfactory conclusion in the end.

A Member: Of course the committee was appointed by the chair. That was the expression of the meeting. They reported a list of officers for election. The motion was made to accept the report of the committee. That was, that the officers were agreeable to the association.

Dr. F. W. PATTERSON: If the gentleman will pardon me, I will announce what my decision was. It was simply accepting the report of the committee. We had just accepted their services. Then we were to take further action hereafter. We did not accept what the committee had done.

Mr. WING R. SMITH: Mr. Chairman, in regard to the question of proxies, I believe it is a conceded fact that there are not enough members here altogether without the use of the proxies to constitute a meeting. We have proxies enough among the members to make a majority. In order to conduct the business properly, the majority must rule. I do not understand how it is that you propose to throw out by a minority vote the proxies which constitute the majority.

The President: The chair is of the opinion that we cannot proceed any further with balloting until the committee reports.

Mr. E. G. FAY: In order to see if we can expedite matters a little, I would move that it is the sense of this meeting that unless some other person is put in nomination for the office of Second Vice-President, that the gentleman who called for the ayes and nays on the question be requested to withdraw that motion; and I move as the sense of this meeting that the meeting request the gentleman who called for the ayes and nays on the question to instruct the President to cast the vote for Mr. W. M. Singerly as Second Vice-President of this association.

Mr. WING R. SMITH: I have a proxy instructing me to vote for one man representing the Holstein Association for one office and the Dutch-Friesian Association for another office. Now, I have no opportunity to do anything of that kind by this method. I insist on the ayes and nays.

The President: The Secretary now has the report of the Committee on Proxies, which may be referred to at any time when the count is taken.

The balloting was proceeded with, and the following officers were duly elected:

For Second Vice-President,	W. M. SINGERLY.
For Third Vice-President,	GEORGE F. JACKSON.
For Fourth Vice-President,	F. C. STEVENS.

FOR DIRECTORS.

G. S. MILLER, two years.	WING R. SMITH, one year.
C. W. HORR, two years.	W. G. POWELL, one year.
C. R. PAYNE, two years.	E. M. WASHBURN, one year.
For Secretary and Editor,	THOMAS B. WALES, Jr.
For Treasurer,	W. C. BRAYTON.

Mr. J. D. GUTHRIE: I move that when this association finally adjourns, that we adjourn to meet at Cleveland, Ohio. It is a long way to come here from Iowa, from Tennessee, and from Missouri. We in the west have been giving our proxies to eastern men, and you have been voting to carry us wherever you please. We have only had one western meeting in six or seven years.

Mr. WING R. SMITH: As I have told Mr. Guthrie, in private conversation, my opinion is, if he were to investigate, he would find that a very large majority, four-fifths at least of the Holstein-Friesian Association will be found east of the west line of New York. But in deference to the gentlemen of the association who are in the west and south, and whose feelings I can appreciate, I second Mr. Guthrie's motion.

The motion was carried.

The President: Gentlemen, you have now elected your officers, and so far completed the organization.

I congratulate you from the bottom of my heart that the thing is an accomplished fact, and I announce to you the death of the Holstein Association of America and the Dutch-Friesian Association, and I announce also the birth of that young child, the Holstein-Friesian Association of America; it has already been christened, and it bids fair to grow and to be one of the strongest associations in America.

We have some other work to do to carry out your ideas, such as the completion of the By-Laws and adoption of rules, etc.

A motion was made to adjourn until 7:30 this evening, which was carried.

PROCEEDINGS, 7:30 P. M., May 26, 1885.

PRESIDENT YEOMANS: Gentlemen, the first thing in order is to look into the By-Laws, and if it is desired, the Secretary will read the report of the committee that had charge of that arrangement. The joint committee that met here some six weeks ago for the two associations, appointed a sub-committee, consisting of Dr. F. W. Patterson, Mr. Thomas B. Wales, Jr., Mr. S. Hoxie, and myself to prepare, in the rough, something in the form of By-Laws to present for the consideration of the new association. The Secretary will proceed to read, by sections, for the consideration of the association.

The Secretary read "By-Laws proposed by the joint committee of the Holstein and Dutch-Friesian Associations, for adoption by the Holstein-Friesian Association of America."

ARTICLE I. OF MEMBERSHIP.

SECTION 1. "Any person of good character, who is a citizen of North America, interested in the breeding of Holstein-Friesian cattle, and the owner of such, may apply for membership in this corporation by filing a written or printed application, in such form as the Board of Officers may prescribe, with the Secretary, with the membership fee of one hundred dollars. The form of application for membership shall give the applicant's name in full, his residence and post-office address, and such other particulars as the Board of Officers may require."

Adopted.

SEC. 2. "Every application for membership shall be submitted to the consideration of the Board of Officers, and if, in their judgment, the applicant is eligible for membership, and ought to be admitted as a member of this corporation, and a unanimous vote of the Board of Officers present to that effect is passed, his name shall be entered on the record as a member, and the Secretary shall issue a certificate of membership to him."

Adopted.

SEC. 3. "Any member of the corporation may at any time withdraw and terminate his membership, by returning his certificate of membership to the Secretary, with a letter expressing his wish and intention to terminate his membership."

Adopted.

SEC. 4. "Any member of this corporation who shall be found guilty of any misrepresentation, deception, or fraud in relation to the registry of animals in the Holstein-Friesian Herd-Book, shall forfeit his membership in the corporation."

Adopted.

SEC. 5. "Each member of the corporation shall be entitled to one copy of each volume of the Herd-Book published after his admission, which shall be forwarded to his address as soon as convenient after its publication."

Mr. WING R. SMITH: I do not know whether I am right in speaking about it, but I think inasmuch as they pay one hundred dollars admission fee, that for the present at least they ought to have the whole set of volumes of the Herd-Books—I mean a man just starting in. I don't think we should oblige him to pay a dollar or two dollars and a half a volume.

Dr. F. W. PATTERSON: There is one thing to be considered; we are working not only for to-day, but for years to come. The time will come when we will have a great many volumes. When we made this draft of By-Laws, we were looking into the future, and considering the large number of volumes which will ultimately be produced.

Mr. WING R. SMITH: I do not make any motion about it. I don't know whether I care for it. I simply wanted it brought up.

The section was adopted.

ARTICLE II. OF THE OFFICERS.

SECTION 1. "The officers of this corporation shall consist of a President and four Vice-Presidents, to be designated as first, second, third and fourth, one Secretary and Editor, one Treasurer, and six Directors, who shall constitute the Board of Officers of this corporation. There shall be three Directors elected at the first meeting for the term of one year, and three for the term of two years. Thereafter at each annual meeting there shall be three Directors elected to serve for the term of two years. The Board of Officers shall appoint inspectors of imported cattle with power to remove for cause and to fill vacancies."

Adopted.

SEC. 2. "The Board of Officers of this corporation, as a Board, shall have and take the entire control and management of its affairs and business, with full power and authority to do what they deem proper and best for its interest, provided that they shall have no authority to contract a debt or obligation against the corporation beyond its current expenses. And in such case, not beyond the amount of cash in the treasury, and that nothing shall be done which is not in accordance with the purpose and spirit of the charter and By-Laws."

Adopted.

SEC. 3. "At any meeting of the Board of Officers, which is duly called, a majority of its members shall constitute a quorum for business."

Adopted.

SEC. 4. "A legal meeting of the Board of Officers of this corporation may be held at any time and place, when and where all the members of the Board are present together and agree to hold a meeting, and all votes and acts done at such meeting shall have the same validity and effect as they could have if passed and done at a regularly called meeting."

Adopted.

SEC. 5. "A meeting of the Board of Officers shall be held on the day of the annual meeting of the members, and a meeting may be called by the President or Secretary, or by any —"

Mr. WING R. SMITH: I would suggest, as an amendment, that in order to call a meeting, a majority of the members of the Board should join instead of any two members of the Board.

Mr. T. B. WALES, Jr.: The President has the power and the Secretary has the power to call a meeting. I think the suggestion is a proper one, that it require a majority of the Board to call a meeting.

Dr. F. W. PATTERSON: I should be inclined to have it a majority of the Board, exclusive of the President or Secretary, because if either of them join, it would be sufficient.

Mr. S. HOXIE: I would suggest that it be called by the President or Secretary, or a majority of the Directors. It strikes me that would be judicious. I will move to amend by inserting "a majority of the Directors" instead of "by any two members of the Board."

The amendment was adopted. Section 5, as amended, was adopted.

SEC. 6. "Notice calling special meetings of the Board of Officers shall be given by the person calling the meeting, in writing, setting forth the date and place of meeting, and the purpose or purposes for which the meeting is to be held, and no other business than that specified in the notice shall be acted on, unless all the members of the Board of Officers are present."

Mr. EDGAR HUIDEKOPER: It seems to me that provides for no business except that specified in the call, to be acted on.

Mr. C. W. HORR: There might be some special matter come up, some incidental matter, which it would be proper to act upon.

Dr. F. W. PATTERSON: The effort is made, if there should be any special meeting, to prevent any undue legislation. Care must be taken of that; and unless the full Board are present, they cannot take up any new matter, otherwise a minority Board might possibly get something through that would be difficult to get rid of.

Section 6 was then adopted.

SEC. 7. "Members of the Board of Officers cannot vote by proxy at meetings of the Board, but any member of the Board who cannot attend a duly called meeting, may address a letter to the Board of Officers, in which he may discuss the purpose or purposes for which the meeting is called, and state how he will vote on the question or questions which may come before the meeting under the notice, and such letter and such votes shall be read in the meeting, and the votes shall be counted and have the same effect as they would if the member was personally present and voted."

Adopted.

SEC. 8. "All notices or calls for meetings of the Board of Officers shall be recorded at length in the Record-Book of the corporation, and the substance of all letters from members of the Board, containing votes on matters set forth in the notice calling the meeting, shall also be recorded; and such letters shall be kept on file, and all proceedings had and votes passed at meetings of the Board of Officers shall be fully set forth and recorded in the Record-Book."

Adopted.

SEC. 9. "The President shall preside at all meetings of the members of the corporation, and all meetings of the Board of Officers, when he is present; and when he is absent or unable to perform the duties of the office, the Vice-President shall act in his stead. The president shall sign all certificates of membership which may be issued."

Mr. C. W. HORR: I would suggest the words "a Vice-President" instead of "the Vice-President."

Amendment accepted and section 9 adopted.

SEC. 10. "The Treasurer shall be the custodian of cash, funds and securities belonging to the corporation, and shall deposit, invest, or otherwise dispose of the same, as the Board of Officers may direct. He shall give a bond with sureties to the satisfaction of the Board of Officers, when required to do so by them."

Mr. J. D. GUTHRIE: Is that right, "that the Treasurer shall invest?" He might make very injudicious investments.

Mr. THOS. B. WALES, Jr.: This is under the direction of the Board, sir. I would suggest one change in this matter, that the words "when required to do so by them" be left off, making it to read, "he shall give a bond with sureties to the satisfaction of the Board of Officers," making it compulsory for him to give it.

The amendment was accepted, and section 10 then adopted.

SEC. 11. "The Secretary shall be the corresponding and recording officer of the corporation, and shall receive and attend to, and dispose of, as the charter and By-Laws require, all applications for membership in the corporation, all applications for registry of animals in the Herd-Book, and all applications for transfer registry of animals in the Herd-Book, and shall sign and issue all certificates of membership and registry, and of transfer registry, and shall keep a record of all such certificates issued."

Mr. THOS. B. WALES, Jr.: Mr. President, I think it is proper for the Secretary to be given authority to purchase, as he may think proper, books and stationery, pay the office rent, etc., of the association. Under these By-Laws he has no authority whatever. I would suggest we add this clause, "he is authorized to expend such sums as he may find necessary for the carrying on of the business of the association.

Amendment accepted; section 11 then adopted as amended.

SEC. 12. "He shall edit and publish the Herd-Book at such times and in such form as the Board of Officers may direct."

Adopted.

SEC. 13. "He shall issue notices of the time and place of the annual meeting of the members of the corporation, and of special meetings of the members which the Board of Officers may order to be called; but no amendments to the charter or By-Laws shall be proposed or made at any meeting, either annual or special, unless thirty days' notice has been given by the secretary in the call for such meeting."

Mr. C. W. Horr: I think it should be "except at an annual meeting." Why should we tie our hands in that way? I do not see why, at our regular annual meeting, we should be tied up. I move that it be made to read, "except at the annual meeting."

Mr. Fred. L. Houghton: These By-Laws constitute every rule of our action, and consequently they are the basis of all acts of the association. It seems to me very necessary that they be upon the firmest basis, and not subject to change at short notice, or anything that may be called up in any meeting. Some unadvisable measure may be called up at the annual meeting and pushed through hastily without consideration. I think the By-Laws should not be subject to amendment unless full notice has been given in the call for the meeting at which such amendment is to be brought up. It is the basis of our whole organization, and should be carefully protected.

Mr. J. D. Guthrie: It has no reference to a change of By-Laws. They have no power to call the meeting at present — to call a meeting as it reads now. I think they should have that power in case of emergency, which the Board of Directors should arrange. With that By-Law reading as it does now, we should have no power.

Mr. Wing R. Smith: Oh, yes, you can, by the Secretary giving thirty days' notice, but in that notice you must state what amendments are to be made to the By-Laws. I think it is perfectly proper. We should not amend these things without due consideration, and you cannot consider it in much less than thirty days.

Mr. Thos. B. Wales, Jr.: I would move that we insert after the word "notice" the words, "of such proposed amendments," reading, then, "but no amendments to the charter or By-Laws shall be proposed or made at any meeting, either annual or special, unless thirty days' notice of such proposed amendments has been given by the Secretary in the call for such meeting."

Mr. E. G. Fay: I would like to inquire whether, if any member of the association should desire to have some change made in the By-Laws or charter, the Secretary would be under obligation to incline that in his notice?

The Chairman: Yes, sir; that is the understanding.

Mr. C. W. Horr: Of course all we want is to do the wisest thing we can. I quite see the force of the remarks the gentleman makes, that the amendment should be well considered and digested. At the same time we have all assembled here without notice, and are adopting all our By-Laws in perhaps one brief session, and yet you are not willing to allow us to make a slight modification at a subsequent annual meeting, which will be more largely attended.

The Chairman: The chair will correct the last gentleman. We have all had thirty days' notice of what we intended to give. The By-Laws are part of the organization.

Mr. C. W. Horr: I received no notice of the character of the By-Laws.

The Chairman: No; but it embraces the whole basis of the organization. At the meeting of the joint committee, which was more than thirty days ago, this meeting was appointed to be held more than thirty days later, in order that the thirty days' notice required under the rule should be given.

Mr. C. W. HORR: What we want — and especially Mr. F. L. Houghton and myself — is to avoid a chance for a technical dispute. As that reads now, it seems to me too strong. You come here under the notice that you are going to propose an amendment to the By-Laws. It seems to me, as that reads now, you cannot vary that at all. The exact proposed amendment must be adopted or nothing. When we get together we will have our hands tied.

Mr. WING R. SMITH: This is the point I make: There are thirty days' notice to be given of the proposed amendment, giving thirty days to digest it and think up some other form, so you can correspond with your neighbors or see your friends, and you have a right to suggest any modification of it, if you know that any such thing is to happen.

A Member: Strike out the word "such," and I think that would meet the objection.

Mr. J. D. GUTHRIE: I think this can be easily remedied by inserting that no amendment of the By-Laws shall be made unless it be at an annual meeting of the association.

Mr. S. HOXIE: As I understand it now, it requires that the precise amendment shall be accepted or rejected. We may want the substance of it, but not in that form. I think the suggestion of Mr. Horr is a good one. We can put in some other form, although it embraces the subject matter.

The Chairman: It seems to me it is quite as important that we protect the action of our annual meetings as any other meeting. We find from experience that only a limited number of our association — and I guess it is so with our neighbors — have attended in person. Now, if notice of the proposed amendments is given thirty days before, gentlemen sending proxies can instruct their attorneys in what manner to represent them. I think it safer to give the notice that the section of the clause provides for.

Mr. C. W. HORR: So do I; but I think it should be that we need not give notice of the precise amendment, so that after we get here we cannot pass a proper amendment, such as would meet the views of the meeting.

The Secretary read the section again, leaving out the word "such."

Mr. S. HOXIE: I move to amend by inserting after the words "thirty days' notice" the words, "of the substance of the proposed amendments."

Dr. F. W. PATTERSON: I move an amendment there striking out the words "shall be proposed or." I will read it as I propose to have it. "But no amendments to the charter or By-Laws made at any meeting, either annual or special, unless thirty days' notice," etc. For instance, I may give notice or make a proposition that I will call up at our next meeting the amendment. It will be giving you all the more notice of such action, and it strikes me by striking out that word, that you allow such a proposition to be made.

Mr. WING R. SMITH: You do not want to strike out the words "shall be."

Dr. F. W. PATTERSON: That is so. Strike out simply the words "proposed or," allowing anybody to propose any amendments at any meeting, to be acted on at the next meeting, so that we have a right to propose something for future action.

Mr. E. G. FAY: I move its adoption, with both of the amendments proposed.

Section 13 adopted as amended.

SEC. 14. "He shall issue notices of meetings of the Board of Officers, when requested to do so by the President, or by a majority of the Directors."

Dr. F. W. PATTERSON: That will have to be amended to correspond with the previous amendment by inserting, "a majority of the Directors," instead of "two members of the Board."

Adopted as amended.

SEC. 15. "He shall record all notices of meetings in the Record-Book of the corporation, and certify therein that they were issued and sent in accordance with the provisions of the By-Laws."

Adopted.

SEC. 16. "He shall keep full and correct records of all the meetings of the corporation and of the Board of Officers, at which he is present, and when he is absent, a Secretary, *pro tem.*, shall be chosen to attend to and perform the duties of the Secretary."

Adopted.

SEC. 17. "He shall keep an accurate account in detail of all moneys received and paid out by him in the performance of his duties, a copy of which he shall transmit to the Treasurer once in each quarter year, during the first month of the quarter."

Mr. W. G. POWELL: I wish to make one suggestion in regard to that. We have now a Secretary who we all know to be perfectly reliable and perfectly responsible. I think this would be a good time to add that he also shall give a bond satisfactory to the Board, same as the Treasurer does. In this present instance, we know that none is required; but would it not be proper to have this proposition inserted now so as to provide for the emergencies of the future?

Mr. THOS. B. WALES, Jr.: If Mr. Powell will put his amendment in writing, so that it can be inserted as an additional clause, I will very gladly second the motion.

Mr. W. G. POWELL: My motion is to add to section 17, "and shall give a bond satisfactory to the Board of Officers."

The amendment was adopted.

SEC. 18. "The Secretary and Treasurer shall receive an annual salary, the amount to be fixed by the Board of Officers, at their last meeting after the annual meeting."

Mr. WING R. SMITH: I would like to ask whether that is before they have accomplished their work or not?

The Secretary: This contemplates the fixing of the salaries for the ensuing year. It does not say they shall be paid. It simply fixes the salary. It has heretofore been customary in our association to make it at the other end of the year.

Mr. FRED. L. HOUGHTON: We have made provision for fixing the salary in advance. Perhaps it would be as well to fix it so that the Secretary would be enabled to draw some salary before the end of the year.

Mr. THOS. B. WALES, Jr.: So far as the present Secretary is concerned, he would not care to have it until the end of the end of the year.

Mr. EDGAR HUIDEKOPER: It strikes me that as a general principal it is better to fix the salary before the officer is elected rather than after.

Mr. J. D. GUTHRIE: I think there is one By-Law that ought to be added there. That in the event of the death or resignation of the Treasurer or Secretary, that the Board of Directors have the power to supply his place.

The Chairman: The chair will state his knowledge of the fact, that under the constitution and laws of the state, the salaries of all judicial and executive officers and others are fixed before the term of office commences. Then a person understands, when he is elected to office, what his salary will be, and if he chooses not to accept the position, he is at liberty to do so. I think the constitution itself prohibits any change during the term of office to which any man is elected or appointed. I think the provision is a wise one.

Mr. EDGAR HUIDEKOPER: I move that the Board of Officers or Directors, at their last meeting before the annual election, so fix the salaries of the salaried officers for the ensuing year.

Mr. C. W. HORR: Possibly you should start that amendment or By-Law by saying, "after the present year."

Mr. EDGAR HUIDEKOPER: This is the amendment in place of section 18, as last read by the Secretary, to take its place: "That the Board of Officers shall, at their last annual meeting, prior to the annual election of officers, fix the salary of all salaried officers for the next ensuing year."

Mr. C. W. HORR: Put in the word "hereafter" after the word "shall."

Mr. Horr's amendment was accepted; then Mr. Huidekoper's substitute, as amended, was adopted as a substitute for section 18.

Mr. C. W. HORR: Where is the power vested now?

The Chairman: For the information of the gentleman, the chair will inform him that the salary of the Secretary of the Holstein Association has been fixed up to the present time for this current year. The association can continue the salaries of the officers for the remainder of this year to the next annual election, or refer it to the new Board of Officers.

Mr. C. W. HORR: Have we not got to have some specific authority granted to the Board of Officers for this year? That resolution, as it now stands, does not apply to this year.

The Chairman: I think there should be authority given them if the Board is to fix it.

Mr. C. W. HORR: I would suggest that there be added, "and that for the present year the Board shall fix the salaries at the first meeting."

Mr. EDGAR HUIDEKOPER: That may be done by resolution after the By-Laws have been accepted. We do not want it in the By-Laws.

SEC. 19. "The Board of Officers shall take cognizance of any and all specific charges made and presented to them in writing against any member of this corporation, or to any of its members, and shall appoint a committee of two members of the corporation to hear the parties and take proofs relavent to the charges, in writing and under oath, and to report the same in full, with their opinion of the matter, to the Board of Officers."

Dr. F. W. PATTERSON: Right there I desire to say a word. After the word "corporation," it should read, "for violation of his obligation to this corporation," making it read, "the Board of Officers shall take cognizance of any and all specific charges made and presented to them in writing against any member of this corporation for violation of his obligation to the corporation." I suggest the interpolation of those words, "for violation of his obligation to this corporation."

So amended.

Mr. W. G. POWELL: Ought not that to go a little farther? Should not we take some cognizance of the transactions of a man with outsiders? Suppose a man is a notorious swindler and swindles every man he deals with, although not a member, should not there be something with reference to it? If a person does an unbusiness-like, ungentlemanly transaction, and continues such acts, the association ought not to suffer by it; and yet he is doing it under the cloak of the membership of the association. I think it would be well to have something to reach that part of it. That was one thing discussed in our meeting at Chicago, in reference to importation. We thought if importation was confined to members, we could have some control over their transactions in importing. I think the resolution should be broad enough to reach that.

Mr. J. D. GUTHRIE: I think the suggestion is a good one. I move that it be adopted.

Mr. WING R. SMITH: I think that all this association is interested in is what the members may do to the disadvantage of the interests of this breed of cattle, or of the association, and that is all covered by the resolution.

The Secretary read again the resolution as amended by Dr. Patterson.

A Member: If a man is swindling the public on the credit of the association, I think we would have a right to deal with him.

Mr. S. HOXIE: I think that sentence, "for violation of his obligation to this corporation," is not specific enough. You do not know what it is. That means any violation. It may be a matter that does not relate at all to our business or the association. It should be more specific, and then add, "or to the public."

Dr. F. W. PATTERSON: Mr. Chairman, the moment you open the door, however, you have got something outside of that that may want to tear your association to pieces. Irresponsible parties may be making charges against members of the association who are entirely honorable. It gives an opportunity for harsh treatment. We desire to be tried by our peers, not our enemies, or scoundrels outside.

Mr. S. HOXIE: Suppose the man injures the public, and people say he is a swindler, and he is given a bad reputation; it seems to me that he ought to be dealt with as much as though he should be dealing with one of us.

Dr. F. W. PATTERSON: I think it would be proper, that charges should be preferred by members.

Mr. S. HOXIE: I would say, then, "violation of his obligations to the association, or swindling any member of the association or the public." He may violate some obligations in reference to questions of temperance or something of that kind, which we would not wish to consider,

A Member: It seems to me we are going beyond our scope. We are not to watch over the morals of our members particularly, only in a general way, as they affect the interests of this association. Of course we expect them all to be moral, but if they violate some of our ideas of morality, and they do not affect the business of the association, we better leave them alone.

Mr. W. G. POWELL: Mr. Chairman, I am very clear in my own mind that the resolution, as it now is, does not reach a person's transactions outside. It is a question whether we do or do not wish to reach that. For myself, I think it is important that our members not only deal honorably and fairly with each other, but that they do so with other people. I think there should be added, "or for unbusiness-like and dishonest transactions." The charges may be preferred only by members.

Mr. C. W. HORR: Better add, "or for unbusiness-like and dishonest transactions in reference to the buying and selling of Holstein-Friesian cattle."

A Member: I move that it be laid on the table.

The motion was carried.

Section 19, as read, with the amendment proposed by Dr. Patterson, was adopted.

SEC. 20. "The accusers and accused shall then, if they desire it, be heard before the Board of Officers, or a majority of them, and after such hearing, or opportunity afforded by the Board to the parties to have such hearing, they shall determine whether the charges made have been proved, and, if so, whether the accused ought to forfeit his membership in the corporation, and take such action in the matter as they may deem advisable.

Adopted.

ARTICLE III. OF MEETINGS.

SECTION 1. "Notice of all meetings of the corporation and of the Board of Officers shall be mailed at least fourteen days before the time named for the meeting."

Adopted.

SEC. 2. "All notices of meetings shall be served by sending a written or printed copy, by mail, to the post-office address of each member entitled to such notice."

Mr. L. T. YEOMANS: I move to add the words, "and shall fully set forth the matters to be acted on at such meeting."

Dr. F. W. PATTERSON: The section below covers it.

Mr. L. T. YEOMANS: I make that motion because section three is almost a repetition of section one.

Amendment accepted, and section 2 adopted.

SEC. 3. "All notices calling meetings of the corporation, or of the Board of Officers, shall fully set forth the matters to be acted on at such meetings."

Mr. WING R. SMITH: Now I move that that section be stricken out because of the adoption of the previous amendment.

The motion carried, and section 3 was stricken out.

SEC. 4. "If the Board of Officers deem it advisable to hold the annual meeting, or any special meeting of the corporation, or any meeting of the Board of Officers, at any other place than Buffalo, N. Y., and so order, the Secretary shall make the notices, calling the meeting, in accordance with the order of the Board."

Adopted.

SEC. 5. "Special meetings of the members of the corporation shall be called when a majority of the members of the Board of Officers join in a request or direction to the Secretary to call such meeting."

Adopted.

SEC. 6. "The travelling expenses of the Board of Officers, when called together for the transaction of business of the association, shall be paid out of the funds of the association."

Adopted.

SEC. 7. "One-third of all the members of the corporation shall constitute a quorum for business at the annual meeting, or at any special meeting duly called."

Adopted.

ARTICLE IV. OF THE HERD-BOOK.

SECTION 1. "This corporation shall publish the Holstein-Friesian Herd-Book at intervals of not less than one year."

Adopted.

SEC. 2. "The Holstein-Friesian Herd-Book shall contain the charter and By-Laws and a list of members of the corporation, the record of the proceedings at all meetings held since the publication of the last volume of the Herd-Book, the reports of the officers, and any other matters of general interest which the Board of Directors may deem advisable to publish, and an accurate registry of all the animals accepted for registry in it, which shall be divided in two parts, one part containing the registry of bulls, and the other the registry of cows. Such registry shall shall set forth the number, the name, the date of birth, the name and residence of the breeder and owner, and if imported, the name of the importer, the markings of the animal sufficient for its identification, and the names and numbers of both sire and dam in the Herd-Book."

Mr. FRED. L. HOUGHTON: I would like to propose an amendment to that section, that in the future volumes of the Herd-Book no plates or engravings be printed, and that there be no publications of any records of animals or anything in the nature of advertising set forth in the Herd-Book at all; that hereafter it simply contain a record of the pedigrees of animals.

Mr. WING R. SMITH: I would like to second Mr. Houghton's amendment that the pedigree of animals may be given. The owners are at liberty to give the pedigree back to importation.

Mr. THOS. B. WALES, Jr.: That is contained in another clause. I would like to make a suggestion that this section commence to read with the words, "each volume of," so as to read, "each volume of the Holstein-Friesian Herd-Book shall contain," etc.

The amendment was adopted, and Mr. Houghton's amendment was then accepted and the section adopted.

SEC. 3. "In the Herd-Book there shall be registered only such animals as are determined, under the rules and regulations of this corporation, to be thoroughbred."

Adopted.

SEC. 4. "Thoroughbred Holstein-Friesian shall be held to mean and refer to only those large, improved, black and white cattle already registered in the Holstein and Dutch-Friesian Herd-Books, and such as are descended from them in direct line, both as to sire and dam, and such imported animals or their descendants as are registered in the Netherlands, Friesian and North Holland Herd-Books, proved by the affirmation of the breeder of the animal, satisfactory to the inspector. No animal having colors other than black and white shall be registered."

A Member: There are three Herd-Books. I move to put in the word "or" instead of "and."

Amendment accepted.

Mr. DUDLEY MILLER: Mr. Chairman, is it not rather superfluous to add at the end of that section, "no animal having colors other than black and white shall be registered?" Does not the first part of it state that an animal shall be black and white?

The Secretary: Yes, sir, that is what it says.

Mr. GERRIT S. MILLER: If you get right down to that nice point, saying no other color than black and white — we all know there are little marks on these animals that are not strictly black and white; but we say the animals must be black and white. Substantially they are so, but the strict wording there might make some trouble. I would move that we leave off the last line or two containing that section.

The words, "no animal having colors other than black and white shall be registered," were stricken out.

Mr. IRWIN LANGWORTHY: Mr. Chairman, it seems to me you are including in this resolution three foreign Herd-Books. There has been an effort made to consolidate here, and that we have but one book, to be known as the Holstein-Friesian Herd-Book. There have been but two books recognized in Europe for any length of time. It seems to me it would be an advantage to the breed of cattle if we would recognize but two European Herd-Books, the

Netherlands and Friesian. I move that the words, "North Holland Herd-Book," be stricken out from the section. I think it is a measure that would tend to the welfare of the breed of cattle. If that is stricken out, you recognize but two Herd-Books in Europe, and one falls flat to the ground. We do not need three books in that country. We should not encourage them any more in that country than in this country. It is just as detrimental there as in America to have so many Herd-Books. I am in favor of our dropping the North Holland Herd-Book, and that we do not recognize the North Holland Herd-Book.

Mr. WING R. SMITH: I would like to ask if the gentleman understands, as I certainly do, that the North Holland Herd-Book is considerably better than the Netherland Herd-Book, as far as the quality of the animals recorded is concerned. They have not the percentage of poor animals that there are in the Netherlands.

Mr. IRWIN LANGWORTHY: I have been laboring for years for a union of these two associations so that we should have but two Herd-Books. I can not see any good policy in recognizing a multitude of European Herd-Books.

Mr. WING R. SMITH: It strikes me as unbecoming in us to dictate to those gentlemen in Holland what they should do, whether they have or not, inasmuch as they already have a Herd-Book, and as they have rules and regulations governing the entry, and the animals that are registered are better than some of the animals originally put into the Netherlands' book, and the percentage is better than the the animals in the Netherlands' book; and I know that to be a fact, and I state it as a fact.

Mr. IRWIN LANGWORTHY: I do not know any authority for the statement.

Mr. WING R. SMITH: I have the authority of those who know it. My authority is from those who have been to Europe and seen the animals.

Mr. IRWIN LANGWORTHY: It doesn't look to me to be a matter of policy for us to labor in America for the establishment of a consolidated association so that we would have but one American Herd-Book — because it is annoying to breeders in America that we should recognize a new book just gone into existence. It has been in existence but a year. If this association does not recognize that Herd-Book, it won't amount to anything. I don't see any good to come of it.

Mr. WING R. SMITH: What is the object of recognizing Herd-Books in Holland if it is not for the purpose of protecting our own own cattle and securing a better grade of cattle. What difference does it make if there are half a dozen Herd-Books if they all have the same object in view, and all are anxious for the highest grade of cattle? As a matter of fact the North Holland Herd-Book does have better cattle and a better percentage. It has the kind of cattle that are brought here, the kind that should be imported. They were established for the reason and object of having a better registry than the Netherlands, and they have got it. They are absolutely a better Herd-Book than the North Holland. So why throw it out when it is better?

Mr. C. W. HORR: It seems to me the real point is this: Is the North Holland Herd-Book a good one? Has it got stringent rules? If they have, why not get the benefit or privilege of buying the cattle recorded in it. To my mind the simple business question is whether the North Holland Herd-Book is a good one. Have they got rules, and are they enforced, and are the cattle of as good a character recorded in that book as in the other book?

Mr. Thos. B. Wales, Jr.: I understand one object in starting the North Holland Herd-Book was to record only black and white cattle. The Netherlands Herd-Book records cattle of other colors as well as black and white. At our last meeting we heard from Mr. B. B. Lord, of Sinclairville, N. Y., who had been to Holland and examined into the subject, and he stated that he thought the animals were fully equal, if not superior, in the North Holland Herd-Book to those in the Netherlands. It seems to me we should not discourage the people there who are recording only fine black and white cattle.

Mr. S. Hoxie: I most heartily agree with what Mr. Wales says. I was opposed to the North Holland Herd-Book, but for the sake of getting all the information I could, I wrote to Mr. McDonald, who was former manager of the Model Farm at Winkel, and he is thoroughly reliable. I will read a little from his letter, with your permission: "Replying to your favor of the 22d ult., I can give you the following information: Our Netherland Herd-Book was started a few years before American buyers came here, and its intention was the improvement of cattle in the whole kingdom. The North Holland Herd-Book was started in November, 1883, as a result of the growing American trade, and mainly influenced by B. B. Lord & Sons. They use a scale of points, a translation of which I hope to send you in a few days; take no other colors than black and white, and then leave the final conclusion about the admittance or refusal of an animal with their inspectors, thereby facilitating matters. The main difference is found in the fact that the Netherlands Herd-Book Association does not admit any females unless they have actually brought a calf and proved to be sound milkers, while the North Holland Herd-Book only requires female animals to be two years old at the time of inspection, no matter if they are in calf or not. The North Holland Herd-Book Association is originated and run by common farmers, who are practical breeders, and I am very sure they aim to do what is right, desire to elevate the breed as well as the Netherland Herd-Book Association, but they do it solely in the hope to get a large share of the American trade. And this purpose, I also fully admit, is a legitimate and laudable one." Now, in reference to this matter, he goes on to say: "Now I do not say this in order to depreciate the latter, but only to show that different opinions and less stringent requirements by the different inspectors, make matters easier." They admit cattle that the Netherlands will not receive. Then he gives the scale of points used by the North Holland Herd-Book:

1	*Head,*		Fine...	3
2	*Horns,*		Thin, smooth, inclining forward.................	3
3	*Eyes,*		Clear, prominent................................	3
4	*Ears,*		Fine, covered with soft hair, not too large.....	3
5	*Nose,*		Dark, with shiny hair around it.................	2

6	*Bearing,*	Docile...	4
7	*Neck,*	Thin, straight.................................	2
8	*Chest,*	Wide, roomy.................................	3
9	*Quarters,*	Broad, square................................	6
10	*Chine,*	Straight, open................................	5
11	*Tail,*	Fine and long................................	4
12	*Barrel,*	Well rounded, with large, but not too deep, abdomen.......................................	2
13	*Legs,*	Straight, with fine bones......................	3
14	*Skin,*	Fine, soft, mellow............................	5
15	*Hair,*	Black and white, well separated, soft, fine......	3
16	*Udder,*	Well developed in front and rear...............	8
17	*Escutcheon,*	Colored Indian yellow, with greasy dandruff.....	5
18	*Teats,*	Well formed, well placed, black, not thick......	6
19	*Hair on Escutcheon,*	Little, fine and silky.........................	4
20	*Mammary Veins,*	Large, crooked, elastic.......................	10
21	*Orifices,*	Two on each side............................	4
22	*Escutcheon,*	Large, broad, without long-haired edges........	6
23	*Size and weight,*	....	6
			100

Mr. JAMES C. POOR: I can testify to these cattle being of a superior quality to look at, and as far as our scale of points goes -- those recorded in the North Holland Herd-Book are superior to those recorded in the Netherland Herd-Book. You will see some distinct colors in those animals. I know this from personal experience, having examined a great many of them last year in Holland.

The amendment offered was lost, and the section as originally read was adopted.

SEC. 5. "American bred animals shall only be registered in the Herd-Book upon application made upon, or following, the form furnished by the corporation, and the payment of a fee of one dollar by members of the corporation, and the payment of a fee of two dollars by persons not members, for the registry of each animal, which must accompany the application. No two animals shall have the same name. A family name shall originate with the female. Only direct descendants of animals shall be entitled to the family name, with numbers prefixed or added, and after the first generation, the family name only in combination. Males shall only be entitled to the family name in combination, in which the family name shall be first."

Mr. WING R. SMITH: I think that is entirely wrong, that the family name should be only given to the female and not to the male. It is not the law of man, and I don't know why it should be the law of animals.

Mr. S. HOXIE: With man, the man gives the name of the family always, but with animals, in all cases, the female gives the name of the family.

Mr. WING R. SMITH? It is not so with horses or dogs.

Mr. S. HOXIE: Here a bull can give a hundred in a season and all belong to the same family.

Mr. WING R. SMITH: And so a man might have a hundred if he was a Mormon.

Mr. C. W. HORR: Certainly, but a man does not want them all to bear his name. [Laughter.]

Mr. F. C. STEVENS: I should think the amount of blood an animal has should entitle it to the name. If a female gives birth to a calf, it is entitled to the family name. It only has fifty per cent. of the blood, being served by some other animal. The amount of blood the animal has determines the relationship, and I can not see why an animal having the proper amount of blood should not have the name.

Mr. W. M. SINGERLY: Why not strike out that sentence, so that they can originate with either? The words, "the family name shall originate with the female," should be stricken out. Also strike out the words " males should only be entitled to the family name," etc.

Mr. S. HOXIE: Why not strike it all out except " no two animals shall have the same name?" That settles the whole question.

Mr. GERRIT S. MILLER: It is generally understood in most Herd-Book Associations, that where numbers are prefixed to the family name, it implies the animal is a descendant from the fountain head; not that it is a full brother or sister.

Mr. THOS. B. WALES, Jr.: I was a member of the committee that proposed these rules. We discussed the matter very thoroughly—Mr. Yeomans, Mr. Hoxie, Dr. Patterson and myself concluded it would be best for the breed generally to adopt these rules.

Mr. WING R. SMITH: It seems to me one way to make that plain would be to say that only males shall take the name of the sire, and only the females the name of the dam in combination.

Mr. W. M. SINGERLY: My motion is to strike out the section, "a family name shall originate with the female," and to make it that it shall be in combination. Strike out the word "only" next to that.

Mr. C. W. HORR: I would like to hear the resolution read that we adopted in Chicago. I think we did a great deal better than we are doing here. There was an important resolution introduced by Mr. Brooks, of Ohio, which has been wholly ignored. I would like to have the resolution read, simply as an argument on the same subject adopted at Chicago.

Mr. W. M. SINGERLY: My amendment in full is this:

SEC. 5. "American bred animals shall only be registered in the Herd-Book upon application made upon, or following, the form furnished by the corporation, and the payment of a fee of one dollar by members of the corporation, and of two dollars by persons not members, for the registry of each animal, which must accompany the application. No two animals shall have the same name. Only direct descendants of an animal shall be entitled to the family name with numbers prefixed or added, and after the first generation the family name in combination. Males shall only be entitled to the family name in combination, in which the family name shall be first."

Mr. S. HOXIE: I move the whole subject be laid on the table.

Mr. L. T. YEOMANS: Now, we have been talking about combinations. I would like to have put right along after Mr. Singerly's amendment, "in all combinations the name of the sire taken in part or full, shall be used as desired by the applicant."

The amendment was accepted by Mr. Singerly, and the whole amendment, as amended, adopted.

Mr. WING R. SMITH: There is another amendment that some gentlemen might want. It was acted on as a separate resolution. That was, "That all titles of distinction and nobility, military or honorary, and all first or given names not in use as family names, should be free for use in combination." I think that should be added at the end of this section.

Dr. F. W. PATTERSON: The gentlemen have been too fast. They have passed the resolution which Mr. Singerly offered, and the section was adopted as read.

The Chairman: No, it has not been adopted.

Dr. F. W. PATTERSON: If it was adopted as read you must rescind the motion.

Mr. WING R. SMITH: We have not passed the section. We just adopted section five. I move to add that.

The Chairman: It was not adopted yet. The amendment only was adopted. This is an additional amendment. Those of you who favor that will please say aye.

Carried.

The Chairman: The question occurs on the original section as amended.

The section, as amended, was then adopted.

SEC. 6. "When application for registry of imported animals is made, the certificate of the breeder of the animal, made upon, or following, the form for such certificates furnished by this corporation, is required."

Mr. THOS. B. WALES, Jr.: I move, as an amendment, to add to the beginning of this section the words, "only members of this association may register imported animals in the Holstein-Friesian Herd-Book."

Mr. L. T. YEOMANS: I will move to insert after the words, "imported animals," the words, "imported from Europe after March 18th, 1885." I would suggest also that you strike out the words, "Holstein-Friesian Herd-Book," because we don't register in anything else.

Mr. W. G. POWELL: It should be stated in that section, or some other one, that the importer's name should appear in the original certificate on the other side. As I understand it, there are cattle perhaps on the water now, or about landing, or having landed, and on the certificate the importer's name is still blank. It is for the purpose of getting around our rule, that no person shall import except members of the association. The object is to find a purchaser or somebody who will act as a cat's paw to have his name inserted, and then have those cattle registered. We must provide for that somewhere. It may be necessary for us to require that they should bring a certificate from the American consul, and that the names all appear on that side.

Mr. WING R. SMITH: The breeder's certificate requires the name of the importer to be at the top of the certificate. All the association requires to show the breeding of the animal, is that the certificate is properly filled out, which includes the signature of the seller and breeder, and acknowledgment that this animal was sold by the seller to the buyer, at the top, which, in itself, requires the name. It must be there if it is honest and properly filled out. It does not require any special statement.

Mr. EDGAR HUIDEKOPER: The present quarantine regulations require that the importer shall notify the Commissioner of Agriculture of this importing of certain animals.

Dr. F. W. PATTERSON: Mr. Chairman, I arise to second Mr. Wales' amendment, that this section should read at the beginning, "only members of this association may register imported animals."

Mr. THOS. B. WALES, Jr.: As amended, then, it would read, "only members of this association may register imported animals which were shipped from Europe after March 18th, 1885." Then follows, "when application for registry," etc.

The section was adopted.

SEC. 7. " Animals *must* be transferred to owners *before their offspring are registered.*"

Adopted.

SEC. 8. " Application for registry of imported animals shall be made to the Secretary, and by him referred to an inspector, who will visit and separately examine each imported animal proposed for registry, and the certificate of the breeder, relating to such animal; and the inspector shall make his report of the result of such examination, in writing on or annexed to the breeder's certificate—"

Mr. W. G. POWELL: Now insert right there, " the importer's name to be inserted in the breeder's certificate before shipment, and to be verified by list from an American consul." I offer that as an amendment. The certificate should state in whose name they are sent.

Mr. C. W. HORR: Suppose somebody should ship without those certificates before they get this information? It seems to me we should go slow and have it apply to cattle exported after a certain date. I believe there is a forfeiture clause of membership that gives us all the protection we want. You have only to read that. I should fully concur with the gentleman if I didn't believe it was fully covered by a preceding section. It seems to me a little bit risky.

Mr. S. HOXIE: I will move that Mr. Koch, who is present here, be heard. I saw that he arose to his feet on this question.

Mr. T. F. KOCH: Mr. Chairman, though not a member of the association, I would like to be heard. I endeavored to be made a member of your association last fall. I was not a resident of the American States then, but I became a resident this spring. I imported some animals last fall and they were recorded in the Holstein Herd-Book last fall. I am a resident of New York, and I shall try to become a citizen as soon as I can, but it will take me five years. I am very much interested in everything in America. I bought 34,000 acres of land with a man in Chicago. I am more interested in New York than I am in Holland, but your laws make it impossible for me to become a member. I would like very much to be allowed to become a member of the Holstein-Friesian Association. I am willing to swear off my own country, because I intend to become a citizen of the United States.

Mr. W. G. POWELL: I appreciate all the gentleman says, but it has nothing to do with this subject. I know that this is a desirable country to live in, and that he wishes to become a citizen of the great country of America, but still I would not accord to him, or anybody else, the privilege of importing cattle in blank certificates and fill up the certificates after they get here.

Mr. C. W. HORR: But would you not be willing to allow our By-Laws to be amended as to read only *bona fide* residents instead of citizen? What is the objection to that?

The Chairman: It seems to me it is not in order to be discussing the question whether the gentleman who is not a citizen of the country can become a member of the association. The question is on the amendment offered by Mr. Powell. Mr. Powell will please state his amendment.

Mr. W. G. POWELL: Insert in the proper place "the importer's name to be inserted in the certificate before shipment, and to be verified by list from an American consul." I do not say it shall be at Amsterdam, or Rotterdam, or any other particular dam, because they may not want to ship from that place. But it should be an American consul.

Mr. C. W. HORR: I move to amend, that this amendment should not apply to cattle shipped from Holland before the 10th day of June, 1885.

Amendment accepted.

Mr. J. W. STILLWELL: I would suggest to the gentleman to make that ten days longer. Suppose a man sends over there and his letter should be miscarried?

The question occurred on the amendment as proposed by Mr. Powell as amended, and carried.

Mr. J. W. STILLWELL: I will make an addition to that section, that this association be authorized to cable to the three Herd-Books in Holland the effect of this resolution, or to the American consul — or that our Secretary be instructed to cable this resolution.

Amendment lost.

The Chairman: The Secretary will read the balance of the section.

The Secretary reads: "No imported animal under one year of age shall be examined or accepted for registry. All imported animals shall be registered in the name of the importer. The application for registry of animals imported in dam must be signed by the importer. All applications for registry of animals which are not filed with the Secretary within one year from date of birth or importation, shall be charged three times the usual registry fee. All animals bred in America shall be registered in the name of the owner, in which case a certificate of service is required from the owner of the bull, and the signature of the breeder to the application. No imported animal shipped from Europe after March 18th, 1885, shall be eligible to registry in the Herd-Book unless the animal or its dam and sire are registered in the Netherlands, Friesian, or North Holland Herd-Book. In recording such imported animal, its breeding, as it appears in the Netherlands, Friesian, or North Holland Herd-Book, with the names and numbers by which its sire and dam are registered in such Herd-Book, shall be spread upon the register of this association. Any person applying to the Secretary for inspection of imported animals shipped from Europe after March 18th, 1885, shall pay to the Secretary of the association, five dollars for each animal to be inspected *before such inspection is ordered*, and after such payment, the Secretary shall be authorized to order such inspection. The registry fee for each imported animal shall be twenty dollars. Inspectors shall receive from the association as compensation, ten dollars for each day, and five dollars for each night occupied in inspecting cattle, and in going to and from places of inspection, all necessary and reasonable travelling expenses shall be paid by the association. No imported animal shall be accepted for registration until it has been passed by an inspector, and the inspector shall be instructed that no animal shall be accepted for registry in the Herd-Book except those of superior excellence that might fairly be ranked as strictly first-class."

A Member: This section does not designate where the animal should be inspected. If the importer saw fit, he could scatter his animals throughout the United States, and the association could charge him but twenty dollars for inspecting and registering the animals. It might cost the association one or two hundred dollars.

Mr. THOS. B. WALES, Jr.: I have the following amendment to offer after the clause relating to inspection: "which must be made within sixty days from date of importation." That will require them to be examined in quarantine before the date of quarantine expires, and before they can get out into the country.

A Member: I would suggest that it be at quarantine or at the farm of the importer.

Mr. THOS. B. WALES, Jr.: The association might be called upon to send all over the United States.

A Member: I think the fee should be as it is, provided the animal was inspected at quarantine, but otherwise, any additional expense should be borne by the importer.

Mr. EDGAR HUIDEKOPER: I think as long as the whole importation is together, and not scattered, that we are entitled to have them examined on our own farm instead of in quarantine, if it suits our pleasure. That would not materially affect the expense.

Mr. J. W. STILLWELL: I move, as an amendment, that they be examined either in quarantine or on the farms of the importers, wherever they desire.

Mr. THOS. B. WALES, Jr.: It seems to me to be important to make some rule regulating the examination of imported cattle. We do not want to send an inspector all over the United States to examine one herd. The inspector may have to go to California, which would cost an immense sum of money. I hope we shall find some way to regulate the matter satisfactorily to everybody, and still not put the association to any excessive expense.

Mr. ISAAC C. OTIS: Mr. Archibald, of Oxford, Miss., had some imported that were not registered, and he now asks that the inspector go and inspect them, and they are distributed around. This is to provide against any such future contingencies.

The Chairman: The amendment proposed by Mr. Miller, as an amendment to the amendment of Mr. Stillwell, is that the cattle be examined at quarantine or on the farm of the importer.

Mr. J. W. STILLWELL: What I mean is that there should be an inspector for California and one about Iowa, and so scatter them along. I don't think it will cost the association any more.

Mr. EDGAR HUIDEKOPER: Mr. Chairman, you can readily see that papers might sometimes come in that needed correction, and would have to be sent back to Holland. They might not get back in time to have the animals inspected in quarantine, and in that case it is but just that a reasonable latitude should be given to the importer that he might take the animals home and have them inspected there.

Mr. F. C. STEVENS: Supposing the importer has a herd of one hundred animals. I think the importer pays a sufficient amount of money for recording them, and that is all that he should be expected to pay.

Mr. THOS. B. WALES, Jr.: I am in favor of the amendment offered by Mr. Stillwell, that the cattle should be inspected either in quarantine or on the farm of the importer.

The Chairman: The question is on the amendment to the amendment, that the cattle be inspected either in quarantine or upon the farm of the importer before they are dispersed.

Amendment carried.

The question then occurred on the amendment of Mr. Miller, as amended.

Mr. GERRIT S. MILLER: I will withdraw my proposition, so he can offer his motion as a substitute.

Mr. Stillwell's amendment was re-considered and then withdrawn. Then Mr. Stillwell offered his motion as a substitute, which was adopted.

SEC. 9. "When an animal is accepted for registry, the Secretary shall issue a certificate of the fact to the owner, giving the number and name, and description the animal will take in the Herd-Book."

Adopted.

SEC. 10. "A register of transfer of ownership of any animal registered in the Herd-Book will be made on application of the owner, and payment of fifty cents by members of the corporation, and one dollar by all other persons.

A certificate of such transfer will be made by the Secretary. A charge of fiffty cents will be made for each duplicate certificate of registry or transfer."

Mr. J. W. STILLWELL: I move that the charge for the transfer certificate be reduced to twenty-five cents. I think that is plenty. The American Jersey Cattle Club have never charged but twenty-five cents.

Mr. C. W. HORR: Well, that is more, according to the size of the cattle, than we charge. [Laughter.]

Motion lost; section 10 adopted.

SEC. 11. Every application for the registry of an animal in the Herd-Book shall be taken as the guarantee of the owner that the animal is thoroughbred, and that all the matters stated in the application are true. No application for registry or transfer will receive attention unless accompanied with the required fee."

Adopted.

SEC. 12. "If, after registry of any animal in the Herd-Book, anything shall be learned which raises a doubt as to the propriety of such registration, the Board of Officers shall cause the matter to be investigated; and if it shall be found that an animal has been improperly registered, they shall cause that registry to be expunged, and take such other steps or measures in the matter as the nature of the case may, in their judgment, require."

Adopted.

ARTICLE V.

"In accordance with the provisions of the charter, a system of advanced registry shall be provided for by the Board of Directors under the supervision of a member of the board, or other person to be named by the board, said registry to be published in a separate volume."

Mr. IRWIN LANGWORTHY: The committee on nominations had a matter under consideration in regard to the Board of Officers. It was thought by the committee that the gentleman having in charge the matter of advanced registration should be a member of the Board of Officers, and it was agreed in that committee to offer an amendment, providing that the superintendent, or whatever you may designate him, of the advanced registry should be a member of the Board of Officers. I make a motion that it be amended, so that the superintendent, or manager of the advanced registry be a member of the Board of Officers so that he may have some standing and act with you for counsel and advice.

Mr. THOS. B. WALES, Jr.: The only objection is that it will give us an even number on our board. We have thirteen now.

Mr. GERRIT S. MILLER: I am in favor of Mr. Langworthy's motion that the superintendent of that work should serve as a member of the board, *ex-officio*.

Dr. F. W. PATTERSON: I rise to a question of order. Our charter has designated who shall be the members of the board, and has designated the officers. I am afraid it has gone too far. I do not see how this can be done.

Mr. ELON G. FAY: The charter has this provision:

SEC. 2. "The officers of said association shall be a President, and four Vice-Presidents, to be designated as first, second, third, and fourth, one Secretary and Editor, six Directors, and such other officers as may be provided for by the By-Laws of this association."

Mr. WING R. SMITH: I suggest that you make the Superintendent of the Advanced Registry an officer, and elect that officer, and then he will be a member of that board.

By direction of the association, the chairman cast a ballot and announced the election of Mr. S. Hoxie as Superintendent of Advanced Registry.

Mr. C. W. HORR: Now I move that these By-Laws be so amended, that the office of Superintendent of Advanced Registry shall appear among the regular officers of this association in the Board of Officers.

The Chairman: I will suggest also they be so changed as to not include the clause that makes this officer appointed by the Board.

Mr. C. W. HORR: But to leave it under the regulations of the rules established by the Board.

Motion carried.

Mr. EDGAR HUIDEKOPER: Mr. Chairman, with your permission, I would like to go back to a previous regulation, section 8, article IV., of the By-Laws, which reads, "in recording such imported animal, its breeding, as it appears in the Netherlands, Friesian, or North Holland Herd-Book, with the names and numbers by which its sire and dam are designated in such Herd-Book, shall be spread upon the register of this association." Now, if that animal itself is registered in one of the Herd-Books in Holland, its name and number should be spread upon our Herd-Book instead of the name of its sire and dam. I move that that be inserted in this clause, so that its name and number shall be spread upon our records instead of the name and number of its sire.

Mr. C. W. HOXIE: I move that resolution be adopted, and the words inserted in the proper place.

Motion carried.

Mr. ISAAC C. OTIS: I would like to inquire if on these certificates appears the name and number that the animal is recorded in the Netherlands Herd-Book, whether that is *prima facie* evidence that they are so recorded, to the inspector. You cannot go back of the returns, can you?

Mr. IRWIN LANGWORTHY: It is certified and sworn to before the burgomaster.

Mr. ISAAC C. OTIS: I am told by some gentleman that that does not amount to anything.

Mr. EDGAR HUIDEKOPER: If the certificate of the Herd-Book is produced, that is sufficient.

Mr. WING R. SMITH: If the animal itself is already recorded in Holland it would be branded on the horn or hoof; so that he would know it.

The Chairman: The Secretary will proceed with the reading of the By-Laws.

Secretary reads:

ARTICLE VI.

"The seal of the corporation shall be a circular-faced die, with the name of the corporation, the date of charter, and the head of a Holstein-Friesian animal so cut on the face of it that the whole can be embossed on paper by pressure, and the minutes of this meeting shall be sealed with it."

Adopted.

Mr. THOS. B. WALES, Jr.: I would like to have some action taken in regard to the matter of this seal. The Holstein Association has a seal now. The imprint is here. We can simply change the lettering around it, and I think it will answer every purpose, and it can be done at a very small expense.

Mr. W. G. POWELL: I move that the Secretary be instructed to have it changed.

Mr. THOS. B. WALES, Jr.: I would further suggest that the certificate of membership be in the form of that of the Holstein Association, changing simply one word in the certificate. It can be done at a small expense. Our plate cost us nearly two hundred dollars. I think it would be a useless expense to have a new plate made, and it will be unnecessary if you will permit me to have that one word changed.

Mr. W. G. POWELL: I move that the Secretary be authorized to arrange the matter of the seal and plate, etc.

Motion carried.

A motion was made and carried that the Secretary be instructed to issue the new certificates to all the members of the Holstein-Friesian Association.

Mr. EDGAR HUIDEKOPER: I would like to go back again and offer this amendment: Section 6, Article IV. "Any person desiring to reserve a family name may make written application to the Secretary, and upon payment to him of a fee of one dollar for each family name, shall have such name reserved for animals of that family only. The Secretary shall issue his certificate therefor and keep a record of the same in a book provided for that purpose. No names now in use as family names shall be used for animals not of such families.

Mr. C. W. HORR: I do not understand the object of the amendment; if you intended to give any different right from that already prescribed.

Mr. L. T. YEOMANS: It is to define what the rights are so that we can act in company. It is not to the individual, it is to the animal.

Mr. C. W. HORR: You cannot use any family name some man has used. You cannot use it in combination unless it is some animal descended from it. We have already got that in our By-Laws.

Mr. T. M. SPOFFORD: I should like to amend the motion by prefixing the word "henceforth," so it will read "shall henceforth be used."

Amendment acccepted.

Mr. GERRIT S. MILLER: Does not the present rule govern that? If you take the name, the descendants are entitled to the name. Others cannot take the name. The first one who gets the name has it. I move the resolution be laid upon the table.

Motion carried.

Mr. ELON G. FAY: Mr. Chairman, I wish to move an additional By-Law that no member of this association, at any meeting of the same, shall represent more than five proxies, unless he be a member of a firm, and then five, and in addition the members of said firm; nor shall he represent proxies from outside of the state in which he resides.

The Chairman: That is entirely out of order, because it conflicts with the charter under which we are organized. You cannot cut off a member from making whom ever he pleases his attorney to act for him.

Mr. WING R. SMITH: I have a matter to bring up here. We have made no provision for the death or resignation of some of the officers. I therefore offer this By-Law or amendment, whatever it shall be, that, "in the event of the death or resignation of the Secretary or Treasurer, the Board of Officers shall have power to fill such vacancies until the next general election."

Adopted.

Mr. GERRIT MILLER: I move that the Board of Officers be authorized to elect or appoint as many inspectors as it deems best, for the purpose of inspecting animals, and that only one inspector be required to serve at a time.

Dr. F. W. PATTERSON: I think that is disposed of in some previous section.

Mr. EDGAR HUIDEKOPER: I move that the Secretary be authorized and instructed to publish, in pamphlet form, the charter and By-Laws of the Holstein-Friesian Association, and the full proceedings of this meeting; containing also a list of the members, with their post-office addresses and the proceedings at the meeting of the Board of Officers; also the first proceedings of the Board of Officers; 3,000 copies to be printed.

Motion carried.

Mr. WING R. SMITH: I offer the following resolution: "That the Secretary be ordered to have printed on separate paper, sections five and six of our By-Laws, relating to the naming of animals, and mail a copy to each member of the association, with the request that they give it their careful consideration and note their criticisms in writing, which may be read and discussed at our next meeting." This I do inasmuch as there are several parties besides myself who are not fully prepared to say that we have decided upon just exactly the rule for naming animals that we might after mature deliberation. We have come together here and in the course of perhaps half an hour, decided one of the most important matters of our whole association, It strikes me that we ought to have more time to consider it. This course will bring it up directly to every member of the association, and they will think it over and correspond and talk about it, and by the time of the next meeting we shall probably be able to come to some definite conclusion. We can adopt some resolution, or amend the By-Laws, if necessary, or retain the present rule in regard to naming animals.

The Chairman: That must necessarily be embraced in the proceedings.

Mr. WING R. SMITH: I want it to be separate so as to bring it before each and every member. Otherwise it will not be.

Dr. F. W. PATTERSON: I will call to Mr. Smith's attention, that this is a good time for him to give notice again that he will call up at the next annual meeting, the question of this new section. The possibilities are that he will want to have it amended. He can now give the notice.

Mr. WING R. SMITH: I am much obliged to Dr. Patterson for the suggestion. I will now give notice that I will call that up at the next meeting of the association; still I would like to have this notice given. I now notify the the Secretary of this matter.

Motion adopted.

Mr. W. G. POWELL: Mr. Stevens, Sr. said, about the time of our adjournment, that he believed there was a provision in the laws of this state that required corporations, under the laws of this state, to meet at least once a year in this state, and that the annual meeting should be held in this state. I move, if that is found to be the case, that our next meeting be held here instead of at Cleveland, if we find it is not legal to go outside of the state, and that the Secretary make the call in pursuance of the law.

Motion adopted.

Mr. WING R. SMITH: I am now ready to present the resolution. The motion made by Mr. Powell, I believe, in regard to the importation of animals, was in substance that the importer's name should be inserted in the certificate before shipment, and after June 10th, is to be verified by list from the American consul. I now move to amend that By-Law as passed, as follows:

"The importer's name to be inserted in certificate before shipment; and after June 10th until July 1st, 1885, it shall be verified by list from an American consul. On and after July 1st, 1885, all certificates must be numbered by the Secretary, who shall fill in the name and address of the importer. The certificates shall bear the official seal of the association. The Secretary shall keep a record of the number of certificates, and to whom issued." I offer it as an amendment to that By-Law, and move its adoption.

Motion carried.

Dr. F. W. PATTERSON: If there are no further amendments, I now move that we adopt the By-Laws, the articles, and sections, as a whole, as we have now passed them in sections, and that we now act upon that motion.

Motion carried, and By-Laws, as amended, adopted.

Upon motion, the meeting adjourned.

BY-LAWS

OF THE

HOLSTEIN - FRIESIAN ASSOCIATION

OF AMERICA,

ADOPTED AT ITS FIRST MEETING, HELD AT BUFFALO, NEW YORK, MAY 26, 1885.

ARTICLE I.—OF MEMBERSHIP.

SECTION 1. Any person of good character, who is a citizen of North America, interested in the breeding of Holstein-Friesian cattle, and the owner of such, may apply for membership in this corporation by filing a written or printed application, in such form as the Board of Officers may prescribe, with the Secretary, with the membership fee of one hundred dollars. The form of application for membership shall give the applicant's name in in full, his residence and post office address, and such other particulars as the Board of Officers may require.

SEC. 2. Every application for membership shall be submitted to the consideration of the Board of Officers, and if in their judgment the applicant is eligible for membership and ought to be admitted as a member of this corporation, and a unanimous vote of the Board of Officers present to that effect is passed, his name shall be entered on the records as a member, and the Secretary shall issue a certificate of membership.

SEC. 3. Any member of the corporation may at any time withdraw and terminate his membership, by returning his certificate of membership to the Secretary, with a letter expressing his wish and intention to terminate his membership.

Sec. 4. Any member of this corporation who shall be found guilty of any misrepresentation, deception, or fraud in relation to the registry of animals in the Holstein-Friesian Herd-Book shall forfeit his membership in the corporation.

Sec. 5. Each member of the corporation shall be entitled to one copy of each volume of the Herd-Book published after his admission, which shall be forwarded to his address as soon as convenient, after its publication.

ARTICLE II.--OF THE OFFICERS.

Section 1. The officers of this corporation shall consist of a President and four Vice-Presidents, to be designated as first, second, third and fourth, one Secretary and Editor, one Treasurer, six Directors, and one Superintendent of Advanced Registry, who shall constitute the Board of Officers of this corporation. There shall be three Directors elected at the first meeting for the term of one year, and three for the term of two years. Thereafter at each annual meeting there shall be elected three Directors to serve for the term of two years. In the event of the death or resignation of the Secretary or Treasurer, the Board of Officers shall have power to fill such vacancies until the next general election. The Board of Officers shall appoint inspectors of imported cattle with power to remove for cause and to fill vacancies.

Sec. 2. The Board of Officers of this corporation, as a Board, shall have and take the entire control and management of its affairs and business, with full power and authority to do what they deem proper and best for its interest, provided that they shall have no authority to contract a debt or obligation against the corporation beyond its current expenses. And in such case, not beyond the amount of cash in the treasury, and that nothing shall be done which is not in accordance with the purpose and spirit of the charter and By-Laws.

Sec. 3. At any meeting of the Board of Officers, which is duly called, a majority of its members shall constitute a quorum for business.

Sec. 4. A legal meeting of the Board of Officers of this corporation may be held at any time and place, when and where all the members of the Board are present together and agree to hold a meeting, and all votes and acts done at such meeting shall have the same validity and effect as they could have if passed and done at a regularly called meeting.

Sec. 5. A meeting of the Board of Officers shall be held on the day of the annual meeting of the members, and a meeting may be called by the President or Secretary, or by a majority of the Directors, when, in his or their judgment, the affairs or business of the corporation make it necessary for the Board of Officers to hold a meeting.

Sec. 6. Notice calling special meetings of the Board of Officers shall be given by the person calling the meeting, in writing, setting forth the date and place of meeting, and the purpose or purposes for which the meeting is to be held, and no other business than that specified in the notice shall be acted on, unless all the members of the Board of Officers are present.

SEC. 7. Members of the Board of Officers cannot vote by proxy at meetings of the Board, but any member of the Board who cannot attend a duly called meeting, may address a letter to the Board of Officers, in which he may discuss the purpose or purposes for which the meeting is called, and state how he will vote on the question or questions which may come before the meeting under the notice, and such letter and such votes shall be read in the meeting, and the votes shall be counted and have the same effect as they would if the member was personally present and voted.

SEC. 8. All notices or calls for meetings of the Board of Officers shall be recorded at length in the Record-Book of the corporation, and the substance of all letters from members of the Board, containing votes on matters set forth in the notice calling the meeting, shall also be recorded; and such letters shall be kept on file, and all proceedings had and votes passed at meetings of the Board of Officers shall be fully set forth and recorded in the Record-Book.

SEC. 9. The President shall preside at all meetings of the members of the corporation, and all meetings of the Board of Officers, when he is present; and when he is absent or unable to perform the duties of the office, a Vice-President shall act in his stead. The president shall sign all certificates of membership which may be issued.

SEC. 10. The Treasurer shall be the custodian of cash, funds and securities belonging to the corporation, and shall deposit, invest, or otherwise dispose of the same, as the Board of Officers may direct. He shall give a bond with sureties to the satisfaction of the Board of Officers.

SEC. 11. The Secretary shall be the corresponding and recording officer of the corporation, and shall receive and attend to, and dispose of, as the charter and By-Laws require, all applications for membership in the corporation, all applications for registry of animals in the Herd-Book, and all applications for transfer registry of animals in the Herd-Book, and shall sign and issue all certificates of membership and registry, and of transfer registry, and shall keep a record of all such certificates issued. He is authorized to expend such sums as he may find necessary for the carrying on of the business of the association.

SEC. 12. He shall edit and publish the Herd-Book at such times and in such form as the Board of Officers may direct.

SEC. 13. He shall issue notices of the time and place of the annual meeting of the corporation, and of special meetings which the Board of Officers may order to be called; but no amendments to the charter or By-Laws shall be made at any meeting, either annual or special, unless thirty days' notice of the substance of such proposed amendments has been given by the Secretary in the call for such meeting.

SEC. 14. He shall issue notices of meetings of the Board of Officers, when requested to do so by the President, or by a majority of the Directors.

SEC. 15. He shall record all notices of meetings in the Record-Book of the corporation, and certify therein that they were issued and sent in accordance with the provisions of the By-Laws.

SEC. 16. He shall keep full and accurate records of all the meetings of the corporation and of the Board of Officers, at which he is present, and when he is absent, a Secretary, *pro tempore*, shall be chosen to attend to and perform the duties of the Secretary.

SEC. 17. He shall keep an accurate account in detail of all moneys received and paid out by him in the performance of his duties, a copy of which he shall transmit to the Treasurer once in each quarter year, during the first month of the quarter. And shall give a bond satisfactory to the Board of Officers.

SEC. 18. The Board of Officers shall hereafter, at their last meeting prior to the annual election of officers, fix the salaries of all salaried officers for the next ensuing year.

SEC. 19. The Board of Officers shall take cognizance of any and all specific charges made and presented to them in writing against any member of this corporation, for violation of his obligation to this corporation, or to any of its members, and shall appoint a committee of two members of the corporation to hear the parties and take proofs relevant to the charges, in writing and under oath, and to report the same in full, with their opinion of the matter, to the Board of Officers.

SEC. 20. The accusers and accused shall then, if they desire it, be heard before the Board of Officers, or a majority of them, and after such hearing, or opportunity afforded by the Board to the parties to have such hearing, they shall determine whether the charges made have been proved, and, if so, whether the accused ought to forfeit his membership in the corporation, and take such action in the matter as they may deem advisable.

ARTICLE III.—OF MEETINGS.

SECTION 1. Notice of all meetings of the corporation and of the Board of Officers shall be mailed at least fourteen days before the time named for the meeting.

SEC. 2. All notices of meetings shall be served by sending a written or printed copy, by mail, to the post-office address of each member entitled to such notice, and shall fully set forth the matters to be acted on at such meeting.

SEC. 3. If the Board of Officers deem it advisable to hold the annual meeting, or any special meeting of the corporation, or any meeting of the Board of Officers, at any other place than Buffalo, N. Y., and so order, the Secretary shall make the notices, calling the meeting, in accordance with the order of the Board.

SEC. 4. Special meetings of the members of the corporation shall be called when a majority of the members of the Board of Officers join in a request or direction to the Secretary to call such meeting.

SEC. 5. The travelling expenses of the Board of Officers, when called together for the transaction of business of the association, shall be paid out of the funds of the association.

Sec. 6. One-third of all the members of the corporation shall constitute a quorum for business at the annual meeting, and at any special meeting duly called.

ARTICLE IV.—OF THE HERD-BOOK.

Section 1. This corporation shall publish the Holstein-Friesian Herd-Book at intervals of not less than one year.

Sec. 2. Each volume of the Holstein-Friesian Herd-Book shall contain the charter and By-Laws and a list of members of the corporation, the record of the proceedings at all meetings held since the publication of the last volume of the Herd-Book, the reports of the officers, and any other matters of general interest which the Board of Directors may deem advisable to publish, and an accurate registry of all the animals accepted for registry in it, which shall be divided in two parts, one part containing the registry of bulls, and the other the registry of cows. Such registry shall set forth the number, the name, the date of birth, the name and residence of the breeder and owner, and if imported, the name of the importer, the markings of the animal sufficient for its identification, and the names and numbers of both sire and dam in the Herd-Book. It shall contain the record of pedigrees, but no plates, engravings, or publication of any records of animals.

Sec. 3. In the Herd-Book there shall be registered only such animals as are determined, under the rules and regulations of this corporation, to be thoroughbred."

Sec. 4. Thoroughbred Holstein-Friesian shall be held to mean and refer to only those large, improved, black and white cattle already registered in the Holstein and Dutch-Friesian Herd-Books, and such as are descended from them in direct line, both as to sire and dam, and such imported animals or their descendants as are registered in the Netherlands, Friesian or North Holland Herd-Books, proved by the affirmation of the breeder of the animal, satisfactory to the inspector.

Sec. 5. American bred animals shall only be registered in the Herd-Book upon application made upon, or following, the form furnished by the corporation, and the payment of a fee of one dollar by members of the corporation, and of two dollars by persons not members, for the registry of each animal, which *must accompany the application*. No two animals shall have the same name. Only direct descendants of an animal shall be entitled to the family name with numbers prefixed or added, and after the first generation the family name only in combination. Males shall only be entitled to the family name in combination, in which the family name shall be first. In all combinations the name of the sire in part, or in full, shall be used as desired by the applicant. All titles of distinction, nobility, military, or honorary, and all first or given names, not in use as *family* names, shall be free for use in combination.

Sec. 6. Only members of this association may register imported animals, shipped from Europe after March 18th, 1885. When application for registry of imported animals is made, the certificate of the breeder of the animal made upon, or following, the form for such certificates furnished by this corporation, is required.

SEC. 7. Animals *must* be transferred to owners *before their offspring are registered*.

SEC. 8. Application for registry of imported animals shall be made to the Secretary, and by him referred to the inspector, who shall visit and separately examine each imported animal proposed for registry, and the certificate of the breeder relating to such animal; and the inspector shall make his report of the result of such examination, in writing, on or annexed to the breeder's certificate. The importer's name to be inserted in breeders' certificate before shipment, and after June 10th, until July 1st, 1885, it shall be verified by list from American consul. On and after July 1st, 1885, all breeders' certificates must be numbered by the Secretary, who shall fill in the name and address of importer. The certificates shall bear the official seal of the association. The Secretary shall keep a record of the number of certificates, and to whom issued. No imported animal under one year of age shall be examined or accepted for registry. All imported animals shall be registered in the name of the importer. The application for registry of animals imported in dam must be signed by the importer. All applications for registry of animals, which are not filed with the Secretary within one year from date of birth or importation, shall be charged three times the usual registry fee. All animals bred in America shall be registered in the name of the owner, in which case a certificate of service is required from the owner of the bull, and the signature of the breeder to the application. No imported animal shipped from Europe after March 18th, 1885, shall be eligible to registry in the Herd-Book, unless the animal or its dam and sire are registered in the Netherlands, Friesian or North Holland Herd-Book. In recording such imported animal, if it be recorded in the Netherlands, Friesian or North Holland Herd-Book, its name and number shall be spread upon the records, if not recorded there, its breeding, as it appears in the Netherlands, Friesian or North Holland Herd-Book, with the names and numbers by which its sire and dam are registered in such Herd-Book, shall be spread upon the register of this association. Any person applying to the Secretary for the inspection of imported animals shipped from Europe after March 18th, 1885, shall pay to the Secretary of the association five dollars for each animal to be inspected *before such inspection is ordered*, and after such payment, the Secretary shall be authorized to order such inspection, the inspection to be made at quarantine or upon the farm of the importer. The registry fee for each imported animal shall be twenty dollars. Inspectors shall receive from the association, as compensation, ten dollars for each day, and five dollars for each night, occupied in inspecting cattle and in going to and from places of inspection. All necessary and reasonable travelling expenses shall be paid by the association. No imported animal shall be accepted for registration until it has been passed by an inspector, and the inspectors shall be instructed that no animal be accepted for registry in the Herd-Book, except those of superior excellence, that might fairly be ranked as strictly first-class.

SEC. 9. When an animal is accepted for registry the Secretary shall issue a certificate of the fact to the owner, giving the number and name and description the animal will take in the Herd-Book.

SEC. 10. A register of transfer of ownership of any animal registered in the Herd-Book will be made on application of the owner and payment of fifty cents by members of the corporation, and one dollar by all other persons; a certificate of such transfer will be made by the Secretary. A charge of fifty cents will be made for each duplicate, certificate, or registry of transfer.

SEC. 11. Every application for the registry of an animal in the Herd-Book shall be taken as the guarantee of the owner that the animal is thoroughbred, and that all the matters stated in the application are true, No application for registry or transfer will receive attention unless accompanied with the required fee.

SEC. 12. If, after registry of an animal in the Herd-Book, anything shall be learned which raises a doubt as to the propriety of such registration, the Board of officers shall cause the matter to be investigated; and if it shall be found that an animal has been improperly registered, they shall cause the registry to be expunged, and take such other steps or measures as the nature of the case in their judgment may require.

ARTICLE V.

In accordance with the provision of the charter a system of Advanced Registry shall be provided for by the Board of Offices. It shall be under the management of a Superintendent to be elected by members of the association, and to be a member of the Board of Officers. Said registry to be published in a separate volume.

ARTICLE VI.

The seal of the corporation shall be circular-faced die, with the name of the corporation, the date of charter, and the head of a Holstein-Friesian animal so cut on the face of it that the whole can be embossed on paper by pressure, and the minutes of this meeting shall be sealed with it.

FIRST MEETING OF THE

BOARD OF OFFICERS

OF THE

HOLSTEIN-FRIESIAN ASSOCIATION

OF AMERICA,

HELD AT BUFFALO, NEW YORK, MAY 26, 1885, AT 11.45 P. M.

Present, Messrs. L. T. Yeomans, Dr. F. W. Patterson, W. M. Singerly, Geo. F. Jackson, G. S. Miller, F. C. Stevens, C. R. Payne, W. C. Brayton, C. W. Horr, W. R. Smith, W. G. Powell, and T. B. Wales, Jr.

Mr. W. R. Smith moved that Mr. Isaac C. Otis, of Jordan, New York, be made temporary inspector, in order that certain imported cattle of Mr. Edgar Huidekoper may be examined at once.

Which motion prevailed.

Adjourned at 12 P. M.

SECOND MEETING OF THE

BOARD OF OFFICERS

OF THE

HOLSTEIN-FRIESIAN ASSOCIATION

OF AMERICA,

AT BUFFALO, NEW YORK, WEDNESDAY, MAY 27, 1885, AT 10 A. M.

Present, T. G. Yeomans, Dr. F. W. Patterson, Geo. F. Jackson, W. C. Brayton, G. S. Miller, C. R. Payne, C. W. Horr, W. R. Smith, W. G. Powell, S. Hoxie, T. B. Wales, Jr.

Mr. J. W. Stillwell requested that a special inspector be named to examine an imported animal near Nashville, Tenn. Ear-mark, No. 253.

It was voted, that an inspector be sent as soon as appointed, which would be during the present day.

Mr. Wing R. Smith moved that a committee be appointed by the chair to investigate the matter of the registration of imported animals by Mr. Chas. W. Wolcott, of Readville, Mass, in his name, when the animals are claimed to have been owned by Mr. C. Stuijt, Jr., of Beemster, North Holland. Report to be made to the Board of Officers.

The motion prevailed.

The chair appointed as such committee, Messrs. Wing R. Smith and Gerrit S. Miller.

Applications for membership were received from G. V. DeGraff, John Hancock, R. N. Stevens, and S. P. Howard, which were accepted.

The applications for membership of Messrs. D. H. Archibald, T. S. Perry, Albert French, and Henry Horn, gentlemen not personally known to any member of the Board, were referred to the Secretary to obtain necessary proof of their eligibility, and to report same by letter to each member of the Board.

The following gentlemen were elected inspectors of imported cattle:

>Dr. F. W. PATTERSON,
>O. P. CHAPMAN,
>ISAAC C. OTIS,
>S. BURCHARD,
>S. N. WRIGHT,
>CAREY R. SMITH.

It was voted that a meeting of the inspectors (excepting C. R. Smith, of California, who is to receive full instruction by letter) be held at Rochester, New York, on the 13th of June, for conference, that a perfect understanding be arrived at in regard to the inspection of imported animals. It was further voted that the expenses incurred by the inspectors attending this meeting, be paid from the funds of the association.

Mr. G. S. Miller then moved to arrange rules to govern the Advanced Registry of the association, and after full and careful deliberation, the following were considered section by section, agreed upon, and on motion of Mr. W. R. Smith, were adopted as a whole:

RULES FOR ADVANCED REGISTRY.

PREAMBLE.

In accordance with the requirements of the Charter and By-Laws of the association, the Board of Officers do adopt the following rules for the establishment of a system of registry, to be known as the Advanced Registry of the Holstein-Friesian Association of America.

RULE I.

The Superintendent of Advanced Registry shall have charge of this registry. Under the general supervision and direction of the Board of Officers, he shall prepare and publish blank forms and circulars, needed in carrying this system into effect; receive and attend to all applications for this registry; make or cause to be made, all examinations of cattle for it; have oversight and direction of all official tests of milk or butter production for it; issue all certificates of registry for it over his signature and the seal of the association; edit and publish all publications of this registry, and perform such other duties as may be required of him by the Board of Officers, to secure the efficiency and success of this system. He shall keep an accurate account in detail of all moneys received or paid out by him in the performance of these duties, a copy of which he shall transmit to the Treasurer of this association, once in each quarter year, during the first month of the quarter. And he shall make a full report of his work to the Board of Officers whenever they shall require it, at least once in each year, at date of annual meeting. He shall give a bond satisfactory to the Board of Officers.

RULE II.

The Board of Officers shall appoint one or more persons to be known as Inspectors of Advanced Registry, whose duties shall be to examine cattle for this registry, and take charge of tests for it, whenever in the faithful discharge of his other duties, the Superintendent is unable to perform this work, in any particular case or cases.

At the opening of each volume of this registry the Superintendent, with the assistance of such Inspectors, shall prepare a schedule of structural and physiological requirements of animals to be admitted to such volume. This schedule shall be submitted to the Board of Officers, who shall have power to alter or amend it. Then it shall become the standard below which no animal shall be received to that particular volume. When such volume is published this standard of requirements shall be given in the introduction.

No one shall examine cattle for this registry over which he has charge, or in which he has a pecuniary interest.

RULE III.

For purposes of convenience in describing cattle offered for this registry, they shall be classified as follows, viz:

All animals from two to three years of age, in a class to be known as the *Two year form.*

All animals from three to four years of age, in a class to be known as the *Three year form.*

All animals from four to five years of age, in a class to be known as the *Four year form.* And

All animals above five years of age, in a class to be known as the *Full age form.*

RULE IV.

An animal to be eligible to Advanced Registry must pass an examination by the Superintendent, or one of the Inspectors, and be reported by him as worthy of such registry. In such report the following particulars shall be given, viz: Name of animal; number in Herd-Book; age at time of examination in years and months, or in years, months and days; comparative size; general form; build so far as relates to structure of chine and levelness of loin, hip and rump; escutcheon; mammary veins; handling; color of the skin and secretions; general appearance and style; and, in case of cows, size and flexibility of udder. Such report shall also give accurate measurements of height of shoulders, height of hips, length of body, length from hook bone to point of rump, width of hips at the hook bones, width at the thurl bones, and girth of chest at its smallest circumference, and the condition, age and weight of the animal at the time of measurement.

'RULE V.

A bull to be eligible to this registry must have proven his superior quality by his progeny, and must scale at least eighty points of the scale adopted by the Board of Officers.

RULE VI.

A cow to be eligible to this registry must have borne a calf, and made one or more of the following records, viz:

If calving in the two year form, a record of not less than ten lbs. of butter in seven consecutive days, or not less than 7,200 lbs. of milk in ten consecutive months, or not less than 396 lbs. of milk in ten consecutive days, previous to eight months from and after date of calving, in which last case she shall have made another record of 132 lbs. in ten consecutive days after such period of eight months.

If calving in the three year form, a record of not less than twelve lbs. of butter in seven consecutive days, or not less than 8,500 lbs. of milk in ten consecutive months, or not less than 473 lbs. of milk in ten consecutive days, previous to eight months from and after date of calving, in which last case she shall have made another record of 154 lbs. in ten consecutive days after such period of eight months.

If calving in the four year form, a record of not less than fourteen lbs. of butter in seven consecutive days, or not less than 10,000 lbs. of milk in ten consecutive months, or not less than 550 lbs. in ten consecutive days, previous to eight months from and after date of calving, in which last case she shall have made another record of not less than 187 lbs. in ten consecutive days after such period of eight months.

If calving in the full age form, a record of not less than sixteen lbs. of butter in seven consecutive days, or not less than 11,500 lbs. of milk in ten consecutive months, or not less than 633 lbs. of milk in ten consecutive days, previous to eight months from and after date of calving, in which last case she shall have made another record of not less than 212 lbs. in ten consecutive days, after such period of eight months.

All of these records shall be made within a period of eleven months from date of calving.

In making each and every such record the cow shall be milked clean at its commencement, and the close shall not extend beyond the number of days reported, reckoned at twenty-four hours each. In each and every butter record reported the butter shall be of good marketable quality, salted at not higher than one ounce of salt to a pound of butter, and worked free from any excess of water or buttermilk.

In reporting each and every record, the date of calving shall be given, the age of the cow at such date, the date of commencement of record, the date of close of record, and the number of pounds of milk or butter produced.

Every such record shall be sworn to by each and every person assisting in making it, including in every case the owner of the animal. Such affidavits shall set forth, that the record, or records, were made in accordance with these rules, and that they are true in each and every particular, to the best knowledge and belief of the subscriber thereto. The examiner shall also certify, that in his judgment, the animal is capable of making such record or records.

RULE VII.

If, in the judgment of the examiner, the registry of any animal ought to be delayed, for further growth and development, or for further records, or ought to be refused for any reason whatever, he shall inform the applicant of such decision within ten days after making the examination. The applicant may then appeal from such decision to the Board of Officers. The Board may act upon such appeal at any time previous to the annual meeting of the association thereafter. They may call in the assistance of other cattle experts, or decide the case without such assistance, but if the action is delayed beyond the date of the annual meeting thereafter, the appeal shall fail and the decision of the examiner shall be sustained.

RULE VIII.

An animal may be examined in each and every form, but no more than one examination of the same animal shall be made in one and the same form. Records of milk and butter production of any cow may be recorded for each and every form, if the rules of the association have been complied with in making such records. Re-entry of cows may be made in different volumes of this registry, when other records have been made in forms not previously recorded, or other offspring have been produced not previously given.

RULE IX.

No pedigree shall be given in Advanced Registry, unless by request of applicant. Upon such request and the payment of the fees required in such cases, a correct pedigree furnished by him shall be recorded in accordance with a uniform mode that shall be maintained throughout the volume of this registry in which such entry is made. Offspring of cows may also be given, together with the sires of such offspring.

RULE X.

Every application for this registry shall be carefully examined by the Superintendent. He shall ascertain that all the requirements of these rules have been complied with, that the name, number, age, pedigree and offspring given are in accordance with the records in the Herd-Book of this association, or in the Herd-Books of the former Holstein or the former Dutch-Friesian Association. If the requirements have been met, and such statements are correct, he shall then enter the animal in a manuscript volume of this registry, and issue a certificate to the applicant in form and language substantially as in the entry. The application and all other evidence, upon which he makes such entry, shall be kept on file by him, subject to examination by any member of this association. In making entries he may correct clerical mistakes and change any diffuse or incorrect language given in the applications, to more concise and uniform expressions, having the same meanings.

RULE XI.

Any incorrect entry may be expunged from the manuscript volume of this registry, and the certificate of such entry revoked by the Board of Officers, upon evidence of its incorrectness. The Board may also expunge any such entry that has been published, and revoke the certificate of such entry, but in such a case they shall cause to be published, in leading cattle journals and in the next following volume of this registry, the revocation of such certificate.

RULE XII.

The necessary travelling expenses of the officers created by these rules, while engaged in their duties, other than examinations, shall be paid by the association.

Travelling expenses incurred in making examinations shall be paid by the applicants, for whom cattle are examined and collected by the Superintendent. If cattle of different applicants are examined at the same time, or during the same trip, the officer making such examinations, shall divide such travelling expenses among such applicants, *pro rata*, according to the number of cattle examined for each.

For time necessarily spent in making the examinations, the examiner shall be paid in the same manner, and at the same rate per day as provided in Article IV., Section 8, of the By-Laws of this association.

For making and keeping this advanced registry, editing and publishing it, and for the performance of such other duties required of him by these rules, the Superintendent shall be paid a just and reasonable compensation, to be fixed by the Board of Officers, on or before the close of each year of such service.

RULE XIII.

The fee for entry in this form of registry shall be five dollars per animal for members, and ten dollars for non-members. The fee for entry of pedigree of animals admitted to this registry shall be twenty-five cents for each name given in such pedigree, providing that the fees in no case shall be less than one dollar, or more than three dollars. The aggregate fees for entry of offsping, in connection with the registry of dam shall be one dollar.

RULE XIV.

In publishing this registry cattle shall be arranged in two divisions, viz.: Bulls and Cows. The entries in each division shall be arranged according to the names of the animals in alphabetical order. New numbers shall in no case be given, but each animal shall appear with the original name and number under which it is recorded in the Herd-Book of this association, or in the Herd-Books of the former Holstein or the former Dutch-Friesian Association. The different volumes of this registry shall be sold at prices fixed by the Board of Officers, but each member shall be entitled to a copy of all such publications, free of charge.

RULE XV.

These rules may be altered or amended by an affirmative vote of a majority of the members of the Board of Officers at any of its regular meetings, previous notice of proposal to make such alteration or amendment having been given in accordance with the provisions of Article III., of the By-Laws of this association.

Mr. T. F. Koch, of Groningen, Holland, was heard in regard to his application for membership, which had been rejected, he not being a citizen of North America.

After mature deliberation by the board, Mr. G. S. Miller moved that the matter be laid on the table, which motion prevailed, and the Secretary was instructed to inform Mr. Koch of the decision.

Mr. Koch then asked that he be allowed to present for registration a lot of sixty head of animals he had already on the water, which were purchased by him in Holland, in the full expectation that he would be admitted a member of the Holstein Association.

Mr. W. R. Smith then offered the following resolution:

Resolved, That under the peculiar circumstances of Mr. Koch, the appended resolution be offered at the next meeting of the association, and that our Secretary be, and hereby is instructed to receive application for the registry of the sixty head of imported animals referred to, to receive the fees therefor, and to hold certificates and money until acted upon by the association, and if acted favorably upon, then to deliver up said certificates of registry, and to place the funds in the treasury of the association, and in case it is acted upon unfavorably, that the registration fee of twenty dollars for each animal be returned to Mr. Koch, and the inspection fee of five dollars for each animal be retained; and further, that Mr. Koch be made fully aware of our action in this matter.

Adopted.

The following is the communication Mr. Smith proposed the board should offer at the first meeting of the association, which was agreed upon:

WHEREAS, Mr. T. F. Koch, now a resident, but not a citizen of North America, has imported and made application for the registration of a certain lot of sixty head of cattle purchased by, or for him, in Holland; and

WHEREAS, Mr. Koch made this importation under circumstances and conditions that to us seem peculiar and unusual, having made due and proper application for membership before the union of the two associations, we therefore suggest and request that the association act on this case, and that such a resolution be passed as will admit to registry this particular lot of animals.

Mr. S. Hoxie was authorized to expend such sums as he may find necessary in carrying out the rules adopted for the Advanced Registry.

The quantity of milk and butter agreed upon as requirements for Advanced Registry was reconsidered, and the inspectors were instructed to increase them in all classes ten per cent.

Adjourned.

NOTE.—The ten per cent. additional requirement, as voted to be added to milk records, is included in amounts given in printed Rules.

MEMBERS

OF THE

Holstein-Friesian Association of America.

AIKEN, M. A.,	Oneida, New York.
ALBAUGH, N. H.,	Tadmor, Ohio.
ALLEN, IRVING W.,	East Syracuse, New York.
ALLEN, WM. H.,	Groton, New York.
ALLIS, JERE,	Isinours, Minnesota.
BABCOCK, F. G.,	Hornellsville, New York.
BAKER, RUFUS,	Fairfield, Michigan.
BARNEY, N. C.,	New York City, New York.
BARR, W. R.,	New York City, New York.
BEAL, PROF. W. J.,	Lansing, Michigan.
BELL, JOHN W.,	Shelbyville, Kentucky.
BEUCHLER, J. R.,	Leesburg, Virginia.
BIDWELL, M. S.,	Monterey, Massachusetts.
BISHOP, W. W.,	Aurora, Illinois.
BLACK, JAMES,	Stanley, New York.
BLESSING, C. L. G.,	Slingerland's, New York.
BLEYKER, J. DEN,	Kalamazoo, Michigan.
BOARDMAN, H. E.,	Rochester, New York.
BORTON, JOB H.,	West Unity, Ohio.
BOWER, B. B.,	Anchorage, Kentucky.
BRACE, H. L.,	West Winfield, New York.
BRADLEY, A.,	Lee, Massachusetts.
BRAYTON, W. C.,	Syracuse, New York.

Brockett, C. Z.,	Bouckville, New York.
Brooks, J. T.,	Salem, Ohio.
Brown, A. W.,	Unadilla Forks, New York.
Brown, Geo. E.,	Aurora, Illinois.
Buchanan, Jas. N.,	Chicago, Illinois.
Buel, W. J.,	Hamilton, New York.
Burch, Robert,	West Schuyler, New York.
Burchard, Sylvester,	Hamilton, New York.
Burrell, David H.,	Little Falls, New York.
Burrell, E. J.,	Little Falls, New York.
Carlisle, N. S.,	Geneva, Illinois.
Carpenter, G. M.,	Waverly, Pennsylvania.
Chaffee, B.,	Springville, New York.
Chapin, Wm. M.,	Sheffield, Massachusetts.
Chapman, O. P.,	Wellington, Ohio.
Chenery, W. L.,	Belmont, Massachusetts.
Clark, W. B.,	Nashville, Tennessee.
Clark, Wm. B.,	Hillsdale, Michigan.
Cole, A. F.,	Pine Woods, New York.
Cole, Ogden,	Rollin, Michigan.
Cole, O. R.,	Solsville, New York.
Comer, J. H.,	New York City, New York.
Coon, Morel,	West Edmeston, New York.
Cooper, Irving C.,	Theresa, New York.
Coy, Edward L.,	West Hebron, New York.
Crandall, W. D.,	West Edmeston, New York.
Crapser, Chas.,	Cresco, Iowa.
Cruikshank, J. W.,	Troy, Ohio.
Cummings, John,	Woburn, Massachusetts.
Curtis, N. B.,	Stockbridge, Massachusetts.
Dale, M. H.,	Scranton, Pennsylvania.
Dean, John L.,	Westmoreland, New York.
DeGraff, G. V.,	Cortland-on-Hudson, New York
Dilger, Hubert,	Front Royal, Virginia.
Dodge, Thos. H.,	Worcester, Massachusetts.
Dorwin, Wm. E.,	Owego, New York.
Downing, A. S.,	Palmyra, New York.
Durnall, Edwin J.,	Goshenville, Pennsylvania.
Dutcher, J. B.,	Pawling, New York.

EASTON, H. S.,	Penn Yan, New York.
ELLIS, A. V.,	Austin, Minnesota.
ELLIS, J. T.,	Flemington, New Jersey.
ELLWOOD, L.,	Schenectady, New York.
EMERSON, S. B.,	Mountain View, California.
EMRICK, G. M.,	Chicago, Illinois.
EWING, WILLIAM L.,	St. Louis, Missouri.
FAY, ELON G.,	Bryan, Ohio.
FIGUERS, T. N.,	Columbia, Tennessee.
FINNEGAN, THOMAS,	Bouckville, New York.
FITCH, C. H.,	Boston, Massachusetts.
FLETCHER, GEO. B.,	Williamsport, Pennsylvania.
FREDERICK, L. S.,	Shelbyville, Kentucky.
FROST, RUFUS S.,	Boston, Massachusetts.
FULLERTON, WILLIAM,	Clifton Station, Virginia.
GALE, H. C.,	Tivoli, New York.
GARDINER, W. L.,	Norwalk, Ohio.
GEBBIE, ALEXANDER,	Lowville, New York.
GEDDES, GEO.,	Fairmont, New York.
GIBNEY, MATHEW,	Doylestown, Pennsylvania.
GIFFORD, W. H.,	Syracuse, New York.
GILBERT, F. M.,	Des Moines, Iowa.
GOODFELLOW, CORNELIUS,	Cato, New York.
GUTHRIE, J. D.,	Shelbyville, Kentucky.
HACK, W. C.,	Orwell, Vermont.
HANCOCK, JOHN,	Barre, Mssachusetts.
HANKE, WILLIAM,	Iowa City, Iowa.
HARVEY, T. W.,	Chicago, Illinois.
HARWOOD, P. M.,	Barre, Massachusetts.
HATCH, H. H.,	Bay City, Michigan.
HAVILAND, JOS.,	Glens Falls, New York.
HEMINGWAY, W. L.,	Jackson, Mississippi.
HENDERSON, JAS. L.,	Washington, Pennsylvania.
HIBBARD, H. G.,	Orwell, Vermont.
HICKS, JOHN H.,	West Chester, Pennsylvania.
HICKS, WILLIAM H.,	Goshenville, Pennsylvania.
HINKLEY, D. J.,	Brookfield, New York.
HINKLEY, O. B.,	Brookfield, New York.
HORR, C. W.,	Wellington, Ohio.

Houghton, F. L.,	Putney, Vermont.
Howard, S. P.,	Fairport, New York.
Howard, Warren A.,	Brocton, Massachusetts.
Howkins, Wm.,	Newark, New Jersey.
Hoxie, S.,	Whitestown, New York.
Hoxie, S. L.,	South Edmeston, New York.
Huidekoper, A. C.,	Meadville, Pennsylvania.
Huidekoper, Edgar,	Meadville, Pennsylvania.
Hunt, Charles,	Delphi, New York.
Hunter, John,	Sterling Valley, New York.
Hush, Valentine G.,	Minneapolis, Minnesota.
Jackson, Geo. F.,	Minneapolis, Minnesota.
Jackson, Wm. O.,	South Bend, Indiana.
Jewett, F. J.,	Farmington, New York.
Jewett, Henry C.,	Buffalo, New York.
Jones, Edgar,	Nashville, Tennessee.
Jones, Leander,	Boone Grove, Indiana.
Keyes, H. W.,	Newbury, Vermont.
Koch, William,	New York City, New York.
Lamb, Anthony,	Syracuse, New York.
Langdon, Samuel A.,	Morrison, Illinois.
Langworthy, Hollum,	West Edmeston, New York.
Langworthy, Irwin,	South Brookfield, New York.
Langworthy, Morgan,	West Edmeston, New York.
Leonard, H. D.,	Crary's Mills, New York.
Ligget, Wm. M.,	Minneapolis, Minnesota.
Lightner, John,	Chester Centre, Iowa.
Lord, B. B.,	Sinclairville, New York.
Lord, C. J.,	Sinclairville, New York.
McAlpin, D. H.,	New York City, New York.
McEwan, Wm.,	Bay City, Michigan.
McGraw, T. H.,	Bay City, Michigan.
McIntyre, S. Maxwell,	Dresden, New York.
McNary, Frank E.,	West Le Roy, Michigan.
McVeagh, Wayne,	Philadelphia, Pennsylvania.
Mann, F. J.,	Gilman, Illinois.
Mann, J. S.,	Elgin, Illinois.
Mann, S. S.,	Elgin, Illinois.
Maxon, F. W.,	Walworth, Wisconsin.

HOUGHTON, CHARLES,	Boston, Massachusetts.
MAXWELL, JOSHUA I.,	Geneva, New York.
MAXWELL, T. C.,	Geneva, New York.
MERRITT, M. F.,	Stamford, Connecticut.
MILLER, DUDLEY,	Oswego, New York.
MILLER, GERRIT S.,	Peterboro, New York.
MITCHELL, JOHN,	Vail's Gate, New York.
MOORE, H. C.,	Fond du Lac, Wisconsin.
MOORE, M. E.,	Cameron, Missouri.
MORSE, L. C.,	Sparta, Wisconsin.
MUNCEY, J. N.,	Jessup, Iowa.
MYER, H. VAN W.,	Madison, New Jersey.
MYERS, M. J.,	Wells, Minnesota.
NAVARRO, J. F.,	New York City, New York.
NEILSON, JAMES,	New Brunswick, New Jersey.
NEWMAN, W. W.,	South Onondaga, New York.
NILES, WILLIAM,	Los Angeles, California.
NOWELL, T. S.,.	North Platte, Nebraska.
ODELL, JOHN K.,	Hobart, New York.
OFFICER, THOMAS,	Council Bluffs, Iowa.
OSTERHOUT, STANTON,	Cobleskill, New York.
OTIS, ISAAC C.,	Jordan, New York.
PACKARD, B. G.,	Medina, New York.
PATTERSON, F. W.,	Lochearn, Maryland.
PATTERSON, W. H.,	Cresco, Iowa.
PAYNE, C. R.,	Hamilton, New York.
PAYNE, L. H.,	Garrettsville, Ohio.
PHELPS, EDWIN,	Pontiac, Michigan.
PHILLIPS, E. R.,	Bay City, Michigan.
PHILLIPS, WM. I.,	Ellington, New York.
PIERCE, GEORGE A.,	Derby Line, Vermont.
POOR, JAMES C.,	North Andover, Massachusetts.
POPE, DE MOTT E.,	South Edmeston, New York.
POTTER, W. H.,	Alpena, Michigan.
POTTER, W. J.,	Glens Falls, New York.
POWELL, E. A.,	Syracuse, New York.
POWELL, JAMES L.,	Springboro, Pennsylvania.
POWELL, WILL, B.,	Springboro, Pennsylvania.
POWELL, W. G.,	Springboro, Pennsylvania.

Pratt, C.,	Syracuse, New York.
Proper, W. W.,	Jefferson, New York.
Ray, E. K.,	Franklin, Massachusetts.
Ray, Joseph G.,	Franklin, Massachusetts.
Reed, Wm. W.,	Erie, Pennsylvania.
Roberts, Chas. W.,	West Chester, Pennsylvania.
Robins, J. N.,	New York City, New York.
Rowland, Lynford,	Cheltenham, Pennsylvania.
Rowley, W. A.,	Mt. Clemens, Michigan.
Russell, Luther,	Burton, Ohio.
Russell, W. A.,	Lawrence, Massachusetts.
Schuyler, R. P.,	West Troy, New York.
Scudder, Ogden H.,	Randolph, New York.
Severy, C. A.,	Leland, Illinois.
Severy, Dexter,	Leland, Illinois.
Severy, Henry A.,	Sandwich, Illinois.
Sexton, W. K.,	Howell, Michigan.
Shallcross, J. W. Jr.,	Louisville, Kentucky.
Sherman, D. H.,	Dover Plains, New York.
Shimer, A. S.,	Redington, Pennsylvania.
Singerly, W. M.,	Philadelphia, Pennsylvania.
Slade, H. F.,	Oneonta, New York.
Smith, C. C.,	Vail's Gate, New York.
Smith, Carey R.,	Santa Ana, California.
Smith, Elizur,	Lee, Massachusetts.
Smith, Eugene,	Madison Station, Tennessee.
Smith, Harlan P.,	East Saginaw, Michigan.
Smith, J. Gregory,	St. Albans, Vermont.
Smith, J. N.,	New York City, New York.
Smith, Thomas R.,	Lincoln, Virginia.
Smith, W. Brown,	Syracuse, New York.
Smith, W. H.,	New Carlisle, Ohio.
Smith, W. J.,	Syracuse, New York.
Smith, Wing R.,	Syracuse, New York.
Spencer, Theodore,	Madison, New York.
Spofford, T. M.,	Pulaski, Tennessee.
Stanford, Leland,	San Francisco, California.
Stanton, T. G.,	Oxford, New York.
Stevens, F. C.,	Attica, New York.

STEVENS, HENRY,	Lacona, New York.
STEVENS, R. N.,	Attica, New York.
STILLWELL. J. W.,	Troy, Ohio.
STOCKWELL, B. F.,	Chester Centre, Iowa.
STONE, J. L.,	Waverly, Pennsylvania.
STURTEVANT, A. R.,	Springboro, Pennsylvania.
SWEET, MARTIN L.,	Grand Rapids, Michigan.
SWEEZEY, C. F.,	Marion, New York.
SWEEZEY, S. W.,	Marion, New York.
TAYLOR, C. C.,	Collins, New York.
TAYLOR, D. H.,	Strawberry Point, Iowa.
TEFFT, E. A.,	South Elgin, Illinois.
THOMPSON, SAMUEL R.,	Stelton, New Jersey.
THOMSON, M. C.,	South Plymouth, New York.
TILTON, W. S.,	Togus, Maine.
TOUSEY, W. H.,	Bay City, Michigan.
TRACY, D. D.,	Erie, Pennsylvania.
TROTTER, HENRY,	Salem, Ohio.
TRULOCK, JAMES H.,	Pine Bluff, Arkansas.
TUCKERMAN, J. B.,	Cassville, New York.
UNDERWOOD, ARTHUR,	Addison, Michigan.
UNDERWOOD, J. M.,	Lake City, Minnesota.
VALE, B. R.,	Bonaparte, Iowa.
VAN DRESER, HENRY,	Cobleskill, New York.
VAN DRESER, J. W.,	Cobleskill, New York.
WALES, THOMAS B., Jr.,	Iowa City, Iowa.
WALES, THOMAS B., 3D,	Iowa City, Iowa.
WALWORTH, C. C.,	Boston, Massachusetts.
WARNER, H. O.,	New Milford, Connecticut.
WARNER, S. L.,	New Milford, Connecticut.
WARWICK, GEORGE,	Dummerstown, Vermont.
WASHBURN, E. M.,	Lenox Furnace, Massachusetts.
WATERMAN, HENRY,	Boston, Massachusetts.
WATERMAN, RUFUS, Jr.,	East Greenwich, Rhode Island.
WEBBER, W. L.,	East Saginaw, Michigan.
WELLS, GEORGE, L.,	Wethersfield, Connecticut.
WESTOVER, WILLIAM,	Bay City, Michigan.
WHEELER, C. A.,	Deposit, New York.
WHEELER, G. D.,	Deposit, New York.

WHITE, HOWARD G.,	Syracuse, New York.
WHITE, JOSIAH H.,	Lakeville, California.
WHITING, G. M.,	Torrington, Connecticut.
WILCOX, A. G.,	Minneapolis, Minnesota.
WILLETTS, W. R.,	Skaneateles, New York.
WILLIAMS, GEO. F.,	Fitchburg, Massachusetts.
WILSON, G. O.,	Baltimore, Maryland.
WILSON, J. B.,	Washington, Pennsylvania.
WILSON, R. R.,	Plymouth, Wisconsin.
WOLCOTT, CHARLES W.,	Readville, Massachusetts.
WOOD, DON J.,	West Exeter, New York.
WOOLSEY, W. W.,	Aiken, South Carolina.
WRIGHT, ALFRED P.,	Buffalo, New York.
WRIGHT, J. F.,	Shell Rock, Iowa.
WRIGHT, S. N.,	South Elgin, Illinois.
YEOMANS, E. L.,	Walworth, New York.
YEOMANS, L. T.,	Walworth, New York.
YEOMANS, T. G.,	Walworth, New York.

PROCEEDINGS

OF THE

FIRST ANNUAL MEETING

OF THE

Holstein-Friesian Association

OF AMERICA,

HELD AT

BUFFALO, NEW YORK, MARCH 17TH, 1886.

———

ALSO ———

Reports of Meetings of the Board of Officers,

HELD AT BUFFALO, NEW YORK,

MARCH 16TH AND 17TH, 1886.

———

Egbert, Fidlar, & Chambers, Davenport, Iowa.
1886.

OFFICERS OF THE

HOLSTEIN-FRIESIAN ASSOCIATION OF AMERICA

FOR 1886-7.

President,	F. C. STEVENS,	Attica, N. Y.
First Vice-President,	G. D. WHEELER,	Deposit, N. Y.
Second Vice-President,	WM. M. SINGERLY,	Philadelphia, Penn.
Third Vice-President,	M. L. SWEET,	Grand Rapids, Mich.
Fourth Vice-President,	DAVID H. BURRELL,	Little Falls, N. Y.
Treasurer,	W. C. BRAYTON,	Syracuse, N. Y.

Directors for Two Years.

W. JUDSON SMITH,	Syracuse, N. Y.
F. L. HOUGHTON,	Putney, Vt.
EDGAR HUIDEKOPER,	Meadville, Penn.

Directors for One Year.

GERRIT S. MILLER,	Peterboro, N. Y.
C. W. HORR,	Wellington, Ohio.
C. R. PAYNE,	Hamilton, N. Y.

Secretary and Editor,

THOMAS B. WALES, JR.,	Iowa City, Iowa.

Superintendent of Advanced Registry,

S. HOXIE,	Whitestown, N. Y.

Inspectors of Imported Cattle, also of the Advanced Registry.

ISAAC C. OTIS,	Jordan, N. Y.
S. BURCHARD,	Hamilton, Ohio.
O. P. CHAPMAN,	Wellington, Ohio.
S. N. WRIGHT,	South Elgin, Ill.
JAMES C. POOR,	North Andover, Mass.
DR. F. W. PATTERSON,	Lochearn, Md.
CAREY R. SMITH,	Santa Ana, Cal.

PROCEEDINGS OF THE FIRST ANNUAL MEETING

OF THE

Holstein-Friesian Association

OF AMERICA.

Held at Buffalo, New York, March 17, 1886.

In pursuance of a notice issued February 12th, 1886, by the Secretary, the meeting was called to order at 10 o'clock A. M., at the Genesee Hotel, Buffalo, New York. President Theron G. Yeomans occupied the chair.

The first order of business was calling the roll, by the Secretary, showing the number of members present in person to be 62, and by attorney, 153; total, 215.

It was moved by Mr. F. L. Houghton that a committee of two be appointed to examine the proxies.

The motion was carried.

The President appointed as committee to examine proxies Messrs. F. L. Houghton and H. Langworthy.

PRESIDENT YEOMANS: I have prepared a few remarks which I wish to make to the Association, and I will ask my son to read them to you, as he can be heard better than I.

ADDRESS OF PRESIDENT YEOMANS.

Gentlemen of the Holstein-Friesian Association of America: It affords me pleasure to be able to say, on this first annual meeting of our Association, that the experience of the official year now closed has shown that the union of the two associations forming the Holstein-Friesian Association of America has proved so eminently harmonious and satisfactory that its members seem to have forgotten, practically, to which organization they heretofore belonged; and thus we may confidently expect to fully realize all the advantages which were anticipated as the result of such union. As a united Association, we are better able to protect and defend our interests, whenever and however assailed, and in far better position to move forward to the accomplishment of the important objects for which our Association was organized.

It may not be known to all of our members that at the meeting of your Board of Officers at Rochester, last August, applications for membership were made by two brothers — foreigners — known as Sluiter Brothers, and their applications rejected, in accordance with our own By-Laws. About that time they imported from Holland eighty head of cattle, which they advertised for sale at auction, in New York, and applied to our Association to inspect and register them; which, of course, was not done. Sluiter Brothers then commenced three actions in the Supreme Court, at Brooklyn, New York, against our Association — one each to compel us to admit them to membership, and one to compel us to inspect and register their cattle.

The complaints in these several actions were served on your President Friday evening, at 8 o'clock, September 11th, and were returnable at Brooklyn the following Tuesday, at 10 o'clock A. M. With this brief notice, he went to Syracuse and consulted Messrs. E. A. Powell, Wing R. Smith, and W. C. Brayton, and employed Hon. Frank Hiscock as counsel, and with him went to Brooklyn to defend the action. Our case was presented by our counsel in a very able and efficient manner, notwithstanding the brief time allowed to investigate the subject.

The several suits were decided in our favor, with costs against the plaintiffs.

These suits have been appealed by plaintiffs, and arguments set down for February 8th, but, on their motion, have been put over to the June term of court. It is believed these appeals are made not so much with an expectation of getting the decisions of the court reversed as to give them time to sell more cattle which they have since imported, and which they may hope to sell to better advantage with the appeals pending than if they had not appealed.

The decision of the court in our behalf is brief and very emphatic, and will be read for your information. Mr. Hiscock is retained for the further defense of these actions.

Upon information which appeared to be reliable, your Secretary and President decided that the law required our annual meeting to be held in the state of New York, where our charter was granted — at least, that it was not safe to hold it elsewhere — and therefore, in pursuance of instructions of the last meeting, it was called at Buffalo. The information upon which this action was based will be given.

It may be remembered that at our organization the question was discussed, and quite a diversity of opinions expressed, concerning the character of the North Holland Herd-Book Association — as to whether we ought to consider it worthy of our confidence. By a majority vote it was decided that we might import animals registered by that association, which, if found individually good on inspection here, could be registered by our Association. I submit to your consideration whether the action of that organization and our subsequent information as to its character have been such as to merit our confidence or recognition hereafter.

The system of advanced registry has had my careful consideration, and I am convinced that it will be greatly for our interest as an association to put it into practical operation to as great an extent as is consistent with attendant circumstances.

The charge is often made by opposing interests that we have no authentic records; that the statements floating about of phenomenal records of Holstein-Friesian cows are merely a "cheap advertising dodge, and not entitled to credit;" and one paper in the Jersey interest, referring to this subject, states that "while the Holstein-Friesian Association has its rules and officers for making tests, and the owners are members of the Association, there is not published the slightest evidence that any effort was ever made to verify the phenomenal yields claimed." Such slurs indicate that some of the Holstein-Friesian records are a surprise to those who have their interests in the Jerseys, and who begin to realize the danger of seeing the Jerseys stand second to the Holstein-Friesians as butter-makers. Evidently the day is not far distant, and is already dawning, when the Holstein-Friesian cow will be crowned queen of the dairy.

It is recommended to persons who contemplate testing their cows with a view to entry in the Advanced Registry to make their records, especially for milk, for the largest specified period of time; also, to make records of both milk and butter, and thus more thoroughly establish, at every stage of our progress, the true merits of this noble breed of cattle. The tests made in pursuance of the rules adopted by our Association will not rest on the same basis as those reported in Canada, or elsewhere, as made by using a quart of sweet cream churned in a two-quart fruit-preserving jar, but upon that primitive, practical, and reliable foundation, the milk-pail and churn, which never mislead, and which common people, in the exercise of their good, plain common-sense, fully understand and appreciate without chemical analysis or intricate scientific research. Consider the absurdity of a test made from one quart of sweet cream from a lanky, leggy, unacclimated, twenty-two-months-old Holstein-Friesian heifer, churned in a two-quart fruit-jar, giving a product of 2.98 pounds of butter from 100 pounds of milk, as indicating the dairy qualities of Holstein-Friesian cows, in comparison with a test of a herd of fifty cows of the same breed made at an Illinois creamery by a disinterested party, owning no cows, showing a product of 4 1-16 pounds of butter from 100 pounds of milk, and another herd of about forty cows averaging 4.69 pounds of butter to 100 pounds of milk. The first is simply fine-spun theory, proving nothing; the latter, practical illustrations of facts fully demonstrated. The system of advanced registry is well calculated to establish the reliability of the records we make, and also act as an incentive to make records more than we otherwise would.

It is my opinion that the present fee for registering in this department is higher than is for the interest of the Association; that a reduction would tend to encourage owners of animals to make the required tests and enter their animals in this registry. Especially is this applicable to non-members who may consider the expense of ten dollars for each animal a formidable obstacle, which, perhaps, may virtually prevent them from taking an active interest in this department. Wisdom would dictate that we should furnish to the breeders who are not members all reasonable facilities for sharing the benefits which, as an association, we can confer. They are chiefly the customers who purchase our stock, and are entitled to our most favorable consideration and encouragement; and, on general principles, a liberal policy is most successful.

It will be remembered, at least by those who attended the Fat Stock and Dairy Show of the Illinois State Board of Agriculture, at Chicago, last November, that a special department was furnished for an exhibit of imitation butter (butterine). That organization has decided to repeat the proceeding the coming autumn. It is my opinion that any state or other agricultural or dairy organization which gives countenance or favor to such a fraud should be classed morally with counterfeiters of coin, or any other commodity intended to defraud the public, and is unworthy the patronage of honorable men. It is no justification for the issue of counterfeit money that it can often be passed for genuine; neither is it a justification for any other fraud that it cannot readily be detected.

The statistical information concerning the business of the Association for the year will be presented by the Secretary and Treasurer; and of the Advanced Registry, by the Superintendent of that department.

In conclusion, I wish to congratulate the Association and all breeders of Holstein-Friesian cattle upon the rapidly increasing popularity of this breed throughout the country. They are destined to grow in public favor just in proportion as their intrinsic merits are carefully and systematically developed.

Mr. GERRIT S. MILLER: I move that the Association tender a vote of thanks to the President for his able address, and also for the efficient manner in which he attended to the law-suits brought against the Association, and that the address be published in the records of the proceedings of this meeting.

The motion was carried unanimously.

The report of the Secretary was called for by the President.

The Secretary, Thomas B. Wales, Jr., read the following report:

SECRETARY'S REPORT.

Mr. President and Gentlemen: I understand it to be my duty at this time to make to you a report of my doings as the Secretary and Editor of our Association during the past year. There are many subjects of importance and of interest to us, which will be presented during the continuance of our meeting, on which I shall desire to express my views, but shall now confine myself strictly to an account of my work during the year, and its results.

I have, as you know, prepared and issued Volume IX. of the Holstein Herd-Book, a work of nearly 600 pages, which completed the registry of the old Holstein Breeders' Association, and closed that registry with a total number of 4,664 bulls and 10,560 cows, or 15,224 animals of both sexes.

I have also revised and corrected the first five volumes of the Holstein Herd-Book, and prepared consolidated transfer lists and indexes of the same, in order that the five volumes may be as easily used for reference as one. An edition of 500 copies of this work has been printed.

The uniting of the records of the old Holstein and of the old Dutch-Friesian Associations has also been brought into the work of the year, and although necessitating a great amount of very careful labor, has been, I am pleased to say, accomplished in such a manner that no confusion of pedigrees, no matter into which of the old records they run, can easily occur.

The regular business of the year has not been allowed to suffer by the attention given to the above mentioned work, for Volume I. of the Holstein-Friesian Registry is well under way; indeed, I have already a part of it in print, and of the extent of this work you will be able to form an estimate when I state that up to the 13th inst., applications for registry in it had been received for 2,290 bulls and 2,901 cows, a total of 5,191 animals, and more to be heard from, as entries only close to-day. This work cannot occupy less than 1,000 pages of a size uniform with our old Herd-Book.

Our membership now numbers 284, having been increased since the union of the Holstein and Dutch-Friesian Associations, on the 26th day of June last, by the admission of eight members.

It is with sadness that I report to the Association the death of one of our most respected and valuable members, and a former officer of the Holstein Breeders' Association, the Hon. J. D. Guthrie, of Shelbyville, Kentucky.

From March 1st, 1885, to March 1st, 1886, there have been registered 2,314 bulls and 3,667 cows, making a total of 5,991 animals. Of these, 137 bulls and 389 cows were imported from Holland, and 189 bulls and 132 cows were imported in dam.

Transfers of ownership have been made of 1,491 bulls and 3,313 cows, which has necessitated the issue of 10,795 certificates of registry and transfer, or thirty-four for each and every working day of the year.

There were registered, up to March 1st, 1886:

In the Holstein Herd-Book,	4,664 bulls.
In the Dutch-Friesian Herd-Book,	730 bulls.
In the Holstein-Friesian Herd-Book,	1,985 bulls.
In the Holstein Herd-Book,	10,560 cows.
In the Dutch-Friesian Herd-Book,	1,937 cows.
In the Holstein-Friesian Herd-Book,	2,459 cows.
Total,	22,335.

From this should be deducted 428 animals registered in the Dutch-Friesian Herd-Book, which were also registered in the Holstein Herd-Book, showing a total registry of 21,907 animals.

The total receipts for the year for membership, registry, and transfer fees, and for herd-books sold, amount to $24,394.14; expenditures, $12,387.04; net profit, $12,007.10.

Included in the expenditures, the largest items are for —

Clerk hire,	$ 2,184 68
Inspection of imported cattle,	2,167 95
Twelve hundred and fifty copies, Vol. 9, H. H. B.,	1,700 00
Five hundred copies, reprint of Vols. 1–5, H. H. B.,	1,413 00

Postage,	583 58
Special premiums at Fat Stock Show,	330 00
Returned to Messrs. Sluiter Brothers, membership and inspection fees,	625 00

The balance being for office rent and fixtures, printing of reports, circulars, and notices of various kinds, expressage, etc., as shown by itemized accounts and vouchers presented herewith. I have paid to our Treasurer the sum of $10,500; I have in my hands a balance of $94.10; and there is a balance due the association, as per ledger accounts, of $1,240.98.

There were on hand March 1st, 1886, of the Holstein Herd-Books:

Volume 1,	452 copies.
Volume 2,	32 copies.
Volume 4,	28 copies.
Volume 6,	104 copies.
Volume 7,	455 copies.
Volume 8,	852 copies.
Volume 9,	994 copies.
Reprint, first five volumes,	500 copies.

Of the Dutch-Friesian Herd-Books:

Volume 2,	318 copies.
Volume 3,	21 copies.
Volume 4,	245 copies.
Total volumes,	4,001

The value of which, at the average sale price, is $10,322.58.

There are also on hand 660 copies of the index books, giving the names and numbers of all cattle registered up to the commencement of Volume 1, Holstein-Friesian Herd-Book.

As an item of interest to the association, I will state that under the late rule placing the registration fee for imported animals at $20 per head there have been recorded 287 animals, and for their registry the sum of $5,740 has been paid.

In order that you may know the number of registered animals owned in the different states, as shown by our records, which necessarily includes animals dead and not reported to me, I read as follows:

	TOTAL.	BULLS.	COWS.
New York,	5971	1861	4110
Illinois,	2431	873	1552
Pennsylvania,	1748	500	1248
Michigan,	1428	492	936
Ohio,	1368	439	929
Iowa,	1334	530	804
Massachusetts,	1280	390	890
Minnesota,	780	267	513
Wisconsin,	668	267	401
Connecticut,	649	169	480
Kentucky,	592	130	462
Tennessee,	368	85	283
Missouri,	352	132	220
Indiana,	345	126	219
New Jersey,	330	95	235
Kansas,	321	120	201
Canada,	290	122	168
California,	288	83	205
Vermont,	251	83	168
Virginia,	186	60	126
Nebraska,	123	62	61
Mississippi,	112	43	69
Maryland,	108	34	74
Colorado,	105	37	68
New Hampshire,	96	37	59
Maine,	84	38	46
Rhode Island,	82	37	45
South Carolina,	73	33	40
Texas,	67	29	36
Dakota,	44	13	31
Oregon,	37	16	21
Montana,	35	13	22
Utah,	30	3	27
Louisiana,	30	13	17
West Virginia,	29	5	24
District of Columbia,	25	10	15
Nova Scotia,	21	4	17
Alabama,	20	9	11
Washington Territory,	19	4	15
Delaware,	19	8	11
Arkansas,	19	11	8
North Carolina,	5	3	2
Nevada,	5	2	3
Mexico,	4	1	3
New Mexico,	4	1	3
Arizona,	3	1	2
Honolulu, Sandwich Islands,	2	2	

Respectfully submitted,

THOMAS B. WALES, JR.,
Secretary.

Mr. C. W. HORR: I move that the report of the Secretary be accepted, and that it be printed in the report of this meeting.

Carried.

The President called for the report of the Treasurer.

The Treasurer, W. C. Brayton, read the following report:

TREASURER'S REPORT.

SYRACUSE, N. Y., March 15th, 1886.

Mr. President and Gentlemen: It affords me great pleasure to make the financial report of this association for the fiscal year, which closes with the date of this meeting, and is as follows:

Balance on hand, as reported at the annual meeting held in Chicago, in March, 1885, $12,022.10.

W. C. BRAYTON, *Treasurer, in account with The Holstein-Friesian Association of America.*

	RECEIPTS.	DR.	
1885.			
March 18,	To balance on hand as per last report		$12,022 10
April 8,	" cash from S. W. Sweezey, life membership fee...........$ 100 00		
May 8,	" " New York draft from Thomas B. Wales, Jr., Secretary, 1,000 00		
July 1,	" accrued interest on balance in Savings Bank, at 4 per cent... 111 25		
Oct. 19,	" cash, New York draft from Thomas B. Wales, Jr., Secretary, 3,000 00		
Dec. 15,	" " " " " " " " " 2,000 00		
1886.			
Jan. 1,	To accrued interest on balance in Savings Bank, at 4 per cent... 145 15		
" 22,	" cash, New York draft from Thomas B. Wales, Jr., Secretary, 1,000 00		
Feb. 26,	" " " " " " " " 2,500 00		
March 11,	" " " " " " " " 1,000 00		
			10,856 40
			$22,878 50
	To balance......................		$15,819 00
	Ledger account..................		1,240 98
			$17,059 98

	EXPENDITURES.	CR.	
1885.			
April 8,	By cash, Thomas B. Wales, Jr., account of services $1,500 00		
" "	" " " G. S. Miller, services to March 18th, 1885,............. 250 00		
" 14,	" " " T. B. Wales, Jr., balance for services to March 18th, 1885, 1,000 00		
" "	" " " W. C. Brayton, services to March 18th, 1885,........... 2 0 00		
May 9,	" " Egbert, Fidlar, & Chambers, on account Herd-Book..... 2,500 00		
June 12,	" " " " " 5,000 copies proceedings,		
	March, 1885,....................... 553 70		
July 11,	By cash, Egbert, Fidlar, & Chambers, balance on Herd-Book... 927 80		
Sept. 12,	" " Telegrams and postage 3 00		
Dec. 1,	" " Hon. Frank Hiscock, services, per order President		
	Yeomans............................... 125 00		
			7,059 50
	By balance.............................		15,819 00
			$22,878 50

Mr. ISAAC C. OTIS: I move, you sir, that the Treasurer's report be received and placed on file.

Carried.

The President called for the report of the Committee on Proxies.

The Chairman of the Committee on Proxies, Mr. F. L. Houghton, reported that there were present by proxy 153 members.

Mr. GERRIT S. MILLER: I move that the chair appoint a committee of three to examine the reports of the Treasurer and Secretary, and report to the meeting.

Carried.

The President appointed as Auditing Committee, Messrs. Miller, Babcock, and Fay.

The chair announced that there were present at the meeting sixty-two members of the Association, and 153 were present by proxy, making a total of 215.

The President called for the report of the Superintendent of Advanced Registry.

Mr. S. Hoxie, Superintendent of Advanced Registry, read the following report:

REPORT OF SUPERINTENDENT OF ADVANCED REGISTRY.

Mr. President and Members of the Holstein-Friesian Association of America: The work of this department, since its organization on the 27th of last May, has been mostly of a preparatory character. In accordance with instructions of the Board of Officers, a meeting of the Superintendent and Inspectors was held, May 29th, at Hamilton, N. Y., to prepare a scale of points and a schedule of requirements of cattle for this registry, to be submitted by letter to the action of the board. Such a scale and schedule was prepared, but failed of receiving the requisite number of votes for its adoption.

Another meeting was held at Rochester, N. Y., June 23d, in connection with a meeting of the Inspectors of imported cattle. The action of this meeting also failing of satisfaction, nothing further was done till August 12th. At that date, a special meeting of the Board of Officers being held at Rochester, N. Y., the scale of points and schedule of requirements prepared by the Inspectors was submitted to their action, and, after amendment, adopted. The rules were also then amended. This made it necessary to have them re-published. This was done, and copies distributed to the members of the Association, about September 1st.

On the 16th of November a paper on the subject of Advanced Registry was read before the convention of Holstein-Friesian Breeders, held in Chicago, Illinois. About the 1st of January, of the present year, the first entries were made, since which time there has been a rapidly growing interest in this work.

Many applications are in preparation. Sixty-five head of cattle have been already examined. The amount of registry fees received to date is $200. Amount of expenses incurred, including purchase of registry-book and index, cattle measures, and a book of 1000 certificates, $126.20. Sixteen days have been spent in inspection of cattle — eight by the Superintendent, and eight by one of the Inspectors.

There has been considerable correspondence consequent upon the fact of its being a new undertaking. Its character and bearings are such that time was required for its consideration. The growth of public sentiment in favor of such a system is necessarily slow, but it is very gratifying to report that, while it is thus slowly received, it grows stable by investigation.

S. HOXIE,
Superintendent.

Upon motion, the report of Mr. Hoxie was accepted.

At the request of the President, Mr. Hoxie read the paper which he had presented at the Holstein-Friesian convention held in November last, as follows:

ADVANCED REGISTRY — ITS GENERAL DESIGNS.

The leading purposes of this registry are to maintain and increase public interest in the milch breeds, to stimulate to rapid improvement, and to furnish information essential in the work of such improvement.

Every milch breed seems to take a common course in its introduction and early history in this country. At first, few animals only are imported. These are selected with much care for the breeding purposes of those who import them. Their owners are not looking for immediate profits. Their rewards are in the future, not among the least of which is the public good that is to accrue from their enterprise. Slowly the breed grows into public recognition and esteem. Then follows an increase of importations, some of which are simply commercial ventures. As profits are realized in these ventures, strong competition in this business grows up. Naturally, all sorts of devices are resorted to to stimulate the market. Booms are created, and to supply the overstimulated demand, cattle of all degrees of merit are rushed into the country. Disappointments follow. Reaction naturally takes place, and the interests of the breed flag. This is a most critical time in the history of every milch breed that has been largely introduced into this country. At this time there is much danger that its reputation will be greatly injured. No degree of general merit in a breed seems to be able to sustain it at this crisis. Wisdom in the public management, and courage in the breeder alone can do this. An inert policy at this time is simply ruinous.

I do not wish to draw attention to any particular breed, but it seems necessary that I should refer to examples to enforce the last proposition that I have made, that an inert policy is ruinous. The Ayrshire breed is one of the most beautiful that has ever been introduced into this country; at the same time it is a breed of great practical merit. At this period in its history its interests became depressed. I need not say more in regard to it. The Jersey breed also followed the course of events that I have pointed out up to the critical period. At this point a new influence began to be felt — an influence that, perhaps, was regarded of little account. I refer to the idea of "standard cows" within that breed. Such "standard cows" are a special class that make a butter record of fourteen pounds a week. Through the influence of this idea the public reputation of the breed has been kept up, and public interest in it intensified. This idea embodies the fundamental principle of advanced registry; and the work of Major Campbell Brown, gathering together such "standard cows," is virtually a system of advanced registry. That work has, no doubt, been looked upon with distrust by many breeders of Jersey cattle. They have feared that it was exalting one class of the breed to the detriment of another class. But this has not been its effects. It is not only saving that breed from the depression that I have pointed out, but it is also advancing the healthy interests of all classes. There is not a respectable herd in America that has not felt the influence of that work, and had its market value increased by it.

The system of advanced registry adopted by this association is much more complex than the one to which I have referred. It has not yet been carried into effect. It was not adopted until about the middle of last August. Since then certain preliminary steps to bring it to the attention of breeders have had to be taken, and consequently it has not been in readiness for the reception of cattle until quite recently. It is not my purpose to discuss the weakness or strength of its details, but to simply speak of its general designs.

First. It is designed to increase and maintain public interest in our breed. In the matter of butter production, its standard cows are required to make a weekly yield of nine pounds if two years old, eleven pounds if three years old, thirteen pounds if four years old, and fifteen pounds if of full age, or five years and upwards. It will be seen that the requirement of a full age cow is a pound higher than that adopted by the Jersey breed. Now, suppose within the coming year a thousand animals should be registered under these requirements. There is not a Holstein-Friesian breeder in America that does not believe that this could be easily done. What would be its immediate effects upon the general interests of this breed? Does any one doubt that it would not greatly increase public confidence in it, and that every breeder would feel that his interests were on a firmer foundation? I need not say that we are now in the critical period that I have heretofore described. I believe we are to successfully pass through it. But we shall not do so by maintaining an inert policy. We must unite in every section of our country to bring out our cattle. The idea of our depending upon a few leading breeders to sustain this reputation, and then clinging to their skirts, is an unworthy one. If any of us have cattle that are not meritorious, the sooner we send them to the shambles the better. The balance will be worth much more without them. Then we must prove by actual performance at the pail and at the churn that our cattle, as a breed, are what we claim for them. We cannot go back. We must maintain what we have advertised by the publication of the rules of this registry. To fail to do so will be disastrous to our interests. We have chosen our methods of proof, and they must be forthcoming. I have the utmost faith in the breed. I know it is capable of much more than we have claimed for it in the standards of this registry. If we show this by generally sustaining this registry, the future prosperity of our breed cannot be otherwise than assured.

Second. One of the designs of this system of registry is to inaugurate a general work of improvement in the breed. As the milch breeds come to this country, they are the products of soils, climates, and markets. Their breeders have been factors in their formation, but not through forethought and skill. The Holstein-Friesian breed has thus been produced by the soil, climate, and markets of Holland, through the intense conservatism of the peasantry of that country. It has had no Bakewells, Collings, or Prices to select, cultivate, and develope it. These cattle come to our shores as virgin material. They may be not inaptly compared to diamonds in the rough — unsorted, uncut, and unpolished. It is for us to truly make of them improved cattle, to beautify their forms, to increase the quality of their milk, and to produce in them a uniformity of transmission of high attainments. By advanced registry we practically unite the breeders in such a work. It stimulates to improvement, and offers a common ideal, toward which all may work. Besides, it furnishes the most valuable kind of information to render such work a success. At the present time breeders are obliged to work very much in the dark. They know next to nothing of the special characteristics of ancestors, to which offspring are very likely to take back. We all know something of the disappointments that, in consequence of this, result often from our most painstaking breeding. This registry gives such information. As it is continued from year to year, the build, style, handling, measurements, milking qualities, etc., of grand sires and grand dams, and back of these, of other ancestors, are easily traced and a flood of light is thrown on the breeder's work. Of what an incalculable value would such a registry be to us now, extending back but a single decade? Is it too soon to commence such a registry?

Lastly, this system is designed to collect observations upon which a science of cattle culture (to coin a much needed term) may be built. This is one of the most pressing needs of cattle-breeders all over the world. At the present time the work of selecting and breeding milk stock is conducted entirely on an empirical basis — on the guess-work system. There have been many works written on selection, but none of the principles advocated have been deduced from sufficient observations, and every one of them is in dispute to-day. This system collects, in a concise form, observations upon the principal points that have been advocated in such works. If carried out, in a few years it would furnish observations upon thousands of the best milch cattle in our country. With such a work before him, a careful student would be able to deduce a science of selection in the full meaning of this term. The same things may be said in reference to the principles of breeding. Almost every one is a matter of dispute. Who can tell when it is wise to inbreed, and when it is wise to avoid inbreeding? Who can tell what qualities and characteristics are transmitted through the male, and what through the female, etc.? Perhaps it may be thought that I am claiming too much for this registry; yet who can question that, with the observations that it collects in connection with the study of relationships, many of the principles of breeding could be settled? Millions of dollars are annually spent in gathering observations in other departments of life that are not a tithe of the practical importance to the world that the observations of such a registry would be. Our vocation as cattle-breeders is a most interesting and important one. It is a field in which investigations may be carried on and improvements made that will be an honor to our age. As individuals, our lives are perhaps too short to promise much; but in our associated capacity we engage in such works with the fullest assurance of success. Our organization is dignified at the thought. In such works it takes its stand among the noblest institutions of our country.

Mr. POWELL: I move a vote of thanks to Mr. Hoxie for this article, and that it be entered upon the minutes and published with the proceedings.

Carried.

Mr. DUDLEY MILLER: I would like to inquire the method of testing these animals.

Mr. S. HOXIE: I cannot spend time to explain it now. It is easily seen in the rules. I am invited to examine a herd. I put a man there and milk certain cows of that herd. I know the measure those cows give, so that we have some basis for estimation. This is done until the Superintendent is satisfied. The owners are allowed to feed them as they see fit. This is continued for a month, if necessary, to satisfy the Superintendent that the affidavits made by the owner are correct.

Mr. C. W. HORR: Under our rules, as I recollect, the Superintendent is not excluded by these affidavits from further investigations. He can go behind the returns if he wishes to. It was distinctly the desire and feeling of the whole board that he should go behind the returns whenever he thought there was the slightest occasion.

The President called for the reading of the resolution passed at the meeting of the Board of Officers, relating to registry of cattle imported by Mr. T. F. Koch.

The Secretary read from the minutes of the second meeting of the Board of Officers as follows:

"The following is the communication Mr. Smith proposed the board should offer at the first meeting of the Association; which was agreed upon:

"WHEREAS, Mr. T. F. Koch, now a resident, but not a citizen, of North America, has imported and applied for the registration of a certain lot of about sixty head of cattle purchased by or for him in Holland; and

"WHEREAS, Mr. Koch made this importation under circumstances and conditions that to us seem peculiar and unusual, having made due and proper application for membership before the union of the two associations;

"We therefore suggest and request that the Association act on this case, and that such a resolution be passed as will admit to registry this particular lot of animals."

Mr. HORR: I move the adoption of the resolution and authorization of registration of the animals.

Mr. Koch, being present, was asked to explain his position to the Association, and spoke as follows:

"*Gentlemen:* By the time I got word that I was not accepted by the Holstein association I was in St. Paul. I did not get any reply before because I was traveling all the time. It was delayed about three weeks after the meeting in Chicago before I knew the effects of the meeting. Then there was not a joining of the Holstein and Friesian associations. Mr. Hoxie did not say that the Dutch-Friesian association could accept me, because they had agreed not to accept members until it was decided whether they would combine with the Holstein association or not I knew that the Holstein association would only accept registered cattle. I telegraphed to Holland, so far as possible, to get the cows and bulls registered in the Holland Herd-Book, so as to make them eligible here. This was done so far as possible. I could not wait for their registry there, as I had made agreement for shipment, and I shipped the cattle about the 12th of May from Europe."

Mr. C. J. LORD: I ask, did he not thoroughly understand that he was debarred from being a member of the Association by his knowledge that he was not a citizen of the United States or Canada? I ask, is it right or justice to the members who have been debarred from registering other cattle to admit these?

Mr. C. W. HORR: Are you not overlooking the fact that at that time there were two associations? that this other association did not have this rule? that Mr. Koch did have reasonable expectation and hope that if he could not get his cattle registered in our book he could in the Dutch-Friesian? He satisfied the board fully. I am opposed to refusing cattle that are good cattle and present good credentials. Because we did one injustice, should we now do another?

Mr. S. HOXIE: According to the evidence before the board, Mr. Koch thought he was a citizen so far as matters had gone. He had already made application to become a citizen, and supposed he had gone far enough to become a member. His money was actually deposited with Mr. Wales.

A MEMBER: It seems to me there is only one point, and that is very clear. We have a resolution excluding this man. In order to admit him, we must first rescind this resolution.

A MEMBER: To all intents and purposes, Mr. Koch is a citizen. I cannot see why he should not be accepted as a member of the Association.

THE PRESIDENT: Application for citizenship does not constitute citizenship.

Mr. I. C. OTIS: Mr. Koch has rights prior to his shipping the cattle to America. He put in his application under the rules governing the registry of the Holstein Herd-Book, paid his money, and made application for membership. The cattle were purchased on certificates furnished by the Holstein Association. He received assurances that he could probably become a member of the Association. On the strength of that he purchased these cattle.

Motion was made and seconded to lay this matter on the table for the present.

Motion was lost.

Mr. J. B. DUTCHER: I have listened very attentively to what has been said. I may not understand the rules of this Association, but if I do, the Association has no right to receive these cattle without first changing the rule. I think I am in favor of accepting those cattle; but let this Association proceed rightly in the matter, and not stultify its record.

Mr. Hoxie asked whether notice was given in regard to changing the rule.

The Secretary read Article V. in the call issued for this meeting, as follows:

"To amend Sections 6 and 8 of Article IV., in relation to the registry of imported animals by members and non-members of the Association, and fees to be charged for the same."

Mr. W. M. SINGERLY: I move that Article IV., Section 6, be suspended for the present.

Mr. C. W. Horr withdrew his motion temporarily.

The motion made by Mr. Singerly was put and carried.

Mr. C. W. Horr renewed his motion that the resolution proposed by the Board of Officers be adopted, and the Secretary authorized to receive these cattle.

Carried.

Mr. W. M. Singerly moved a reconsideration of the resolution regarding the suspension of Article IV., Section 6.

Carried.

Moved by Mr. C. W. Horr that the meeting adjourn to 2 o'clock P. M.

Carried.

AFTERNOON SESSION.

The meeting was called to order at 2:45 p. m., by the President.

The President stated that Mr. Singerly's motion for a reconsideration of the resolution to suspend Article IV., Section 6, having passed, the question now before the meeting was whether that article should remain suspended; that a negative vote would restore the article to its original force.

The question was put, and decided in the negative.

THE PRESIDENT: The question now before the meeting is, as stated in the call, to petition the state of New York for an amendment to our Charter, granting the right to hold the annual meeting of the Association in any state in the United States.

Mr. C. W. HORR: I move that the President and Secretary be authorized to make the petition in the name of the members of this Association, and to take the necessary steps to obtain the needful legislation to carry out the recommendation.

THE PRESIDENT: I would state that the impression I have gained in regard to this is that the legislature had an object in providing that all bodies incorporated by this state should hold their meetings in this state. Whether the legislature will be induced to depart from that I am not at all prepared to say. If there is a reason that covers all except special cases, they will construe that as covering ours with the others.

A MEMBER: Have you ever examined the constitution of the state to see whether it would be in violation of the constitution for the legislature to charter a company to hold meetings out of the state?

THE PRESIDENT: I will read a letter I have received from a gentleman in Georgia on the subject. This letter is from a Mr. Randolph, who was Secretary of a corporation known as the Garnet Water-Power and Mining Company, whose business was transacted exclusively in Georgia.

"*T. G. Yeomans, Esq.*— DEAR SIR: In reply to your letter of the 4th, I would say that if your company is incorporated under the laws of New York, your annual meeting for election of Directors must be held in the state, and in the city or town mentioned as your principal place of business. If you do not hold a meeting, such Directors hold over. If you do hold a meeting, it must be in the state, and nowhere else."

Mr. F. C. STEVENS: At the request of our Secretary, I have consulted a lawyer in this city in regard to the possibility of our holding our meetings outside of the state. He told me that under the present charter we could not, but that we could get the charter amended so as to permit it, by special act.

Mr. W. G. POWELL: The laws of several of the states require that all corporations and associations doing business in those states shall be chartered by and hold their meetings in those states, with certain exceptions. Also some of the states require that a majority of the officers or those constituting the Board of Directors shall reside in that state. We must be careful where we go to, or we may be liable for a tax. It is also provided by some of the states that business done, except in accordance with such legislation as is stated, is illegal.

Mr. C. W. HORR: I live in Ohio, and I begin to feel that it is unsafe for a man to get up here and talk. I supposed this was not a monied corporation, and there was no capital stock that they could assess. I had supposed that this sort of an institution was different from a co-partnership that comes and seeks the benefit of your laws in the transaction of their business. I do not believe there will be any difficulty in getting the relief from your legislature. There will not be unless you have a constitutional difficulty. The advice of the lawyer whom Mr. Stevens consulted would indicate that there would be no such difficulty. Consequently, it is very safe to pass this resolution, and also to conclude that the Secretary and President will get the help from the state.

A MEMBER: I was not here at the last meeting, but as I understand it, it was the generally conceded idea that this Association was to be chartered by this state but the meetings could be held at any point we might select throughout the country. Unless there is some constitutional provision that prohibits us, I am in favor of that. We like to have these gentlemen meet us here, but if they do not want to, we are willing to meet them half way. I am in favor of passing this resolution, and if the committee find it impossible to get such a law, we cannot help it; let us do the best we can.

THE PRESIDENT: The question is upon Mr. Horr's resolution, that the President and Secretary, in the name of the members of this Association, petition the legislature of the state of New York for an amendment to our charter, granting the right to hold the annual meeting of the Association in any state in the United States, and to take the necessary steps to obtain the needful legislation to carry out the recommendation.

Carried.

THE PRESIDENT: The next matter in order is the proposition to amend Section 19 of Article II. of the By-Laws of the Association so as to facilitate action in certain cases coming under this section. The Secretary will please read the section.

The Secretary read Section 19 of Article II., as follows:

"The Board of Officers shall take cognizance of any and all specific charges made and presented to them in writing against any member of this corporation, for violation of his obligation to this corporation or to any of its members, and shall appoint a committee of two members of the corporation to hear the parties and take proofs relative to the charges, in writing and under oath, and to report the same in full, with their opinion of the matter, to the Board of Officers."

THE PRESIDENT: The question alluded to in that article was this, there have been one or two cases before the Board of Officers, and the board yesterday expelled one gentleman for misconduct. The idea suggested by that was that where a person was charged with misconduct, by which he ought to lose his membership, that when he should be notified that he was so charged, and failed to appear or answer, that this failure might be construed as an acknowledgment of his guilt, and that we might act upon it without all the preliminary steps provided for in this section.

Mr. F. L. HOUGHTON: I move that the matter be referred to a committee to prepare a proper amendment to that By-Law, to have it presented at the meeting and passed upon.

Carried.

The President appointed Messrs. F. L. Houghton and W. C. Brayton as such committee.

THE PRESIDENT: The next matter in order is the proposed amendment of Section 4, Article IV., omitting the words "North Holland."

The Secretary read Section 4 of Article IV., as follows:

"Thoroughbred Holstein-Friesian shall be held to mean and refer to only those large, improved, black and white cattle already registered in the Holstein and Dutch-Friesian Herd-Books, and such as are descended from them in direct line, both as to sire and dam, and such imported animals, or their descendants, as are registered in the Netherlands, Friesian, or North Holland Herd-Books, proved by the affirmation of the breeder satisfactory to the Inspector."

Mr. WING R. SMITH: I would ask why the North Holland Herd-Book should be stricken from that list?

Mr. C. PRATT: I move that the resolution be adopted, omitting the words "North Holland."

Mr. W. G. POWELL: I move that the Board of Officers be instructed to make investigation as to the character of that book, whether it is conducted for the interests of the breed or for speculative purposes, and also be authorized, if in their judgment, after a thorough investigation, the words "North Holland" should be stricken out, to strike them out.

This motion was seconded.

Mr. J. B. DUTCHER: I move to amend by striking out the last clause, and insert that the Board of Officers shall make their report to this Association, instead of striking out.

Amendment seconded.

Mr. W. G. POWELL: I accept Mr. Dutcher's amendment.

The President: The question is to refer this matter to the Board of Officers, as a committee, to report to this Association.

Mr. Wing R. Smith: It seems to me that it is strange that this should be referred to such a committee without their being anything said on the subject. I doubt whether anything can be said by any one present against the North Holland Herd-Book. If there is any one here who will say anything against the North Holland Herd-Book, I will be in favor of the motion.

Mr. Gerrit S. Miller: I move that the whole question be laid upon the table.

Carried.

The President: Next in order is the proposition to amend Section 5 of Article IV., making it necessary that the application for the registry of American-bred animals be made by the breeder, or owner at date of birth.

The Secretary read Section 5, Article IV., as follows:

"American-bred animals shall only be registered in the Herd-Book upon application made upon or following the form furnished by the corporation, and the payment of a fee of $1.00 by members of the corporation and of $2.00 by persons not members for the registry of each animal, which *must accompany the application*. No two animals shall have the same name. Only direct descendants of an animal shall be entitled to the family name with numbers prefixed or added, and after the first generation, the family name only in combination. Males shall only be entitled to the family name in combination, in which the family name shall be first. In all combinations the name of the sire or dam, in part or in full, may be used as desired by the applicant. All titles of distinction, nobility, military, or honorary, and all first or given names, not in use as *family* names, shall be free for use in combination."

Mr. E. M. Washburn: There is no one specified to make the application. Any one can make an application for the registry of an animal. This specifies who shall make the application.

It was moved that the proposition be laid upon the table.

Carried.

The President: The next proposition is: That firms or corporations, where one or more members of such firm, or stockholders of such corporation, are members of the Holstein-Friesian Association, be entitled to register and transfer their animals for fees charged to members; also in relation to the naming of animals.

A Member: Some fault has been found by firms and by corporations whose members are not all members of our Association. Such firms have been refused registration at member's fees because all their members were not members of our Association. It has been proposed to change this so that such firms can register and transfer animals at member's fees, provided a certain number of their members are members of the Association.

Mr. G. M. CARPENTER: I would say that I am a member of a firm of which two members are members of the Association. We make the motion that where members of firms are members of the Association stock shall be registered the same as for members of the Association.

The motion was seconded.

Mr. C. W. HORR: It seems to me that something is needed, but it seems to me that this resolution does not quite hit it.

Mr. THOMAS B. WALES, JR.: Mr. President, I find that there are some thirty such firms, a portion of whose members only are members of this Association, and in justice to them, I make the following motion: That "firms or corporations composed of two members or stockholders shall be entitled to register and transfer animals for member's fees, when one member or stockholder is a member of this Association. When such firms or corporations are composed of three or more members or stockholders, such firms or corporations shall be entitled to register and transfer cattle at member's fees when two or more members or stockholders are members of this Association.

Mr. POWELL: I would call attention to the article that prohibits those not American citizens from registering cattle. Suppose that I, as a member of this Association, see fit to form a co-partnership with somebody in Holland, for instance, would that resolution let us in? We have another section that prohibits that. I would amend that resolution by saying that it shall not affect prohibiting the importation and registration of cattle by those not American citizens.

A MEMBER: I move the adoption of this amendment, with this amendment put to it, where it speaks of corporations, that they should be corporations within this country; residents of our own country.

THE PRESIDENT: The chair understands that the motion is on the resolution offered by Mr. Wales, with the additional provision that those corporations must be composed of American citizens.

A MEMBER: Should that not specify that those animals be recorded in the name of the corporation or firm?

A MEMBER: My idea is that half, or a majority, of the corporation or company should be members of this Association.

Mr. C. W. HORR: Is there not one trouble yet? Here is a firm of Smith & Brown; if Smith & Brown are allowed to record cattle because Smith is a member of the Association, Smith ought not to be entitled to record cattle individually.

It was moved and seconded that the resolution be referred to a committee of three.

Mr. S. HOXIE: Let us take an illustration. Here is Carpenter, father and son. Father and son have a certain number of cattle. As I understand it, the movement is to arrange it so that only one member of the firm can register.

Suppose you limit the number to twenty. If the firm is so large as to desire to register more than that — take the firm S. Pope & Son; one member is a member of the Association. They desire to register at $1.00 per head. Let them have the benefit of that to a certain degree — say ten animals. If they have more animals than that, they both should become members of the Association.

A motion was made that the subject be laid upon the table.

Mr. M. A. AIKEN: Supposing a company, or corporation, as you are a mind to have it, own a few Holstein cattle. They do not do it as an entire business, but they have a few cattle. It is one of their interests. One member of the firm becomes a member of this association. What benefit, if you make this law, can it possibly be to that corporation if that member becomes a member of this Association?

THE PRESIDENT: As a member of the Association, he will get the Herd-Books, and all other publications issued by the Association, free of charge.

The motion to lay the matter on the table was withdrawn.

Mr. WALES: Mr. President, no rule having been established by this Association, a short time ago I asked the Board of Officers to instruct me on the point in question. It instructed me to charge firms full fees where all its members were not members of the Association. This affected some thirty firms, one or more of the members of those firms being members of the Association. This ruling of the board having caused much dissatisfaction, I have proposed such a rule as I think would prove satisfactory to all concerned.

Mr. C. W. HORR: I move that this question be referred to a committee of three, for immediate action.

Carried.

The chair appointed as such committee, Messrs. Horr, Langworthy, and W. B. Smith.

THE PRESIDENT: The next question before the meeting is the proposition to amend Sections 6 and 8 of Article IV., in relation to the registry of imported animals by members and non-members of the Association, and fees to be charged for the same.

Mr. HOXIE: I would say that Dr. Patterson said he offered it. Section 6 reads: "Only members of this Association may register imported animals shipped from Europe after March 18th, 1885." The idea was to strike that out.

Mr. T. B. WALES, JR.: Mr. President, by this it is proposed that others than members of this Association may register imported animals shipped from Europe after March 18th, 1885. In doing that we open our registry for imported animals to anybody, provided, only, that the animals come up to our requirements.

It was moved and seconded that the resolution be laid on the table.

The motion to lay the matter on the table was withdrawn.

Mr. GERRIT S. MILLER: It seems to me that animals of equal value, no matter who the owner is, should have the privilege of being registered in our Herd-Books. Our Association, as I understand it, is for the purpose of improving the breed. When we have two animals of equal merit, because one is owned by A and the other by B, I see no reason why one should be kept out and the other registered.

Mr. E. A. POWELL: This brings up the most important question before the body for consideration, on several accounts. You see the bearing of this. You must not take the thing as it appears to-day; we must go into the future. We are starting in to build up a breed of cattle, to make them superior to what they are now, and to what they are now in their native country. This we can do by breeding on the principles followed in America. To get to where the cattle are at the present time has been the work of centuries. Their advancement in their native country is but a slight advancement in a century. The Hollander does not breed from any established principle of advancement, or any established principle to produce certain results. The animal as bred in Holland is an accident. We can make more advancement in ten years than they can in a century. The Hollander cannot keep an ordinary cow. They have been compelled to have them selected, and keep the better animals. Hardly a man in Holland is breeding on the principles that we use. Our friend, Mr. Jewett, will show you what can be done in a very few years. In Holland their registers are not established on purity of breeding at all. They do not estimate an animal from the purity of its blood. They estimate it from its appearance to-day. We want to establish something beyond that. We must advance on the principle that we can combine certain necessary elements to produce certain results which advance rapidly, from one generation to another. We want to look still further. The Hollander, while he may import just as good cattle as the American — that will appear to the eye just as well, that will sell, providing it was not for the record, for just as much money — has no interest in this country or the cattle beyond the time the money is paid to him under the auctioneer's hammer. The American who imports cattle feels the responsibility. To show you an illustration of what the effect of breeding is on the general estimation of the public, the other day, in Kentucky, a certain horse was sold at auction and bought for $4,700. That horse was sold, and some days passed before it was discovered that there was a question about the breeding of the horse. During that time the Hollander would be half across the Atlantic. The claim that was spoken of — I do not know what the result was — was that the damage was $4,000. There is the difference in one case. Gentlemen, we are acting for the people of this country. We are acting to not only improve the breed in America, but to improve it as Americans. As such, I claim that we are bound to protect Americans from any chance of fraud. Any man who has imported cattle from Holland knows that the Dutchmen are not so different from Americans, so far as honesty is concerned. You will find all classes of men there. You can go to Holland and buy an animal with any kind of a pedigree that you want to write out, and have it testified to before the Burgomaster. You also know — any man that has been there — that it takes the utmost care in buying your animals to know that they are carefully bred. The Hollander, living there, knows the men from whom he can buy; he can go to those men who have such cattle that a good breeder from this side would not touch. He can bring those cattle here and have them registered. They will pass inspection, because no inspector can detect the difference between pure blood and a good grade. He sells those cattle under advantages which an American would not have. He buys them cheaper, because the best importers would not buy them. With the view that we are going to breed better and advance faster than they do there, and that we want to build up a lot of cattle, not to sell to-day, but for all time, and a breed of cattle that are going to stand higher and higher; that we are going to assume a certain responsibility, to stand between the breeder and the importer, we want to be very careful what gates we throw open. If we admit one foreigner we cannot exclude another until we prove that he is not importing that class of cattle. We will be establishing a precedent that will be very dangerous, and we do not know where it is going to end. A foreigner who lives in that country has an opportunity of buying cattle, fine in appearance, that will pass inspection, that are not pure, and that Americans would not have. We cannot be too careful in opening our doors to foreigners not interested in this country.

Mr. O. P. CHAPMAN: This is the first time I was aware that the breeding of the Holland cattle was an accident. I had supposed it was done with great care. It seems to me that Mr. Powell's whole argument is based on the fact that Hollanders are dishonest and Americans honest. If you have a Hollander — we will take this position — if you have a Hollander that is a good, square, honest breeder, he cannot get his cattle registered by this Association. He has got no way of getting them in. You have a dishonest importer in this country, and still you allow him to record his cattle just the same.

Mr. E. A. POWELL: Our By-Laws do not admit a man unless he is voted in by the board.

Mr. DUDLEY MILLER: I know it is a difficult thing to establish a pedigree on the other side. What is the difference between establishing it on this side or the other side? Whether the American goes there and gets it, or it is brought to him from there?

Mr. E. A. POWELL: Do you believe if you write to a firm in Holland to send you a certain number of cattle, that they would take the same pains in selecting them that you would?

Mr. MILLER: No man would act so much for my interest as I would. I see no difference from judging them on this side and judging them on the other.

Mr. W. G. POWELL: This restriction is not alone against the Hollander, against the German, or against the Englishman. It is against any one not a member of the Association. One of the principal arguments in favor of the rule was this: You notice Article I., Section 4, says: "Any member of this corporation who shall be found guilty of any misrepresentation, deception, or fraud in relation to the registry of animals in the Holstein-Friesian Herd-Book shall forfeit his membership in the corporation." That was the principal reason for throwing this safeguard around the importation of cattle, confining it to the members of the Association. It was believed that by this rule we had some safeguard thrown around the pedigree. On this side we can reach the man, if he is anywhere in the United States, if he has done a fraudulent transaction. There is a difference between him and the foreigner who skips the country as soon as he is done. . The same restriction applies to any person not a member. We are glad to receive any American citizen who can come with a reasonable reputation as to character and standing; if he is willing to pay the $100 membership fee, the board will be glad to receive him. If membership in the Association is not worth that to him he ought not to go into the business.

Mr. E. A. POWELL: There is one point that covers this case. A short time ago there was a firm of foreigners advertised their stock to be sold in New York under the hammer. The statement was made that they would be responsible for those cattle, pedigree, etc., but that any claim for fraud or misrepresentation must be made to them before the steamer sailed on a certain date.

Mr. S. BURCHARD: Mr. President, I agree with every word that the Messrs. Powell have said in regard to this matter; but there is one point I wanted to bring before the Association. That is this: In the first place, this Association has established a scale of points supposed to represent a perfect animal. With our ideas of breeding, we expect to breed up, some day, to that point. The Short-horns have been bred up nearly to that point. Any man riding along the roads can point out one of these animals. As the Holstein-Friesian cattle have been bred, if it was not for the color, I defy any man to tell them. We have a type that we have established; we want to breed up to that standard as fast as we can. As has been said, we can make more advancement in ten years than the Europeans can in one hundred years, because (I affirm what has already been said) these cattle are an accident in that country; they are produced by the soil and climate and the circumstances surrounding them. Any one who has been to Holland knows that it is the greenest, freshest looking country in the world; and these cattle, feeding on those low lands all these ages, have come up to what they are now, to their present condition, and not through any skill in the people of Holland in breeding them. Their ideas of judging cattle are altogether different from our own. Any one who has been in Holland and been around their markets has seen their cattle-men with a staff or whip with knots tied in it, and the animal that measures the most knots is the best animal. We have established this scale of points. We want to breed up to that scale of points — to that standard — as fast as we can. Allowing those men, with their ideas, to bring their cattle into our country retards our advancement in this direction. If there is any man in this Association who can form a better plan of getting our cattle that Hollanders would select to put upon our shores, and, as they would suppose, to improve our breed, we would be ready to accept it.

Mr. G. S. MILLER: I think the Association would be wise if it confines itself to the provinces of a herd-book in this matter. In my opinion, that province consists in establishing a pure pedigree, and then requiring high individual excellence. We have asked the Hollanders to protect us on the pedigree question by establishing herd-books. They have established herd-books, and we have recognized those herd-books for pedigrees. We have appointed inspectors, and they must satisfy themselves that these pedigrees are correct. In my judgment, it is very good policy for us to receive all animals that come with such recommendations through our examining committees. I wish to call your attention to the fact that a few years ago the Holstein Association considered themselves strong enough to give the cold shoulder to their opponents, thinking that they would not establish a herd-book. It was thought so by many of our prominent members at that time. We went on our headstrong way, and you all know the result: A very strong, formidable competitor was organized against us, and finally we made favorable terms and granted concessions and united; and we are a stronger association than when the two existed. If we compel these foreigners to establish a herd-book over here, and they import the same animals that we import — the same class and family of animals that are recorded in those herd-books — the public are going to buy those animals. They are going to make just as good records as the animals we import. The public will not sustain us in this fight. We had better be liberal, and accept all that come up to our standard; leave our doors open to those who will bring all that we require.

Mr. E. A. POWELL: Let me correct one mistake of Mr. Miller's. That was, that we accept the foreign herd-book as authority upon pedigrees. We do not accept it at all upon pedigrees. We ignore it by asking the importer to go before the Burgomaster. They have not a herd-book that is authority on pedigree. They select a better class of animals, as a general thing.

Mr. MILLER: I merely wish to explain myself. Of course the herd-book in Holland has been started within the past few years, and a certain limit was placed on time for the foundation to be recorded. The first animals we imported came without pedigree. The only pedigree they have is that which traces back to the first record in our book. It is so with the animals. If you get young animals, they can trace back to the time to which the herd-book goes. We require that the animal shall be recorded in one of those herd-books before we accept it here.

Mr. BURRELL: I think we all wish to be consistent. I sympathize fully with what Mr. Powell has said in regard to putting safeguards around the importation of stock. If it is necessary that stock should be owned in this country for a year or so, let that condition be imposed. As for barring out any citizen from abroad, I am opposed to it. Take it in the department of cheese and butter making, or almost any department, we are dependent upon them for almost all the success we obtain. We must not forget that the Holstein-Friesian cow was not bred in this country. Why we should discriminate against these parties who bring their cattle up to our standard I cannot understand.

Mr. W. G. POWELL: I wish to renew the remark I first made, that this is not a restriction against the foreigner; it is a restriction against any man who is not a member of the Association, simply because he is not a member; it is a restriction against Americans and foreigners alike.

Mr. S. BURCHARD: I have here a scale of points of the North Holland Herd-Book. I want to read a few points to show their ideas of judging cattle. "Chest, wide and roomy, three points; tail, fine and long, four points"— the tail one point more in value than the chest. "Barrel, well rounded, with large but not too deep abdomen, two points"— of only half as much importance in their scale as the tail. "The udder, eight points; the teats, six points"— of almost as much importance as the udder.

Mr. C. W. HORR: This is a question that has been debated, more or less, in the board, and there are some differences of opinion in that august body on this question. It is very important. It is one that needs the most careful consideration of every member of this society. I think it is, in the first place, a good thing for us all to try to get into a good, candid temper. First, you make a rule that excludes these foreigners from becoming members; then you turn around and say because they are not members they cannot import. This does not seem quite fair. It is a grave question with me whether the correct remedy is not to allow any man of good character to become a member; then you can expel the foreigner, the same as an American, if he practices any fraud upon the Association. I believe the correct solution of the question is to say to any respectable man upon the earth who desires to join us, "We are a little better than you, but we will take you in provided you come up and pay the little hundred dollars." It might help him somewhat. I like the church better that keeps the wide door — that does not have a long list of questions which they propound to its members — that says to any man who wants to learn to live a better life, "Come in," on the theory that it will do him good and will not do you any harm. If a man comes into this Association who has not been educated up to our view — who has not the interests of the Holstein cattle down to the bottom of his heart — perhaps we will help him along. We are inconsistent; because we require every animal imported to be recorded in the books of these Holland men, whom you do not want to trust in the next breath. If I am not correct, I wish to be corrected. Those Holland books over there, now, will not record an animal not descended from black-and-white cattle. We do not allow any animal to be imported that is not recorded.

Mr. S. HOXIE: For every animal the color is given.

Mr. C. W. HORR: Let us take a look at a little picture, like this: Here is a man of this country with some cattle. He knocks at the door of our institution. He is a foreigner, and cannot speak our language. He does not have anything to do with the selection of an inspector. He has to submit to our rules, and comes with that knowledge. We have adopted the most rigid rule in regard to inspection and affidavits. We have required them to pay $25 for registration. He has to knock at our door and ask for admission. Let us look again. Here present to-day are about four importing firms who have in their pockets enough proxies to control, absolutely, this Association. Tell me whether there is more danger that this inspector will do injustice influenced by the money of the foreigner or influenced by these great firms that control the institution and hold his official existence in the hollow of their hands. It seems to me we can trust ourselves to inspect these cattle that come to our shores. I think we should say to any man whose character is good that he can become a member; and we shall have done the wise thing. The only thing we can do to protect these Herd-Books is to allow these men to become members and have the same rights of registration that we have.

A MEMBER: If we are to protect ourselves and advance these cattle, we must do it ourselves, and for ourselves, not for those not connected with us. I am clearly of the opinion that if we would protect our rights in the matter, we must do it as an association, and not by letting everybody in.

Mr. C. PRATT: The gentleman last up has been mistaken, I think, in Mr. Horr's opinion. I understood him not to say let everybody in, but everybody of character. I am in favor of letting in everybody with character good enough to get in. I am myself in favor of taking anybody into this Association whose character is all right. I think we made a mistake in discriminating against the Sluiter Brothers. We want just the same character from the Messrs. Sluiter Brothers that we would from any Americans.

Mr. DUDLEY MILLER: What is the use of keeping these other animals out if we can breed them so superior in this country?

Mr. POWELL: While we may breed those animals so superior, while they are flooding the country with animals not so well bred, the tendency is downward.

Mr. MILLER: Our inspectors only protect us so far as the eye is concerned.

Mr. POWELL: I wish Mr. Miller to say whether he can tell from the appearance of an animal whether it is a pure-bred animal.

Mr. MILLER: I do not pretend to.

Mr. POWELL: Then what are we going to do as an association?

Mr. MILLER: We take their Herd-Books as one guarantee, and use our own inspection as another, and the affidavit as another.

A MEMBER: It seems to me that we will make a great mistake in this matter if we undertake to pursue the policy of confining the cattle to be registered to the American importers. I do not know whether the Hollander has got life enough to protect himself; but if when he imports just as fine cattle as we do, and we shut him out from the market when we will not allow him to record in the Herd-Book, what else have you left that man only to protect himself by starting a Herd-Book for himself. What will be the result, on the supposition that they import as good cattle as we do? It will resolve itself to a question of merit. If they import better cattle, on the merits of the cattle, finally, they will succeed; and it seems to me there can be but one side to this. I have no interest in the matter, as far as importing is concerned, but I do want to keep the Association in such a situation that we shall not be in such a position as forces us to shut the door to the honest Hollander, and open the door to the dishonest American.

Mr. DUTCHER: I move to lay the whole question on the table.

Carried by a rising vote.

The President called for the report of the Committee on Amendment to the By-Laws.

Mr. F. L. HOUGHTON: Mr. President and gentlemen, the committee desire to report as follows:

To amend Section 19 of Article II. of By-Laws. "The Board of Officers shall take cognizance of any and all specific charges, made under oath and presented to them in writing, against any member of this corporation, for violation of his obligation to this corporation or to any of its members, and shall appoint a committee of two members of the corporation, which said committee shall notify the alleged offending member at his last known place of residence, of the specific charges, fully set forth in writing, and designate a place and day when and where he may have a hearing before said committee, who shall hear the parties and take proof relevant to the charges, in writing and under oath, and report the same in full, with their opinion of the matter, in writing, to the Board of Officers. All notices of such hearings shall be given to the alleged offending members not less than sixty days before the time set for such hearings. In case of a wilful failure of the alleged offending member to appear and answer the charges made, at the time and place named, the Board of Officers shall be hereby empowered to act the same as though said charges were true, and take such measure in regard to the same as they may deem proper and advisable under the charter."

THE PRESIDENT: The question is upon the adoption of the report of the committee.

Adopted.

The President called for the report of the Committee on the Amendment to Section 5 of Article IV.

Mr. C. W. HORR: I am compelled to make a majority report — two agreeing, and one dissenting. We recommend that to Section 5, Article IV., there be added the following clause:

"All firms and corporations, all of whose members are citizens of North America, shall be entitled to the privilege of registration and transfer of American-bred animals, in the name of the firm, in our Herd-Books, by paying the fees charged to members, when one-half or more of the members of said firms or corporations are members of this Association."

Mr. WING R. SMITH: Mr. Chairman and gentlemen, the reason why I differ from the majority of the committee is, in one instance the case has just been stated. I will suppose that the two gentleman who just went ont with me are members of the Association. They are in company with me in business. I am not a member of the Association. I am the manager, however, of the cattle; know more about them than they do; have charge of them, and care of them. I can play any sort of tricks on them. They are not responsible for my acts at all. I think the more you tamper with this thing, after we have spent a month trying to revise it and get it into shape, I think we had better let it alone. The reason is that some firms have one or two of their members — they could not get their partners into the Association if they made application — who are members of the Association, and they are going to shoulder their partners. I really believe, and my firm conviction is, that it is a step in the wrong direction to undertake to open the bars and let one man cover another man's responsibility.

Mr. C. PRATT: I would say, in answer, that in many instances the barn is under the management of a foremen.

A MEMBER: I move the following amendment to the resolution:

"Before the Secretary shall accept entries, a full list of the members of the firms and also of the corporations, shall be reported to the Board of Officers, and they shall pass upon the character and standing of those different members."

Adopted.

Mr. SMITH: It seems to me the question is, what is our object in becoming members? If a man belongs to the firm, and the firm sees fit to let him record cattle in his own name, he has a right to do so.

THE PRESIDENT: The question before the Association is upon adopting the report of the committee, as amended.

Motion lost by a rising vote.

THE PRESIDENT: The next business in order is the submission to the Association of a proposition regulating the use of proxies at the meetings of the Association.

A MEMBER: I move that the consideration of the matter be laid upon the table.

Motion lost.

Mr. THOMAS B. WALES, JR.: I was written to by several members that they would make such a proposition at this meeting.

Mr. B. B. LORD: I, for one, wrote to the Secretary in regard to the use of proxies. Proxies, as used at the present time, I think, are dangerous. There should be some way of regulating their use; throwing them out entirely, or limiting the number that members should hold.

A MEMBER: I doubt whether the Association has the power to take away the right of a member of the Association to delegate any other member to vote, whether he votes as he sees fit, or delegates him to vote definitely.

Mr. POWELL: Section 3 of our charter says that while a person is a member in good standing he is entitled to vote personally or by proxy, and to all the privileges of such membership. I make it as a point of order.

Mr. HOUGHTON: Every man has a right to appoint an attorney, and constitute him as his attorney to act for him.

Mr. DUTCHER: I do not think there is any question that any member has a right to vote. For myself, I do not want any office. I would not accept any office; but the impression seems to have gone abroad that this Association is run in the interest of one or two firms. Whether that is true or not, I do not know, and do not care, but it is injuring the character and standing of this Association very much. I know a gentleman now, in good standing, who would become a member of the Association if it was not for this fact. If any arrangement or understanding could be made about the use of proxies, I think it would be beneficial to the Association. I do not question the right of any member to send his proxy. This made serious trouble last year, and will continue to make trouble as long as the Association exists.

A MEMBER: I move that the committee already appointed to have the charter so amended that the annual meetings may be held outside of the state shall also have Section 3 of the charter amended so that the section shall read "is entitled to vote personally," leaving out the words "or by proxy."

Motion seconded.

Mr. POWELL: There is no question but there has been more or less dissatisfaction in regard to the use of proxies. I really am unable to see how this matter can be remedied, unless we might do this: That the parties giving the proxy shall instruct particularly the party who holds the proxy on the question to be brought before the Association. I think that proxies ought to be used as seldom as possible.

A MEMBER: I move that the question be laid upon the table.

Motion carried.

THE PRESIDENT: The next business in order is the consideration of the proposition "that the widow or minor children of a member of the Association be allowed to register and transfer animals for member's fees."

Mr. C. PRATT: I made that proposal.

Mr. DUTCHER: I move the adoption of the resolution, with the additional proviso that when any male member of the family arrives at majority, that privilege shall cease.

Motion seconded.

Mr. POWELL: That is, that the executors or administrators of the estate shall have the same benefit of the Association that the member of the Association shall have.

THE PRESIDENT: The chair understands Mr. Powell to offer an amendment that it be for the executors and administrators representing an estate.

Mr. F. L. HOUGHTON: I second that amendment.

Carried.

Question upon the original resolution, as amended, was put and carried.

THE PRESIDENT: The next question is in reference to an appropriation for butter, cheese, and beef premiums.

Mr. SMITH: I have understood that it is proposed to admit in competition with butter, the imitation article — butterine and oleomargarine — at the Chicago fat stock and dairy show. I would like to suggest that an exception be made in reference to this show. I move that the Chicago fat stock and dairy show be excluded in whatever premiums this Association may see fit to offer for Holstein cattle or butter or cheese premiums, for that reason.

Mr. S. N. WRIGHT: I move that a committee of three be appointed by the chair to take into consideration the action of the Board of Agriculture of the state of Illinois in regard to admitting bogus butter at the fat stock show next fall.

THE PRESIDENT: How would it do to offer a resolution requesting our Board of Officers not to make any appropriation for any show that admits butterine or oleomargarine?

Mr. DUTCHER: If any gentleman is afraid to put his butter by the side of butterine, the sooner he goes out of the butter business the better. I think it is to the interest of every agricultural man in the United States to have butterine shown by the side of butter. I am opposed to this industry as much as any man in the country; but for this Association to say they will not show their butter in any show where butterine is shown, I think, is boys' play.

A MEMBER: I think the gentleman is under a misapprehension. I have had a talk with a member of the Board of Agriculture. They do not enter it in competition with butter. They enter it as butterine or oleomargarine.

THE PRESIDENT: The question is upon the proposition of Mr. Smith, that the Board of Officers of this Association be requested not to offer premiums to associations where butterine is accepted in competition with butter.

A MEMBER: I want it put upon record that this Association condemns the whole manufacture of butterine.

THE PRESIDENT: The first question is upon the amendment offered by Mr. Wright, that this matter be referred to a committee of three.

Mr. SMITH: I accept Mr. Wright's amendment.

Mr. POWELL: I would suggest that this committee also formulate some resolution petitioning Congress to take action in regard to the manufacture of this article. The trouble is that this is sold as butter, used as butter, and eaten as butter, when it is a fraud. It is nothing more than the circulation of counterfeit money, because it looks so much like good money that you cannot tell them apart. There are a very few men, representing, perhaps, about

$2,000,000, engaged in the manufacture of this imitation of butter, selling large amounts of it at an expense of about seven cents a pound. It goes into market looking like butter, and sells as butter. It brings down all the butter and all the dairy interests of this country to that level. If there is anything this Association can do to put a restriction upon the manufacture, it is our duty, not only as an association, but as citizens, to do it. There is a bill before Congress providing that a tax of ten cents shall be levied upon every pound sold. It shall be put under the department of revenue. Every package shall be stamped the same as a package of cigars or whisky. It is only just that such a law should be passed and enforced. The reason why it should be put under the department of revenue is because it is then under the control of the United States, and would be enforced in every state alike.

Mr. WRIGHT: I accept the suggestion of Mr. Powell.

A MEMBER: I would ask Mr. Powell if he knows that any man can make any article in this country that is not detrimental to health.

Mr. POWELL: It is detrimental to health physiologically. It is proven to a demonstration that it is. Supposing, under deception, lard is put before you and you eat it, is it detrimental to health? At seventy degrees trichinæ is not killed. Trichinæ is introduced into the butter. That butter, under the sanction of the general government, is put before the public and consumed. Nine hundred and ninety-nine thousand parts of it are consumed under a misapprehension to one that is not.

THE PRESIDENT: The question is upon the amended resolution offered by Mr. Wright, that a committee of three be appointed to consider this subject, and report to the Association.

Carried.

The President appointed as such committee Messrs. S. N. Wright, E. A. Powell, and O. P. Chapman.

Mr. F. L. HOUGHTON: I move that the Board of Officers be authorized to offer such an amount of money for premiums for butter, beef, milk, and cheese as they deem proper.

Carried.

Mr. W. M. SINGERLY: I move that we proceed to the election of officers.

Carried.

Mr. C. W. HORR: I wish to preface my nomination by congratulating this Association upon our happy selection, a little less than a year ago, of the honorable gentleman who has so impartially presided over our deliberations. I nominate Mr. T. G. Yeomans for President of the Association.

Mr. POWELL: I wish to say a word in regard to Mr. Yeomans' qualifications for this office. I think I have an opportunity of appreciating as much as any member present the amount of work Mr. Yeomans has had to do this past year. Mr. Yeomans has managed in the very best manner possible, and I think to the satisfaction of every member here. I doubt if it would have been possible for any person here to have stepped into his shoes and managed the affairs of the Association more ably than he has done. You understand the suits that have been brought up the past year required not only time, but ability and expense. We are under a debt of obligation to Mr. Yeomans for the able manner in which he has conducted the affairs of the Association.

Mr. T. G. YEOMANS: I appreciate the compliments of the gentlemen who have mentioned my name. I was placed in the position I have occupied unsolicited, by my friends. Not only so, but it has given me pleasure to render what services I have been able to. But there are many men, younger members of the Association. It is but just that a position of this kind, which I conceive to be very honorable, be passed around. I wish very respectfully to decline the nomination you have tendered me. I hope you will proceed to the election of a successor to my office.

Mr. MILLER: I heartily endorse all Mr. Powell has said in regard to Mr. Yeomans and his faithful fulfilment of all the requirements of the office. I must say I also agree with the view Mr. Yeomans has put forth — that there are younger men, and a good many men, in the Association who are aspiring to fill this office of honor. It seems to me it will give better general satisfaction if we consider that from this time forward the office of President is to be filled simply for one year — that there is to be a change at each of our annual meetings — and with that feeling on the subject, I take great pleasure in nominating for President one of our prominent members — a man who has always striven to maintain a herd of very high standard, and sets his standard as high as any one of us. I nominate Mr. F. C. Stevens, of Attica, New York.

Mr. SMITH: I second the nomination. I move that the President cast the ballot of the Association for Mr. F. C. Stevens, for President of the Association.

Carried.

The President accordingly cast the ballot of the Association for Mr. F. C. Stevens for President of the Association.

It was moved that the President cast the ballot of the Association for Mr. G. D. Wheeler for First Vice-President of the Association.

Carried.

The President cast the ballot of the Association in accordance with its vote.

Mr. S. N. Wright moved that the President cast the ballot of the Association for Mr. W. M. Singerly for Second Vice-President of the Association.

Carried.

The President cast the ballot of the Association in accordance with its vote.

Mr. HOXIE: I move that Mr. George F. Jackson be the Third Vice-President.

Mr. THOMAS B. WALES, JR.: Mr. President, I understand that Mr. Jackson has, or is about closing out his cattle interest, and if I am informed correctly, I would suggest that some other name be substituted.

It was moved and seconded that the President cast the ballot for Mr. M. L. Sweet for Third Vice-President.

Carried.

The President cast the ballot of the Association according to its vote.

Mr. HOXIE: I move that the President cast the ballot of the Association for David H. Burrell for Fourth Vice-President.

Carried.

The President cast the ballot of the Association in accordance with its vote.

It was moved and seconded that the President cast the ballot of the Association for Mr. W. C. Brayton for Treasurer.

Carried.

The President cast the ballot of the Association in accordance with its vote.

The report of the Financial Committee was called for by the President.

Mr. GERRIT S. MILLER: Your committee would report that they have given the accounts of the Secretary and Treasurer careful attention. The accounts of the Treasurer are correct, agreeing with the vouchers. The accounts of the Secretary are correct, agreeing with the vouchers. They find a few small errors in footing. There is an error of two dollars in favor of the Association. On the debtor side there is an error of twelve cents in one place, and ten cents in another, against the Association.

It was moved and seconded that the report of the Finance Committee be accepted.

Carried.

THE PRESIDENT: The next business in order is the election of three Directors for the term of two years.

Mr. E. G. FAY: I move that we proceed to ballot, as we did last year for officers; that the ballot be cast for the three at one time.

Carried.

Messrs. F. L. Houghton, H. Langworthy, W. J. Smith, E. Huidekoper, J. B. Dutcher, and W. G. Powell were nominated as members of the Board of Directors.

Messrs. J. B. Dutcher and W. G. Powell declined the nomination.

THE PRESIDENT: I wish to suggest that every gentleman who votes any proxies put his name on the back of the card, and the number of proxies he is entitled to. I will appoint Messrs. Babcock and Chapman tellers.

The tellers reported the result of the ballot to be as follows: F. L. Houghton, 90; John W. Shallcross, Jr., 27; Wing R. Smith, 31; Edgar Huidekoper, 90; H. Langworthy, 54; W. Judson Smith, 99; W. G. Powell, 55; B. B. Lord, 14; M. L. Sweet, 3; H. C. Gale, 1.

The President declared Messrs W. Judson Smith, F. L. Houghton, and Edgar Huidekoper elected.

Mr. C. W. HORR: I move that these gentlemen be declared the unanimous choice of the Association.

Carried.

It was moved and seconded that the President cast the ballot of the Association for Mr. Thomas B. Wales, Jr., for Secretary and Editor.

Carried.

The President cast the ballot accordingly.

It was moved and seconded that the President cast the ballot for Mr. S. Hoxie for Superintendent of the Advanced Registry.

Carried.

The President cast the ballot in accordance with the vote.

Mr. GERRIT S. MILLER: I move that the Association offer a vote of thanks to the New York Central & Hudson River Railroad, and the Boston & Albany Railroad, for the courtesy shown in allowing members of the Association half rates on the return passage.

Carried.

Mr. C. W. HORR: I move that when we adjourn, we adjourn to meet in Cleveland, provided the committee succeed in getting the charter amended so that it would be legal; if not, to meet at Buffalo, N. Y.

It was moved and seconded to amend Mr. Horr's motion by inserting the word "Chicago" in place of the word "Cleveland."

Motion lost.

The motion as originally made by Mr. Horr was carried.

The President called for a report of the committee on resolutions regarding imitations of butter.

Mr. S. N. WRIGHT: Mr. Chairman, your committee beg leave to report the result of their deliberations as follows:

"*Resolved*, That this Association will pay no premiums at fairs where oleomargarine, butterine, or other fraudulent imitations of butter are recognized as worthy articles to be put on exhibition; and

"*Resolved*, That we recommend legislation on the part of Congress, placing a stamp tax of ten cents a pound on all imitation butter, and putting it under the supervision of the revenue department, for the protection of the dairy interest and consumers of dairy goods; also

"*Resolved*, That each member of this Association urge upon his member of Congress all honorable efforts to secure such legislation."

It was moved and seconded that the report of the committee be accepted and adopted.

Carried.

Mr. THOMAS B. WALES, Jr.: Mr. President, I desire to offer the following resolution.

"WHEREAS, A committee from the National Cattle Growers' Association is at present at Washington, D. C., endeavoring to secure adequate national legislation for the suppression and eradication of contagious diseases, and for the regulation of the manufacture of imitation butter, and

"WHEREAS, Urgent requests have been made for financial aid to meet the legitimate expenses of their work; therefore

"*Resolved*, That the Holstein-Friesian Association of America authorizes its Board of Officers to appropriate $250 from the funds of this Association for the work mentioned."

It was moved and seconded that the resolution offered by Mr. Wales be adopted.

Carried.

Mr. C. W. HORR: I would inquire if the charter or By-Laws fix the date of our annual meeting?

THE PRESIDENT: It does.

Mr. C. W. HORR: I move that we adjourn.

Carried.

FOURTH MEETING

OF THE

BOARD OF OFFICERS

OF THE

Holstein-Friesian Association of America

HELD AT THE

GENESSEE HOTEL, BUFFALO, NEW YORK, TUESDAY,
MARCH 16TH, 1886.

The meeting was called to order at the hour named in the call, 3 o'clock P. M.; President Theron G. Yeomans in the chair.

The roll was called, and the following-named gentlemen were present: T. G. Yeomans, William M. Singerly, F. C. Stevens, W. C. Brayton, Gerrit S. Miller, C. W. Horr, C. R. Payne, Wing R. Smith, W. G. Powell, S. Hoxie, Thomas B. Wales, Jr.

The Secretary reported that a quorum was present.

The President called for the report of the committee appointed to investigate the charges against Mr. J. K. Odell.

The Secretary read the report of the committee, by Mr. I. C. Otis, chairman; also the letter from Mr. J. K. Odell referred to in the report of the committee.

The secretary reported that he had notified Mr. Odell to be present at the meeting this afternoon, at 3 o'clock, to answer to the charges preferred against him.

It was moved and carried that the report of the committee be accepted.

It was moved and carried that Mr. J. K. Odell be expelled from the Association, for the false registry of cattle, and that the animals registered as "Cartwright Maid (5941 H. H. B.)" and "Lady Cartwright (5942 H. H. B.)" be dropped from the registry of the Association.

The President called for the report of the committee in reference to charges preferred against Mr. Charles W. Wolcott.

Mr. Wing R. Smith reported that he had not taken action in the matter, on account of ill health; that he had written to Mr. Wolcott twice, but had received no reply from him.

It was moved and carried that further action in the matter be postponed until to-morrow, at the annual meeting of the board.

The following-named gentlemen having applied for membership in the Association, upon motion, their applications were accepted, and they were elected members of the Association: Amos Edmunds, Disco, Illinois; Dr. Henry Foster, Clifton Springs, New York; H. B. Hammond, New York City; E. A. Hoffman, Fort Wayne, Indiana; Edward P. Taft, Providence, Rhode Island; D. M. White, Hudson, Wisconsin; J. M. Curtis, Wilmington, Delaware; Everett Smith, Waltham, Massachusetts; F. H. Hagerty, Aberdeen, D. T.; James S. Sanborn, Boston, Massachusetts.

W. B. Barney, Hampton, Iowa, made application for membership upon condition that his firm, of which one member is already a member of the Association, be allowed to register their animals at the fees usually charged to members.

It was moved and carried that the application be laid upon the table and made a special order of business at the next meeting.

It was moved by Mr. Hoxie that Rule XIII. of the Advanced Registry be amended so as to read: "The fee for entry in this form of registry for members of this Association shall be three dollars per animal; the fee for non-members shall be six dollars per animal."

It was moved and carried that the subject be laid upon the table for the consideration of the meeting of the board to-morrow.

It was moved by Mr. Hoxie that Rule XIV. of the Advanced Registry be amended by striking out the words "The entries in each division shall be arranged according to the names of the animals in alphabetical order," and substituting therefor the words "The entries in each division shall be arranged according to number in the order in which the animals are received."

Motion carried.

It was moved and carried that the President appoint a committee of three to retire, and, as soon as possible, make a recommendation to the board as to the salaries of officers for the past year and for the coming year.

The president appointed as such committee Messrs. Horr, Singerly, and Miller.

Mr. Horr reported for the committee, recommending that for the past year Mr. Wales be allowed $3,000, and that the sum of $2,500 be allowed him next year, and that he be allowed to hire what assistance he requires, the same to be paid for by the Association; also, that Mr. W. C. Brayton be allowed $250 for the last year, and the same sum for the coming year; also, that Mr. Hoxie be allowed $250 for the last year, and $500 for the coming year, provided that he shall not be paid more than one-half of the sum received for registration in the Advanced Registry for the coming year; also, that both Mr. S. Hoxie and

Mr. S. Burchard be allowed the authorized per diem rate of the Advanced Registry for the inspection of cattle recently inspected for Messrs. T. G. Yeomans & Sons and Messrs. Powell Brothers.

It was moved and carried that the report of the committee be accepted.

It was moved by Mr. Smith that the registration fee of the Advanced Registry be reduced to three dollars.

Adopted.

It was then moved by Mr. W. M. Singerly that the registry fee of three dollars in the Advanced Registry be the same for members and non-members of the Association.

The meeting adjourned until March 17th, at such hour as should be agreed upon.

FIRST ANNUAL MEETING

OF THE

BOARD OF OFFICERS

OF THE

Holstein-Friesian Association of America

HELD AT THE

GENESSEE HOTEL, BUFFALO, NEW YORK, WEDNESDAY, MARCH 17TH, 1886.

The meeting was called to order by President F. C. Stevens.

The Secretary called the roll, which showed the following gentlemen to be present: F. C. Stevens, G. D. Wheeler, W. M. Singerly, M. L. Sweet, D. H. Burrell, Gerrit S. Miller, C. R. Payne, C. W. Horr, W. J. Smith, F. L. Houghton, S. Hoxie, Thomas B. Wales, Jr.

Applications for membership were received from Messrs. W. B. Barney, Hampton, Iowa; C. T. Riley, Troy, Ohio; and J. O. Beal, Rollin, Mich.; all of which were accepted.

THE PRESIDENT: At the request of Mr. J. W. Stillwell, of Troy, Ohio, I again bring before the board his request for the return of a part of the charge made by inspectors for the examination of one imported animal. He wished me to state that the inspector was appointed before he had an opportunity of getting the necessary papers to him. He asks that $100 be refunded.

Mr. G. S. MILLER: I move that we do not allow Mr. Stillwell's claim.

Carried.

Mr. S. N. WRIGHT, of Elgin, Ill.: Mr. President and gentlemen, it is always unpleasant to me to enter into any litigation with any gentleman, especially a man who has been accepted by this Association, and is now, at this time, a member of the Association. The charge that I have to make is against W. A. Pratt, of Elgin, Ill. In the spring of 1884, somewhere about the 1st of May — I would state, Mr. President, that I had these charges all written out and in my desk. I neglected, however, to bring them with me, which I much regret. My charge is this: In the spring of 1884 I bought a lot of heifers. Among the lot was one that I did not get the certificate of. The certificate was not ready, and the representation he made to me was this: that there was something wrong in regard to the registry in Holland, and they had to go back to be rectified. I took that for granted, of course. I waited, perhaps four or five months — long enough for the papers to go to Holland and return — and I spoke to him again, and he said he had not received them, but I should certainly have them as soon as they came; he would guarantee it was all right. I waited a reasonable length of time and went at him again. He said the papers had come and the certificate was issued and was in the hands of William Koch, and he was unable to get it — that Koch would not deliver the certificate to him. I wrote to Mr. Koch about it, to inquire the reason why, and he said there was some difficulty between them — that he would not deliver the papers until he settled with him for the heifer. After a reasonable time William Koch sent a carload of cattle to Elgin, and sent a young man as his agent to sell those cattle for him. I went to this young man and asked him about the certificate. He said he had it, and that her name in the herd-book was Elgin Lass. I then asked him if he would show me the certificate. The certificate does not describe the heifer in dispute that I bought of Mr. Pratt. I went to Mr. Pratt about it, and he said he would certainly make it right with me, and it ran along for some time, and I at him again. He got up on his ear and said he would not do anything about it; that he could not get the papers of Mr. So-and-so, and did not know he was bound to do so for me. I finally sued him in one court and obtained a judgment. He appealed it to the Circuit Court. This last term I went to the clerk, and he said he had failed to docket it. My attorney tells me he is responsible under the bond he had to give in order to make the appeal.

THE PRESIDENT: What charge do you make?

Mr. WRIGHT: My charge is that he is not a worthy member of the Association, and I desire to have him expelled on the ground of false representations.

THE PRESIDENT: Under the present By-Laws, amended to-day, the complaint must be made in writing and sworn to, after which the board appoints a committee of two to investigate the charges.

Mr. Wright stated he would put his charge in proper form.

Mr. C. W. HORR: Mr. President, I desire to offer the following:

Resolved, That we authorize the Secretary of our Association to offer a prize of $100 for the best essay upon the following subject, and upon the conditions hereinafter stipulated: "The Breeding of Holstein Cattle, including practical suggestions about the Care, Food, and Exercise of Calves; also as to the Selection of Sires and as to how they should be cared for during the season of service in order that their offspring may be large and healthy, and to obtain a full transmission of milking and other desired qualities." *Conditions:* Each essay to be forwarded to the President, and also to the Secretary, by February 1st, 1887; each essay to contain from 3,000 to 5,000 words, and to be printed or very plainly written; each of these officers, without exchange of views, to forward the three essays that he thinks show most merit to a referee, to be selected by the Board of Control; the referee's decision as to the relative merit of the different articles to be conclusive; the successful essay to become the absolute property of this Association upon the payment to the author of $100; essays to be forwarded to the President and Secretary, and by them to the referee, without signatures or anything that would give the referee any possible information as to their authorship.

Carried.

Mr. BURRELL: I move that the decision be referred to the President and Secretary, and that Mr. Horr be made referee.

Carried.

Upon motion, the board adjourned until 8:30 P. M.

EVENING SESSION.

The meeting was called to order, at 8:30 P. M., by President Stevens.

Mr. C. W. HORR: Mr. President, I move that Mr. I. C. Otis be appointed one of the Inspectors of Imported Cattle.

Carried.

Mr. SMITH: I move that Mr. S. N. Wright be appointed one of the Inspectors of Imported Cattle.

Carried.

A MEMBER: I move that Mr. O. P. Chapman be appointed one of the Inspectors of Imported Cattle.

Carried.

Mr. HOXIE: I move that Mr. S. Burchard be appointed one of the Inspectors of Imported Cattle.

Carried.

Mr. HOUGHTON; I move that Mr. J. C. Poor be appointed one of the Inspectors of Imported Cattle.

Carried.

Mr. HORR: I move that Mr. S. Burchard be appointed one of the Inspectors of the Advanced Registry.

Carried.

Mr. HOXIE: I move that all the Inspectors of Imported Cattle be also Inspectors for the Advanced Registry.

Carried.

Mr. G. S. MILLER: I would like to move that in future the department of advanced registry be known by the name of the Holstein-Friesian Test-Book.

My reason for this is that the simple fact of our having a registry bearing the name "Advanced" would seem to throw discredit on our Herd-Book Registry. That under some other name it would be less objectionable to the mass of breeders who cannot, for many reasons, go to the expense and trouble of keeping records of their cattle. I therefore propose that the name "Advanced Registry" be changed to "Holstein-Friesian Test-Book."

Motion seconded by Mr. Wales.

Mr. C. W. HORR: I move that we lay the matter on the table.

Carried.

THE PRESIDENT: The case of Mr. C. W. Wolcott, laid over from the last meeting, is now in order.

Mr. F. L. HOUGHTON: I have received the following telegram from Mr. Wolcott, which I will read to the board:

"*F. L. Houghton:*

"Unable to go to Buffalo, on account of estate business, please notify Board of Officers. Say that I deny the charge of Mr. Otis.

[Signed.] "C. W. WOLCOTT."

Mr. SMITH: I think I understand the state of the case. It was in substance, that Mr. Wolcott was charged with allowing cattle to be registered in his name, when the man who owned them was not a member of the Association. I have a slight acquaintance with Mr. Wolcott. What little I know of him I think well of him. I also know the Hollander referred to, and although I do not know anything about the Hollander, it occurs to me that the circumstances under which he made the statement were very trying. It is a very serious question whether the charges against Mr. Wolcott are true.

Mr. HOUGHTON: The By-Laws were quite specific on the subject, and are now made more so. Shall we act under the old By-Law, or the present one? I would recommend that the charges be made now under the new By-Law, under oath, in writing, and that a new committee be then appointed.

THE PRESIDENT: The Chair would state that this is not a matter of this board. It was made under the old By-Law, and this committee is continued.

Mr. HOUGHTON: Mr. Otis said he knew nothing about the matter personally; that he made the formal charge at the request of some member or members of the board.

It was moved and seconded that Mr. Houghton be substituted on the committee, in the place of Mr. Wing R. Smith.

Carried.

THE PRESIDENT: The next thing in order is consideration of the distribution of the $2,000 for premiums for cattle and dairy products.

Mr. SMITH: I move that $1,500 be devoted to the cattle enterprise, and $500 for butter and cheese.

Carried.

It was moved and seconded that the $1,500 be expended in the best way the board could devise to secure a good exhibit at the Chicago fat stock and dairy show next fall.

Carried.

Mr. C. W. HORR: I move that we first duplicate the premiums offered at the Chicago fat stock and dairy show for Holstein-Friesian cattle, and put the balance of the $1,500 in the hands of our President and Secretary, to be expended as they deem best in connection with the exhibition of fat grade or full blood Holstein-Friesian cattle.

Carried.

A MEMBER: I move that the $500 be divided into sums of $250, for butter and for cheese, to be divided up at the different fairs in the country, duplicating premiums for butter and for cheese wherever taken by Holstein-Friesian butter or Holstein-Friesian cheese.

Motion seconded.

A MEMBER: I move to amend, that it be given at State Dairymen Association exhibitions.

Amendment accepted.

Mr. C. W. HORR: I move that the $500 be expended as the President and Secretary may deem best.

Carried.

Mr. C. W. HORR: I move that we instruct our Secretary to include Mr. Powell's article in the publication of the proceedings of this meeting; and that we request the agricultural papers of the United States to publish the same in their columns; that the Secretary send them a copy of the article.

Carried.

Mr. SMITH: I move that we investigate the worthiness or unworthiness of the North Holland Herd-Book, in order that we may decide whether it is advisable for us to accept that registry as one of our standards.

Motion seconded.

After considerable discussion, the motion was withdrawn.

Mr. SMITH: I move that we appoint ourselves a committee of the whole to investigate the matter of the North Holland Herd-Book.

Carried.

Mr. SMITH: I move that the Treasurer be requested to take proper means to secure bonds to the amount of $15,000, to the satisfaction of the President of the Association.

Carried.

Mr. C. W. HORR: I move that Mr. Brayton be instructed to deposit the funds of the Association in such banks as receive the approval of a committee composed of the President, Mr. D. H. Burrell, and Mr. W. J. Smith, and that it be deposited in the name of the Holstein-Friesian Association of America, W. C. Brayton, Treasurer.

Carried.

A MEMBER: I move that we adjourn.

Carried.

TESTS OF DAIRY COWS.

By E. A. POWELL, Syracuse, New York.

My attention has been several times called to an article written by Valancey E. Fuller, of Ontario, under the above heading, which appeared in the *Rural New Yorker* of October 17th. This article purported to show the comparative merits of the Jerseys, the Ayrshires, and the Holsteins for the dairy. The tables contained therein are said to have been compiled from the "advance reports" of Prof. William Brown, of the Ontario Experimental Farm. I do not wonder that Mr. Fuller, one of the leading Jersey breeders of the country, should seize upon this report and take steps to publish it in every agricultural paper throughout the country. It was a golden opportunity for the Jersey breeders, providing they could convince the dairymen of the country that the tests were impartial, and that the cows selected for the trial fairly represented the various breeds — that each cow was an average of the breed to which she belonged.

I beg your indulgence, even at this late date, to correct some erroneous impressions that may have been created in the minds of those not familiar with the actual facts. I do not wish to question Prof. Brown's good intentions, nor the accuracy of all his calculations; but, either through lack of knowledge of the Holstein-Friesian breed or from some other cause, he started on a false basis by taking as a representative of this breed a heifer of the very poorest class — inferior in size, in appearance, in quantity of milk, and in quality of milk for both butter and cheese.

A single moment's reflection will convince any intelligent breeder that no one cow can fairly represent any breed of tens of thousands of cows any more than a handful of sand will represent a sea-shore, and especially when that one is a poor, insignificant heifer. As well might Prof. Brown, from the analysis of a handful of soil from some solitary sand-hill, write a treatise on the agricultural possibilities of the Dominion. Had he given the various dairy breeds a fair, impartial trial by having a competent committee, interested equally in all the breeds, select at least half a dozen good representative cows of each, and had them given the same care and kind of food for a year previous to, as well as during, the time of trial (for it is now an admitted fact, proven by actual experiment, that previous condition and food have almost as much to do with the product of the cow as her present ration), he would have done a work of incalculable value to the whole dairy world. As it is, his report is misleading, conveying an erroneous impression, and is a great damage to the dairy interests of not only the Dominion, but the whole country. Any misleading tests are decidedly worse than none.

I wish here to say that Prof. Brown doubtless was prompted by the best of motives — a desire to give the people of the Dominion an equivalent for their outlay in maintaining an experimental station — but he was too hasty, and made his report without the proper material to make it from.

Let us review some of the statements therein. The Holstein is given in the report as Verapina, three years old, weight 895 pounds, and dropped first calf in January, 1883. Prof. Brown describes her as "lanky and leggy." Nothing is said of her breeding. No herd-book number or date of importation is given, but by reference to the Holstein Herd-Book I find the heifer to be Verasina (10450, Vol. IX.), calved March 15th, 1883, imported in May, 1884, and must have come out of quarantine the August previous to dropping her calf in January. This record and the name are confirmed by Prof. Brown in reply to a letter from me asking him for the dates of birth and importation, with herd-book number, of this heifer.

It will thus be seen that this representative Holstein-Friesian was only one year old past — a yearling — only twenty-two months old when she dropped her calf, and commenced her record at twenty-two and a half months, instead of being three years old, as stated in no less than six different places in Prof. Brown's report, and confirmed by Mr. Fuller's letter. She dropped her calf in January, before being acclimated, and before she became accustomed to the severe winters of Ontario, or to the feed and water in use there. All importers know full well the bad effect of such changes, not only in quantity, but in quality, of milk. Many good cows are almost worthless the first season after importation. Verasina may, therefore, yet prove to be a good cow.

Why this heifer's name should have been misspelled, why her Holstein Herd-Book number, the date of importation, and the fact that she was not acclimated, were all withheld in the report, and, above all, why she should be called a three-year-old cow when in fact she was but twenty-two and a half months — why a "leggy and lank" little unacclimated heifer should be selected by such an institution as the Experimental Farm of Ontario to represent the Holstein-Friesian breed in such an important trial — are facts beyond my comprehension.

We will compare this heifer with the average of some of the largest herds of the same breed in the country, in order to see if she is a fair representative. In doing so I will be pardoned for referring to a herd in which I am interested. I am compelled to do this, as I have the necessary data at hand from only this herd and that of Messrs. Yeomans & Sons.

For the present milking year, now nearly closed, the Lakeside herd had in milk for five months (the length of time which the report in question covers), in all, fifty-seven head of two-year-old heifers. Their records were carefully kept by weighing each milking. The entire lot averaged for five months 5,575 pounds. For the previous year there were, in all, in the same herd, of the same age, milked through the season, twenty-six head. The entire lot averaged for five months a little over 5,350 pounds, and for the year 10,810 pounds, although a few did not complete the year. Fifteen of the number averaged 12,307½ pounds. In 1882 Messrs. Yeomans & Sons reported fourteen heifers two years old (their entire herd of that age), which averaged for the year 11,118 pounds and 3 ounces. I have not their exact records for five months, but they must have averaged fully as much as the Lakeside herd for this season (5,575 pounds), and probably more if a large majority of them dropped their calves in the spring, and thus had the benefit of fresh feed. Here we have ninety-seven two-year-olds, all recorded Holstein-Friesians, embracing the entire milking herd for two consecutive years in the Lakeside herd and the entire number for one year in the Yeomans herd, which nearly all dropped their calves at from twenty-two to twenty-eight months of age, and the entire lot averaged for five months 5,515 pounds.

Verasina gave for the same time, according to Prof. Brown's report, 3,239 pounds, showing a balance in favor of each of the ninety-seven head of 2,286 pounds for five months.

Verasina weighed, at twenty-five and one-half months, 895 pounds. At the same age all the heifers at Lakeside referred to above averaged over 1,050 pounds, and those in the Yeomans herd, I judge, were fully as heavy, showing this representative cow to be 155 pounds under weight even as a two-year-old, instead of three, as in the report.

In butter I cannot give a comparison with the whole herds, as only part have been tested. In the Lakeside herd seventeen two-year-olds averaged for a week 10 pounds and 8 ounces. Messrs. Yeomans, in their report on butter tests, give nine two-year-olds which averaged 12 pounds and 13½ ounces per week; so that twenty-six heifers averaged 11 pounds and 7 ounces. Verasina made, in 151 days, 108 pounds, showing an average of 5 pounds per week, or considerably less than half the average of the twenty-six. Of course Verasina here had the disadvantage of the longer trial, but it is probably safe to conclude that if the test of the twenty-six head had been continued for the same time they would, on the average, have nearly, if not fully, doubled her record.

This will be enough to show the character of this "representative" Holstein-Friesian as compared with some of the entire large herds of the same breed. It shows her to be 155 pounds under weight, her milk for five months to have been 2,286 pounds below the average, and her butter about one-half.

Let us now turn our attention to the Jersey. Prof. Brown, in his report, describes her as follows: "Beauty o' the Mill may be described as a Jersey that pokes her nose into everybody's pocket — an uneducated pet. With such a disposition we have had much pleasure in handling this cow. Cream-colored, even, roomy, a fine skin, but with little milk mirror, and medium udder." Three years old, weight, May 1st, 832 pounds, which shows that she was above the average of her breed in size, and the Professor's description shows that she was of just the type and disposition to insure the largest results. The report shows just what we could expect from such an animal, viz.: That her combined milk, butter, and cheese product for the five months is far above the average of her breed. In fact, it is far above the average of any entire herd of Jerseys of a dozen heifers of the same age we have ever seen published. It should be borne in mind that this heifer was fully acclimated — accustomed to the severe winters and feed of Canada. A few more singular facts regarding her are worthy of note. She is given in the report as a Jersey, three years old; but date of birth and herd-book number are not given. To get more definite information regarding this cow, I went to the office of Mr. Hand, the Secretary of the American Jersey Cattle Club, and to my surprise learned that no such cow was on record. I then wrote Prof. Brown, who kindly replied that she was dropped in 1882, and was not recorded. I was not a little surprised that an unregistered animal should be taken as a representive Jersey, especially by such a breeder as Valancey E. Fuller. The question naturally arises: Is she a grade, and does this fact account for her large flow of milk, and the fact that her milk is much superior for cheese to any registered Jersey of which we have yet seen an account?

In order that a fair estimate of the two breeds (the Jerseys and Holstein-Friesians) for the dairy may be formed, we will compare the product of this heifer with that of entire herds of the same age.

In the Lakeside herd of Holstein-Friesians, this last season, twenty-four three-year-olds (entire number in milk for the time) gave by actual weight in five months an average of 6,114 pounds for each cow, while this Jersey gave 2,944 pounds, leaving a balance of milk in favor of the black-and-white cows of 3,170 pounds per cow in five months; or in other words, the Holstein-Friesians each gave 226 pounds more than double the amount given by the Jersey.

Our tests for butter do not comprise the whole herds, but I will make as fair a comparison as the data at my command will admit.

In the Lakeside herd thirteen heifers three years old have been tested, and they averaged 13 pounds 6 ounces of butter per week. Messrs. Yeomans & Sons, in their recent butter reports, give four three year-olds which averaged 17 pounds 6 ounces per week. It will thus be seen that seventeen three-year-olds average for a week 14 pounds 5 ounces. In all the butter tests, in both the Yeomans and Lakeside herds, the butter was worked dry and weighed before salting.

This Jersey made an average for the five months of a little over eleven pounds per week, a difference of 2 pounds 12 ounces per week in favor of the spotted cows. This I will frankly say is hardly fair for the Jersey, on account of her longer test, but it will convey a good idea of the merits of each, and will satisfy any one that these seventeen Holstein-Friesians far excel her for butter.

I will make a few comparisons by taking, as a basis, the number of pounds of milk for a pound of butter, and as the following tests were made when the cows were in full flow and fresh, I think the fairness of the comparison will be conceded, for I believe it is an admitted fact, that as the time after calving lengthens and the flow diminishes, the milk becomes richer, taking a less amount for a pound of butter.

The following table will show the results of the tests of seven heifers in the Lakeside herd — four three-year-olds and three two-year-olds. It gives the amount of butter made by each in a week's test; the average weight of milk required for a pound of butter; the amount of milk given by each for five months, and on this basis the amount of butter each would have made in that time:

NAME.	Age at time of test.	Butter per week.		Pounds milk to make pound butter.	Pounds milk given in five months.	Pounds butter in five months at same rate.
		Lbs.	Ozs.			
Netherland Belle (1876),	3	16	7	22.34	7,191	321
Netherland Countess (2634),	3	15	15	20.88	5,724	274
Netherland Jewel (2642),	3	15	3½	26.31	6,667	253
Alexander's Queen (6998),	3	15	4	21.93	6,028	274
Benola Fletcher (6891),	2	16	9	18.11	6,634	366
Soldene (2896),	2	13		24.93	7,068	283
Aaggie Sarah 2d (7142),	2	12	1½	24.41	6,301	258
Total,						2,029

Average of the seven head for five months, 289 pounds; Jersey for five months, 248 pounds; balance in favor of Holsteins, 41 pounds.

The "funny" part of this whole affair, the one which makes all dairymen smile, is the claim that the Jersey leads all other breeds for cheese. This is the first instance on record that has come to my knowledge where such a claim has been made. One of the prominent Jersey breeders of the country recently remarked to a large gathering of dairymen, that "the superiority of the Holsteins for cheese was conceded by everybody excepting Valancey E. Fuller." Nearly all former tests have shown the Jersey milk, while superior for butter, to be inferior for cheese. It should be borne in mind, that to obtain the results for cheese which are apparent in the report and in Mr. Fuller's letter, that the same "lanky and leggy" little unacclimated twenty-two and a half months heifer had to be pitted against older native competitors.

I cannot give results in cheese production from personal experience, for I have made no tests, but will take Prof. Brown's own figures, as used by Mr. Fuller, and concede for the time being, that the Holstein-Friesian Heifer would represent the breed in quality of milk for cheese (a statement that no intelligent breeder will believe to be a fact), and what is the result? It shows that it required 8.95 pounds of the heifer's milk for a pound of cheese. The twenty-four three-year-olds referred to above averaged for the five months, 6,114 pounds of milk, and hence would have made 684 pounds of cheese, while the Jersey, of the same age, made 456 pounds, leaving a balance in favor of the Holstein-Friesian of 228 pounds per cow, or in other words, they excelled her for cheese just fifty per cent. The fact that Holland is the greatest cheese country of the world, making more cheese, not only in proportion to the area of the country, but in proportion to the number of cows, should be satisfactory proof of the superiority of her cows for that purpose.

A comparative test made by J. E. Grant, the owner of several large cheese factories in Illinois (who did not own any Holstein-Friesian cattle), with the milk from a herd of fifty pure-bred Holstein-Friesians, in comparison with the milk of the other herds brought to his factory, showed that the Holstein-Friesians made six and one-half per cent more cheese from the same amount of milk. He declares the test to have been a fair one, the conditions being similar in all respects.

What are the conclusions to be drawn from the above facts?

First. The Holstein-Friesian gave over 107 per cent more milk.

Second. The Holstein-Friesian made $16\frac{1}{2}$ per cent more butter.

Third. The Holstein-Friesian made 50 per cent more cheese.

If we call the average milk of the twenty-four Holstein-Friesians equal to that of the Jersey for cheese (and we verily believe it to be better), they would have made 107 per cent more cheese.

From the above we feel fully justified in quoting Mr. Fuller's conclusion: "It seems, therefore, that there is little doubt as to which is the best all-around cow."

As to the test made at the exhibitions at London and Toronto, we will only say that so much depends upon the condition of the cow, the amount and quality of her previous rations, her care and treatment, the length of time in milk, when due again, the distance shipped, whether fully acclimated or not, etc., that such tests have no practical value as an evidence of the actual merits of the cows tested, and we will spare you a useless discussion regarding them. We will simply add that these tests were made "by the same experts" as those given in the report referred to above.

PROCEEDINGS

OF THE

SECOND ANNUAL MEETING

OF THE

Holstein-Friesian Association

OF AMERICA,

HELD AT

BUFFALO, NEW YORK, MARCH 16TH, 1887.

———

— ALSO —

REPORTS OF MEETINGS OF THE BOARD OF OFFICERS,

HELD AT BUFFALO, NEW YORK,

MARCH 15TH AND 16TH, 1887.

Egbert, Fidlar, & Chambers, Printers, Davenport, Iowa.

1887.

OFFICERS OF THE

HOLSTEIN-FRIESIAN ASSOCIATION OF AMERICA,

FOR 1887-8.

President, ... WILLIAM M. SINGERLY, . Philadelphia, Penn.
First Vice-President, . GERRIT S. MILLER, . . . Peterboro, N. Y.
Second Vice-President, . M. L. SWEET, ... Grand Rapids, Mich.
Third Vice-President, . W. G. POWELL. . . . . . Springboro, Penn.
Fourth Vice-President, . W. M. LIGGETT, ... Benson, Minn.
Treasurer, ... WILLIAM BROWN SMITH, Syracuse, N. Y.

Directors.

F. L. HOUGHTON, ... Putney, Vt.
EDGAR HUIDEKOPER, ... Meadville, Penn.
EUGENE SMITH, ... Nashville, Tenn.
C. W. HORR, ... Wellington, Ohio.
C. R. PAYNE, ... Hamilton, N. Y.
D. H. BURRELL, ... Little Falls, N. Y.

Secretary and Editor.

THOMAS B. WALES, JR., ... Iowa City, Iowa.

Superintendent of Advanced Registry.

S. HOXIE, ... Whitestown, N. Y.

Inspectors of Imported Cattle.

ISAAC C. OTIS, ... Jordan, N. Y.
O. P. CHAPMAN, ... Wellington, Ohio.
S. BURCHARD, ... Hamilton, N. Y.
S. N. WRIGHT, ... South Elgin, Ill.
J. C. POOR, ... North Andover, Mass.
CAREY R. SMITH, ... Santa Ana, Cal.

Inspectors of Advanced Registry.

All Inspectors of Imported Cattle, and—
JERE ALLIS, ... Isinours, Minn.
J. N. MUNCEY, ... Jessup, Iowa.
J. L. STONE, ... Waverly, Penn.
A. R. STURTEVANT, ... Springboro, Penn.
H. D. WARNER, ... New Milford, Conn.

SECOND ANNUAL MEETING

OF THE

HOLSTEIN-FRIESIAN ASSOCIATION OF AMERICA,

Held at the Genesee House, Buffalo, N.Y.,
Wednesday, March 16th, 1887.

The meeting was called to order at 10 o'clock A. M., by the President.

THE PRESIDENT: Gentlemen, at the last meeting of the Holstein-Friesian Association, at which I was elected, I had not the opportunity to thank you for the honor you conferred upon me by electing me to the position I now hold. I now thank you for that honor, and I would say for myself that I have tried to perform the duties devolving upon me to the best of my ability, and trust that they have been satisfactory to you. I shall forego the pleasure of delivering the customary President's address, for, under the circumstances, knowing the feeling which exists among many members of the Association, myself included, I could not, in duty to myself, restrain from saying some things which might be better left unsaid. Consequently, I thank you again, and we will proceed to the usual order of business. The Secretary will call the roll.

Upon roll-call it was ascertained that the following members were present, and that 193 were represented by prox :

Jere Allis, E. P. Beauchamp, H. E. Boardman, James Black, W. C. Brayton, J. T. Brooks, A. W. Brown, Sylvester Burchard, David H. Burrell, G. M. Carpenter, B. Chaffee, N. B. Curtis, G. V. DeGraaf, P. M. Harwood, C. W. Horr, F. L. Houghton, S. Hoxie, S. L. Hoxie, Edgar Huidekoper, Charles Hunt, Henry C. Jewett, Leander Jones, Anthony Lamb, Hollum Langworthy, William M. Liggett, John Lightner, C. J. Lord, F. W. Maxon, Dudley Miller, Gerrit S. Miller, James Neilson, Isaac C. Otis, C. R. Payne, L. H. Payne, James C. Poor, W. J. Potter, E. A. Powell, Will. B. Powell, W. G. Powell, C. Pratt, W. A. Pratt, E. K. Seabury, Dexter Severy, W. K. Sexton, W. M. Singerly, W. Brown Smith, W. J. Smith, Wing R. Smith, F. C. Stevens, J. W. Stillwell, Martin L. Sweet, C. F. Sweezey, S. W. Sweezey, E. P. Tafft, C. C. Taylor, Henry Van Dreser, Thomas B. Wales, Jr., George L. Wells, G. D. Wheeler, Alfred P. Wright, S. N. Wright, E. L. Yeomans, L. T. Yeomans, T. G. Yeomans.

Mr. Lamb moved that a committee of three be appointed to examine the proxies and report to this meeting.

Seconded and carried.

The chair appointed Mr. Anthony Lamb, Mr. C. R. Payne, and Mr. C. J. Lord as such Committee on Proxies.

The committee so appointed proceeded to collect the proxies, and retired to examine them.

THE PRESIDENT: While the Committee on Proxies are investigating the subject, we will listen to the minutes of the last meeting.

Mr. Houghton moved that the reading of the minutes of the last meeting be dispensed with.

Motion seconded and carried.

The President called for the report of the Secretary for the past year.

The Secretary read as follows:

SECRETARY'S REPORT.

Mr. President, and Members of the Holstein-Friesian Association of America: Another year has passed, and it is with pleasure that I am able to report to you a year of marked success in our business affairs—by far the most prosperous, financially, of any that has preceded. Our little family of over three thousand breeders, whose interests are largely in our keeping, appear to have been fully satisfied, and I believe quite generally appreciate what I have been able to do for them in the line of recording the pedigrees of their cattle, furnishing them promptly their certificates of registry and of transfer registry, as well as in keeping them in line when occasionally the rather difficult question of naming some of their animals arises—our rules in that regard being somewhat indefinite.

Therefore, with no trouble to report, so far as my department is concerned, certainly we have just cause for congratulation.

Since our last annual meeting we have admitted fourteen members, which increases our membership to 314.

Volume I. of the Holstein-Friesian Herd-Book has been issued, in which are recorded 5,687 animals. An expression by the Association as to whether the work is satisfactory, as regards its style and general make-up, would be thankfully received by me, in order that I, or my successor in office, may be guided thereby in the future.

From March 1st, 1886, to March 1st, 1887, there have been registered 3,109 bulls and 3,709 cows, of which thirteen bulls and 268 cows were imported animals.

During this period the ownership of 2,998 bulls and 3,286 cows has been transferred on our records, necessitating an issue of 13,102 certificates of registry and transfer, being an increase of 2,307 over the previous year.

Volume II. of our Herd-Book is now being printed, 976 pages having already been completed. It will contain something over five hundred pedigrees more than are contained in Vol. I.

Seven thousand four hundred letters have been received and answered.

To some, no doubt, the financial statement which I have to offer will prove most interesting, and to such I respectfully ask that they try to realize, from a consideration of the above statement, the great amount of work which must have been done.

The receipts for the year ending March 1st, 1887, are as follows:

RECEIPTS

Cash on hand March 1st, 1886	$ 94 00
Received for membership fees	1,900 00
Received for register of imported bulls	260 00
Received for register of imported cows	5,360 00
Received for register of bulls	5,302 65
Received for register of cows	5,849 00
Received for transfer register of bulls	1,476 00
Received for transfer register of cows	2,499 50
Received for duplicate certificates	48 50
Received for inspection of imported cattle	915 00
Received for Herd-Books	684 49
Received for sundry old accounts paid	905 64
Received for fees not yet charged to personal accounts	663 34
	$25,958 12

EXPENDITURES.

For expenses Board of Officers	$ 356 36
For clerk hire	2,616 99
For expense account, including office rent for year, $270.00	2,407 23
For printing, including reprint of volumes I.-V	2,371 55
For inspection of imported cattle	563 18
For special premiums	520 00
For annual dues to National Cattle-Growers' Association	102 00
For Stamps	434 52
For balance paid to W. C. Brayton, Treasurer	16,586 29
	$25,958 12

We have on hand Herd-Books as follows:

Holstein :—

    Volume I. . . . . 450 copies. ⎫ Not valued, having been
    Volume II. . . . . 32 copies. ⎬ included in reprints of
    Volume III. . . . . 28 copies. ⎭ Volumes I.-V.
    Volume VI.,   92 copies, at $2.00 . . . . $ 184.00
    Volume VII., 538 copies, at 2.25 . . . . 1,200.00
    Volume VIII., 830 copies, at 4.00 . . . . 3,320.00
    Volume IX., 952 copies, at 2.25 . . . . 2,142.00
    Reprint of Vols. I. to V., 467 copies, $3.00 . . . . 1,401.00

Dutch-Friesian :—

    Volume II., 314 copies, at $1.50 . . . $ 471.00
    Volume III., 17 copies, at 2.00 . . . . 34.00
    Volume IV., 239 copies, at 2 00 . . . . 478.00

Holstein-Friesian :—

    Volume I., 1,091 copies, at $4.00 . . . . $4,364.00

    Total Volumes, 4,540.   Total value $13,594.00

And this closes my report as Secretary for the past year. It means, in a few words, that the Holstein-Friesian Association, as looked upon from a business standpoint, is at least equal in standing to any other like association in the world. It goes on from year to year increasing the respect in which it is held, not by our breeders alone, but by all who take note of the conduct of such organizations. That we may be able to command such respect in the future is my most hearty wish.

Respectfuly Submitted,
THOMAS B. WALES, JR.,
Secretary.

Mr. Liggett moved that the report of the Secretary be accepted, and printed in the proceedings of this meeting.

Seconded and carried.

The President called for the report of the Treasurer, which was read by Treasurer W. C. Brayton, as follows:

TREASURER'S REPORT.

SYRACUSE, N. Y., March 15th, 1887.

Mr. President, and Gentlemen of the Holstein-Friesian Association of America: It affords me great pleasure to make this, our second annual financial report of this Association, for the fiscal year which ends with the date of this meeting, and is as follows:

Balance on hand, as reported at the annual meeting held at Buffalo, in March, 1886, $15,819.00.

RECEIPTS.

1886.				
March 17.	To balance, as per last report			$15,819 00
June 10.	To cash, Thomas B. Wales, Jr., Secretary, with quarterly report	$4,553 01		
July 1.	To accrued interest at savings bank, at 4 per cent	120 00		
July 1.	To accrued interest on monthly balance, Trust and Deposit Co., at 3½ and 3 per cent	52 75		
Sept. 23.	To cash, Thomas B. Wales, Jr., Secretary, with quarterly report	2,258 98		
Nov. 1.	To cash, Thomas B. Wales, Jr., Secretary	1,500 00		
Dec. 15.	To cash, Thomas B. Wales, Jr., Secretary, with quarterly report	255 40		
1887.				
Jan. 1.	To accrued interest at savings banks	120 00		
Jan. 1.	To accrued interest at Trust and Deposit Co., at 3½ and 3 per cent	164 86		
March 1.	To accrued interest at Trust and Deposit Co., at 3½ and 3 per cent	51 02		
March 9.	To cash, Thomas B. Wales, Jr., Secretary	8,018 90		
	Cash receipts for fiscal year		— 17,094 92	
				$32,913 92

EXPENDITURES.

1886.				
March 20.	By cash, Thomas B. Wales, Jr., account of services, year ending March 17th, 1886	$3,000 00		
March 20.	By cash, S. Hoxie, Superintendent Advanced Registry, year ending March 17th, 1886	360 30		
March 20.	By cash, W. C. Brayton, Treasurer, services year ending March 17th, 1886	250 00		
July 1.	By cash, W. C. Brayton, expense attending annual and special meeting	15 71		
Oct. 2.	By cash, Thomas B. Wales, Jr., account of services six months, to Sept. 1st, 1886	1,250 00		
Oct. 19.	By cash, Egbert, Fidlar, & Chambers, account of publishing Herd-Book	1,169 15		
Nov. 1.	By cash, Egbert, Fidlar, & Chambers, balance due publishing Herd-Book	3,182 65		
1887.				
Jan. 1.	By cash, Bagg & Nottingham, attorneys, drawing up Treasurer's bond	5 00	9,232 81	
	By balance		23,681 11	
			$32,913 92	

Upon motion, the report of the Treasurer was accepted as read.

THE PRESIDENT: It has been customary to appoint a Finance Committee to examine the accounts of the Secretary and Treasurer. Shall we have such a committee at this meeting?

Mr. C. Pratt moved that the President appoint a committee of three for that purpose.

Seconded and carried.

The chair appointed as such committee, Mr. C. Pratt, Mr. S. Burchard, and Mr. C. C. Taylor.

The committee, as named, proceeded to act.

The President called for the report of the Superintendent of the Advanced Registry.

Mr. Hoxie read the report, as follows:

REPORT OF SUPERINTENDENT OF ADVANCED REGISTRY.

To the President and Members of the Holstein-Friesian Association of America: During the official year closing with this annual meeting there has been received into the Advanced Register of this Association 341 entries, including those received up to date of last annual meeting—a total of 381. The first volume has been published, containing entries of 350 cows and thirty-one bulls. Of the cows thus entered, 212 butter records are given on the basis of a higher standard of requirements than that adopted by any other association or any other publication in this country. This, indeed, is a matter for congratulation. Hitherto the supremacy of our cattle as milk producers only has been acknowledged. These records will go far toward establishing their supremacy also as butter producers.

Several tests have been commenced under the supervision of the Superintendent and Inspectors. Some of these are not yet completed. Those that have been completed are the largest received in their forms, and the establishment of their reliability has closed the mouths of all doubters and questioners, both in this country and in England. In thus doing, the reputation of the breed has been established on a firmer foundation than it ever before occupied.

It seems almost unnecessary to add that these tests have done much toward strengthening public confidence in the wonderful records reported by our breeders in the past, and hence, toward our reputation as an association. It is not too much to say that the interests of every individual breeder have thus been advanced.

During the year this department has published 5,000 copies of blank applications, nearly all of which have been distributed among breeders. It has also published 4,000 copies of a small pamphlet of eleven pages, containing our scale of points and rules for Advanced Registry. These have been distributed free of charge. The edition is entirely exhausted. In accordance with a vote of the Board of Officers, we have also published 500 copies of the first volume of the Advanced Register. In accordance with the requirements of the rules, 299 copies have been distributed to members of this Association — 297 copies by mail, and two by personal delivery. The Board of Officers directed that the retail price of this volume be fixed at or about fifty per cent above the net cost of printing and binding. This net cost was ninety-seven and one-fifth cents per copy. Accordingly, the retail price was fixed at $1.50 per copy, if personally delivered, or at $1.65 if delivered by mail.

The accounts of this department may be briefly summarized, as follows:

ADVANCED REGISTRY.

	DR.	
To fees for 341 entries	$1,023 00	
To 297 copies Advanced Register mailed to members, at $1.65 per copy	490 05	
To two copies personally delivered, at $1.50 per copy	3 00	
To 201 copies, at net cost of printing, 97 1-5 cents per copy	195 37	$1,711 42

CONTRA.

	CR.	
By stationary	$ 9 91	
By postage	62 64	
By traveling expenses	18 15	
By express charges	3 30	
By telegraph and telephone communications	1 90	
By purchase of seal	15 00	
By purchase of certificate book for bulls	15 00	
By paying for engraving	9 00	
By clerk hire	2 75	
By printing Advanced Register	486 00	
By other printing	61 01	
By salary of Superintendent	500 00	
By paying Inspectors	475 00	$1,659 66
Balance on hand		51 76
		$1,711 42

All of which is respectfully submitted.

S. HOXIE, *Superintendent.*

Upon motion, the report was received and ordered published with the proceedings of this meeting.

Mr. E. P. Tafft suggested that the report of the Superintendent of Advanced Registry be referred to the committee to which was referred the reports of the Secretary and Treasurer.

Motion seconded and carried.

MR. YEOMANS: I would like to see, when we get through, and when the proceedings are published, a list of the names of the gentlemen who were in attendance. Some come a long distance to attend, and I think it would be very well to know who it is who come from a long distance to our meetings.

THE PRESIDENT: If there be no objection to the suggestion, it will be adopted.

MR. C. W. HORR: If you have read the action of our Board at the last meeting, you will discover we offered a hundred dollars for a prize essay according to the rules therein stated. They are, briefly, as follows: The President was to select the three essays which he liked best, and the Secretary the three which he liked best, and those were to be forwarded to a referee, and the referee, from that number, was to select the one which he liked best, and which was to receive the prize. The Board did me the honor to select me as referee, and our worthy President selected three, having one that the Secretary did not send, and the Secretary sent three, having only one that the President did not send; and I selected the one that the President sent and that the Secretary did not. It was written by a foreigner, and, notwithstanding the language was not quite as rhetorical as the language of some of the others, indeed, not nearly so, it seemed to me to be the fullest of real practical hard sense; so I had to sustain the judgment of our President, and I award the prize, as the referee, to this essay. I do not know who wrote it. I was not to know, and I do not now know.

The Secretary moved that the successful essay be printed in the report of this meeting.

Motion seconded and carried.

Mr. Horr moved that the successful essay be included in the report of the annual meeting, but be omitted from the Herd-Book. Also moved that the second choice be published, if the gentleman will consent to have it published.

Mr. Wales accepted the amendment.

The chair put the question as amended, which was carried.

Mr. Horr called for the name of the successful competitor.

MR. WALES: His name is T. M. Koldyk, of Friesland. He is at present in Iowa City, in my employ, taking care of a part of my cattle. I will say further, that I never gave this young man one single point of information of any kind; that I never knew of his doing the work until he brought me his manuscript the day before the entries closed, and asked me to consider it with the others.

MR. NEILSON: I would make a motion, that whereas there are some three thousand breeders of Holstein cattle throughout the country who do not get any of the reports of this Association; and, as men who first buy Holstein cattle naturally do not know about the various operations of the society, such as the recording of them, they do not know that we have Herd-Books; the whole thing is more or less a mystery to them; such matter as to us seems a matter of course is not so to a great many of the new breeders. Now, in order to inform them, and to widen the interest in this breed of cattle, I move that the proceedings of this meeting, which will also contain this essay, be printed in pamphlet form and several thousand extra copies be printed and sent to all the Holstein breeders, as far as we can reach them.

Motion seconded.

The motion was amended so as to include Canada and Mexico.

Amendment accepted.

Question put as amended, and carried.

Mr. Huidekoper moved that hereafter all books and properties in the hands of any officer of the Association be estimated and put into the inventory at cost price.

Seconded and carried.

THE PRESIDENT: At the meeting of the Board yesterday, Mr. Wales was requested to present to you a matter that will be of interest, and he will take this opportunity, there being nothing particularly before the meeting at this time.

MR. WALES: I was authorized by the Board to recommend some resolutions, which are as follows, and explain themselves:

"WHEREAS, The American Jersey Cattle Club has asked the co-operation of this Association in its endeavors to procure the passage by each state legislature of 'an act to punish false pretenses in obtaining registration of cattle and other animals, and to punish giving false pedigrees;' it is therefore

"*Resolved*, That this Association does hereby heartily approve and endorse the timely action of the American Jersey Cattle Club in this most important matter, and assures it of the cordial support and assistance of this Association."

MR. E. A. POWELL: I am glad, indeed, that our Secretary has been thoughtful enough to bring that matter before the Association. I think it is a very important one. The American Jersey Cattle Club have taken a good move in the right direction in urging the passage of such a bill. They have been in correspondence with quite a number of breeders of this Association, who have heartily, I think, endorsed and have taken pains to encourage the passage of that kind of a bill, and it looks as though it was a step in the right direction. We want to put our foot on fraud wherever we find it. And it seems to me that not only would the breeding of cattle be benefitted, but all improved stock. I believe this bill has already passed both houses of this state, and I think a general bill covering the same ground should be encouraged.

Mr. Burrell called for the reading of the bill.

The Secretary read the bill, as follows:

"AN ACT To punish false pretenses in obtaining registration of cattle and other animals, and to punish giving false pedigrees.

"*The people of the State of*   , *represented in Senate and Assembly, do enact as follows:* SECTION I. Every person who by any false pretense shall obtain from any club, association, society, or company for improving the breed of cattle, horses, sheep, swine, or other domestic animals, the registration of any animal in the herd register, or other register of any such club, association, society, or company, or a transfer of any such registration, and every person who shall knowingly give a false pedigree of any animal, upon conviction thereof shall be punished by imprisonment in a state prison for a term not exceeding three years, or in a county jail for a term not exceeding one year, or by a fine not exceeding one thousand dollars, or by both such fine and imprisonment.

"SEC. II. This act shall take effect immediately."

MR. W. G. POWELL: The bill is before the Pennsylvania legislature. I have assurances, as one of a committee to defend its passage, that it will pass, and also the assurance of the Governor that it will receive his sanction.

MR. YEOMANS: That bill, as read, is substantially a bill that has passed our state legislature (New York) and has received the sanction of the Governor.

Mr. Smith moved the adoption of the resolution.

THE PRESIDENT: I think it would be well to have a copy of this resolution sent wherever the Secretary or President deem advisable.

The motion for the adoption of the resolution was seconded and carried.

THE PRESIDENT: The chair will state that Mr. Houghton was instructed by the President to present a matter before the Association, and he will now present it, there being nothing particularly before the meeting.

Mr. HOUGHTON: This Association, about a year and a half or two years ago, joined what is now known as the Consolidated Cattle-Growers' Association. In that association there are no personal members. It is an association that consists only of bodies. The object of that association is to promote generally the interests of cattle-breeders and owners all over the country. The membership fee is $15.00, and a yearly assessment upon each association, according to the number of its members, of fifty cents for each member. The past year this Consolidated Cattle-Growers' Association has been engaged in the good work of securing legislation by Congress which would prevent the spread of pleuro-pneumonia, and other matters that are generally for the interest of cattle-breeders everywhere. In that attempt they have spent considerable money, and now they ask us, not alone, but with almost every other association that is interested in cattle, to contribute a certain amount towards those expenses. It is a perfectly just request, and should be consented to and promptly honored. For this association is the only association of the kind in the United States, and is undoubtedly using its best efforts to promote the interests of all cattle-breeders. Among the other societies that have been assessed, I see the names of the American Jersey Cattle Club, the American Hereford Breeders' Association, the Dakota Fine Stock Breeders' Association, and numerous agricultural societies and stock-breeding associations all over the country. The amount requested of our Association is $250.00. Small associations are not charged quite as much as the others. I also see that the largest railroads are asked to contribute the same amount. As I have said, it seems to be a very proper thing to do. We are members of that association, and should keep ourselves in good standing with that work.

SECRETARY WALES: I will state that the delegates appointed from this Association took part in the election of officers of the Consolidated Cattle-Growers' Association at its annual meeting at Chicago, in November last.

MR. J. W. STILLWELL: I move you, sir, that the Secretary of our Association be instructed to notify the Secretary of the Consolidated Cattle-Growers' Association that we will honor their draft for $250.00 for this purpose.

MR. W. G. POWELL: I will call upon our President, who has given this matter more attention, and probably knows more about it than the rest of us. He has been in Washington, and I want a fair and square statement in regard to what he thinks, after seeing the ins and outs and ups and downs of the matter this winter. I would like his opinion upon it.

PRESIDENT STEVENS: This puts me in a very unpleasant position.

MR. POWELL: I knew it would.

PRESIDENT STEVENS: Thank you, sir. It puts me in an unpleasant position for this reason, that I am a member of this Association, and I heartily co-operate in everything that will benefit the breeding of cattle and their general welfare. I have tried to do everything I could for their support; and I also represented this Association at the meeting of the Consolidated Cattle-Growers' Association held in Chicago last fall. You, gentlemen, are well aware of the action taken by that association, and it would be a long, tedious, and tiresome thing for you to listen to, were I to recite to you the ins and outs of the whole matter, as I understand them and have looked at it. The proceedings of that association have been published, and you can all draw your inferences whether it was a politic thing to do or not. Nevertheless, it was done, and the result followed. We stand to-day without any legislation whatever in regard to the matter, with the exception of an appropriation to be expended by the Commissioner of Agriculture. We have no commissioners to investigate or to stamp out pleuro-pneumonia. The committee that represented the National Cattle-Growers' Association of America undoubtedly did as they themselves thought for the best interests that they represented. Whether they did is a question for those interested to judge; not for me. I think that inasmuch as we have a large cash balance on hand, it would not deplete our deposit a great deal to appropriate the the $250.00. If I should be called upon to vote, I should vote, under the circumstances, to pay the $250.00.

Mr. Sweet: Would it be on the ground of services rendered, or what would it be on?

President Stevens: It would be, sir, on general principles.

Mr. Huidekoper: Mr. President, did not the representatives from this Association meet with the National Cattle-Growers' Association in Chicago, and take part in the proceedings of that association? Did we not appoint representatives to represent not only the National Cattle-Growers' Association, but, through our representatives, to represent us at Washington? Did we not incur this liability? If we have made a mistake in the representation that we had at Washington, and have failed entirely in our purpose, did we not at all events incur a liability which we are under obligations to pay?

The President: I will say this, that we did take part in the election of the officers of the National Cattle-Growers' Association. We voted for them on the nomination. They, as officers, or as President of the Association, appointed the Congressional Committees.

Mr. Powell: Mr. President, we have a list of associations, railroad companies, etc., from whom they have asked contributions. We have no list of those who responded. Now, I would suggest that instead of our having this absolutely determined now, that it be referred to the Board of Officers. If, upon inquiry, they satisfy themselves that other associations and companies have responded, and that this money is to be legitimately used, that they appropriate it. If not all, such portion of it as the Board, in their discretion, think advisable.

THE PRESIDENT: The chair would suggest that Mr. Houghton did not read the letter from the Secretary of that association to the Secretary of our Association, in which he says that all requests have been promptly responded to, and nearly all of them have answered by sending their checks.

(Mr. Wales read the letter referred to.)

MR. SMITH: It seems to me very clear from the statements that have been made here in regard to this Association that we are honorably bound to pay this assessment, no matter whether we have realized any benefits or not. The only question is to look out for the future. If you have any instructions to give to your officers in the future, now is the time to do it, and I move that the amount be paid.

Mr. Sweet seconded the motion.

MR. YEOMANS: Is this for expenses already incurred in the past, or to be incurred in the future?

THE PRESIDENT: It is my understanding that it is for legislative expenses of the past winter. There was a committee at Washington for some two months, and they have necessarily incurred some expenses, and the chair understands it is to defray these expenses that the assessment is made.

The chair put the question, which was carried.

The chairman stated that the Finance Committee was ready to report.

The chairman of the Committee, Mr. C. Pratt, presented the following report.

Mr. President: Your committee would state that they have gone over the Secretary's, Treasurer's, and Superintendent of Advanced Registry's accounts, and find them correct. All of which is respectfully submitted.

It was moved that the report of the Finance Committee be received and adopted.

Seconded and carried, and the committee discharged.

MR. HORR: It seems to me that we are going to be a little crowded for time. There has to be a meeting of the Board of Officers at the intermission; would it not be well to adjourn and let the Board of Officers have their meeting, and then we can get back early.

THE PRESIDENT: The chair would state that the Board of Officers adjourned yesterday for a certain purpose; that purpose has not been accomplished, and until all the members of the Board are present he does not see that the Board can meet. I understand that Mr. Singerly is on the way here; he is a member of our Board.

The President called for the report of the Committee on Proxies.

Mr. Lamb, as Chairman of the Committee, read his report, as follows:

The committee appointed to examine proxies respectfully report that the following members are entitled to vote the number of proxies set opposite their names:

F. L. Houghton,	32
Anthony Lamb,	30
F. C. Stevens,	25
Thomas B. Wales, Jr.,	20
H. Langworthy,	16
S. Burchard,	12
S. Hoxie,	12
T. G. Yeomans,	10
Watkin G. Powell,	5
C. J. Lord,	4
C. R. Payne,	4
W. M. Liggett,	3
D. H. Burrell,	2
Dexter Severy,	2
J. W. Stillwell,	2
G. M. Carpenter,	2
J. W. Stillwell & F. C. Stevens,	2
John Lightner,	1
Henry Van Dreser,	1
Jere Allis,	1
George L. Wells,	1
S. N. Wright,	1
James C. Poor,	1
A. W. Brown,	1
W. J. Potter,	1
C. W. Horr,	1
Blank, signed by D. H. Taylor,	1
Whole number of proxies,	193

Mr. Huidekoper moved that the report of the Committee on Proxies be accepted, and the committee discharged.

Seconded.

Mr. W. G. Powell moved that the report of the Committee on Proxies be received, and that the committee hold over until afternoon.

Mr. Huidekoper accepted the amendment.

The question, as amended, was put and carried.

Upon motion, the meeting adjourned until 2 o'clock P. M.

AFTERNOON SESSION.

The President called the meeting to order at 2 o'clock P. M.

THE PRESIDENT: The chair would state that all the preliminary business has been transacted, and we now come to the regular business of the meeting, brought before it in the order of the call. The first matter to be considered is that the fees for registration and transfer of animals be reduced.

MR. J. W. STILLWELL: I believe that that proposition originated with myself. At the time, I expected to continue in the Holstein business, but since then, through force of circumstances, I, to a certain extent, lost the interest which I expected to have in the matter. As far as I am concerned myself, really I have not any pecuniary interest in it at the present time.

THE PRESIDENT: The gentleman who represents this call makes no motion upon that question. Is there any other gentleman in the house who entertains the same view, or desires to have this matter brought to the attention of the Association? If not, the matter will be dropped without further consideration.

MR. POWELL: It would seem to me from the present financial condition of our Association, with the amount of money in the treasury, that we can, at least for the coming year, during the present stringency in the stock business of the country, relieve, to some extent, the breeders from what has seemed to some embarrassment. We can reduce the expense of registering and transfer to the members of our Association to a point that will just cover the actual running expenses, and if we do that we are dividing the advantages of our Association with our fellow-breeders. At times when we have needed funds our breeders have responded liberally. I believe there has never been a protest against any fee that has been charged for registry or transfer, or anything of the kind, by the Association. Now, it seems to me that on the part of this Association we can show something of an appreciation by relieving them partially at this time; and, although I had not expected to do so — I supposed the party who offered this call would bring the matter in shape — and as that is not done, I now move that for all members of this Association the record of all American-bred animals and the transfer of all animals be reduced one-half for the coming year.

Motion seconded.

MR. YEOMANS: I would propose to amend that slightly. The transfer fee is now small, and I would not divide it. I would make the transfer fee nothing; make it free, and reduce the registry one-half. I move that as an amendment.

Mr. Powell accepted the amendment.

The chair put the question, which was carried.

THE PRESIDENT: The second question is that the registry fee for bulls be increased to twenty-five dollars. I would state, at the request of a member of the Association who is not here, and did not expect to be here, I put this in the call for him. I do not approve of it myself, but acted at his request.

A member moved that it be laid on the table.

Motion seconded and carried.

THE PRESIDENT: The third proposition is as follows: That when one member of a firm or corporation is a member of the Association, such firm or corporation be entitled to the registry and transfer of animals for member's fees. The Secretary has a letter from Mr. Shallcross relative to this matter. He is one of the gentlemen who made the call. The Secretary will read Mr. Shallcross' views in regard to the matter.

The Secretary read the letter referred to, as follows:

Mr. President, and Gentlemen of the Association: The only explanation that can be offered of the action of this Association at its last meeting, in passing the rule requiring all members of a firm to become members of the Association before they can register their cattle for the same fees exacted from individual owners of herds, is that the wisest assemblies sometimes frame laws lacking in both wisdom and justice.

Why this Association refuses to follow the common usage in regard to firms is past finding out. In the commercial world, it is only necessary to transact with one member of a firm; through him the firm speaks and acts. We conduct our negotiations with one, not with each member separately, he representing his associate or associates in the matter.

The law draws no distinction between firms and individuals, but places both upon the same footing, looking upon any one partner who may represent his firm in the courts as if he were the firm itself. But so far as the charges for registering cattle are concerned, this Association will not permit a firm of breeders to derive any benfit by reason of one of its members being a member of the Association, nor will it admit a firm as a firm. It requires each and every member of a co-partnership to become members of the Association, independent of their joint ownership of the cattle they desire to register, before they will allow them to register their stock at the same rate it charges where the ownership is vested in a single person who is a member. In other words, it, in its wisdom, sees fit to draw a decided distinction between firms and individuals, putting such an impost upon the former that to a firm it becomes a question whether it would not be more profitable to remain outside the Association altogether, and pay the fees exacted from non-members. Let us take an example: Two parties join together for the purpose of breeding Holstein-Friesian cattle, say on a moderate scale. They collect a herd of twenty-five females. To curtail the cost of registering the produce of their herd, they are willing for one of them to become a member of the Association, or are willing to join the Association as a firm, but they find that their firm cannot join as a firm; and to accomplish their object, both must join at a cost of $200.00, while their neighbor and competitor, who owns as an individual 100 head, has obtained the privileges they wish at a cost of $100.00. It would require four years of registering the produce of their herd to get back this most unjust overcharge.

It is not at all likely they would suffer such an imposition, nor would their opinion of the fairness and judgment of the Holstein-Friesian Association be very elevated.

Suppose this incident should occur: A merchant of Buffalo goes to take out his city license. "How much business do you do?" he is asked. "$200,000.00 a year." "How many are in your firm?" "Six." "You will have to take out six licenses at $100.00 each — $600.00."

Before the merchant can recover from his astonishment his competitor steps up for a license. "How much business do you do?" "$500,000.00 a year." "Have you any partners?" "No." "You will need only one license, $100.00."

Rome might not, but I venture to say Buffalo would, howl. What would be said if the license law of the City of Buffalo was such that an incident like this could occur? Yet the rule of this Association regarding the registration of cattle belonging to firms is identical in kind to such a law — equally as absurd, equally as narrow in policy, equally as discriminating.

It may be urged in favor of the existing rule, that where a firm is represented in the Association by only one partner the Association cannot reach his associates in case they commit acts for which, if they were members, they could be held amenable. As a firm is responsible for the partners, so the partner is responsible for the firm, and the member of a firm who is also a member of the Association stands as bondsman for his partners, and consequently must be prepared to bear himself whatever penalties the misdeeds of his partners deserve. But the Association has yet a more effectual weapon for controlling these outside members of a firm. It can erase the names of all their cattle from the Herd-Books, depreciating the value of the stock to that of mere grades, and it can prevent their ever afterwards registering and transferring cattle, virtually destroying their business. Even if they were so inclined, with such consequences staring them in the face, they would be slow to commit practices which would bring down upon them the wrath of the Holstein-Friesian Association.

It may be advanced that where only one member of a firm belongs to the Association his partners derive, in the matter of registration, benefits to which they are not entitled, but a moment's reflection will reveal the fallacy of such an argument. As well say that the junior member of a firm of cotton-dealers is not entitled to his share of the firm benefits derived from the cotton exchange because only the senior partner is a member of the exchange. The expense of having one of them a member of the Association is equally divided among a firm of breeders, and in proportion to the cost they obtain no more advantages than does Mr. Jones, who is sole owner of his herd. It is the herd of cattle at last; and the Ashland herd, owned by four men, asks no more at the hands of the Association than the herd of Mr. Jones — it simply does not wish to be discriminated against. The fact that some firms have all their members members of the Association proves nothing. It sets no precedent and makes no law to guide this Association. It is a matter which concerns those firms alone. Most of them became members when it cost considerably less than it does now, and they became members to use their vote.

There is another question which forces itself to the surface in this discussion. How will you deal with corporations and companies? It is not so long since that the project was bruited in Kentucky to form a company and buy a body of land for the purpose of breeding Holstein-Friesians. Say this design had come to a head, and the company consisted of ten men, who, on investigation, found that every one of them would be compelled to join this Association, at a cost of $1,000.00, before they could register their cattle at membership rates; what would have been the result? The probabilities are strong that the undertaking would have been dropped at once. Is this the way to encourage the dissemination and breeding of our cattle?

While the rule as it now stands is unjust in all its operations, and a grave mistake when considered from a purely business standpoint, it is especially oppressive to those firms of which one of their members is a member of the Association, and which, prior to the last meeting, had for some time been allowed to register their cattle at membership rates. To them it is retroactive in effect, and it is not necessary to tell you gentlemen that no court of equity will sustain a retroactive law. These firms paid their money in good faith, and thought themselves secure in the privileges they bought. One, at least, was so assured by an officer of the Association —and enjoyed them for a length of time — which of itself should make them inalienable. Then this rule is passed, whose working most unreasonably goes into the past over a period of years, and revokes rights for which full value has been given. True, there was no law covering the point, but the action of the Association in receiving from those firms the fees for one of their members becoming a member of the Association, and allowing them to register their stock at membership rates for such length of time, became of itself, as between those firms and the Association, an unwritten law, guaranteeing and vesting rights which are indefeasible.

Now, it certainly seems that the proper thing for this Association to do is to do away with the present illiberal and proscriptive rule — a rule unworthy of a body of enlightened men — and allow firms to become members as a firm, *with only one vote*, and to register their stock at membership fees on account of one of their members being a member of the Association.

Believe me, the present rule is hurtful to the interests of the breed, and is calculated to antagonize where we should conciliate.

This Association is a National one now, and not run for the benefit of a few. Certainly the finances of the Association do not call for this rule, and I move you that the rule be abolished.

Respectfully,
JOHN W. SHALLCROSS, JR.

Motioned seconded.

MR. MILLER: I would like to make an amendment to that motion. It seems to me that it would be fair to all corporations which are members of our Association, and to those which are members in part in our Association, to regulate the fee for entering animals in proportion to the fractional portion of membership of those firms. Let me illustrate: If there is a firm of two people, one of them is a member of the Association and one is not, I would favor admitting one-half of their cattle at membership fees, the other half at non-member's fees. If there is more than two, I should take the same fractional portion as represented by the members of this Association in the corporation, whether one-half, one-third, or three-fourths, or whatever it may be. In that way we would be giving to members of our Association simply their just dues, and to outsiders their just dues.

MR. STILLWELL: I sympathize with Mr. Shallcross myself, to the extent of a hundred dollars. About a year ago I was advised by the honorable Secretary that there would be no more cattle registered for J. W. Stillwell & Co. at membership fees until the remaining partner joined the Association. At the same time, I knew there was considerable feeling among some of the members, and also with one or two of the Board. We had a meeting of our company, and I told them "we are liable now to get into a very nice little pickle here. For instance, suppose Mr. Riley, a member of our firm, should not be admitted to the Association. Practically, then, J. W. Stillwell and G. W. Cruikshank, another member of our firm, also a member of this Association, could receive no benefit whatever by being members of this Association. The only privileges that they would be allowed would be to come and vote (which they could do at home just as well as here). That was one reason why, if you will remember, one year ago I had a sale on the same day that you met in Buffalo. It was said to me, why do you have the sale on the day of the meeting of the Association? I made the remark that I thought the Association did not care very much for me, and I cared less for them; that I would make the sale when I got ready, and would consult nobody. I think the rule has been arbitrary. It is radically wrong. You have no right to say that all the members shall join the Association before they can reap any benefits from it at all. While I feel in sympathy with Mr. Shallcross, I would vote for his resolution in full, but at the same time how are you going to reconcile those whom you have compelled to pay this $100.00; and as an amendment to Mr. Miller's amendment I would suggest that the first member be charged $100.00, the second one $50.00, and the balance admitted for nothing, and then register their cattle as members of the Association. I think this would be fair. There are seldom more than three men connected in this way, and I think that that would be a fair compensation to the Association, and I would offer that as an amendment— that the first one of the firm be charged $100.00, the second one $50.00, and the balance admitted free of any charge.

MR. HUIDEKOPER: I would like to ask the speaker, when this firm dissolved partnership, what are you going to do with their membership? You have got six members and six partners who would be made members for $150.00. Those four members then retain their memership for life for nothing, and the Association gets no benefit of it.

MR. STILLWELL: The Association has had the benefit of the $150.00. If the firm has retired, they would simply say, "I have no interest in this; I do not wish to vote either way," and they do not vote at all, the same as I have done with Mr. Stevens. I sent in the proxies of J. W. Cruikshank and Mr. Riley, and told Mr. Stevens that under the existing circumstances I should stand and look on, and that he might take these proxies and vote himself and I would not vote. If our firm goes out of existence, I do not suppose either of us will vote in the Association again, unless we have cattle. If you have any difficulties whatever, I think it is proper and right that you should settle them among yourselves. The gentleman speaks of six members; I do not suppose you would find to-day in the Association any four men connected in a company.

MR. C. PRATT: I know of five.

MR. W. G. POWELL: We have rules prohibiting membership by foreigners—those who are not residents or citizens of the United States and the Dominion of Canada. Suppose I, myself, should see fit to form a partnership with some foreigner, and under that rule, as proposed, how would it prohibit importation of cattle in that way, or their registration? What would be effected by this rule and the modification of it? There are certainly some things very fair about Mr. Miller's suggestion that a proportion, pro rata, of the cattle of a firm should be registered. As has been suggested by Mr. Stillwell, that the first member should pay $100.00, the second $50.00, and all thereafter should be admitted free, that would put us in a position that we would be compelled to admit any scalawag that any member might see fit to form a partnership with. Now, do we want to do that? If we so modify the rule as to admit registration, as suggested by Mr. Miller, pro rata with the membership of the firm, then there should go with that some restriction that it should not apply to the importation of cattle, or cattle not of American birth. For myself, I have no special preference in the matter. I recognize some justice in Mr. Shallcross' argument. On the other hand, I think he has gone to an extreme when he proposes that these are rules that are not in accordance with what should be in a respectable body of men.

Mr. E. P. TAFFT: The remarks made by the gentleman referred, as I understand them, to firms where there are several members. But you take the case of a corporation chartered by law, how are you going to operate with them? They own the cattle and want to register, and one of their officers may be a member of the Association. How are you going to cover their case? That is properly a corporation, and not a co-partnership of several members.

Mr. SMITH: We have discussed this question at two or three meetings, and the question of companies and large firms seems to be a very difficult and almost impossible one to handle. There seems to be a good many ways suggested. It seems to me, as I think of it, the question is at once, why is there an injustice? Is it because the membership fee is too high? If it is too high, make it less. If $100.00 is too much, make it $50.00. If it is not worth $50.00 to be a member of this Association, make it $25.00, or $10.00, or whatever it is worth. We cannot undertake to give the benefits of this Association broadcast over the country, regardless of where they may strike. It seems to me that the system proposed might answer the purpose. In the cases — of which I believe we have twenty-five or thirty — where there are more than one member in the firm, and one of those members is a member of this Association, why would it not be proper for this Association to transfer free the cattle in the name of the firm to the name of that individual who happens to be a member of this Association? That is, of course, provided the firm saw fit to accept that. They could then transact their business in their firm name and register their cattle in the name of the one member of the firm who happened to be a member of this Association.

THE PRESIDENT: The question before the house is, when one member of a firm or corporation is a member of the Association, shall such firm or corporation be entitled to register and transfer animals at membership fees? The amendment offered by Mr. Miller is, that it shall be done pro rata: where there are two members of the firm, one-half of the cattle shall be registered at the original charge and the other half at the fee of membership.

Mr. SMITH: I make my suggestion in the shape of an amendment.

Amendment seconded.

Mr. HUIDEKOPER: I move that it be applied only to American-bred animals.

Mr. Smith accepted Mr. Huidekoper's amendment.

Mr. HORE: You do not mean imported animals that have already been registered.

Mr. POWELL: My idea is that it shall not apply to the original registration of imported animals.

Mr. Houghton: Mr. President, I would like to ask Mr. Miller if he will explain how he would keep the accounts of those firms with the Association. I think there is a practical difficulty; that we would need to establish something in the nature of a clearing-house in the Secretary's office in order to keep an account of the registry fees. Will Mr. Miller please suggest a plan for doing it?

Mr. Miller: That would be work for the Secretary's office to do. It could easily be done by a system of percentage. If there are three members of a firm, and only one member is a member of this Association, one-third of the cattle offered by that firm should be accepted at membership rates. If it is for transfer, nothing should be charged for that one-third. For the other two-thirds charge full rate. The same in regard to recording. Of course it would make a little more work in the Secretary's office.

Mr. Tafft: In the case of a corporation, what would you do?

Mr. Miller: They would have to pay non-members' fees unless they are members of this Association.

Mr. Tafft: It hardly seems to me to be justice to the corporation that is represented by only one individual.

The President: The last amendment is that offered by Mr. Smith, that the Association transfer to the member of a firm who is a member of this Association. Are you ready for this amendment?

Mr. E. A. Powell: I offer the amendment that this rule should not apply to the registration of imported animals.

The President: That amendment was accepted.

Mr. Wales: Mr. President, I really do not see how this rule is going to work, as proposed by Mr. Miller. I am sorry to disagree with Mr. Miller. I very seldom do. I hope we can find some other manner of satisfying gentlemen belonging to these firms owning cattle, and also corporations. It is a pretty difficult question to decide what is best. I think as stated in the call is a fair way to do, but I would not include any foreigner as a member of a firm; any firm that had a foreigner as a member I would not allow the privileges under this proposed change in the By-Laws.

Mr. Smith: Will Mr. Wales be kind enough to state the particular objection to Mr. Miller's proposition. It looks to me to be a very fair one, but there may be things about it that I do not understand.

Mr. Wales: That is my trouble. I do not fully understand it either. If Mr. Miller will explain how it is going to work I will try and be satisfied. We would have to keep an account of just how many cattle every firm owns and divide it up.

Mr. Miller: You would only have to consider the number of animals that were offered for registry and transfer, and at each transaction send in your bill for the amount, or require payment of the amount. Whenever they send you fifty animals, and one-fifth of them are to be entered at membership rates, it is easy enough to arrive at the amount due.

Mr. WALES: I think that would not be very difficult.

Mr. WHEELER: I would be interested personally in having this amendment, as my son and myself are together, and owning cattle together; but I have thought it perfectly proper that it should remain just as it was, in view of the difficulties that we all seem to apprehend in this matter; and I move that the question be laid on the table.

Motion seconded.

Motion to lay the matter on the table put and carried.

A division was called for.

A standing vote was taken, and the motion to lay the question on the table was declared carried by a vote of 46 to 18.

THE PRESIDENT: The next topic under discussion is the amendment to Section 2 of Article II. of the By-Laws.

The Secretary read Section 2 of Article II.

Mr. WING R. SMITH: I would move to amend Section 2 of Article II. so as to read as follows: "The Board of Officers of this corporation, as a board, shall have and take the entire control and management of its affairs and business, with full power and authority to do what they deem proper and best for its interest; but nothing contrary to the expressed wish of the Association"—"but nothing contrary to the expressed wish of the Association," I wish to have put in—"and they shall have no authority to contract a debt against the corporation beyond its current expenses, and in no case beyond the amount of cash in the treasury, and nothing shall be done which is not in accordance with the purpose and spirit of the Charter and By-Laws;" and here I add, "But shall in all cases execute every expressed will of the Association as expressed at any regular meeting."

Motion seconded.

Mr. HUIDEKOPER: If we are limited to this, to transact only such business as is the expressed wish of the Association, then the Association has got to attend to all the business.

Mr. SMITH: Allow me to explain. If, for instance, the Association pass a resolution that a certain thing shall or shall not be done, the object of the resolution is that the Board of Officers shall not have it in their power to go on and do that thing, contrary to the expressed will of the Association, which has been done in the past.

Mr. C. PRATT: I understand this a little different. At our annual meeting last year there was a resolution offered and adopted to the effect that this Association should give no premiums where oleomargarine was on exhibition. After we had adjourned there were circulars issued by the Board to each one of the members, asking the privilege of appropriating a certain sum, as I understand, for premiums at that show. We had expressly stated here that we should not exhibit. I understand that the Board did appropriate money for exhibitions there.

Mr. STILLWELL: I remember that circular very well myself, and I ask for enlightenment if I am wrong; I never heard how the vote stood on that. I remember distinctly that we voted, and I do not believe that it was ever announced how that vote stood by the Secretary. I see that the Board went on and did it anyway.

THE PRESIDENT: The chair is not able to answer that question; but as soon as the Secretary has an opportunity, he will no doubt furnish the desired information.

The chairman put the question on the amendment to Section 2 of Article II., which was carried.

THE PRESIDENT: The next call is in reference to amending Section 6 of Article IV.

The Secretary read the section referred to.

MR. HORR: I move that we lay that upon the table.

Seconded.

THE PRESIDENT: I do not think it is necessary to lay this question on the table. The mover of the amendment is not present, or if he is, he does not seem to be anxious to bring it up. The Secretary will read Section 8.

The Secretary read Section 8 of Article IV.

THE PRESIDENT: Is the gentleman present who desires to have this amended?

MR. G. V. DEGRAAF: I would like to have the Secretary read the amendments which I have offered.

The Secretary read the petition of Mr. DeGraaf, as follows:

To the Holstein-Friesian Association of America:

Your petitioner, Garret V. De Graaf, a member of the above named Association, respectfully asks that the By-Laws of the said Association be changed, amended, or modified, in the following respects and particulars, viz.:

First. That Section 6 of Article IV., page 19, shall be changed, amended, or modified to such an extent that in case *any member or members of the Association shall purchase an animal or animals within the United States of America* (instead of Europe), that any said member or members shall have and shall be allowed and entitled to all the registration privilege contained in said section and article, and as if the said animal or animals had been shipped from Europe.

Second. That Section 8 of Article IV., pages 19 and 20, shall be changed, amended, or modified to such an extent that any member or members of the Association *shall be vested with the right and power to make application to the Secretary* of the Association for the *registry of any animal or animals purchased within the United States*, and to be given and to be controlled by the same privileges and rights governing applications for the registry of imported animals.

Third. That Section 8 of Article IV., page 20, about line 18, which reads, "unless the animal or its dam and sire are registered," shall be changed or amended so as to read, "*unless the animal or its dam* OR *sire are registered.*"

Fourth. That Section 8 of Article IV., page 20, about lines 24 and 25, shall be changed, amended, or modified to such an extent as to read as follows: "*Any person or persons applying to the Secretary for the inspection of imported animals shipped from Europe or animals purchased in the United States.*"

Fifth. That Section 8 of Article IV., page 20, about lines 29 and 30, shall be changed, amended, or modified so as to read as follows: "The registry fee for each imported animal *or each animal purchased in the United States* shall be $20.00."

Sixth. That Section 8 of Article IV., page 20, about lines 33 and 34, shall be altered, amended, or modified so as to read as follows: "No animal or animals imported *or purchased within the United States* shall be accepted for registration until it has been passed by the Inspector."

Seventh. That Section 8 of Article IV., page 20, about line 29, shall be changed, amended, or modified so as to read as follows: "*Or upon the farm of the importer or purchaser.*"

Your petitioner further asks that the members of the Association above named will give this petition their earnest and careful consideration, and that the said members will take favorable action upon the same as soon as practicable, inasmuch as your petitioner sincerely believes such action would prove highly beneficial to the best interests of this Association, of which your petitioner is a member.

Very truly yours,
G. V. DE GRAAF.

Mr. Singerly moved that the subject be laid upon the table.

Amendment seconded.

Motion to lay upon the table put and carried.

MR. POWELL: I desire to make a motion that all Inspectors hereafter be allowed $8.00 per day, with no extra fees for traveling nights. I think the times and the depreciation in the business in which we are all engaged are such that all parties would feel that it was proper and right, and I think there is no Inspector here — I have talked with several — who would object to that change, and I therefore make that motion, that the By-Laws be amended so that the fees hereafter be $8.00 a day, and nothing for night travel.

Motion seconded and carried.

MR. LIGHTNER: I desire to call attention to this: "All applications for registering animals which are not filed with the Secretary within one year," etc., "shall be charged three times the usual registry fee." In two or three cases with myself I could not tell at the end of the year whether the animal was a breeder or not. So far as I am concerned, I would like to have that read something like this: "All applications for registry of animals which are not filed with the Secretary, before known as to whether they were breeders." In two or three cases I have myself written to Mr. Wales: "Will I have to register within a year?" "Yes, you will have to register within a year." And I registered; and before the two years were out I saw that the animal was not a breeder and had to butcher the animal. Some times, with regard to a bull, we do not know at the end of the year whether he is worth anything or not; and would it not be better to have it understood that we have the privilege of holding the registry until we know whether the heifer or the bull are breeders?

MR. LORD: I would say, if this motion had been passed some time ago it would have saved me $40.00, in the case of an imported animal, which the Board discussed yesterday, and decided it was right for us to pay the full amount. In this case we had a heifer which we were quite certain was not a breeder, and we did not register her. Of course it ran over the year, and she proved finally to be a breeder. If this fee for the animal was $20.00, $10.00, or something of that kind, I would think it was worth while to take action of this kind; but while it is only $1.00 it seems to me it is not risking a great deal to pay the dollar and have it registered within the year and keep our records straight.

MR. WALES: I hope the gentlemen will not vote for any such change. I think it will interfere very seriously with the business of the Association.

The chair put the question, which was declared lost.

MR. POWELL: In reference to Section 10 of Article IV., in regard to registration and transfer. Has that not already been amended upon motion of Mr. Yeomans?

THE PRESIDENT: That has already been amended, as the chair understands it, so that the transfer of animals by members is free for the coming year.

MR. LORD: I would like to offer an amendment to Section 10 of Article IV., so that it will read: "That a register of transfer of ownership of any animal registered in the Holstein-Friesian Herd-Book will be made on application of the owner on the payment of fees, if there are any, by the owner; and in case the signature of the owner, or of the person in whose name the animal now stands, could not be obtained for any reason, from death or any other cause, we will go on, without a lawsuit, or something of that kind, to obtain this signature from any unfriendliness that may come up; that upon the affidavit of the present owner of the animal the Secretary shall be instructed to issue this certificate." Now, I wish to bring this matter up. We had a heifer which we took back as payment for stock. We sold it on time, and the person could not meet his payments, and the heifer came back to us, and this heifer had been purchased from another party by the party who we received her of, and he had neglected to get a transfer from the first party to him, and when we bought the heifer he signed a transfer from himself to us. We took no further trouble about the matter, supposing that the heifer had been transferred to him. We found, on sending the certificate to the Secretary, that she never had been transferred from Mr. Leavitt to Mr. Williams. The Board failed to pass it yesterday for me, and I do not know whether we will ever get the transfer or not. We are ready to make affidavit that the heifer is in our possession, and also ready to come and defend this Association from any damage whatever, if they will transfer it for us; and I want to get it in such shape that if anything of the kind arises again the present owner of the animal can make affidavit to his ownership of the animal, setting forth the causes and reasons why he could not obtain the signature, and then, if it looks reasonable to the Secretary, that he shall issue this certificate. If it does not look reasonable to him, and he thinks there is a catch in it in any way, carry it to the meeting of the Board. If it looks straight to him, let him issue a certificate of transfer.

MR. POWELL: I would suggest, without making a motion, that the better way would be for the parties to make their proofs and bring their case before the Board, and, if necessary, the Board submit it to the meeting. If Mr. Lord had his transfer here I have no doubt we would instruct the Secretary to give a certificate, but, in the absence of this transfer, it would be a loose and indefinite method of adjusting the matter.

MR. WALES: This is the first case of the kind that has ever come up. The probability is there will not be another one in five years. I think we should do very wrong to make any change in our rules in regard to such a matter as this. This case came before the Board, and I informed Mr. Lord that he would be expected to make further endeavors to obtain a proper application for the transfer of the animal; and told him, in addition, that it was the sense of the Board that in case he could not, after using all the means in his power, get the proper papers, that we would consider it further, and probably the matter could be arranged.

The chair put the amendment of Mr. Lord to Section 10 of Article IV., which was declared lost.

The chair stated that the next order of business was in reference to Article V. of the By-Laws.

Mr. Houghton: Mr. President, I regret that the views expressed in my pamphlet have called forth such excited utterances from the advocates of the Advanced Registry.

I desire to express for my constituents (a large number of breeders in all parts of the country) our views of the system as we understand it, and as evidenced by the volume just received from the hands of our enthusiastic Superintendent.

I wish to disclaim any intention to bring about any of the untoward results which have been suggested in the circular replies to my pamphlet. I desire to act only in the true interests of the Association, and in perfect harmony with all, if possible.

I will state that no gentleman has sent me a proxy without at the same time expressing his views on this subject.

With your permission I will read extracts from a few of the letters received.

Having presented my views at some length in my pamphlet, I will confine myself to some points not touched therein.

My sincere belief that a herd-book is simply a register of pure-blooded animals is the sole incentive for all that I have said and done.

It has been said in reply to my statement in this regard, that such a system was expressly authorized under these words of the Charter, viz: "That this corporation is for the purpose of improving Holstein-Friesian cattle; ascertaining, preserving, and disseminating all useful information and facts as to their pedigrees and desirable qualities, and the distinguishing characteristics of the best specimens." I would not detract in the least from the power and meaning of those words; but I would ask you to read the following lines of the Charter, viz: "And *generally* for promoting and securing the best interests of the importers, breeders, and owners of said cattle," which is my argument in a nut-shell, viz: That the present system is not for the best interests, generally, of the owners of these cattle.

It seems to me that the creation of a class within the record can not fail to discriminate in favor of those having superior advantages in the way of means and peculiar situations, inasmuch as it forces every owner to great trouble and expense to place himself upon the level of those who have cattle recorded in the Advanced Registry.

My most serious objection is the name, "Advanced Registry." It implies tacitly a connection with the pedigree registry, and, indeed, when published, as has been this volume, under the name of a register, and not as contemplated by the rules, a *registry*, the public may be easily led to infer that there is a connection in fact, when it is, or rather should be, a record of authenticated tests.

We now have the first volume of the record as it is presented to the public. It contains, in addition to the already published (and seldom believed by the public) statements of the owners, that these records have been made at some distant period, a statement of the measurements and general description of the animal, and the fact that an Inspector has seen the animal and believes her capable of having made the record. In what way does this generally benefit the owners, except as an advertisement? It is not an authenticated official test of the animal, such as the rules have provided for. I do not believe that the Association has any right to guarantee records made in this manner.

I do not understand that the advocates of this system claim it to be perfect, and I desire to disclaim any carping criticism on the results of what must have involved immense labor upon the part of its Superintendent, but I sincerely wish to aid the Association in establishing a system which shall work practical results without conflict or prejudice to the interests of any individual.

A few words on the form of the record in Volume I.:

Rule 5 says: "A bull, to be eligible to this registry, must have proven his superiority by his progeny, of which the examiner must see and examine at least three animals."

Question. What right has a bull who has no progeny tested, under the rules, to record in the Advanced Register? I find, for instance, an animal two years and seventeen days old when he was examined and accepted for record, who could not have had any progeny old enough to be tested (see No. 30), undoubtedly one of the best bred bulls in the book, but still, to my mind, ineligible for record, for an examination of his progeny at that age could not determine his superiority as a sire of dairy stock.

Again, No. 24, two years four months and twenty-eight days old, is open to the same criticism.

Again, Nos. 21 and 22, also No. 13, No. 10, and No. 2.

A cow, to be eligible, must have born a calf. To carry out the objects of this system, the superiority of a bull's progeny as dairy cattle cannot be determined until the progeny have born a calf and been tested.

Rule 6 provides for certain tests of milk or butter in certain specified periods. I do not find, except in isolated instances, any record of these tests, but in lieu thereof I find statements of records made, in one case, five years prior to the establishment of this system (see No. 38, also No. 1, three years, No. 4, four years).

I also find instances where the examinations were made in December, 1886, where the sole record published was made during 1884–85 (see Nos. 321, 230, and 233), that is to say, these records were made and closed prior to the establishment of this registry, and not under the supervision of any Inspector, according to the rules. No. 233 closed her record in 1883.

What authority is there for the publication in this book of records other than those required by the rules. Rule 8 says that records of milk and butter productions of any cow may be recorded for each and every form *if the rules of the Association have been complied with in making such records.*

It does not appear that the rules were complied with in the instances mentioned — Nos. 1, 2, and 38 — for there were no rules at that time. Such records in this registry are worthless.

Such a record or system should be entirely separate and independent of the record of purity of blood, and should be called by a name plainly indicating its purpose, as, for instance, test-book, and not one implying a class of cattle better than another class of the same blood.

I think that a test-book, on the plan of that of the American Jersey Cattle Club, would be entirely unobjectionable. I have with me a copy of the forms and rules. I have partially outlined a set of rules which would seem to me something upon which all might unite:

First. A book should be kept by the Superintendent, to be known as the Holstein-Friesian Test-Book, in which all tests hereafter made by the Association shall be entered.

Second. The Superintendent shall be appointed by the Board of Directors, and shall hold his office during the pleasure of the Board, and receive such compensation as the Board may decide. He shall have the power, subject to the approval of the Board, to appoint deputies to assist him.

Third. Any person making application for a test shall bear the traveling expenses of the Superintendent or deputy, which must be fully paid to the Secretary on the completion of the test, and before the test is entered in the official test-book. He shall also pay a fee of $3.00 for each animal tested.

Fourth. Each deputy shall be paid by the Association $5.00 per day for each day he is necessarily engaged in conducting the test; and under no circumstances shall any payment or gratuity to the Superintendent or his deputies be made or permitted from the owner of the animal, or any one interested in it. Any violation thereof shall invalidate the test.

Fifth. The report of the Superintendent and his deputies shall be retained by the Secretary of the Association as a permanent record, and shall be published entire in the test-book.

Sixth. The following tests, and these only, shall be fully made: For a milk or butter record: One test, at not less than thirty days after calving, of three days; one test, at not less than eight months after calving, of three days; and the production in said tests, to entitle the animal to registry, shall be not less than three-tenths of present standard in the different forms. In every test a complete statement of the amount and kind of grain and fodder consumed by the animal during the test shall be kept, and published in the record.

It has been asked, where would the breed be to-day if it were not for the records of such and such cows? I answer, the breed did not reach its present position under the fostering care of any advanced registry, but reached its position as the result of individual enterprise and sagacity, not even a herd-book having been kept until within the last seventeen years. There need be no fear but that the best animals will receive proper recognition, and their owners receive money enough for them, without creating an aristocracy in the Herd-Book.

I dislike to have my position construed as one in any way opposing improvement and progress, and I think that a fair construction of my acts will show that I am simply opposing discrimination, and advocating equal rights.

The progress of the introduction of Holstein-Friesian cattle into this country we know has been far more rapid than that of any other breed in the same period of time. This we have been told by the very persons who are advocating the present system, which they openly admit is for the purpose of still faster forcing the merits of these cattle upon the public, and creating a still greater demand.

I greatly fear that if such should be, and is, the effect of the Advanced Registry, that this forcing process would result in an unhealthy condition of things in a short period.

I do not wish to work any hardship on those gentlemen who were induced to form this Association upon belief that this identical system of Advanced Registry should be maintained as a feature of this Herd-Book, nor do I wish to be accused of acting in bad faith by those gentlemen. I think, when you fully understand what I mean, you will be satisfied that I am acting in harmony with the best interests of all concerned.

Upon the formation of this Association, we simply agreed to provide for a system of advanced registration. I think no one desired to gain advantage over another.

If we find to-day, after two years' trial of the system, that it is likely to, and does, result in giving advantages to a certain class, we are at liberty to change and modify the rules for the system without incurring the displeasure of any member or violating any agreement.

If the adoption of this identical system was an error, it should be at once corrected, so that all shall be treated alike, and this without giving rise to personal feeling or rupture of harmonious union.

I would therefore move you, Mr. President, that a committee of five be appointed by the chair to revise Article V. of the By-Laws, and the rules established under it, with a view to providing a system of milk and butter tests in a more authentic form than under the present system.

Motion seconded.

Mr. Yeomans: I would move, as a substitute, that this matter be referred to the Board of Officers. They certainly have more knowledge of this matter than any committee, and I think they are the proper ones to take charge of this matter, and I move that this subject be referred to the Board of Officers. It makes no difference who the individual members of that Board are.

Mr. Horr: I suppose within two hours, if we have good luck and all keep our heads, we will have a new Board of Officers, and consequently it will be referred to the Board of Officers that we are to select. Now, while I am talking extemporaneously, I would be very much obliged to

Mr. Houghton if he will refer to the rules and show me which rule it is that requires that these tests should be made under the supervision of the Inspector. I simply speak from memory, and say that there is nothing of the kind in the rules at all; not only nothing like it in explicit words, but nothing that squints towards it. The oath of the man who milks the cow, with the record before him of three years ago, is as good as the oath of the man who milked the cow six weeks ago; and consequently there is nothing in those rules that contemplated it.

Let us discuss this good-naturedly. A few running comments in my rough and extemporaneous way upon my friend Houghton's argument: First, he gives us a long chapter of correspondence that he has been having. I see by that that he has been having some correspondence with the members of the Association, and I notice that the attempt was to influence the vote of the members present by reading from letters, in most cases giving almost no reason at all, but simply stating that the writer of that letter was in favor of discarding advanced registration. If the truth was to be elicited in that way, a great deal of the progress that has made for us the civilization that we are all so proud of we never would have had. If because some men think things are right they are right outside of any argument, why, where would the reformations and advancements of the world go? Consequently it is a unique method of establishing a position to simply read some letters from gentlemen who have received a misleading circular from my friend Houghton — letters written in reply to a misleading circular, as it seems to me. Again, Mr. Houghton, if I did not misunderstand him — and if I did he will put me right — started out by saying that he was opposed to advanced registration. I certainly think the first two or three paragraphs of his address clearly took the position that he was opposed to advanced registration. If he is opposed to it, then we should be cautious in accepting his rules; because if this system is against his judgment, I do not think he has given to it that kind and candid consideration that would enable him to give to this Association his advice. I am in favor of advanced registration. About two years ago some of us came here and met a like number of gentlemen who then belonged to the Dutch-Friesian Association, and for a whole day we consulted with those gentlemen with a view to the union of the two associations. From the outset we were told by those gentlemen that they wanted a system of advanced registration; that they would not join us unless we would promise to give the system of advanced registration a fair trial. Throughout that discussion no gentleman present objected to the words, "Advanced Registration." When we came to our By-Laws the phrase, "Advanced Registration," was used. Not one present raised his voice in protest against it. Those gentlemen came with their small society and joined our large one, with a pledge on our part that we would give them a system of advanced registration, and that we would give to it a fair trial. As honorable men, not only the members of the committee representing the old Holstein Association, but every one of the members whose accredited representatives we were are bound by that pledge; a pledge that will not be shrunk from by the gentlemen in my presence, nor by any considerable number of them. Your Board got together to carry out the pledge that we had given to them — to carry out the By-Laws that had put the construction of those rules into our hands; and what did we do? Did we act hastily? Those present know we did not. Hours, and hours, and hours, were spent; some gentlemen who perhaps now sympathize with Mr. Houghton were present and assisted him. We went home and spent weeks and months in discussing and writing about these rules, and we came back here again and spent another day or two in doing nothing but canvass all these rules and regulations. Gentlemen, up to that time — I challenge contradiction — there had never been a single syllable uttered in our deliberations against the name that had been used in our old negotiations for the consolidation. Under that we put these rules into the hands of Mr. Hoxie, who had had charge of a similar attempt in the old association, and Mr. Houghton says that we now have two years' experience. I beg his pardon; we have not had two years' experience. His circular was sent out before you had seen the first volume. The public had no opportunity of passing judgment or turning over in their minds the work before he sent that circular to them. They never had an opportunity of seeing this work until the circular had been put in the hands of every member of this Association; and yet he stands before us and says that after two years' trial it must be pronounced a failure; and that is the sort of backing that Mr. Hoxie, who is willing to consecrate all the energy and talent that he possesses, is to receive from the old members of this Association to-day in fulfilment of our sacred promise. I do not think that will be the result of our deliberations to-day. I feel sure it should not. Now let us see whether this helps or hurts the large breeder and the small breeder. Smiths, Powell & Lamb have shown themselves tolerably well able to advertise without our assistance. Go where you will, their herd is known. Take up an agricultural paper, the first thing you see is the nice stories those gentlemen tell. They do not need us. Every record that is made, which is a creditable one, by a Holstein cow contributes somewhat to the value of every other Holstein cow in the United States. Just as we are proud, as men, of the achievements of every one of our distinguished patriots and soldiers and statesmen, so Holstein breeders are proud of the achievements of these distinguished members of the Holstein family. When they have made these large records, they have made them with a Holstein, not with a Jersey; they have made them with an animal bred as our cattle were bred; and when Echo made her celebrated record every man who owned a relative of her was directly benefitted. Every man owning a Holstein was indirectly helped. These gentlemen who are doing advertising for themselves are doing it for me, and they cannot help themselves. When they convince the world that Holstein cattle are superior to other breeds, they have convinced them for my herd as well as for their herd; and when, by the collection of the statistics that we are offering in this advanced registration, we show that the Jerseys and the Ayershires and the native breeds, and all others, are far inferior to ours, then we have shown that fact just as much for the man who has but a single cow of that family as for those who have many. We have furnished here an opportunity for a man who owns but three cows to advertise on an equality with Mr. Powell's firm. They may be able to get up their pictures, and get out grand catalogues, that a man with ten cattle can not do; but the man with ten can enter those ten in the advanced registration for $3.00 apiece, and Powell has also got to pay $3.00 apiece to get his in; consequently that man who has ten can put his in on a ground of perfect equality. Now, I simply say, I trust that this Association will not put their hands upon this child before it is fairly a year old; that they will allow it at least room and life and freedom, and that they will put it into the hands of its friends and not its enemies, and that they will let its friends nurse it, and not those who wish for its destruction, so that it may grow into something that will be helpful. I own sixty-five head of Holsteins. I never have paid out $25.00 for advertisements in my life. I am in the same boat with most of the gentlemen in whose interests Mr. Houghton is making this motion. I believe advanced registration will help them. I believe it will help you, and there can not be too many grand records made, whether by men who own many or few. I would like all the cows to be grand, and I would like to have their performances collected in this Herd-Book in such shape that we can present them to the world.

Now, as to these authentications. I would be in favor myself of having these records authenticated by an Inspector, if it is practicable. You cannot get them too strict to suit me, only so that you do not get them so strict that nobody will make them. Now, you could not have them all tested on the same day. It would cost you, to get a single cow in, twenty or thirty or forty dollars in spite of everything, if you had to have a Superintendent stand over the milk-pail, etc. It would be impracticable.

Again, judging from fast horses — I never had anything to do with fast horses myself, but I happened once to ride with a gentleman who is all horse, and I found there that a horse's position is made almost wholly in the standard book, what they call their standard stud-book, by trotting records made by dam, or sire, or grand-sire, or grand-dam, or by the animal himself, or by his progeny. I hope the time will come when we talk about a bull just as they talk about their Hambletonian and Dictator. They will say such and such a bull has got so many grand-daughters who has given so much; and when we will begin to judge of bulls in an intelligent way, copying after the fast horsemen; and I predict to you, if the advanced registration receives the fostering care that I believe it will at your hands, it will not be twenty years, nor ten years, before that sort of a statement will be in all our catalogues and throughout all our newspapers; and the time will come when the bull that really has rank has it because his daughters, or grand-daughters, or great grand-daughters have made these performances in the milk-pail that correspond with 2:20 and 2:15 upon the trotting-track.

I hope the intelligence and sense of justice of this Association will lead them to adopt this amendment, and send this work where our by-laws leaves it—with the officers of the Association.

MR. HOUGHTON: Mr. Horr asked me for the rule. I will read Rule I. (Reads the rule referred to). Those are the words which I referred to. Now, to take just a moment more of your time, I do not think the argument is a good one, or strong one. The fact that we did not see at that time, when we adopted the name of advanced registry, that it would not work well — the mere fact that we did not discover it at that time is nothing against us. If we made an error we want to correct it. Mr. Horr has made a great deal of talk, and I have been very happy to listen to it; but whether or not it has been to the point is another question. I have not argued against this advanced registry particularly in itself. I have simply asked for accurate tests that no one could discredit, and that is what I want now. I want it amended. I want this child to grow, but I want the tests to be accurate, so that nobody can discredit them.

MR. W. G. POWELL: I will have to differ somewhat with my friend Mr. Houghton in reference to his position. He did not see fit to send me one of his circulars. I suppose it was because he thought I would not appreciate it. He knew what my position was. A friend sent me one, and, after reading it, somebody asked me what I thought its strongest point was, and my answer was, I thought its strongest point was its weakness. When he states now that he is not opposed to advanced registry, why has the whole burden of his argument, not only in the circular, but to-day, been against advanced registry, as he calls it? He is opposed to it. He is opposed to it undoubtedly from the bottom of his heart.

MR. HOUGHTON: That is not very far.

MR. POWELL: If he is not opposed to it, why all of this argument that it is favorable to the large breeder and opposed to the small one? What different would any other system be? He gets up, and one part of his argument is in favor of abolishing it and that it is all wrong, and the rest is in favor of some other rule; that the rules we have got are all wrong. After that, he proposed to refer this whole thing to a committee. My point is that the registry system is not in favor of the large breeder and against the small one. Only a few years ago the system was made for the admission of trotting-horses to what is called the standard record. The main argument against that was that it placed the wealthy breeders, etc., in a position to develop their animals, and the small breeders not.

The man is a fool to-day who will stand up and argue that the standard registration was a detriment to the trotting-horse, or that it was a detriment to the small breeder, and the same thing is true here. Every man who owns a dollar of Holstein-Friesian stock is benefitted by every record that is made, every record that is given the standard, whatever that is, and the argument that this is against the small breeder is simply, to use plain language, all bosh. It is not the fact; it is not the case in practice. A man who holds a single animal has the same opportunity to weigh his milk as the cow is milked as the man who owns a hundred. There is no restriction that he shall not weigh it, or that he shall not have somebody else weigh it. If he does his own milking, he weighs it and gives his oath. If somebody else does it, that man weighs it and takes his oath to it; and any argument that this is against any particular breeder, and favorable to others, simply falls of its own weight. Our Honorable President, I understand, issues a circular. He, like Mr. Houghton, forgot me. I have not seen it, but I understand that he has issued one. I understand that he is opposed to advanced registry. I am surprised that a man known and believed to have the wide-awake business principles that our President has should take that position. He may have opposition to our rules, but that does not affect the principle of advanced registry. If our rules are wrong, amend them; they are subject to amendment. But when we come to the question of advanced registration, the principle is right. All animals are not equal. It is desirable to know the valuable ones and those that are not. It makes no difference whether owned by one man or a firm, or somebody else. If they are worthy of registration in the advanced registry, give them a chance. Now, I happen to be interested in some animals that are in there, and others here are, and if I had not any in, I would want to get in on as fair a basis as the rest. I would not be fool enough to let the rest in and not get in myself. I would like, also, to get in the same door that they got in at.

THE PRESIDENT: The question is on the amendment, that this be referred to the Board of Officers.

Question put, and carried as amended.

Mr. William M. Singerly moved that the matter of the 6th, 7th, 8th, and 9th Articles of the By-Laws be referred to the Board of Officers, the same as the last.

Motion seconded and carried.

Mr. Houghton asked for the call of the roll.

MR. STILLWELL: Mr. Horr says there was nobody who made any objection to these things a few years ago. He is mistaken. Mr. Horr, nor any other man, has a right to come here and promise what I shall do. I never gave him that privilege, and I voted against advanced registry first, last, and all the time. If you look at the proceedings of the meeting you will find that I made the remark that there would be another consolidation inside of three or five years of the Holstein-Friesian Association and the advanced registry. These things are unfair, and I want to vote, even if I do not have but one voice.

The Secretary, by direction of the chair, proceeded to a call of the roll.

MR. MILLER: I desire to be excused from voting, and to briefly state my reasons: I have opposed the name of Advanced Registry from the beginning, and oppose it now, because I consider it a virtual endorsement of all records of that registry. I think that endorsement should be given to no record except an official one, and for that reason I favor a full discussion of the question before this meeting — to trying some other means to come to some understanding of the matter. However, I will withdraw my request to be excused from voting and vote no.

The Secretary announced as the result of the count that there were 165 ayes and 81 noes.

The chair declared that the vote was in favor of the ayes.

THE PRESIDENT: The next thing is Article X. — that there be an Association Inspector in every state.

MR. SMITH: I offer a resolution that the Association advise or recommend the Board of Officers to appoint at least one Inspector in each state, where it is practicable to do so.

MR. C. PRATT: I move as a substitute that this be referred to the Board of Officers.

Mr. Harwood seconded Mr. Smith's motion.

The chairman put the question as amended by Mr. Pratt, which was declared lost.

The chair put the original question, which was carried.

THE PRESIDENT: The next call is that the By-Laws be so amended that at the annual meeting of the Association matters may be acted upon without previous notice of the same being given.

A motion to lay this matter on the table was seconded and carried.

THE PRESIDENT: The next call is that a charter be obtained from the national government granting the right to hold annual or special meetings of the Association in any state.

Mr. Langworthy moved that the matter be laid upon the table.

Motion seconded.

MR. MILLER: I trust this motion will be voted down.

MR. LANGWORTHY: I withdraw the motion.

MR. MILLER: I move that this Association take steps to get a national charter. It seems to me that the Association can exert a wider-spread influence among its members, and among cattle men generally, by holding annual meetings occasionally in other states than New York. It causes members living in the western states a very long journey to attend the annual meetings if held here every year. If we hold a majority of the meetings in this state, where we can accommodate the greater number of members, it is very proper, but that we should hold a meeting every two years in Ohio, Illinois, Wisconsin, or in any of the western states, I think would be very proper also.

The motion was seconded.

Mr. Neilson asked whether anybody could cite an example of a charter granted by the general government.

MR. J. T. BROOKS: I was going to suggest that I have very grave doubts whether it is within the power of the national government to grant a charter, but still the object desired, I think, can be accomplished.

MR. HORR: I would suggest that we all constitute ourselves a committee to see if we can obviate this difficulty. If we can get Mr. Brooks interested in it, it will be queer if he will not find some way out of it, so that it seems to me we had better postpone it to another year.

THE PRESIDENT: In accordance with the instructions of the Association a year ago, I went to Albany and staid there several days and tried to procure an amendment to our present charter, so that we could hold our annual meetings outside of the limit of New York state. The Governor and members of both houses, and also the Attorney-General of the state, decided that we could not, under the constitution of the state, go outside.

MR. W. G. POWELL: I have made some inquiry of those who pretend to know, and I believe who do know, and among them members of congress, and they say we might just as well save our time and expense as to undertake any such thing. They say there are associations who would give a million dollars to get a charter, just such as we ask for, through congress, authorizing them to do business anywhere throughout the United States, and that is the reason I second the motion to lay this matter on the table, because I am satisfied that it would amount to nothing.

About the states; I made the same remarks a year ago, and I make them again, that there are some states in which the laws require that the majority of the directors of any association shall live in those states. The laws of some of the different states require that. While I am not partial to this state or any other state, I do think that it is a pretty good thing to let well enough alone. I am a member of several associations, perhaps a dozen of them, and I will say that there is more interest manifested in this Association than in any one or two or three that I belong to now; and that even at Chicago at the time of their annual gathering there, there was no association that could show anything of such a nature as this Association brings here, and I do think it is a good thing to let well enough alone.

Mr. William M. Singerly moved to lay the matter on the table.

Seconded and carried.

THE PRESIDENT: The next call is, that under the auspices of the Association a monthly or semi-monthly journal be published in the interests of the Holstein-Friesian breed.

MR. DUDLEY MILLER: I offered that resolution, and I have a few words to read on the subject:

"THE HOLSTEIN-FRIESIAN JOURNAL."

The thirteenth proposition on the list of subjects to be discussed at the second annual meeting is, "That under the auspices of the Association a monthly or semi-monthly journal be published in the interests of the Holstein-Friesian breed." All will admit that a well edited paper is a power.

The tendency of papers at present is toward specialties. An agricultural paper covers so much ground that it is unable to do justice to each branch. This has caused the publication of "Live-Stock Journals," "Breeders' Gazettes," and the like—all very useful and well in their way.

The field still seems too broad for one paper to do full justice to the many varieties of live-stock, hence the appearance of journals published in the interest of the horse, as "The Horseman," cattle, swine, sheep, poultry, etc., etc.

The desire for more knowledge of particular breeds of cattle, and the great interest the public takes in them, has prompted the publication of such papers as "The Jersey Bulletin," which has been substantially supported by Jersey breeders, and doubtless has accomplished much good for the breed. Then the "Guernsey Breeder," published in New York, under the auspices of the Guernsey Breeders' Association.

"The Holstein-Friesian Register" appeared about a year since, and though championing our favorite breed, has not been equal to representing it as well as could be desired, perhaps owing to the neglect of its managing editor in not devoting to it the requisite time, owing to his law business, stock-farm, and large interests in real estate.

That there is ample field for a paper published in the interests of the breed seems evident. There is much of value relating to our breed appearing in journals throughout this country and in the European press. During the past year I have obtained much valuable information regarding the breed from Scotland, England, Germany, Holland, and France, whence I receive newspapers.

No breeder of Holsteins would probably want to go to the expense of taking from fifty to one hundred papers to acquaint himself with all the useful information appearing in them regarding the breed, and if unfamiliar with German, Dutch, and French, could not readily obtain it if he desired to. From the concentration of the best matter relating to Holsteins which appears in the American and European press, and the co-operation of our most intelligent breeders in the way of letters, records, and advertisements, a valuable paper might be published if conducted by a careful, energetic editor.

Mr. Stillwell: I move that the matter be laid on the table.

Motion seconded.

Upon the motion being put the chair declared itself in doubt as to the result.

A rising vote was taken, which resulted in 17 in favor and 11 opposed.

The chair declared the motion carried.

The President: The next call is that appropriations be made for special premiums and other purposes.

Mr. Stillwell moved that the matter be laid on the table.

Seconded.

The question to lay on the table was put and lost.

Mr. E. Pratt: I move to give that to the Board, with power.

Seconded.

Mr. Miller: I wish to state to the Association that there is a fair to be held in New York City, in May, in which the dairy breeds only are to be represented individually and by their products. Liberal premiums are offered for Jerseys, Guernseys, Holsteins, and Ayrshires by those who are interested in getting up the fair in New York. The fair is to be held in Madison Square Garden, and it is the intention of the management to call out the very best representatives of each of the different breeds. We have offered, in addition to individual prizes, two sweepstakes prizes of $150.00 each, one for the cow giving the largest yield of milk in one day during the exhibition; the other for the cow giving the largest yield of butter during one day of the exhibition. It seems to me that those sweepstakes prizes are of great value to us as breeders of Holstein cattle. If a Holstein cow should be successful in winning each of those sweepstakes prizes it would be worth a great deal to the interests of all who are breeding Holstein cattle. I am in favor of this Association making an appropriation to be offered for Holsteins securing those prizes. For that purpose, I would move that we authorize the Board of Officers, in their discretion, to appropriate moneys of this Association to be used in giving premiums to successful Holsteins at this fair, not to exceed $500.00.

Motion seconded.

Mr. Wales: Mr. President, I approve heartily of what Mr. Miller says, and think we ought to do something in this way. We have heretofore, and I think it has been a very great benefit to us. I would go further than Mr. Miller proposes, and offer to duplicate premiums which are awarded to our cattle at state fairs and such shows as Mr. Miller describes, when our cattle come in competition with cattle of other breeds. I think we can get no better reputation for our cattle than when we win these large premiums in competition with Jerseys, Ayrshires, Guernseys, and Devons. We can almost always do it. It seems to me that the little money we have spent in this way has done, in the past, a great deal of good, and I think it can in the future.

MR. A. P. WRIGHT: How would it do to award a certain sum to each exhibitor? If we could get twenty gentlemen here who would subscribe $25.00 each — that would be $500.00 — that would help pay the expenses of the gentlemen who exhibited their cattle, and then let the winner take the money. Nobody would take their cattle there to get the $25.00, because it would cost them a great deal of money, but that would be a great help toward the expenses. I only make the suggestion.

MR. E. A. POWELL: It seems to me that the opportunity that is now offered for this breed of cattle to make a good showing before the public at New York is greater than almost any similar opportunity that has ever been offered, and it is directly where our breed of cattle ought to be at the front, and I believe in giving all necessary encouragement, and heartily approve of Mr. Miller's motion to put this matter in the hands of the Board of Officers, and they can decide in just what way it is best to offer it, and whether $500.00 is the proper amount, or whether it ought to be increased. Perhaps, if Mr. Miller has looked at the matter, the sum named is sufficient.

MR. W. G. POWELL: If I understand Mr. Miller's motion, it is for an appropriation for a specific purpose for this one show. Am I right?

MR. MILLER: You are right; for this particular dairy show.

An amendment was offered making the limit not to exceed $1,000.00, to be distributed at the discretion of the Board of Officers.

The motion as amended was put and carried.

MR. POWELL: It occurs to me, that between now and the next annual meeting there will be several fairs at which it will be very important that we should have fine exhibitions, and among them the fat stock show at Chicago, and, providing the trouble about disease should get away from there, we ought to make a fine show, and I move you that the Board be authorized, at their discretion, to use an amount not to exceed $2,000.00 at the various fairs between now and the next annual meeting, aside from this present appropriation. It does not instruct them to use it, but to use it at their discretion.

MR. SMITH: Will that be a sufficient sum to duplicate the premiums?

MR. WALES: It is entirely sufficient in my opinion.

MR. STILLWELL: I do not think that would come anywhere near to it, and I would be in favor of doubling it, and if I could get a second to the amendment, I would make the amendment.

Amendment seconded.

Mr. W. G. Powell: I have no idea that the Board of Officers will use any more than is actually necessary, and at a very few of the leading fairs. If we make an exhibit, we want to do it creditably. At the fair in New York, I have no doubt it will be necessary to use not more than $500.00, but I merely suggest this so that the Board of Officers can, in emergency, use it.

The chair put the question as amended by Mr. Stillwell, making the limit $4,000.00.

Question as amended put and lost.

The original question, making the limit $2,000.00, was put and carried.

Mr. Huidekoper moved that the meeting proceed to the election of officers.

Mr. Yeomans: For the sake of facilitating the business, I move you that an opportunity be given to name candidates, and in case where there is but one candidate named for a given office, that the President be directed to cast the ballot of the Association for that officer. If there are more than one candidate named for any given office, of course a vote will become necessary.

Motion seconded and carried.

Mr. Powell: I suppose the first officer to be elected will be the President for the next year. I wish to say that about ten years ago, or nearly that, when we were a small society and met at Syracuse, we were very glad to see any stranger from outside come in to help us. About that time a gentleman came who was almost an entire stranger to us here — I think, knowing only one person at that meeting. He came with a very pleasant face, and a manner that soon won our hearts, and we were always glad to see him come. From that time to this, whether stormy weather or fair, he has always been with us. We have always been glad to greet him. He came from a little town down in the Key-Stone State, I believe called the City of Brotherly Love. He has brought that brotherly love with him, and whenever there has been anything exciting, or a difference of opinion where we could not agree, he has always been ready to pour the oil of reconciliation upon the troubled waters. We have occasionally called him to the chair, and he has presided so handsomely that we have often taken occasion to call him to that post. This gentleman is not a breeder in the ordinary sense of breeding stock to sell, but generally he has taken this same interest with us. I feel great pleasure in nominating him as our next President, and I believe that every person here will heartily endorse that nomination. Perhaps it is not necessary to say that I refer to William M. Singerly, of Philadelphia.

There being no further nominations for the office of President, the chairman cast the ballot of the Association for Mr. Singerly for that office.

THE PRESIDENT: I take great pleasure in being able to cast the vote for a gentleman whom I have known so many years, and who has always been with us, and acted for our very best interests.

Mr. Isaac C. Otis presented the name of Gerrit S. Miller for First Vice-President.

There being no further nominations for the office of First Vice-President, the chairman cast the ballot of the Association for Mr. Miller for that office.

Mr. Boardman presented the name of M. L. Sweet, of Grand Rapids, Mich., for Second Vice-President.

There being no further nominations for the office of Second Vice-President, the chairman cast the ballot of the Association for Mr. Sweet for that office.

Mr. H. Langworthy presented the name of W. G. Powell, of Pennsylvania, for Third Vice-President.

There being no further nominations for the office of Third Vice-President, the chairman cast the ballot of the Association for Mr. Powell for that office.

Mr. Horr nominated Mr. W. M. Liggett, of Benson, Minn., for the office of Fourth Vice-President.

There being no further nominations for the office of Fourth Vice-President, the chairman cast the ballot of the Association for Mr. Liggett for that office.

Mr. Yeomans nominated Mr. William Brown Smith, of Syracuse, N. Y., for Treasurer.

There being no further nominations for the office of Treasurer, the chairman cast the ballot of the Association for Mr. Smith for that office.

Mr. William M. Singerly nominated Mr. C. W. Horr, of Ohio, for Director of this Association, to hold office for two years, in the place of Gerrit S. Miller.

There being no further nominations for this office, the chairman cast the ballot of the Association for Mr. Horr for that office.

Mr. C. F. Sweezey presented the name of C. R. Payne, of Hamilton, N. Y., for the office of Director, in the place of C. W. Horr.

Mr. Stillwell nominated Mr. Dexter Severy, of Illinois, for the same office.

There being two candidates placed in nomination, the ballot was taken, Mr. Otis acting as teller.

The President announced as the result of the vote, that the total number of votes was 236, of which Mr. C. R. Payne received 149 and Mr. Dexter Severy 87.

Mr. Hoxie nominated Mr. David H. Burrell for the office of Director.

Mr. Houghton nominated Mr. C. J. Lord for the same office.

A ballot was taken, which resulted in the election of Mr. Burrell by a vote of 158 to 86.

MR. HUIDEKOPER: I take pleasure in nominating for the office of Secretary, Mr. Thomas B. Wales, Jr.

There being no further nominations for the office of Secretary, the chairman cast the ballot of the Association for Mr. Thomas B. Wales, Jr., for that office.

Mr. Horr nominated Mr. S. Hoxie for the office of Superintendent of Advanced Registry.

There being no further nominations for the office of Superintendent of Advanced Registry, the chairman cast the ballot of the Association for Mr. Hoxie for that office.

MR. W. J. SMITH: I had hoped that we might have a representative in the Board from a section of the country that is very much interested, and that ought to be represented, which I believe never has been, and that is the line below the Ohio river. Particularly in Tennessee there is a section containing a large number of very fine Holstein-Friesian cattle, and at the same time some of the best Jersey cattle in the country. They are running a strong opposition, and I am so anxious that that part of the country should be represented, and properly, and knowing as I do a gentleman of ability, integrity, and sterling worth, who can properly represent that section, and inasmuch as another member of my family has been favored with a position—it seems to me that one in a family is enough—I therefore beg leave to resign my position as one of the Directors of the Holstein-Friesian Association; and I would say, by way of explanation, that I desire to have the privilege, if this resignation is accepted, of offering the name of the gentleman to whom I have referred for this place.

Mr. Horr moved that the resignation of Mr. W. Judson Smith as a member of the Board be accepted.

Motion seconded and carried.

MR. SMITH: It gives me great pleasure to place in nomination Mr. Eugene Smith, of Nashville, Tennessee. I move his election. I would say that the family of Smith is pretty extensive. I suppose we are connected through Adam, but I do not know of any closer relationship between Mr. Eugene Smith and me.

There being no further nominations for the office of Director, the chairman cast the ballot of the Association for Mr. Eugene Smith for that office.

Mr. Horr moved that the meeting extend a hearty and cordial vote of thanks to President Stevens for the excellent manner in which he has presided over the meeting, with the same thanks to the other officers.

Seconded and carried.

Mr. Powell moved that when this meeting adjourns, it shall adjourn to meet at this place.

Seconded and carried.

Upon motion the meeting adjourned.

MEETING OF THE BOARD OF OFFICERS

OF THE

HOLSTEIN-FRIESIAN ASSOCIATION OF AMERICA,

Held at the Genesee Hotel, Buffalo, N. Y., March 15th, 1887.

The meeting was called to order by President F. C. Stevens.

Upon roll call there were found to be present the following officers: G. D. Wheeler, First Vice-President; M. L Sweet, Third Vice-President; D. H. Burrell, Fourth Vice-President; Thomas B. Wales, Jr., Secretary; W. C. Brayton, Treasurer; S. Hoxie, Superintendent of Advanced Registry; and the following directors: Gerrit S. Miller, C. R. Payne, W. J. Smith, F. L. Houghton, E. Huidekoper.

Upon motion, the reading of the minutes of the previous meeting was dispensed with.

The next order of business being the election of members, the following names were presented, and the gentlemen elected members of the Association:

MONS ANDERSON,	LaCrosse, Wis.
N. F. SHOLES,	Earlville, N. Y.
GEORGE C. FISK,	Springfield, Mass.
I. C. WADE,	Jamestown, D. T.
CHARLES SIEDLER,	Jersey City, N. J.
WILLARD WHITE,	Boston, Mass.
JOHN R. McPHERSON,	Belle Mead, N. J.
CHARLES A. BROWN,	Portland, Maine.
JERE BAXTER,	Nashville, Tenn.
W. T. RADFORD,	Pembroke, Ky.
JOSEPH A. FRYE,	Marlboro, Mass.

MR. MILLER: I move that the question as to the admission of Mr. Henry Klepinger as a member of this Association be referred to a committee of two, Mr. Wales and Mr. Smith, and if, upon making proper inquiry, they are satisfied that he is an American citizen, and will make a desirable member, that he be admitted.

The Secretary read a communication from Mr. James B. Wilson in reference to the transfer of twenty-six cattle.

Mr. Smith: I would say that Mr. Wilson wrote me on that subject about a year ago, I being personally acquainted with him, and wrote him then, as I have since, that from the appearance of things I should judge that he had a just claim, but it was a question in my mind — which is not settled yet — as to just how much his claim is. I presume the transfer of those twenty-six animals would be fair, but the question in my mind is just what benefit he has already had from his membership. I think there is a credit and debit side to the account, which, perhaps, may already be balanced. I would inquire of Mr. Wales in reference to it.

Mr. Wales: I cannot say now, but my impression is that he has received some benefit from his membership.

Mr. Smith: I move that the Secretary be instructed to transfer twenty-six head of cattle from J. B. Wilson & Son to J. B. Wilson without charge.

Motion seconded and carried.

The Secretary read a communication from Messrs. B. B. Lord & Son, asking that the registration fee on an imported heifer, after one year from date of importation, be made $20.00 instead of $60.00, as called for under the By-Laws.

Mr. Smith: Mr. Lord asked me to request the privilege of being heard whenever this question came up, and I told him I would advise him.

Upon motion it was determined to admit Mr. Lord to a hearing.

The President: Mr. Lord is with us, and desires to be heard.

Mr. Lord: *Mr. President, and Gentlemen:* My father and myself owned a heifer which we supposed was a barren heifer. The year ran past and some time over, and she proved to be in calf, and dropped a calf, and as soon as she did so I wanted to get her registered. I sent to Mr. Wales, and he issued a certificate, saying that he would charge us $60.00 upon the books, and if the Association saw fit to register her at the old fee, that would be all there was of it.

In reference to the other matter: We have sold some cattle to Mr. Williams, of Picton, Ontario. We have had a great deal of dealings with him one way and another. We had a bill of sale for the cattle which we had sold him, and we found it necessary to have him turn those cattle over to us again. We went to him and told him that we felt we were unsafe; we wanted it straightened up, and he sold us the cattle back again with the increase, with several animals, and in the lot was a heifer which he had evidently bought from Mr. Leavitt, of Picton. As I understand the matter, Mr. Williams sold Mr. Leavitt some stock; Mr. Leavitt gave him a note in payment for the stock, but the understanding was that he was to pay up this stock in calves at a stated price; I don't know what the price was, but he was to pay him back year after year until this original stock was paid for in calves, and this heifer was one of that lot. Mr. Williams evidently has neglected to get a transfer from Mr. Leavitt. Mr. Williams signed a transfer from him to us, and when we came to send the transfer to Mr. Wales we found she had never been transferred from Mr. Leavitt to Mr. Williams. We have never had occasion to be in Picton since. If we were there, probably it could be arranged, but I can't get a word out of either one of them. Mr. Williams has failed, financially. He is not worth, probably, a dollar in the world, and has compelled Mr. Leavitt, I understand, to pay the cash for the balance of the cattle, and it has created an unfriendly feeling, so that we cannot get anything out of either of them. We cannot get a signature for this transfer. We would like to get it transferred in some way.

MR. WALES: Have you got anything to show that this heifer went from one party to the other properly?

MR. LORD: We have not a thing. All we have got is the heifer, and we feel that she came into our hands legally. I have got the certificate of registry in my pocket. We have nothing to show, one way or the other, and we cannot get a word out of them by mail. This heifer is recorded as owned by J. B. Leavitt, of Picton, Ontario. If the Association does not see fit to grant me a transfer, I shall have to go over there, probably. My request is to get the transfer worked through in some way. I will make affidavit, if necessary, that the heifer is in our possession, and has come into our possession legally, so far as that is concerned. I would like to get the transfer.

Upon motion, it was decided to sustain the ruling of Mr. Wales, and refuse the request of Mr. Lord.

The President read a communication from Prof. J. W. Sanborn, of the Missouri Agricultural College, and the Secretary read the correspondence in reference thereto.

MR. MILLER: I move that the Board recommend at the annual meeting to-morrow that the Association furnish the required number of calves to Prof. J. W. Sanborn.

Seconded and carried.

The next question in order being the appropriation of $100.00 awarded for a prize essay, Mr. Huidekoper moved that the Secretary be instructed to draw an order upon the funds of the Association for $100.00 for that purpose.

Seconded and carried.

The President stated that the next question was in reference to co-operation with the American Jersey Cattle Club in matters of legislation in relation to those convicted of recording animals fraudulently.

MR. BURRELL: I move that the Secretary be requested to draft a resolution covering the question, which shall be submitted to the annual meeting to-morrow, recommending its passage, and that the Secretary shall thereupon send the result of this vote to the Legislature, couched in such language as he may deem proper.

Motion seconded and carried.

The Secretary referred to the matter of the contribution to the fund of the Consolidated Cattle-Growers' Association for the payment of $250.00, and stated that this Association was asked to contribute $250.00 as its portion. The Secretary read the correspondence in reference thereto.

MR. BURRELL: I move that Mr. Houghton be appointed a committee to present to the meeting to-morrow the question of the assessment made by the National Cattle-Growers' Association, for them to take such action as they deem proper.

Motion seconded and carried.

The Secretary put before the meeting the question of registering a calf without horns.

Mr. Smith moved that Mr. Wales be instructed to register the calf when application is made, if there is no disqualification.

Seconded and carried by a vote of 5 to 4.

MR. WALES: I desire to ask what sum it is proper to charge for the transfer registry of an animal on an application signed by a member of the Association in favor of a non-member, said application being presented by the purchaser, a non-member. As an illustration: Mr. Miller sells an animal to some person who is not a member of the Association, and sends him the application for transfer; this gentleman, knowing that Mr. Miller is a member of the Association, sends 50 cents, instead of $1.00. I write him, our charge against you is $1.00. He says it is all the same thing; send me back the application and I will send it to Mr. Miller, Mr. Miller will send it to you.

The opinion of the Board was that the transfer fee in such cases should be that charged to non-members.

The Secretary read a communication from G. W. Thompson, on which no action was taken.

MR. BURRELL: I move we now adjourn.

THE PRESIDENT: The motion is that this meeting now adjourn, subject to the call of the President.

The motion, as put by the President, was carried, and the meeting was declared adjourned.

ADJOURNED MEETING OF THE BOARD OF OFFICERS.

Held at Noon, Wednesday, March 16th, 1887.

President Stevens called the meeting to order.

Mr. Horr moved that the Secretary's salary for the year be the same as it was last year, viz.: $2,500.00.

Motion seconded and carried.

Mr. Horr moved that the Treasurer's salary be the same as for the past year, viz.: $250.00.

Mr. Smith offered as an amendment that the office of the Treasurer be a non-salaried office.

Amendment seconded by Mr. Payne.

Mr. Horr stated that he did not accept the amendment.

MR. BURRELL: I do not think it is best to pass that resolution. I think it is best for the Association to have control of its own funds; that the funds be deposited in such bank as the Association deem proper, in the name of the Association. If all that is done, I should think that there ought to be a salary attached to the office.

The chair put the question on the amendment, which was lost by a vote of 12 to 2.

The chair declared the amendment lost.

The chair put the original question, which was carried.

Mr. Singerly moved that the annual salary of the Superintendent of Advanced Registry be $1,000.00.

Seconded by Mr. Sweet, and carried.

The application of Mr. E. P. Beauchamp was presented for membership.

Mr. Horr moved that the application of Mr. Beauchamp, of Terre Haute, Indiana, be accepted.

Seconded.

Mr. Houghton recommended Mr. Beauchamp for membership.

Upon motion, Mr. Beauchamp's application was accepted.

Mr. Smith stated that he recommended the application of Mr. Henry Klepinger, whose name was presented at the meeting yesterday, for membership.

The meeting, upon motion, accepted the membership of Mr. Klepinger.

Upon motion, the meeting adjourned.

ANNUAL MEETING OF THE BOARD OF OFFICERS.

March 16th, 1887.

President Singerly called the meeting to order at 7:30 P. M.

Upon roll call it was found that all the members but one were present.

The Secretary stated that Dr. Nelson B. Gregory, of Unadilla, New York, was an applicant for membership; he was recommended by Mr. Miller.

Mr. Smith moved that he be received as a member.

Seconded and carried.

The name of M. B. Shallcross, of Louisville, Ky., was presented for membership by Mr. Wales.

Mr. Shallcross was admitted to membership.

MR. MILLER: Mr. President, at the dairy fair to be held in New York there are several prizes offered for butter in packages of different sizes. I would propose that we use a portion of the money to be appropriated in premiums at that show in duplicating any premium that the society offers for butter, in case it be won by Holstein butter. There are two sweepstakes premiums offered of $150.00 each, for the milch-cow giving the largest amount of milk during one day of the exhibition, and the cow giving the greatest quantity of butter during one day. I would propose to duplicate those premiums, in case a Holstein cow is the winner. This fair comes on the 10th, 11th, 12th, 13th, and 14th of May. I propose duplicating the $150.00 prizes.

Motion seconded by Mr. Burrell.

Carried.

MR. MILLER: Now, I move, in regard to premiums offered for butter, that we duplicate any premium that is won by Holstein stock at that exhibition.

W. G. POWELL: Are they all first-class prizes?

MR. MILLER: Some of them are second.

W. G. POWELL: If Holstein butter should take the second prize, then what?

MR. MILLER: Duplicate the prize, that is all.

The motion made by Mr. Miller was seconded and carried.

MR. MILLER: Then there are prizes offered for Holsteins as a class by themselves. A prize of $250.00 is offered for a herd. I would not propose adding anything to that. A prize for a bull, of any age, with four of his progeny, females. I would leave that just as it is. But when we come to the individual prizes — there is one for a bull two years old — $100.00, $50.00, and $25.00; first, second, and third; and for a cow, a two-year-old, a yearling, and a calf. I would propose to add to each one of those premiums the amount of the first prize; add to each class the amount of the first prize.

Mr. Sweet seconded the motion.

THE PRESIDENT: The question before us is that the amount of the first prize be added to the classes and be divided pro rata among any premiums distributed at this fair.

MR. MILLER: We will restrict that, from prize number 21 to 27 inclusive. That shuts out the herd prize and the bull.

THE PRESIDENT: Classes from number 21 to 27.

Question put as stated, and carried.

Mr. Wales moved that the butter premiums offered at the different state fairs be duplicated by this Association for the butter produced by Holstein-Friesian cattle.

Seconded by Mr. Hoxie.

MR. W. G. POWELL: Does that include all the states in the Union?

MR. WALES: Wherever they offer prizes for butter.

MR. HUIDEKOPER: I offer as an amendment, that it be referred to a committee to offer those premiums — the President, the Secretary, and Mr. Miller.

MR. SMITH: Is it not possible for Mr. Wales and some of these other gentlemen to designate a certain number of states in which they will exhibit butter, and define now and here just where they will exhibit? I suggest that you select your states and decide how much you will appropriate in each state.

MR. MILLER: I move that we authorize the President and Secretary to offer premiums at state fairs, using their own discretion as to which, duplicating their butter premiums in every case where that premium is won by Holstein butter in competition.

MR. HORR: I offer as a resolution, that the President and the Secretary of this society, on consultation with members of the Board in the various states where they propose to offer premiums, may offer not to exceed $300.00, to be divided according to their judgments. That in the states where there is no member of the Board, that the Secretary and President be authorized to use their discretion.

Mr. Wales: Do I understand that that covers cattle and butter and cheese?

Mr. Horr: Yes, cattle and butter; the Holstein interest. If you went into some state where there was no member, the President and Secretary would be authorized to take care of it. That puts it wholly into your hands.

Mr. Huidekoper: Mr. Horr stipulates the sum of $300.00. That will only go to six states. I would suggest that that figure be put two or three hundred.

Mr. Horr: It is from one cent to three hundred now; it says "not exceeding" that.

The President: The proposition of Mr. Horr is that the amount of premiums shall not exceed $300.00 to be appropriated to any one state by the President and Secretary, on consultation with the resident member of that state.

Question put and carried.

Mr. Horr: I move that the President and Secretary and Mr. Miller be authorized to offer any amount they like, not exceeding $600.00, for everything in the Holstein interest at the Chicago fat stock show. Of course we have got to keep within $2,000.00 in all of these matters.

The President put Mr. Horr's proposition, which was carried.

Mr. Wales presented the matter of furnishing ten calves to the Missouri Agricultural College.

Mr. Burrell moved that the President be authorized to appoint a committee to examine Holstein calves for the purpose of securing fine specimens to be sent to the Missouri Agricultural College for experimental feeding.

Motion seconded.

Mr. Payne. I move that this matter be put into the hands of Secretary Wales, and that he be authorized to spend any sum that he likes, not to exceed $500.00, to furnish the Missouri State Agricultural Society with ten calves for the purpose of feeding.

Seconded and carried.

It was moved and seconded that an amount not exceeding $1,000.00 be appropriated, under the direction of Mr. Wales and Mr. Liggett, to send ten calves to the Missouri Agricultural College for the purpose of feeding.

After considerable discussion, the question being put, was lost.

The chair stated that the next thing in order was the appointment of Inspectors.

It was decided that Inspectors, in order to hold over, should be re-elected at this meeting.

A motion to re-elect F. W. Patterson was lost.

The following Inspectors were chosen: O. P. Chapman, of Wellington, Ohio; Isaac C. Otis, of Jordan, N. Y.; S. Burchard, of Hamilton, N. Y.; S. N. Wright, of South Elgin, Ill.; Jere Allis, of Isinours, Minn.; J. N. Muncey, of Jessup, Iowa; J. L. Stone, of Waverly, Penn.; A. R. Sturtevant, of Springboro, Penn.; Carey R. Smith, of Santa Ana, Cal.; J. C. Poor, of North Andover, Mass.; H. D. Warner, of New Milford, Conn.

Upon motion, it was decided that the appointment of Inspector for Tennessee be left to Mr. Eugene Smith, member of the Board in Tennessee, and Mr. Hoxie; also that the appointment of Inspector for Michigan be left to Mr. Sweet and Mr. Hoxie.*

The election of Inspectors was declared closed.

Mr. Hoxie moved that the advanced registration fee be $2.00, instead of $3.00.

Seconded and carried.

MR. HOXIE: I desire to take advice of the Board in this matter. My original plan in this work was to obtain an authenticated record, even of dead cows, in order to preserve them. I was advised by the friends of the Advanced Registry that it would not answer; there were a good many authenticated records of dead cows sent to me, and I had to reject them; not that they be recorded, but there must be some place where the records may be preserved.

Mr. W. G. Powell moved that the Superintendent of advanced registration be authorized to receive and accept authenticated records of deceased cows, to be catalogued in his book of Advanced Registry.

Seconded and carried.

MR. HOXIE: Now, the rules provide for a re-entry. Suppose a cow has made fifteen pounds of butter. Suppose the coming year we have an authenticated record for twenty pounds. They would be glad to have the record appear. Now, I want you to fix the fee for that single record. It is a re-entry of the record; not of the animal itself.

MR. W. G. POWELL: I move that the fee be fifty cents.

Seconded and carried.

The matter of the Treasurer's bond and of the investment of the funds of the Association was considered, and the following gentlemen were appointed a committee to attend to the matter: Gerrit S Miller, D. H. Burrell, L. T. Yeomans.

Upon motion, the meeting adjourned.

---

* Mr. W. A. Rowley, of Mt. Clemens, Mich., has been made Inspector for that State.

PRIZE ESSAY.

By T. M. KOLDYK, *Weidum, Friesland.*

"*Breeding of Holstein-Friesian Cattle, the Selection of Sires, and their care during the Season of Service, to the end that they Transmit to their Offspring Health, Strength, and Superior Milking and other desirable qualities. Also suggestions on the care and feeding of calves.*"

ORIGIN OF THE HOLSTEIN-FRIESIAN CATTLE.

The Holstein-Friesians, as they are now called, originated in the lowlands of Holland, in what at present are the provinces of Friesland and North Holland. They most probably descend from the "Auerochs," the wild cattle once native in Northern Europe. The Friesians, a German tribe, who settled Holland about 2,000 years ago, owned large herds of these cattle, which grazed the abundant pastures in the lowlands during summer; in winter, when these pastures were flooded, the cattle and their owners retired to the higher woodlands. When the country became more settled, other tribes took possession of those higher lands, leaving the lowlands for the Friesians and their cattle. Then necessity compelled the Friesians to accomplish a work which is admired even by the present generation, and shows what can be done by constancy and unity. With their primitive tools and implements they succeeded in throwing up hills, sometime a mile in circumference, high enough to offer a safe retreat from the water.

On these hills (*terpen*) they built their villages and wintered their stock. As little else could be obtained, the Friesians were compelled to gather hay for their cattle in summer to feed during winter, and thus we find in the beginning of the Christian era, in the lowlands of Holland, cattle sheltered and fed. This extra care during winter and the abundant pasturage during summer had a favorable effect upon the cattle, and they soon excelled the cattle of the surrounding countries in size and shape.

When Northern Europe emerged from barbarism, Holland became famous for its cattle and dairy products, for, though civilization gave Holland windmills and dykes, and thus kept the water within its boundaries, the country remained a low country — too low and wet to be of much value for agricultural purposes.

Step by step the black and white cattle advanced, until they reached the high point of excellence at which they now stand. But it must be admitted their success is due more to centuries of care and unusually favorable circumstances for their development than to scientific breeding. The majority of the breeders of Dutch cattle in their native country have but little idea, even at the present day, of the most simple principles of breeding. But for centuries they kept the best cattle for themselves, simply because they knew that these paid the best; and they kept the bulls of their best cows simply because they knew, as a rule, these made the best bulls. And with these limited ideas of breeding they succeeded in producing some of the best cows yet known. Nothing shows better the possibilities of the breed, and American breeders having, as a rule, a better knowledge of the art of breeding than their Dutch predecessors, and having herd-books to guide them, will doubtless succeed in producing a race of cattle as far above the present Holstein-Friesian as these are superior to the native or "scrub" cattle of the United States. To accomplish this, however, will require close study and untiring labor for generations to come.

SELECTING THE HERD.

"A good beginning is half the work." This is as true in breeding cattle as in anything else. To begin with, one should have a distinct idea of the animal he wants to breed, and have a definite object in view; this object should always be kept in mind when selecting the foundation of a herd. By doing so, and never purchasing animals, however excellent, that are not of the type desired, breeding will be greatly simplified and success is more sure to follow. It is much easier to find a bull to head the herd if the cows are uniform in type; and this alone would render uniformity in the most important points desirable; besides, the fact remains that the nearer the foundation stock is to your "beau ideal," the less faults will there be to overcome.

But there are several other things equal in importance to uniformity, and never to be lost sight of when selecting a herd; and first of all, to secure such animals only as are healthy and vigorous themselves and have sprung from healthy stock. To ascertain the last may be exceedingly troublesome, but it is worth the while to have as much light thrown upon it as possible. Little profit and pleasure can be expected from unhealthy stock, even if they are of high merit and can be secured at small expense.

Since Holstein-Friesians are a dairy cattle, the next thing to ascertain is what the cow has done at the pail and churn; in fact, as much about her value as a dairy cow as is possible to be learned should be known. When her individual value as a dairy cow has been proven, the next thing to be ascertained is, who and what were her ancestors, and, if there be any, who and what are her near relatives. If the animal is young and has not yet been able to give any account of herself, this is of the more importance, for although milk and butter indications may be seen on a young heifer, they are not so much to be relied upon as in matured cows, since further developments may work radical changes. But for all that, these milk and butter signs should not be neglected, even if the animal has shown herself to be a superior dairy cow. The cow that shows the best milk and butter indications, viz: wedge shape, fine hair and hide, yellow skin, etc., is preferable to the cow that shows only little of them. Although their value for the dairy may be the same, the former is more likely to transmit the dairy qualities to her offspring than the latter.

The perfect dairy cow and the perfect beef cow cannot be combined in the same animal, since the highest development for producing milk and butter is antagonistic to the highest development for producing beef.

But some of the best breeders of Holstein-Friesians maintain that a great capability for producing milk and butter does not necessarily shut out all possibilities for producing fair beef, and some of their cows are living proofs of the truth of that assertion. And there is no reason why this should not be possible. Dairy cattle have many points in common with beef cattle. The successful beef cow, as well as the successful dairy cow, has to be a healthy, strong cow, with great digestive and assimilative powers; in both, fine bones, fine skin, and good handling are desirable points. But in the dairy cow the posterior part of the body will always be the larger, on account of the larger digestive and milk-secreting organs. This prevents her from being the *most* profitable butchers' beast, but does not prove that she can not be turned into profitable beef when necessary. For though she be lacking in chest and shoulders, with broad and level hips, broad back, well developed loins and quarters, and deep flanks, she will be able to make a good butchers' beast.

Taking this into consideration, the man who intends to build up a herd of Holstein-Friesians is not likely to neglect the beef points, as the block is the only thing to fall back upon when the cow becomes unfit for the dairy or fails to breed; and as long as he cannot control the sex, he cannot afford to forget that *every year* there will be some bull calves that had better be made into steers.

Since black and white is the only eligible color, there can be but little choice of color, and it is to be hoped Holstein-Friesian breeders never will get the color craze, and seek their salvation in either dark, light, mottled, or piebald cattle. Merit is independent of color.

But the breeder of cattle cannot be blamed for trying to make his cattle look as attractive as possible in his own eyes, and in those of his patrons; and if he has a preference for certain markings, he is perfectly right in breeding in that direction, if he only takes care never to place fancy before actual merit.

MANAGING THE HERD.

As said before, the Holstein-Friesian cattle are more the product of soil and climate, combined with careful management, than of scientific breeding. Though Holland's soil and climate can not be imported into America, by careful study human skill will overcome this, and the cattle will be placed in equally as favorable conditions as they are in their native country.

Holland's magnificent pastures are the special feature that tended to develop the black and white cattle into what they are, and there, where good pastures are found, the Holstein-Friesians stand the best chance of a favorable reception and further development. But since green corn, sorghum, oats, roots, etc., largely take the place of grass, Holstein-Friesians need not be a failure here, where climate and soil are less favorable for excellent pastures. Even there, where pastures are excellent, one or more of the above-named crops should be raised, to be fed when pasturage fails.

The Holstein-Friesian cow is simply an improved machine to transform feed into milk and butter, and the dairyman's aim should be to have the greatest amount of feed transformed into milk and butter with as little waste as possible. As soon, then, as the cow shows signs of shrinking in milk she should be fed so as to prevent this as much as possible. If she gets all the coarse food necessary, her ration of grain should be increased. Grain, or other concentrated food, should be given during the whole season of milking, for, as a rule, the cow can digest more than she can eat of coarse food, and as she should always be fed to her full capacity when milking, she should have the balance in a more concentrated form. A great deal has been said and written about feeding cattle, and a great many experiments have been made; and guided by these, every cattle-feeder can find out very easily which is the most economical food for him to feed. That a dairy cow should always be fed to her full capacity seems as clear as that an engine pays the best when used the most. When a dairy cow is not transforming all the food she can into milk and butter she is not only paying smaller profits than she is capable of doing, but is also impairing her future usefulness. Especially is this the case with young heifers; and everything should be done to stimulate the secretion of milk and to develop the milk-secreting organs.

As already said, a good deal can be accomplished by feeding. Other conditions that greatly influence the milk product are warm stables and good milking.

Some people have accused the Holstein-Friesians of not being a hardy breed of cattle, while others have claimed them to be one of the hardiest breeds in existence. However this may be, the man who wants very hardy cattle had better get some Buffaloes or Texans, and leave all improved breeds alone, and especially the dairy breeds. If he wants his cattle to fight the battle of life alone, he can get no better than those that nature fitted for it. But nature does not provide us with cows that give twenty thousand pounds of milk in a year, or make twenty pounds of butter in a week; for if there is anything impossible, it is that a cow can give much milk when kept in a place where the mercury goes below zero. I believe it would prove more economical to the breeder of any kind of cattle to provide warm stables than to provide the increased amount of food that his cattle will consume when not properly housed during cold weather. But it must be admitted that of all breeds of cattle the dairy breeds are most in need of a warm stable, for the following reasons:

First. The dairy cow is expected to give a large amount of milk, and in order to do this she must consume feed to sustain herself—feed to produce milk, and feed to keep her body at the proper temperature. If left out in the cold, she cannot eat and digest the amount of food it would require to perform these different functions, and consequently she will fall off in milk.

Second. When a cow has been turning her food into milk all summer she will be thin in flesh when winter comes, and thus be in a far worse condition than a well fleshed animal.

Third. The dairy cow, in order to produce a large amount of milk, will have to drink a large amount of water, which, unless warmed, will cause the temperature of the animal's body to go down considerably.

To heat the water for cattle in winter will, I feel sure, in the course of time become a common practice, since it is more economical to heat the water before the cow drinks it than afterwards. The decreased amount of food required will pay for the labor, and we will gain this: That the cow can turn all her energy to her purpose; that is, to the production of milk. Setting this aside, the danger of contracting disease will be greatly lessened. But though the stable should be warm, it should be well ventilated and lighted, since air and light are necessary for life, and withholding them will cause disease and sickness.

It will also prove very beneficial to have the cattle tied so that when in the barn they feel really comfortable. In some stables the cattle are forced to assume unnatural positions, which often leads to serious consequences. The cattle should have moderate exercise, summer and winter. Moderate exercise is necessary to maintain health, and it has a stimulating effect on the milk-production, as it promotes appetite and digestion. Over-exercise has the opposite effect, since the food used to recover the waste will be deducted from the food the cow consumed, leaving less to produce milk from. If practicable, it might prove best to keep the cattle in the stable during extreme cold days.

Good milking is of the greatest importance, for it develops the milk-secreting organs. The milk should be drawn from the cow as fast as possible, but at the same time so that the animal likes it. The milking should take place at regular intervals, twice a day, and when the amount of milk is very large, oftener.

A regular milk-record of each cow should be kept during the whole season, and an occasional butter test will greatly add to the value of each record. Also keep account of the feed, time of calving, and other items that influence the milk and butter product. Tests that endanger the life of the cow and impair her future usefulness should be avoided.

Breeding at too early an age is another thing that never should be done. It dwarfs the size, and thus greatly injures the future usefulness of the cow.

It is almost superfluous to say that cattle should always be treated kindly and kept free from excitement.

SELECTION OF SIRES.

"The bull is half the herd," is an expression very often heard amongst breeders of cattle, and it proves that they are well aware of the fact that the bulls in use greatly determine the value of the future herd. A bull, to be worthy to head a herd of Holstein-Friesians, should fulfill the following requirements:

First. He should be vigorous and healthy, and descended from healthy stock.

Second. He should spring from parents that are themselves animals of superior merit — the dam having shown herself to be a great milk and butter producer, and the sire a superior stock-getter.

Third. His sire's dam should have proven herself to be a great dairy cow; and the more of his ancestors and relatives that have distinguished themselves, either in the dairy or as sires, the greater will be his value.

Fourth. The bull himself should be an animal of superior merit, showing all the characteristics of the breed; exhibiting the most important dairy points and showing great digestive power. If he is handsomely built, and possesses a form that permits laying on flesh economically and rapidly, he is of the greater value. (I do not think it necessary to copy a scale of points that every man who breeds Holstein-Friesians, or contemplates breeding them, should be acquainted with.) Of course every breeder must judge for himself which bull is best suited for his herd. The bull should be especially strong in those points in which his herd is lacking the most.

Fifth. The bull should be of kind disposition. It hardly pays to pay a high sum for a breeding animal and dispose of him after a short time on account of viciousness. Besides, his calves are liable to inherit his vices, and are thus greatly deteriorated in value.

I should give the preference to a mature animal that has proven himself to be a good stock-getter. One has then the advantage of seeing the bull's calves, and he can then form an idea how the bull will mate with his cows.

Young bulls should be used sparingly, and only on less valuable cows, till they have proven themselves superior stock-getters.

Some of the first improvers of Short-Horn cattle let their young bulls to their neighbors, and those that proved the best stock-getters they afterwards used in their own herds. Perhaps this plan might be adopted by some of the most extensive breeders of Holstein-Friesians.

When the bull is getting so old as to lose his strength and vigor, he should be discarded.

In breeding, coupling the bull with his near relatives should not be practiced; for though great success has been attained by inbreeding, it is a proven fact that inbreeding causes loss of vigor and fertility. Without these the improvement can not be a lasting one; and as the aim of breeding should be not only to produce animals that are of high merit themselves, but such as will in turn produce animals of high merit; any course that does not lead to this result should be avoided.

CARE OF THE BULL.

When a bull has been secured, he should be kept in the best possible condition, so as to produce the best results and retain his usefulness as long as possible. As said before, the bull should not be used extensively till fully matured, to avoid dwarfing his size and causing him to lose his vigor at an early date. Care should also be taken to use no bull too often. The service bull should never be in any more than moderate flesh. Fat is not a sign of health, as often supposed, but an abnormal condition. A fat bull, aside from the fact that he is almost worthless while fat, on account of his inability to do service duty, is not likely to get healthy calves, being in an unhealthy condition himself. If a bull has once been very fat, he will never entirely recover his former vigor, and if kept fat, premature decay is sure to follow.

The bull should have regular exercise, and such as compels him to use every muscle and limb is the best. As a rule, the bull is kept indoors during the whole year, as this is the most convenient way. His stall should fulfill the same requirements that are recommended for the cow-stable. Care should be taken to keep it dry and clean. His attendant should study his nature, and treat him accordingly. As a rule, gentle treatment is the best, but he should be taught to obey. This is most effectually done by putting a ring in his nose and by using a staff when handling him. Everything that tends to worry, vex, or excite him should be avoided. Regular currying and cleaning will not only promote his health, but will also render him more gentle.

As many bulls are called upon to do service duty during the whole year, there is no reason for slacking at any time, especially as neglect, even for a short time, impairs the animal for a much longer time, sometimes for life.

SUGGESTIONS ON THE FEEDING AND CARING FOR CALVES.

The care of the calf commences as soon as it is born, or rather before it is born, the breeder being supposed to do everything within his power to produce a healthy calf. If he has done so, it will be born in a well bedded box-stall. As soon as it is born, the first thing to be looked after is that it be well cleaned; if the cow fails to do this, the calf should be cleaned by rubbing with straw or a rag. It should never be denied to suck the cow for the first two days, as it needs the first milk to clean its bowels, and should get it in the most natural way. It needs no introduction to do this, and unless very weak, should not be interfered with. After being weaned, the calf has to be fed by hand. For the first few days it should have its mother's milk, directly after being milked; later the milk may be changed, but care should be taken to feed it at the natural temperature. Some contrivance to prevent the calf from drinking too fast will prove very beneficial. By drinking too fast the milk does not go to the true digestive stomach, and this is one of the causes of "scours." After six or eight weeks the calf may be fed skim-milk; care should be taken to make the change gradually, and to heat the milk to the natural temperature. As skim-milk is lacking in fat, something should be given to take its place; steeped linseed or scalded oil-meal will be found to answer the best. The calf, no matter what time of the year it is born, should be kept indoors for the first weeks of its existence. The best way is to have it loose, in company with others of the same age, in a box-stall. Extra pains should be taken to keep the floor of the stall dry and well bedded. The calf-stable should be free from sudden changes in temperature, and draughts especially should be avoided. As soon as the calf will eat — and it will do this a few days after birth — it should have some nice early cut hay, and when it gets an appetite for the hay it should have all it will eat. A little grain might also be fed, but always sparingly. Young cattle should never be allowed to grow fat, and young dairy cattle the least of all. Oats and bran are the best to feed the calves in addition to the hay, as they are not fat-forming. By feeding thus the digestive powers of the calf will *develop better* than if feeding more concentrated food. The calves born in the spring can be turned out when about two months of age, but they should have a good pasture, with a shed for stormy and hot weather. When the pasture fails, hay and grain should be fed. The calf should be kept growing right along. The smaller and weaker calves should be kept separate from the larger and stronger, and when five or six months old the bull calves should be separated from the heifers.

If skim-milk is plenty, there is no need of weaning calves before they are six months old; and even when older than that skim-milk may be fed to them with profit. The weaning should be done gradually, and at the same time their grain ration should be increased, so that they will never stop growing on account of weaning.

While young stock will be able to stand more cold than milch-cows, they should not be exposed to rough weather.

During winter, calves should be curried regularly, as they need it more than any other stock. A sharp lookout should be kept for lice, and these eradicated as soon as discovered.

BREEDING OF HOLSTEIN-FRIESIAN CATTLE.

Essay of Mr. Dudley Miller, of Oswego, N. Y., Offered in Competition for the Association Prize, and Designated as Second Choice by the Referee.

BREEDING OF HOLSTEIN-FRIESIAN CATTLE.

"*The Selection of Sires and their Care during the Season of Service, to the end that they Transmit to their Offspring Health, Strength, Superior Milking and other Desirable Qualities. Also Suggestions on the Care and Feeding of Calves.*"

Breeding Holstein-Friesian cattle has been the occupation of the inhabitants of Holland for hundreds and hundreds of years, with various purposes in view, according to the locality in which they have been kept. Hence the name "general-purpose," so appropriate to the breed which excels in the different uses for which it is bred.

This is clearly illustrated by referring to the dairy products of the provinces of Holland, in the "Verslag over den Landbouw in Nederland" (the agricultural report) for 1884, where it is seen (page 553) that of the 17,653,703 kilograms (2 2-10 lbs., 1 kilo) of butter sold, 7,854,000 kilograms, nearly one-half the entire marketed product, are credited to Friesland, the area of which is perhaps not more than one-tenth of the whole kingdom.

All the cheese sold during the same period, and in the same country, amounted to 20,280,067 kilograms, of which 13,882,612 kilograms, nearly seven-tenths of the whole product, were sold in the province of North Holland, which is about one-third as large as Friesland, where 133,339 milch cows were kept, to 149,832 in North Holland.

It is plainly seen from the above where butter cows and cheese cows predominate in Holland. All ultimately go to the block, and no heifers are raised for beef which can be profitably used in the dairy.

There is a large trade in veal calves and in steers and cows fattened at the distilleries, one of the principal features of which is exporting to England.

The thrifty Hollanders have found it more prudent and safer to breed their cattle with a view to ultimate beef, rather than devoting all their energies to establishing a special-purpose breed, adapted solely to the production of milk, cheese, beef, or butter, as has been done with other more modern breeds.

Although their efforts have been made with the general purpose in view, they have produced a breed, individuals of which have excelled all others for milk and for butter, for certain periods, also for the early maturity of young stock, though these facts are in direct contradiction to the ground held by many wise and plausible theorists.

Owing to the variable climate of Holland, these cattle acclimate remarkably well, perhaps better than any other breed, whether exported to warm or cold climates. Many comparisons have been made by importations of European breeds to various parts of America. One in particular comes to my mind, of an importation of Holstein-Friesians and the notoriously hardy Aberdeen-Angus. These cattle were imported from Europe together, were three months in quarantine in New Jersey, and thence removed to southern central New York. They were kept there a year or two; thence removed to Kansas, where the bones of the Angus are now bleaching on the prairies. The Holstein-Friesians were shipped to New York and sold at public auction, where the aged bull which headed the herd, and several aged cows, sold for from $500 to over $650 each. This may be an example of "the survival of the fittest."

In America Holstein-Friesians have been bred with intelligence and great success. The greatest milk record for one year was made twice by an American-bred cow, viz: Echo, when she milked 18,120 pounds and 8 ounces, and the following year 23,775 pounds and 8 ounces. During part of the time of both these records she was carrying calves, viz: one calf for part of the time of the first record and triplets for about half the duration of the second record.

This record for one year has been excelled by Clothilde, milking 26,021 pounds and 2 ounces, but she was farrow during the entire record.

The greatest two-year-old milk record, 18,484 pounds and 13 ounces, was made by Albino 2d, an American-bred cow, as was also the greatest two-year-old butter record for seven days, 21 pounds and $10\frac{1}{2}$ ounces, made by Netherland Princess 4th. The greatest butter record for ninety days, 304 pounds and $5\frac{1}{2}$ ounces, was made by Aaggie 2d, an imported cow.

Some of the greatest gains in live weight have been made by American-bred calves, among which is one who gained $5\frac{1}{3}$ pounds for thirty days in succession. Cows bred here have attained a live weight of over 1,900 pounds, and bulls 2,500 pounds and upwards.

The progress of the breed in America, with the Holland statistics given above, amply indicates the wonderful power of the Holstein-Friesian, whether it be bred for beef, butter, cheese, or milk. Hence it is apparent that one may pursue any one of the above branches of the dairy or the raising of fat stock without resorting to other breeds than the Holstein-Friesian.

SELECTION OF SIRES, ETC.

In selecting a sire to head the herd, it is necessary that one should be chosen which not only possesses in a marked degree all the characteristics that we desire, but should have the power of reproducing his own qualities.

Sometimes we meet with excellent individuals that utterly fail to breed true, their blood being impotent to stamp their own good qualities on their offspring. Such animals should be carefully avoided.

Never use a bull, if it can be avoided, unless you have proof positive that he is not only individually superior for the purposes required, but that his direct antecedents have also the same characteristics clearly and strongly defined; and better yet, if possible, secure a bull that, in addition to the above, has proven himself a sire of superior animals. The time and money wasted by using inferior, I might say, worthless, bulls is incalculable. It is an easy matter to select a sire of good individuality from a family that has proven itself of superior excellence, and at a slight increase to the cost of an ordinary and, perhaps, worse than useless animal. The good sire from a good family will, with almost certainty, reproduce his own good qualities. He who buys the poor, cheap sire will waste his time, feed, and patience, and fail in the end, which is tenfold more expensive than securing a good animal on the start at a little higher price.

Do not be dazzled by pedigree alone. Some animals of most excellent families have been so bred in and in, to produce great results, that their weak points have been so intensified as to undermine their constitutions. The greatest results have often been attained by inbreeding, but, as a rule, it is a failure in cattle as well as in the human race, unless the animals inbred are thoroughly strong and vigorous in all particulars, which is rare.

The first and most essential quality, whether we desire beef, milk, cheese, or butter, is a strong, vigorous constitution; second, an animal that is a strong feeder and assimilates his food well; third, an animal with a quiet, equable disposition; fourth, one that is large and well developed, as this is a good indication of health and vigor.

Nearly all of the great milk, butter, cheese, and beef producers regardless of the breeds to which they belong, have been of the large rather than of the medium or smaller types of their respective breeds. From experiments made in Germany, and from results obtained in America, it has been conclusively demonstrated that not only the larger breeds, but also the larger cattle of the same breed are the most economical producers.

In selecting sires for the purpose of most successfully breeding beef cattle, early maturity is of the utmost importance. Why? Because it has been frequently demonstrated, and can be proven by any one who will take the trouble to count the cost, that beef can be grown at far less expense on young animals, from twelve to eighteen months old, than on two-year olds; and growing beef on three and four-year olds costs, generally, more than it sells for.

Therefore, the first consideration for a breeder of beef cattle in selecting a bull is early maturity, which is usually found with cattle having good digestive organs, easily assimilating their food, and having quiet dispositions, wasting no adipose tissues in nervous excitement; the second, good size, long, deep, well-rounded barrel, long, broad hips, deep, full thighs, fine head, neck, and legs; and the third consideration should be to select animals which "finish up" well, having the fat well interlarded with the lean, called marbled, and not put on in bunches fit for the manufacture of oleomargarine.

The sire of beef cattle should stand straight and firm, with front legs wide apart, giving plenty of lung room and more capacity for beef than cramped, narrow-chested animals afford. The stand behind should be straight and legs wide apart, giving ample room for the formation of flesh on the thighs both outside and inside. The skin should be soft and mellow, with oily secretions, and loose on the body, so that it can be readily gathered up in the hand.

The sire of good dairy stock, be it for milk, butter, or cheese, should be strong and vigorous, of large size, indicative of a good constitution, with a fine, clean-cut head, slightly dishing forehead, a large, mild eye, a medium-sized horn, a large muzzle, a fine neck of medium length, and the barrel long and deep, with well-sprung ribs, wide apart, giving plenty of room for well-developed digestive organs; for success depends upon the amount of food consumed and the facility with which it is digested.

The hips should be long, broad, and straight. This formation admits of and is generally found with capacious, well-formed udders in the cows, and in the males and fat stock is best adapted to growing the greatest amount of beef. The fore legs should be wide enough apart to give ample room for heart and lungs, and the hind legs should be straight and wide apart, affording room for large udders, which are apt to inconvenience the walking of cows that stand close behind.

By many, a crooked leg is deemed an essential characteristic of a good milch cow. It is, however, a most objectionable feature, for it is generally found on cows with hocks so close together that every time they step their large udders are in the way and are usually injured by being banged about, first by one leg and then the other, until the cows are so hampered that they fail to graze with freedom, and consequently produce less.

The udder should be large and evenly quartered, extending far forward, spreading on the belly, well tucked up, reaching far back and up between the hind legs, and with soft, pliable skin which shrinks to almost nothing when milked dry. The teats should be of good size, evenly placed, and wide apart on the udder. Avoid a large, fleshy bag, which when milked out still appears large, and as though it contained milk. The escutcheon is greatly admired by many, but though most good milkers possess it, it is by no means a sure sign of a great milch cow. Much more important are the milk veins and holes on the belly, to be found both on males and females, but far less developed on the former.

These are features rarely, if ever, found in poor dairy stock. The larger, the longer, and the more crooked the milk veins, and the larger and the greater the number of milk holes at the ends of the veins, the better the cow.

The fluid which passes through the milk veins and holes from the udder is the waste or surplus from which the milk has been taken. The greater the amount of milk produced, the greater the amount of refuse to be carried off, consequently the greater the development of these veins and holes in a great producer.

The same characteristics which are desirable in a good milch cow are equally requisite for a good cheese or butter cow, but with the latter something more is needed. The distinction between a good milch cow and a good cheese cow is found only by actual experience and by the analysis of respective milks; that is, there are no exterior indications whereby one good dairy cow can be distinguished from another as being superior for the production of cheese. It is, however, different with the butter cow.

While there is no absolute rule (without exception), it is generally true that those cows whose skins have a yellow, oily appearance and touch are good butter cows, and the more yellow and oily, the better butter cow. This yellow, oily skin is just as desirable in bulls as in cows.

During the service season bulls should be in a perfectly healthy, vigorous condition; and to attain this they should be fed in accordance with what is required of them. Daily exercise and grooming is necessary if the best results are desired.

Service bulls in Holland are reported to have covered three and four hundred cows in a single year. One case in particular I have in mind, of the bull Artis, which is reported to have served over five hundred cows within that time. If a good bull is fed strong, nourishing food, and is well exercised, groomed, and cared for, there is no reason why he should not be allowed to serve a cow daily for six months. The usual number, however, will probably range somewhere between fifty and one hundred for the season of three or four months.

One of the most successful breeders of my acquaintance has an average of from twenty to twenty-five females to breed annually, and for the purpose he keeps four or five bulls. This is not done because one bull is thought unequal to the task, but for the purpose of more readily combining different good qualities and intensifying them in his young stock.

The proof of the excessfulness of this breeding is not only apparent when representatives of this breed compete in the show ring, but they have become notorious throughout the country as great producers. Four cows bred in this herd have each given over ninety pounds of milk in a day; one of them 101 pounds, another 102 pounds (milked within twenty-four hours, but secreted in twenty-six hours), and the third twice excelled the greatest annual record (before mentioned).

THE CARE AND FEEDING OF CALVES.

If improperly raised, the best bred calves will amount to naught. One must not only know how to raise calves as they should be, but must see that they have the best of care. Calves are often fed too little, and after the first month or six weeks, are allowed to make shift for themselves, which results in their being half-starved and growing up to poor, miserable, undersized animals. If a calf has been abused in this manner, it is next to impossible for it to entirely recover.

The natural and best way ever invented or known to raise a calf is to let it run in the pasture with a cow. It may be said that it is not good for the cow. True, but if you have not the misfortune to own some old cows, or three-teated cows, on which the best calves can be raised, they can be fed the milk of their dams by hand.

The calf should be kept in a thrifty, growing condition, not fat, as this impedes the growth of bone and muscle.

It should be fed three or four times daily when young, because feeding but twice often causes it to become so hungry that it takes more at a time than it can readily digest.

This is injurious, and frequently results in what is called pot-bellied calves.

At about two months old, rowen, and a little oat-meal or ground oats should be put in a convenient place for the calf to taste when inclined. By degrees, with increasing age, it will learn to like and take more of both, and gradually becomes weaned from milk at eight, ten, or twelve months old, according to the desire of the owner.

A large pen, having a floor covered with straw, should be provided for the hand-fed calf, so that it can get plenty of exercise.

A run in a yard without grass would also be beneficial. Care should be taken to have the calf-pen dark enough to exclude flies in fly-time, as they are a great annoyance and injury to the most favorable growth of calves.

The dangers of over-feeding calves, as well as of starving them, are great, particularly with breeders who take a pride in having large, show animals.

In one respect shows are an absolute injury. I mean the tendency they have to induce breeders to over-feed their stock for the purpose of taking premiums with large, fat animals.

Many and many a good animal has been ruined for breeding and dairy purposes by excessive feeding, which dwarfs the growth of bone and muscle and induces a tendency to take on fat, and diminishes, if not utterly ruins, the milking characteristics, and, worse than all, so affects the organs of generation that re-production becomes impossible.

Some of the most promising animals in America, by being over-fed, have had their usefulness greatly impaired, and others have been rendered totally unfit for breeding purposes, and consequently were condemned to a premature and ignoble death on the block.

Breeding Holstein-Friesians includes a large and interesting field for the intelligent breeder, as their characteristics are of more varied excellence than those of any other breed.

It now stands far in advance of all others as the greatest milk producer, is excelled by none for cheese, is successfully contending for honors as a butter breed with those specially bred for that purpose, and surpasses for beef all other dairy breeds.

There is ample room for the improvement of this breed in concentrating and intensifying their good milk, butter, cheese, and beef qualities.

Under this improving process the breed is now making wonderful progress in America; in fact greater than it has made in Europe. This is evident from the fact that the best and highest priced Holstein-Friesians are now found in America.

PROCEEDINGS

OF THE

THIRD ANNUAL MEETING

OF THE

Holstein-Friesian Association,

OF AMERICA,

HELD AT

BUFFALO, NEW YORK, MARCH 21ST, 1888.

ALSO

REPORTS OF MEETINGS OF THE BOARD OF OFFICERS,

HELD AT BUFFALO, NEW YORK,

MARCH 20TH AND 21ST, 1888.

Egbert, Fidlar, & Chambers, Printers, Davenport, Iowa.

1888.

MEETING OF THE BOARD OF OFFICERS

OF THE

HOLSTEIN-FRIESIAN ASSOCIATION OF AMERICA,

Held at the Genesee Hotel, Buffalo, N. Y.,
March 20th, 1888.

Upon roll call, the following were found to be present: President, William M. Singerly; Gerrit S. Miller, M. L. Sweet, W. G. Powell, W. M. Liggett, William Brown Smith, F. L. Houghton, Edgar Huidekoper, C. W. Horr, D. H. Burrell, S. Hoxie, and Thomas B. Wales.

The next business in order being the consideration of applications for membership, the Secretary presented the application of John A. Beauchamp, of Nashville, Tenn., a member of the firm of W. B. Clark & Co.

Upon motion, he was declared elected.

The Secretary next presented the name of Benjamin W. Folger, of Kingston, Ontario.

Upon motion of Mr. W. G. Powell, the Secretary was instructed to make inquiries in reference to the fitness of Mr. Folger to become a member, and, upon satisfactory proof, to enter his name upon the roll as a member.

The Secretary next presented the name of H. V. Pugsley, of Plattsburg, Mo., and recommended his election.

Upon Motion, Mr. Pugsley was received as a member.

The Secretary next presented the name of Truman G. Avery, of Buffalo, N. Y., recommended by A. P. Wright.

Upon motion, Mr. Avery was declared elected.

The Secretary next presented the name of Charles Robinson, of Barre Plains, Mass., recommended by Mr. F. L. Houghton.

Upon motion, Mr. Robinson was declared elected.

The Secretary next presented the name of George R. Morehouse, M. D., of Philadelphia, Penn., recommended by E. A. Powell.

Upon motion, Mr. Morehouse was declared elected.

The Secretary next presented the name of H. F. W. Breuer, of Charleston, S. C.

Upon Motion, Mr. Breuer was declared elected.

The Secretary next presented the name of J. B. Collins, of Minneapolis, Minn.

Upon Motion, Mr. Collins was declared elected.

The Secretary next presented the name of William Farrington, of San José, Cal.

Upon motion, Mr. Farrington was declared elected.

The Secretary next presented the name of William S. Gurnee, of New York, N. Y., and recommended his election.

Upon motion, Mr. Gurnee was declared elected.

The Secretary next presented the name of F. B. Knowles, of Worcester, Mass., recommended by F. L. Houghton.

Upon motion, Mr. Knowles was declared elected.

The Secretary next presented the name of Joseph V. Phelan, of Wellingington, Ohio, recommended by C. W. Horr.

Upon motion, Mr. Phelan was declared elected.

The Secretary next presented the name of O. P. Potter, of Potter Building, 38 Park Row, New York, N. Y.

Upon motion, Mr. Potter was declared elected.

The Secretary next presented the name of C. E. Rumsey, of Pittsburgh, Penn., recommended by John Hayes, President of the Bank of Pittsburgh.

Upon motion of Gerrit S. Miller, it was decided that the application of Mr. Rumsey should be referred to the Secretary to make inquiries of Mr. J. T. Brooks, of Salem, Ohio, for further information in reference to the application, the name to be entered on the roll as a member if the information is satisfactory to the Secretary.

The Secretary next presented the name of J. Rust, of North Greenfield, Wis.

The application of Mr. Rust was referred to the Secretary under the same conditions as the application of Mr. Rumsey.

The Secretary next presented the name of Daniel W. True, of Portland, Maine, recommended by Charles J. Chaplain, mayor of Portland.

Upon motion, it was decided that the application of Mr. True should be received when the recommendation of Mr. C. A. Brown, of Portland, is procured.

The Secretary next presented the name of C. H. Vandevort, of Amity, N. Y., recommended by C. H. Demarest and S. Case.

This application was referred to the Secretary in the same manner as those of Mr. Rumsey and Mr. Rust.

The Secretary next presented the name of W. A. White, of Wahpeton, D. T.

Upon motion, it was decided that the application of Mr. White should be received when the recommendation of Mr. Liggett is procured.

The Secretary next presented the name of Henry A. Whitney, of Nantasket, Mass., and recommended his election.

Upon motion, Mr. Whitney was declared elected.

The Secretary next presented the name of E. M. McGillin, of Cleveland, Ohio, recommended by Mr. C. W. Horr.

Upon motion, Mr. McGillin was declared elected.

The Secretary presented the name of J. W. Howard, of Aberdeen, Miss., recommended by Eugene Smith.

Upon motion, Mr. Howard was declared elected.

Mr. F. C. Stevens, of Attica, N. Y., was introduced, and said:

Mr. President and gentlemen, I have a matter to present for your consideration. In 1873 I imported a heifer which was called "Hollander" in Holland, in the Holland Herd-Book. I brought her to this country and they called her "Hollander" here. Two years after she dropped a heifer calf. That animal I named "Hollander Second." Last year she dropped another female. I made application to Secretary Wales for permission to use the name "Hollander Third," which was refused, on the ground that there was already an animal in the old Dutch-Friesian Herd-Book named "Hollander Third." I then referred Mr. Wales to the rule which governed me in the matter, saying that the progeny of animals should receive the name of sire and dam with the numbers prefixed or added. He referred me to the rule which provides that no two animals shall have the same name. I told him that I should have to appeal from his decision in this matter, because I did not regard the rules of the Holstein-Friesian Association as applicable to the old Dutch-Friesian Association.

This is a statement of the case, and I ask your consideration of the matter.

I have another request to make. I have an animal, a daughter of "Mechthilde," called "Chelonis." I would like to change that to "Mechthilde 2d."

Mr. WALES: The point I made was this: That having an animal in our register named "Hollander Third," no other animal should be allowed to receive that name. I look upon the old Dutch-Friesian Herd-Book as a part of our record, and I refer to them as a part of our records, the same as I refer to the book we published last year.

Upon motion of Mr. Huidekoper, permission was granted Mr. Stevens to use the name "Hollander Third," and also the name "Mechthilde 2d."

Mr. D. B. Whipple was introduced, and said:

I have a case somewhat similar to that which Mr. Stevens has presented. I would like to have the names of some of the members of the "Pietertje" family changed in rotation with the original. "Pietertje Second" has three daughters and a son. The son is the oldest of her progeny, named "Holland King." The oldest daughter is "Millet." The second daughter is "Pietertje Second Netherland." The third daughter is "Netherland Duke's Pietertje." I would like to have those named in rotation, "Pietertje Third," "Pietertje Fourth," "Pietertje Fifth," etc.

In the case of "Holland King," I would like his name to be "Pietertje's Holland King."

Upon motion, the request of Mr. Whipple was granted.

SECRETARY WALES: On the 10th of January, 1887, I received an application for the registry of a bull to be named "Prince of Cedarside 9th," from W. A. Pratt, of Elgin, Ill. On examination it was found to conflict with an application afterwards received from S. N. Wright, of South Elgin, Ill., for the registry of the heifer "Pride of Elgin." The latter was born April 15th, 1886, and the first March 2d, 1886. I investigated the matter, and found that Mr. Pratt did not own this animal, and that Mr. Wright had a perfect right to register his animal according to his application. I wrote to Mr. Pratt explaining the matter to him, and asked him to return the certificate of registry, but I have never been able to get a word of response from him. My position is that this animal "Prince of Cedarside 9th," No. 4246, should be thrown out of our registry entirely. I do not think there ever was such an animal.

Upon motion, it was decided that the registry of "Prince of Cedarside 9th," No. 4246, should be expunged from the Holstein-Friesian record.

The Secretary read a letter from Mr. William A. Hinds, Secretary of the Oneida Community, New York, to Mr. G. S. Miller, in regard to fees charged to that company.

Upon motion of Mr. Huidekoper, the matter was laid upon the table.

Mr. Horr called for the amount of funds now in the treasury.

Treasurer William Brown Smith reported a balance on hand of $225,413.36.

Upon motion, the chair appointed the following committee to fix the salaries of officers for the ensuing year: Mr. C. W. Horr, Mr. D. H. Burrell, and Mr. M. L. Sweet.

Adjourned until March 21st, 1888, at 8:30 A. M.

ADJOURNED MEETING OF THE BOARD OF OFFICERS,

Held March 21st, 1888, at 8:30 a. m.

The committee appointed at the last session to fix salaries of officers for the ensuing year reported as follows:

Salary of Secretary and Editor, $2,500.00; Superintendent of the Advanced Registry, $1,000.00; Treasurer, $250.00.

Upon motion, the report of the committee was accepted, and the salaries voted as reported.

Upon motion, the meeting adjourned.

Treasurer William Brown Smith reported a balance on hand of $25,113.36.

ADJOURNED MEETING OF THE BOARD OF OFFICERS,

Held March 21st, 1888, at 8:30 a. m.

The committee appointed at the last session to fix salaries of officers for the ensuing year reported as follows:

Salary of Secretary and Editor, $2,500.00; Superintendent of the Advanced Registry, $1,000.00; Treasurer, $250.00.

Upon motion, the report of the committee was accepted, and the salaries voted as reported.

Upon motion, the meeting adjourned.

THIRD ANNUAL MEETING

OF THE

HOLSTEIN-FRIESIAN ASSOCIATION OF AMERICA,

Held at the Genesee Hotel, Buffalo, N. Y.,
Wednesday, March 21st, 1888.

The meeting was called to order at 10 o'clock A. M., by the President.

Upon roll call, it was ascertained that the following members were present:

Jere Allis, Sylvester Burchard, David H. Burrell, O. P. Chapman, John A. Frye, C. W. Horr, F. L. Houghton, S. Hoxie, Edgar Huidekoper, H. Langworthy, William M. Liggett, C. J. Lord, D. H. McAlpin, Dudley Miller, Gerrit S. Miller, T. S. Nowell, Isaac C. Otis, F. W. Patterson, E. A. Powell, W. G. Powell, W. M. Singerly, Harlan P. Smith, W. Brown Smith, F. C. Stevens, J. L. Stone, Martin L. Sweet, C. F. Sweezey, S. W. Sweezey, Thomas B. Wales, G. D. Wheeler, Dallas B. Whipple, Don J. Wood, S. N. Wright, L. T. Yeomans, T. G. Yeomans, and that 189 were represented by proxy.

It was moved that a committee of three be appointed to examine the proxies, and to report to this meeting.

The chair appointed Mr. F. C. Stevens, Mr. Langworthy, and Mr. B. Chaffee as such Committee on Proxies.

The committee so appointed proceeded to collect the proxies, and retired to examine them.

THE PRESIDENT: The next thing in order is the reading of the Secretary's report.

The Secretary read as follows:

Mr. President, and Members of the Holstein-Friesian Association of America: Another year's work has been completed, and I am glad to be able to make what I trust may prove a satisfactory report of my doings as Secretary. At any rate the business of the Association has had my undivided attention, and I have given to it my best efforts. Each year brings largely-increased work, and I presume such will always be the case; at least it is to be hoped so, for that only means continued prosperity and success.

It seems remarkable to me that with such a large number of correspondents, resident from Canada to Florida, and from Maine to California, and in all conditions of life, that I hear so few complaints. I sometimes think that this comfortable state of affairs is, in a measure, owing to the pleasure and satisfaction our breeders take in the care and interest in their quiet, gentle, Dutch cows.

You will not be surprised to learn that our membership is rapidly increasing. During the year applications for membership have been received from twenty-one breeders. If all are admitted, we shall then number three hundred and thirty-one (331).

Two deaths have been reported — Mr. William McEwan, of Bay City, Mich., and Mr. F. W. Maxon, of Walworth, Wis.

Since our last meeting Volume II. of our Herd-Book has been completed. As you know, it was printed in two parts. The one for bulls contains the reports of meetings and the pedigrees of 2,948 bulls; and the part for cows, 3,472 pedigrees; the number of pages is 1,438.

Volume III. has closed, and about 1,000 pages are already in print. I expect it will include at least 2,000 pages. The transfer lists for this volume are by far the largest of any yet published.

During the year I have issued 4,225 certificates of registry of bulls; 1,959 certificates of registry of cows; 2,357 certificates of transfer of bulls; 4,045 certificates of transfer of cows, and 147 duplicate certificates, making a total of 15,733 certificates.

The registry of the year includes but seventy-six imported animals. We have registered to date a total of 37,685 animals — 14,258 bulls, and 23,427 cows.

There has been expended during the year for special premiums $1,837.00, and I think all will agree that the money could not have been put to better use. I am sure its offering brought out a finer display of our cattle than if it had not been made. Our great victories over all other breeds of dairy cattle at the largest and most important shows of the country are certainly owing in part to our liberal policy in this regard, and I trust such policy will continue.

The receipts and expenditures for the year ending March 1st, 1888, are as follows:

RECEIPTS.

Received for membership fees	$ 2,200 00
Received for registry of imported bulls	60 00
Received for registry of imported cows	1,460 00
Received for registry of bulls	5,082 00
Received for registry of cows	6,034 00
Received for transfer of bulls	1,267 50
Received for transfer of cows	1,572 50
Received for duplicate certificates	73 50
Received for inspection of imported cattle	320 00
Received for Herd-Books	415 11
Balance of ledger	542 98
	$19,027 59

EXPENDITURES.

For Board of Officers, traveling expenses ....$	429	88
For Clerk hire	3,005	70
For Expenses, including office rent	1,073	41
For Printing	1,129	40
For Inspection of imported cattle..............................	65	19
For Special premiums...	1,122	00
For National Cattle Growers' Association	250	00
For Stamp account, government envelopes, wrappers, etc	646	75
For Missouri Agricultural College	183	43
For prize essay...	100	00
For sundry personal accounts, fees refunded, drafts returned for endorsement	165	42
For balance remitted to W. Brown Smith, Treasurer	10,856	41
	—$19,027	59

Respectfully submitted,

THOMAS B. WALES, JR.,

Secretary.

Mr. W. G. Powell moved that the report of the Secretary be accepted, and printed in the proceedings of this meeting.

Seconded and carried.

The President called for the report of the Treasurer, which was read by Treasurer W. Brown Smith, as follows:

TREASURER'S REPORT.

Mr. President, and Gentlemen of the Holstein-Friesian Association of America: I herewith beg leave to make the following report of the receipts and expenditures of this Association for the fiscal year ending with the date of this meeting:

Balance on hand, as per report of Treasurer at last annual meeting, Buffalo, March 16, 1887, $23,681.11.

RECEIPTS.

1888.

March 16.	To balance, as per last report............................	$23,681	11
April 1.	Accrued interest to date, as per report of W. C. Brayton,	91	70
		$23,772	81

EXPENDITURES,

AS PER REPORT OF W. C. BRAYTON, AND VOUCHERS FURNISHED.

1887.

March 17.	Thomas B. Wales, salary six months, to March 1, 1887	$1,250 00		
March 17.	W. C. Brayton, salary one year............................	250 00		
March 17.	Bill, account of Advanced Registry, S. Burchard...........	210 00		
March 17.	Bill, account of Advanced Registry, S. Hoxie.	170 00		
March 17.	Bill, account of Advanced Registry, S. N. Wright..........	95 00		
March 17.	Postage...	10—$	1,975	10
	Balance turned over to W. Brown Smith, Treasurer.......		21,797	71
			$23,772	81

RECEIPTS.

1887.
April	11.	Cash from W. C. Brayton, Treasurer..................................		$21,797 71
June	8.	Cash from Thomas B. Wales, Secretary, as per quarterly report...$	941 14	
June	30.	Accrued interest on deposit, Salt Springs National Bank,	100 00	
		Accrued interest on deposit, Onondaga County Savings Bank..	30 00	
		Accrued interest on deposit, Syracuse Savings Bank.......	30 00	
Sept.	7.	Cash from Thomas B. Wales, Secretary, per quarterly report..	3,500 00	
Dec.	7.	Cash from Thomas B. Wales, Secretary, per quarterly report	822 44	

1888.
Jan.	1.	Accrued interest on deposit, Onondaga County Savings Bank..	60 00	
		Accrued interest on deposit, Syracuse Savings Bank.......	60 00	
		Accrued interest on deposit, Salt Springs National Bank,	242 02	
March	5.	Cash from Thomas B. Wales, Secretary, per quarterly report..	5,589 53	
		Total receipts for fiscal year...........................		11,378 13
				$33,176 14

EXPENDITURES.

1887.
April	12.	S. Hoxie, account of Advanced Registry.....................$	188 66	
April	12.	Hiscock, Doheny & Hiscock, legal services, Sluiter Bros. vs. Holstein-Friesian Association........................	178 90	
April	18.	Durston & Co., account books for Treasurer.................	2 40	
May	16.	John I. Holly, Secretary, premium paid at New York Dairy Show, offered by Association....................	415 00	
May	16.	Smiths, Powell & Lamb, sweepstakes premium at New York Dairy Show...................................	300 00	
May	21.	F. C. Stevens, special premium for butter at New York Dairy Show..	55 00	
June	27.	S. Hoxie, account of Advanced Registry.....................	51 17	
June	27.	J. N. Muncey, account of Advanced Registry..................	17 05	
July	30.	Egbert, Fidlar, & Chambers, publishing Herd-Book.......	4,006 60	
Sept.	6.	Thomas B. Wales, salary six months, to Sept. 1, 1887......	1,250 00	
Nov.	28.	J. N. Muncey, account of Advanced Registry..................	16 00	
Nov.	28.	S. N. Wright, account of Advanced Registry.................	8 00	

1888.
Jan.	13.	J. N. Muncey, account of Advanced Registry.................	24 00	
		S. Hoxie, salary..	1,000 00	
		W. Brown Smith, salary...	250 00	
		Total expense for fiscal year...............................		$ 7,762 78
		Balance on hand..		25,413 36
				$33,176 14

Respectfully submitted,

W. BROWN SMITH,

Treasurer.

Upon motion, the report of the Treasurer was accepted as read.

The President next called for the report of the Superintendent of Advanced Registry.

Mr. S. Hoxie read the report, as follows:

REPORT OF SUPERINTENDENT OF ADVANCED REGISTRY.

To the President and Members of the Holstein-Friesian Association of America:
In offering this report I am happy to say that there is a growing interest among our breeders in the subject of Advanced Registry, and a more general knowledge and approval of its objects and methods. Breeders who entered cattle in the first volume assure me that they are already realizing great advantage from it.

It is also attracting the attention of other breeders of thoroughbred cattle. Leading men in other associations are recognizing the importance of the principle upon which it is based, and the coming necessity of a similar system for the registry of their own cattle. At the annual meeting of the Devon Cattle Club, held in this city (Buffalo) on the 25th of January, steps were taken toward establishing a similar system for Devon cattle. If I am correctly informed, the subject is being widely agitated among Short-Horn breeders. And it is a matter of gratification to learn that the Jersey Cattle Club has adopted rules somewhat similar to ours for verifying butter records by affidavits. Indeed, it is a matter in which we all feel a degree of pride, that our Association, handling the breed latest introduced into this country, is leading other associations in this movement as well as in other important movements. We have assumed in this respect the highest position of any association in the world. We have shown a progressive tendency that is drawing public attention to our breed perhaps more than to any other breed in our land. It now remains for us to hold this position, and prove that our cattle are worthy of the attention that is being fixed upon them.

During the past year the work in this department has been mainly in giving information to breeders in regard to the character and requirements of this registry, and in preparing material for a second volume.

Two hundred and twenty-seven animals have been examined and accepted so far as requirements of structure are concerned. As a rule it has been the practice to not issue certificates until the final revision of entries previous to publication. For this reason fees have not been paid, except in a few instances; and the bills for service of Inspectors have been sent to the Treasurer as they have been received and approved.

The immediate receipts and expenditures of my office have been as follows:

RECEIPTS.

Fees	$ 50 00
For books	19 50
From Treasurer	51 17
Total	$120 67

EXPENDITURES.

For postage	$ 24 08
For printing	14 87
For measures	56 05
For stationary	4 40
For express	1 15
For telegraph	35
For traveling expenses	1 25
	$102 15
Balance due the Association	$ 18 52

Upon motion, the report was received, and ordered published in the regular proceedings.

THE PRESIDENT: It has been customary to refer the reports of the Secretary, the Treasurer, and the Superintendent of Advanced Registry to a committee for examination. What is the pleasure of the meeting in that regard?

Mr. Huidekoper moved that such a committee be appointed.

Seconded and carried.

The chair appointed as such committee Dr. Patterson, C. J. Lord, and D. B. Whipple.

THE PRESIDENT: The next business before the meeting is the proposition to amend Section 5 of Article I. of the By-Laws, so that each new member shall receive a full set of the Herd-Books free of charge. The proposition was sent by Mr. I. C. Wade, of Jamestown, D. T. Mr. Wade is not present.

Mr. Yeomans moved that the matter be laid upon the table.

Mr. HOUGHTON: In deference to those whom I represent, I will say that eight or nine of them speak very decidedly in favor of having the complete set of Herd-Books furnished to new members. I simply state that I have their proxies, and they request me to favor the matter.

Mr. POWELL: Is it simply the books of the Holstein-Friesian Association, or does it refer to the old association?

SECRETARY WALES: I think the intention of the gentlemen was to include all publications of the Association, and that includes the old Dutch-Friesian and the old Holstein Herd-Books. As I understand Mr. Wade's letter, that is what he intended to ask for.

The motion of Mr. Yeomans that the proposed amendment be laid upon the table, was seconded and carried.

THE PRESIDENT: The next subject before the meeting is a proposition to amend Section 8 of Article IV. of the By-Laws so as to read: "Upon application to the Secretary by members of this Association for the inspection of imported animals, and having deposited with the Secretary a sufficient amount to cover the fees and expenses of the nearest Inspector, the Secretary shall then order such inspection; the registry fee shall be the same as is made and provided for home-bred animals."

It was moved that the matter be laid upon the table.

Mr. E. A. POWELL: I think it is due to Mr. Lord, who proposed this amendment, that he be permitted to give his reasons for proposing it, Mr. Lord being out on committee work.

The motion to lay the proposed amendment upon the table was withdrawn for the present.

Mr. M. L. SWEET: Mr. President, at the annual meeting of the Holstein-Friesian Association of Michigan, I was instructed to offer a resolution at this meeting to have the membership fees reduced from $100.00 to $25.00, and on my arrival home, I sent it to Mr. Wales, who received the notice too late to include in his notice of this meeting, and there can be no action taken upon it this year, but I wish to bring the matter to the attention of the Association.

THE PRESIDENT: The next subject for consideration is the matter of appropriation for special premiums. Mr. Wales, anticipating requests for special premiums, included the necessary notice in his notice of this meeting.

Mr. E. A. POWELL: Mr. President, we have heretofore each season made an appropriation for a certain amount to be placed in the hands of the Board, to be offered at their discretion for special premiums, in order to induce exhibitions of the best class of stock, and in order to stimulate a general interest in the breed, and I think it has been money well expended. I believe no money has been used that has reflected greater benefit upon the Association than this. During the coming season there are to be a number of exhibitions where it is very important indeed that this breed of cattle should come to the front, and I therefore move that $4,000.00 be put into the hands of the Board of Officers, to be used at their discretion during the coming year for premiums to be paid for exhibitions of stock, etc., as they shall deem best, the sum not to exceed $4,000.00. Of course it is not necessary that that amount should be used.

Motion seconded.

Mr. YEOMANS: Would it not be well for some gentleman who is posted upon the subject to state something in reference to the Ohio Centennial of this year, so that before we vote upon the question we may be advised of the fact.

THE PRESIDENT: The chair would state for the information of the Association, that last year $2,000.00 was appropriated, of which a little over $1,800.00 was used. Perhaps Mr. Powell, or Mr. Miller, or Mr. Wales can give us further information.

Mr. MILLER: Mr. Wales has given me all the information I have, which is very limited. I think he knows much more about it than I do.

Mr. WALES: I will state, Mr. President, that I was written to by Mr. L. N. Bonham, Secretary of the proposed Centennial Exhibition to be held in September and October of the present year at Columbus, Ohio, asking that our Association appropriate moneys to be offered there as special premiums for Holstein-Friesian cattle and their products. I replied to him that I thought we would like to do something in that way, as I considered Ohio was a good place to exhibit our cattle, and that we could make a very good showing there. They agreed to give us every facility. They intend to erect special buildings for dairy cattle. I think tests of three or four weeks will be made of the different dairy breeds, and I thought it would be a good place to show what we could do. I wrote Mr. Bonham that I would present the matter to the Board, and I did so by letter, asking the Board to give me authority to promise Secretary Bonham the unexpended $800.00 from last year's appropriation; and the Board voted unanimously to do so. I therefore informed Secretary Bonham that he could have this money, and the special premiums were arranged by Mr. C. W. Horr and myself, as authorized by the Board. Having only $800.00 to use, and there being some very important prizes to be offered, Mr. Horr and myself agreed that we would ask the Association for a liberal appropriation the present year, in order to enable us to offer further premiums than we have already offered. The tests for milk and butter, as I understand, are to extend over thirty days. The premium lists are not yet printed, and I gather this from the letters of Mr. Bonham.

Mr. W. G. POWELL: I would suggest that the premiums are not given alone for butter. I think we are overlooking other very important features and characteristics of our breed in which they undoubtedly excel.

THE PRESIDENT: The motion is that $4,000.00 be placed in the hands of the Board of Officers to be used in their discretion. It does not confine it to butter, or milk, or anything else.

The motion of Mr. Powell was put to a vote, and carried.

Mr. ISAAC C. OTIS: It has been customary to divide this money, or to duplicate premiums in the states. I move that the committee in charge be directed to take into consideration the prominent fairs in Canada. It will stimulate the breeders there.

Motion seconded.

Mr. YEOMANS: Do I understand that Mr. Otis simply makes this as a recommendation to the Board of Officers?

Mr. OTIS: Certainly.

Motion to include Canadian Fairs was carried.

Mr. M L. SWEET: I wish to bring up a matter for the consideration of the members. I have here a report on feeding from our agricultural college; also President Johnson's report on agriculture — his letter to me. I have not had time to read it or to look over these papers before I left home. My clerk sent me the papers, and I have run over the letter hastily, and I see nothing out of the way in it at all. I will present the report to the Secretary, so that he may read what transpired there in regard to feeding those cattle.

Mr. Horr moved that the reading of the report referred to be dispensed with, and that the Secretary be instructed to include in the report of this meeting such portions of it as he considers best.

Seconded and carried.

Mr. E. A. POWELL: There is one other matter that properly comes up at this time; I am in possession of a letter sent to me by Dr. Collier, the superintendent of the experimental station at Geneva, N. Y. It should have gone to Mr. Singerly, but for some reason it was sent to me, and I will therefore take the liberty of presenting it to the Association. It is rather an important matter, and I think you will all agree with me that it is well to give it due consideration. Dr. Collier is the new director of the experimental station at Geneva, N. Y.; has just come into the charge of that institution:

"GENEVA, N. Y., March 1st, 1888.

"*My Dear Sir:* Upon assuming the directorship of this station, it has appeared to me that there was a wide field for careful scientific investigation which could not but prove of immense practical value to the agricultural interests of the state, and especially the dairy interest, which I need not inform you is of almost pre-eminent importance to our people.

"I beg leave to submit to your consideration the following points which have occurred to me, and shall be happy to receive from you any suggestions by way of criticism of the plan proposed, or of amplification of the details of the proposed investigation.

"I shall be pleased, also, to have your suggestions as to how I may secure most economically for the station the animals needed for the purpose of such investigation and experiments, and any information which shall tend to make the results of the highest value to the people of the state:

"*First.* At a public institution devoted to the advancement of agriculture through experimentation, the stock should be representative animals of the breed from which they are selected.

"*Second.* The dairy interest in New York State being the most important branch of the stock industry, it should be the first to receive attention.

"*Third.* The average butter yield per cow in this state does not exceed 130 pounds per year, whereas it should not fall below 300 pounds. This being true, the station can do no better service for the dairymen of the state than to unite with them in working out the problems of feeding, individual variations, and breed characteristics, with the allied subjects, which, when better understood and practiced, shall help to raise the standard and bring the yield up to double the present amount.

"*Fourth.* The breeds which should first be selected are the Holstein, Jersey, Guernsey, Ayrshire, Short-horns, Devon, and one or two of the Polled breeds.

"*Fifth.* In building up a herd to be used in experimental work, young animals should be selected — animals under one year, or better, but a few months old. By having young animals, under like feeding they can be grown to maturity, making the conditions for all the same, so that experiments with these animals would be much more valuable and conclusive than if their earlier feeding and environments had been widely different.

"*Sixth* The yearly growth of the animals under like conditions and feeding, and the amount of food consumed for the several breeds in proportion to their live weight, is of value and importance to the dairymen, and would form a part of the trial.

"*Seventh.* At least four animals of each breed should be had—two heifers and two steers. The two heifers from each breed would be the beginning for a herd, finally enabling us to study the breed characteristics in the production of milk and butter. Two steers from each breed, fed and grown to maturity and fattened, would show much as to the relative values of the dairy breeds for beef.

"*Eighth.* The question of which is the more profitable for the dairy, a small cow or a large one, is of much importance, and what place is better fitted to investigate this subject than an experiment station?

"*Ninth.* Whether with two foods of similar composition both will affect equally the milk and butter yield, or whether one will tend more to the production of body fat and less to an increase of the milk.

"*Tenth.* The influence of the various grains fed separately and combined in rations, and to what extent the chemical and physical properties of butter are influenced by different foods.

"I have but briefly indicated the general scope of the proposed investigation, but I cannot but think it will meet your entire approval and receive your co-operation, and that of your associates, in this important branch of our agricultural industry. Sincerely yours,

"PETER COLLIER,
"*Director.*"

Mr. POWELL: I will say that the scope of the experiments is broad; it takes in nearly everything—or is intended to take in everything—for which a breed of cattle is used. It seems to me that we have a breed of cattle that is better adapted to make a fine showing in that respect than any other. I also feel that experiments in this line will be of greater value than almost any others that can be made with any breed of cattle. This matter has been brought to our attention before it has been acted upon by any of the other associations, and it seems to me that prompt and favorable action on the part of this body would tend to place us before that institution in a favorable light, showing our hearty co-operation, and we would not fail to get a fair and just, and it seems to me a valuable, report, which would be to the advantage of our breed, providing we can furnish the right animals. The important thing to be considered is the kind of animals we shall furnish. He does not ask us to contribute any animals, but he asks us in what manner animals may be obtained by the experimental station at the least possible expense. If it is left for those gentleman to purchase their own cattle, I am afraid they will not purchase as judiciously as it is for the interest of this Association to have it done, and it seems to me proper to refer this matter to the Board of Officers, to make such selection of animals as they deem best; for instance, two animals for beef purposes, adapted to that particular purpose, and instead of two females, I would suggest four, and let the proposition be made with the understanding that we comply with this. We make a report to them that we will furnish four females and two males, providing any four other breeds of those mentioned by him will do the same. That would be my idea of making the report.

Mr. MILLER. I would heartily endorse all that Mr. Powell has said, but I would suggest that if we confine the number to four females it would make the herd so large at the experimental station that the experiments will not be as thorough as though the number were smaller. If they have five or six breeds, and take six animals of each, it will make a pretty large herd to experiment with. I think I would leave the matter of numbers to the Board of Control of the experiment stations.

Mr. POWELL: You will notice he says that he wants these heifers for the purpose of nucleus. If that is his idea, he will not object to taking four animals to start with. If he has four intstead of two, he will be so much further advanced, and my idea is that it is risky to stake the reputation of any breed of animals on one or two animals selected as calves. Any man who has experience in the matter sees the danger of risking the reputation of even a family on one or two calves. By selecting four it gives us a better opportunity than if we only select two.

Mr. MILLER: As a breeder of Holsteins, I agree with Mr. Powell entirely, but as a member of the Board of Control of the experiment station, I would say that the expense of such a trial would be considerable. It is hard for us to get all the appropriation from the state that we now need, and for that reason I think it would be more practicable if the number is confined to two steers and two females.

Mr. POWELL: The proposition that we make establishes them a precedent of having these animals furnished without any expense to the station, which evidently in his report he does not expect. My idea is that we establish the precedent of furnishing them without charge, and while it is not absolutely imperative, I should insist pretty strongly on having four representatives.

Mr. MILLER: I would add to Mr. Powell's motion that we make an appropriation to the Board of Officers to draw upon the Treasurer for, say $2,000.00.

Mr. POWELL: My idea is that we should leave it to the Board of Officers to draw what in their judgment is necessary.

THE PRESIDENT: The chair would state that in the St. Louis Experimental Station, or at the Agricultural College of Missouri, who sent us two or three communications with a great flourish of trumpets as to what the different breeds of cattle were going to do, that when they found the Holstein-Friesian Association were ready, and our calves were ready for delivery, all the others backed out, and I think you will have about the same experience here.

Mr. YEOMANS: I think the interest of the Association would be better served to have the number not less than four, and, perhaps, if the Board of Officers have charge, they might say four, more or less, and I would suggest that if there are no competitors there, it would be almost folly to send animals and have to pay for them; but if there are two or more breeds willing to come in as competitors — not necessarily four, but two or more — I would favor it.

THE PRESIDENT: As the chair understands the motion of Mr. Powell, and the remarks which have followed it, the question before us is that the Association is ready to enter into competition with any other breeds that may be sent there. Are you ready for the question?

The question was called for, and carried as stated by the President.

Mr. HUIDEKOPER: Mr. President, I desire to call the attention of the gentlemen present to the matter of bulls. We all know that there are a great many cheap bulls put upon the market — a great many bulls that are not fit to be used as bulls. While this matter is not advertised in the call of the meeting, it strikes me as being a subject that may be discussed to advantage. I understand the Hereford Association requires breeders to send in their list of bull calves for registry, and the breeders may strike out a percentage of those bulls — I forget whether it is ten per cent or twenty per cent; whether it is one bull in ten or one bull in twenty. If the owner of those bulls does not strike out one bull in ten, the Secretary strikes out one in ten, and only records nine in ten. It seems to me if we could devise some satisfactory means of culling our bulls it would be an advantage to the breed, although I do not quite see how it can be done satisfactorily.

Mr. E. A. POWELL: I would like to hear the ideas of our President upon the subject.

PRESIDENT SINGERLY: I think the registry last year was 4,000 bulls and about 6,000 heifers; about that proportion. Now, there is not a member of this Association who does not know that the ratio of registered bulls to that of registered calves and heifers is out of all proportion to the use or the services required, or the necessity of that service. I attempted to bring this matter up two years ago before this Association. We ought to have some rule adopted in regard to the registration of bulls. It is not the mere fact that a bull is descended from a registered sire and dam, but for the purpose of the improvement of the breed, and for the general benefit of the Association. If some rule was adopted after the manner of the standard registry of trotting-horses, that is, that no bull calf should be registered except from a dam eligible to the advanced registry list, or from a dam producing a certain amount of milk a year, which would entitle her to the advanced registry list, and even that, I do not believe, will last us more than a year or two, for the reason that on account of the development of the cows, I think that in the next two or three years practically all of those of which any care at all has been taken in the breeding will be eligible to the advanced registry list. I say if some such rule as this was adopted, it would be the right thing to do. I would like to hear from any gentleman who is opposed to it; I can conceive of no reason, either as regards advantage to the individual breeder or the advantage of the Association, why we should not cut down the registry of bulls seventy-five per cent. I think instead of registering four thousand bulls this year, it would be better for every one present to have registered one thousand.

Mr. HORR: It seems to me that it is very fortunate that our President has introduced this subject before the Board, because there are a good many present, and I presume that among us we can devise something between this and next year. At the same time, if we do hit upon a plan that gives substantial help, we will be the first to do it. The real trouble is that nature is against us. A dam can have one, or at the very most two calves in a year; while the sire can get fifty or one hundred, and there has been only one relief found, and that has been the knife. We hear of no trouble among the fast horses of the country. People have come to see that it is not advisable to leave their colts for stallions unless they are wonderfully well bred, and so they castrate them; and castration is the simple solution of this matter finally. Whether we can enforce castration or not by some rule remains to be seen.

THE PRESIDENT: We cannot enforce it, but we can turn around and enforce rules of registration.

Mr. HORR: I should be very much in favor of that, but there would be a great deal of objection. As I understand it, there are not perhaps more than twelve, or twenty firms at the out side, represented in our registration books, unless you go back to the Dutch-Friesian. The great bulk of the owners and breeders of Holsteins have not a single animal recorded in the advanced registration, and therefore they will have to have their knives well sharpened or else we would force them to registration. How is eligibility ascertained except by the inspection and the proper certificates? And they would have to go through precisely the same form to establish the fact of eligibility; and having to incur the expense, they would presumably take their certificates. Now, I am not talking in this strain because I am not in favor of it; I am in favor of as rigid a plan as can be devised which will be just and equitable.

Mr. HUIDEKOPER: I move that a committe be appointed to present to this association at the next meeting plans with this object in view.

Mr. HORR: Will you not add to that, and serve the proper notice.

Mr. HUIDEKOPER: That is covered as a matter of inference.

Mr. G. D. WHEELER: I move that that committee consist of the Board of Officers.

Motion seconded and carried.

THE PRESIDENT: The question before us is that the matter of the registration of bull calves be referred to the Board of Officers, they to report at the next meeting.

Question put as stated, and carried.

Mr. Stevens, Chairman of the Committee on Proxies, made the following report: That Smiths, Powell & Lamb are entitled to 61 proxies; S. Hoxie, 2 proxies; H. Langworthy, 14 proxies; S. Burchard, 14 proxies; George D. Wheeler, 1 proxy; J. L. Stone, 2 proxies; Jere Allis, 2 proxies; T. G. Yeomans, 4 proxies; C. W. Horr, 3 proxies; C. J. Lord, 1 proxy; W. M. Liggett, 4 proxies; S. N. Wright, 3 proxies; W. G. Powell, 3 proxies; F. C. Stevens, 1 proxy; F. L. Houghton, 18 proxies; Thomas B. Wales, 44 proxies; M. L. Sweet, 12 proxies. Total, 189.

On motion of Mr. Miller, the report of the Committee on Proxies was accepted and placed upon the minutes.

THE PRESIDENT: The next thing in order is the election of officers. We have to elect a President, First, Second, Third, and Fourth Vice-Presidents, Treasurer, three Directors for two years, Secretary and Editor, and Superintendent of Advanced Registry. The unwritten law of the association is that the President is only elected for one year.

Nominations for President are now in order.

Mr. HORR: I have the very great pleasure of nominating my friend from Michigan, Mr. M. L. Sweet, as candidate for President of our Association for the ensuing year.

Upon Motion of Mr. Liggett, the nominations for President were declared closed.

Mr. YEOMANS: I move that in this, as well as the subsequent elections, where there is only one candidate named, that the Secretary be authorized to cast the ballot of the Association for that candidate. Motion seconded and carried.

The Secretary cast the ballot of the Association as directed, and Mr. Sweet was declared elected.

Mr. Yeomans presented the name of Mr. Edgar Huidekoper, of Meadville, Penn., for First Vice-President.

There being no further nominations for the office of First Vice-President, the Secretary cast the ballot of the Association for Mr. Huidekoper for that office, and he was declared elected.

Mr. Langworthy presented the name of Eugene Smith, of Nashville, Tenn., for the office of Second Vice-President of the Association for the ensuing year.

There being no further nominations for the office of Second Vice-President, the Secretary cast the ballot of the Association for Mr. Smith for that office, and he was declared elected.

Mr. William Brown Smith presented the name of Mr. F. L. Houghton, of Putney, Vt., for the office of Third Vice-President for the ensuing year.

There being no further nominations for the office of Third Vice-President, the Secretary cast the ballot of the Association for Mr. Houghton for that office, and he was declared elected.

Mr. Burrell presented the name of Mr. William M. Liggett, of Benson, Minn., for the office of Fourth Vice-President for the ensuing year.

There being no further nominations for the office of Fourth Vice-President, the Secretary cast the ballot of the Association for Mr. Liggett for that office, and he was declared elected.

Mr. Burchard presented the name of William Brown Smith, of Syracuse, N. Y., for the office of Treasurer for the ensuing year.

There being no further nominations for the office of Treasurer, the Secretary cast the ballot of the Association for Mr. Smith for that office, and he was declared elected.

Mr. E. A. Powell presented the name of Mr. William M. Singerly, of Philadelphia, Penn., for the office of Director for two years.

First Vice-President Gerritt S. Miller took the chair, and declared that there being no further nominations to the office of Director for two years, the Secretary was authorized to cast the ballot of the Association for Mr. Singerly for that office.

Mr. Singerly was declared elected.

President Singerly resumed the chair.

Mr. L. T. Yeomans presented the name of Mr. W. G. Powell for the office of Director for two years.

There being no further nominations for this office, the Secretary cast the ballot of the Association for Mr. Powell, and he was declared elected.

Mr. Huidekoper presented the name of Mr. Gerritt S. Miller as a Director of the Association for two years.

Mr. Horr presented the name of T. G. Yeomans for the same office.

There being no further nominations for this office, the meeting proceeded to the election by ballot.

Mr. Isaac C. Otis and Mr. Dudley Miller were appointed tellers by the chair, and reported that a total of 198 votes had been cast, of which Mr. Yeomans received 146 and Mr. Miller 52.

Mr. Miller moved that the election of Mr. Yeomans be declared unanimous. Motion seconded and carried, and Mr. Yeomans was declared elected.

Mr. D. H. Burrell was nominated as a Director of the Association for two years.

There being no further nominations for this office, the Secretary cast the ballot of the Association for Mr. Burrell, and he was declard elected.

Mr. W. G. Powell presented the name of Mr. Thomas B. Wales, of Iowa City, Iowa, for the office of Secretary and Editor of this Association for the ensuing year.

There being no further nominations for this office, Mr. Wales was declared elected.

Mr. Huidekoper presented the name of Mr. S. Hoxie for the office of Superintendent of Advanced Registry.

There being no further nominations for this office, the Secretary cast the ballot of the Association for Mr. Hoxie, and he was declared elected.

Mr. STEVENS: Mr. President, I desire to call the attention of the members of the Association to the fact that there has been a new organization formed in this city for the purpose of getting up an exposition in September next, from the 4th to the 14th. Half a million dollars has already been subscribed, and they desire to have the co-operation of all breeders of live-stock and of all the different interests that we represent. We would like to have all members of this Association, and all other similar associations, join us in making this a success, and we would be very happy to receive contributions to the capital stock, so as to make it extend all over the country. We ask this for the purpose of insuring success, and that the interest may be wide-spred. We would also like this Association to furnish to the Secretary, Mr. C. W. Robinson, who is present, the names of some parties who are considered competent judges of Holstein stock. We would also ask breeders representing other cattle to do the same. We would also like to receive suggestions from other parties who have exhibited cattle heretofore as to the best manner of building sheds, etc., for the cattle. We would also like this Association to remember us in the distribution of special prizes, and we would ask that they duplicate the prizes where Holstein stock comes in competition with other breeds. We intend to make a butter and milk test that will be different from any previous one. We would like a committee to formulate these premiums and make it a success. We have here a cut of the building of which the plans are already drawn. It will be the largest building of the kind in the country. Now, I would like to have Mr. Robinson make any statements in reference to the matter that he may desire.

Mr. ROBINSON: Mr. President and gentlemen, I do not know that I have anything to add to what Mr. Stevens has said. I will simply state that the object of this fair is to give the most liberal premiums that have ever been given for live-stock — that is, where they have considered all different classes together. You can easily ascertain who its incorporators are if you so desire. The money has been put up. We would be glad to have you take stock in it if you would, not but that the stock has already been taken, and those who have it are willing to retain it, but we feel the importance of having such representative men as form this Association interested in it, so that if any one does desire to take any of the stock, whether a small amount or large, they may do so, although the stock is all taken.

Now, the incorporators of this institution are moneyed men, and are in favor of the advancement of the breeding interests of the country and the industrial interests generally, and they propose to put up larger amounts of money than have ever been put up, and to hold out what they think are better inducements than have heretofore been extended, and they desire the hearty co-operation of this Association.

Mr. E. A. POWELL: If there are no further suggestions or discussion of the subject, I move that the chair appoint a committee of five to take into consideration this matter of recommending a list of names from which the different associations can select judges to pass upon this breed of cattle.

I move that such a committee of five be appointed to report at a later session of the meeting.

Motion seconded and carried.

THE PRESIDENT: Mr. C. J. Lord has given notice that he will bring before the meeting a motion to amend Section 8 of Article IV. of the By-Laws. The chair would state for the information of the Association, that the object of the amendment is to do away with the present fee of $25.00 attached to imported animals.

Mr. C. J. LORD: My object in presenting this question before the Association was that at the present time there seems to be no money made in the importation of cattle from Holland to this country. The prices have fallen here below those to which these cattle would come if imported and brought over as a matter of business or as a matter of speculation, to take them as a general importation. The only possible object that I can see in importing animals to this country now would be representatives of some particular family that a breeder or importer might own and desired to get more of the same family that were still left in Holland; and as I said before, it being a fact that it is almost impossible to import them as a matter of speculation, it seems to me it would be better to reduce this fee, and make the fee the same as that made and provided for home-bred animals, and give the person who desired to import these few animals the advantage of importing them at such fees. It is a matter that I am not particularly interested in myself, but it would seem to me that it would be better for the Association to encourage the bringing of a few superior animals. And certainly if the family is not a superior one, they would not desire to add any more animals to it of that family, and it would seem to me that rather than keep them from importing these animals by a $25.00 registry fee, it would be better to lower the fee and thus encourage the importation.

Mr. HORR: Mr. President, with due respect to Mr. Lord, I move that this matter be laid upon the table. We have voted upon this subject every time that I have been present, and I believe that there is almost a unanimity upon the subject, and that it is not necessary to occupy the time of the Association in discussing it. It seems to me to be a very plain proposition, that, since for three years we have made importers pay $25.00, we do not now want to change the rule.

Mr. Horr's motion to lay the matter upon the table was seconded and carried.

Mr. W. G. Powell moved that when the meeting adjourn, it adjourn to meet in Buffalo next year, the third Wednesday in March.

Mr. Liggett moved to amend by naming New York City in place of Buffalo.

The nominations for places being closed, a *viva voce* vote was taken, which resulted in the selection of New York City as the place of the next meeting.

The chair announced as the committee of five provided for in Mr. Powell's resolution in connection with the fairs, Messrs. E. A. Powell, H. Langworthy, Jere Allis, C. W. Horr, and M. L. Sweet.

Upon motion, a recess was taken until 2 o'clock P. M.

AFTERNOON SESSION.

The President called the meeting to order, and announced that Professor I. P. Roberts, of Ithaca, N. Y., would read his paper on —

THE PRODUCTS OF THE DAIRY COW.

Why should the husbandman keep dairy cattle for the production of food for man, when plants of innumerable varieties and kinds furnish all the life-sustaining elements in much simpler and more inexpensive forms? We raised 72,000,000 acres of corn for 63,000,000 of inhabitants, or twenty-three bushels of corn for every man, woman, and child in the United States. The noted German investigator, Dr. L. Landois, gives the following as a daily ration for a man at moderate work:

Albuminoids	4.6 ounces.
Carbhydrates	14.4 ounces.
Fats	3. ounces.
Salts	1. ounce.
	23. ounces dry matter.

This gives a nutritive ratio of 1:4.7.

Corn alone does not give a properly balanced ration; but if we mix with a bushel of corn ten (10) pounds of cotton-seed meal we have, in the required proportions of Albuminoids and carbhydrates, forty-three (43) daily rations for a grown man. This gives a basis for computation. To feed our 63,000,000 of people one year would require 534,760,000 bushels of corn and 2,673,800 tons of cotton-seed meal.

Deducting the corn consumed from last year's crop, we have a surplus of 921,400,000 bushels. Suppose 7,500,000 horses and mules are necessary for the production of the corn and cotton, and suppose we feed each one a peck of corn per day, there would still be left 231,000,000 bushels of corn.

We raise 6,300,000 bales of cotton or 2,835,000,000 pounds. For every pound of cotton raised we must raise two pounds of seed, and as the cotton-seed meal that can be produced is but 7-20 of the seed used in its production, we have in round numbers 1,000,000 tons of cotton-seed meal; this is not enough, and in order to supply the deficiency the 231,000,000 bushels of surplus corn may be traded for 60,000,000 bushels of beans, and these added to the cotton-seed meal furnishes the proper amount of food.

This corn, beans, and cotton-seed meal, if mixed and properly baked, will make better bread than is attainable by 10,000 human beings in other countries. Then why should not Americans use these cheap and abundant foods? Why not dispense with our milk and honey, butter and cheese, fruits and vegetables, and devote the larger share of our time to the acquisition of knowledge, to recreation, and to enjoyment? Why all this toil and expenditure of mental energy to make food dearer? Is not the indulgence in aromatic and concentrated foods but yielding to vicious and depraved appetites? These are fair questions although they may be new, and if we cannot answer them, we have no excuse for our meeting here to-day; neither have we any excuse for breeding dairy cattle, although they may be unexcelled in the production of milk, butter, and cheese.

The use of cheap kinds of food such as are mentioned above may, under stress of circumstances, be necessary for short periods, but when used for generations, who can foretell the results on civilization? "The fall of Egypt," says Buckle, "was due to an abundance of cheap food more than to any other cause." It is believed by close students that abundant unconcentrated food led to the extinction on this continent of the people who resided here long anterior to the advent of the Europeans.

History does not furnish a single instance of a nation rising to any degree of civilization whose food was composed of a few unconcentrated vegetable products. Not a single valuable variety or breed of domestic animals has been developed or improved without improving their food?

It is all well enough to talk of economy, and compute the amount of nutrients in various foods, yet it is far more important that we ascertain the quality and the power required to digest them.

Tell me the kinds of food a nation uses, and I will indicate the exact point of civilization to which that nation has arrived. The worm, which uses the same elements as man to sustain life, takes them direct from the soil, unconcentrated and unmanufactured. Its powers of instinct and reason are so small that it is totally incapable of protecting itself from the early bird.

Other classes of animals feed upon plants. These have advanced one step in animal development simply because the quality of their food has been improved.

Advance a step further, and we find carniverous animals. The fox that has surrounded the spring chicken is quite as cunning as the African, and the lion that lies down with the lamb — inside of him — is more courageons than the Eskimo.

True, enlightened man eats of both the vegetable and animal kingdoms, but he takes the first opportunity to so force and improve the grasses that they shall direct all their final energies to the production of the highly concentrated seed. He so selects, and dungs, and grafts, and dwarfs the trees of the forest that in time they bring not leaves alone, fit only for food for the lower animals, but luscious digestible peaches and yellow appetizing pippins.

He gathers the golden grain already twice concentrated, but he is not content; so he feeds it to the waiting kine, and once more the elements of life are worked over into juicy steaks. Still he is not satisfied; he would make this food yet more perfect, so he calls to his aid the fire to improve this thrice refined product in order that it may be meat indeed for man made in the likeness of his creator.

With this improved diet man is now enabled to construct, invent, and create. With this added knowledge he soon discovers that there is a still higher class of food. Immediately he selects and breeds and feeds that complex organism the cow, and lo! the land flows with milk — the perfect food.

He also finds that he may divide and improve for various uses this fourfold rectified food, and lo! he has enchained a golden grain of butter that has slipped down to him from the Gods on a sunbeam. And now you still ask me why we breed and feed the dairy cow; why labor and toil to concentrate, rectify, improve, and develop the appetizing volatile oils and aromas in the food which sustains our bodies?

For your answer I bid you to a feast. Come with me to the wretched home of the Indian. In his cold and cheerless wigwam, composed of poles and skins of wild beasts, sit we down as guests of human beings less cleanly and less companionable than the brutes of the field. A single stolen kettle contains the putrid entrails and carcass of some wild animal, garnished, perhaps, with a few kernels of maise and the bitter roots of some wild plant of the wood. It cannot be denied that he lives most economically and with little toil and thought. His highest reach at improvement is the bow and arrow. He could not originate or invent if he would. This is the type of men which is produced by the use of a too primitive food.

And now I bid you to another feast. One of butter and milk, sugar, luscious fruits, and beautiful flowers. And what effect have these dear and concentrated foods upon the man who consumes them? Immediately he seizes upon all the forces of nature and binds them to his chariot wheels. He calls upon the lightnings, and they carry his messages to the uttermost parts of the earth. He harnesses the energy of the bowels of the earth, and it transports him from land to land and from sea to sea. He speaks, and dumb wheels and levers and cams record his thoughts and preserve them for the use of untold millions. He talks, and flinty steel and iron hear and remember, and years afterwards the child may listen to the father's kindly words of wisdom, may hear the very tones and recognize the voice of one whose body has long since returned to dust.

Isaiah prophecied that when Christ should come "He should eat butter and honey, that he might know to refuse the evil and choose the good."

He who spends his energies in determining how to procure the greatest amounts of nutrients for the least expenditure of mental and physical force has only half learned how to live. But he who has learned to sustain the body by foods which require the least amount of energy to transform them into noble enduring thoughts and deeds and God-like aspirations has solved the problem of how best to make them minister to our higher natures.

A pound of fat pork costs one-half or one-third as much as a pound of butter; the pork is best utilized by vigorous exertion in the open air; but the very exertion required to utilize it consumes its energy and leaves little to sustain those organs which are brought into active use in mental labor; butter, on the contrary, requires little expenditure of vital power to convert it into heat and energy for the brain and nerves.

So our province as farmers is not so much to produce quantity as quality; not so much to furnish physical force as brain energy.

Does the product of the cow furnish this energy in the most available form? H. Critchett Bartlett, an eminent authority on the digestion and assimilation of fat in the human body, answers, "Whatever description of fat may have been eaten, it must be so far transformed as to approach in composition to that of butter, or the fat of milk which has passed through the mammary glands." And this is the reason why butter is better food for man than cotton-seed meal or tallow and lard; it "has passed through the mammary glands." The tenderest infant partakes of milk, and without visible exercise, transforms it most rapidly into healthy living tissue. As the child grows older and requires food for thought, he eliminates the water from the milk and has the concentrated products — butter and cheesy matter. He adds to the skill of the manufacturer that of the chemist, and transforms the cheesy matter into a rich, digestible, nitrogeneous food. But in this operation the sugar is lost; he seizes the tropical cane, wrings out the glistening crystals, and his food is again perfected.

The author quoted above adds: "It may not be generally known that butter is, to a certain extent, easily rendered soluble in water" by a process similar to the action of the digestive fluids in the small intestine, while if other fats are treated in like manner 95 per cent will be found to be insoluble and floating on the surface of the liquid; and "it is this peculiarity that affords the distinctive difference between pure butter and the common fats with which it may be adulterated."

If these things be so, and if I draw my conclusions logically, may we not without egotism feel an honest pride in the improvement we have wrought in a noble breed of dairy cattle, already good when we received them from the dike-girt polders of the Netherlands. No people on the face of the round globe are advancing so rapidly in knowledge, in the arts of peace, and in all that goes to make up beautiful, happy, enlightened homes, and secure their perpetuation, as the Americans; and no people consume so much butter and sugar per capita.

Abraham, when he entertained the three angels, set before them butter and milk; so I make no excuse for spreading before men food fit for angels — butter of Holsteins, cheese of Friesians, and milk of Holstein-Friesians.

THE PRESIDENT: The next address upon the programme is by Mr. C. W. Horr, of Wellington, Ohio, subject —

FARMS AND FARM LIFE.

Mr. President, and Gentlemen of the Association: It is with very great regret that I commence a few remarks, which I shall offer for your consideration with an apology; but I have been so overwhelmed with business since I received our Secretary's kind invitation to address you upon this occasion, that it has been utterly impossible for me to reduce to writing what I should say. So you must pardon me for talking extemporaneously, and if the reporter will kindly afford me an opportunity to revise what I shall say before its publication, I will give it such grammatical and rhetorical revision as it may require.

We hear in the United States a great deal said about the dignity of labor. Newspapers are full of it, political speakers particularly so, and yet, when you get right down to the very bottom of the American heart, labor — and I mean work with the hands — is regarded as ignoble, and is practically so regarded. How many gentlemen who are now listening to me, and who are, as probably most of you are, fathers of sons, are planning to make real good farmers of your boys? If you have a boy who is especially bright, with what pleasure do you listen to his little declamations. If he writes an essay which is well expressed, you forthwith say, "there is a boy of whom I can make a lawyer;" if piously inclined, possibly a minister, or perhaps you will say a physician. If he seems to be a fellow who has a business turn, but not very fond of books, you will make a merchant of him, or perhaps a railroad man will enter your vision. But who of you would think of saying, "I have a boy who is so bright and so full of energy and thoroughness that I can make a successful farmer of him? This other boy, who does not seem to do anything well, who has perhaps got barely a gift of gab, why that fellow would not make a good farmer, I will have to let him be a doctor or a lawyer, or, perhaps, a minister?" Did you ever hear of such a sentiment in your life? When we speak of the dignity of labor and the farmer's calling, most of us mean that we would like to have our neighbor's boy be a good farmer, and our own boy a good professional man. "Ah," says the proud father, "I am going to educate my boy. I am going to save him from the hardship and labor that I have had to endure, and put him in a position where he can get his living without labor."

Now, the birds of the air practically get their living without work; the fish of the sea do not have to labor in order to live; the beasts of the field may get a very comfortable living without daily labor. Mankind cannot do this; and yet do you claim that the Heavenly Father in creating us has put us at a disadvantage, and has given every bird that wings its way through the air, and every fish that swims in the sea, and every beast that roams through the forest an advantage over the human family? I say no. And I want to preface what I have to say about farms and farm life with the assertion that labor is not a curse. We have no occasion to shed tears because we have to get our living by the sweat of our brow. If I were called upon at this moment, without reflection, to describe the most unhappy creature upon the face of the earth, I should instantly describe it to be the person who has nothing to do with brain, with hand, or with heart. Supposing there should come a Vanderbilt here who should say to you gentlemen, " I want to hire every one of you for $20,000.00 a year." "Is it very laborious?" "Not at all; but I want to hire you, and I will pay you $20,000.00 a year." "What for?" "I want to hire you ten hours a day to go out and sit where you can see nothing but waste and look at a post, that is all. For one year I want you to sit down and look at a post — $20,000.00." Is there a man who would accept that situation? No; there is not a man who knows enough to buy Holstein-Friesians who would not know enough to reject that offer. No man who is worthy of being called such could live through a year sitting in absolute idleness, doing nothing, and getting $20,000.00 for it. Now, if I was asked to describe the most fortunate man on the face of the earth, it would be the man who has the most complete opportunities for the use of his brain; opportunities best adapted to his peculiar mind, who is surrounded by the best, the most loving, and the most intelligent family, and who has the most to do, providing it was not too much. To tell us that God has made us with these fingers, and this wonderful thumb-arrangement so that we can handle tools, wield axes and hoes and spades, and then that it is a misfortune that this work had to be done, is to accuse providence itself of the very grossest lack of wisdom. To tell me that there is any more dignity in sitting down in your office and listening to the testimony in a divorce suit, and then going into court for the purpose of separating that man from that woman than there is in going upon a farm and clearing it up and developing it, is asking me to believe one of the most absurd things that a man ever listened to.

The first thing that I want to do is to try and get those who hear me to go home and think that it would be a nice thing if you happen to have a boy who knows enough so that you can, with reasonable expectation of success, make a farmer of him. If you have one boy in your family who you are afraid is not going to amount to much, make a lawyer of him; or if you are so pious that you could not conscientiously do that, make a preacher of him. It is not as difficult to point the way to heaven as it is to take hold of a farm and do justice by it. If you have another boy who has but little brain, and no very large amount of muscle, who you really do not know what to do with, you go then into your village, and go to the dry goods merchant and say, "here is a fellow who looks first rate; he is not very bright, but I think he could measure calico and ribbons and silks, and sell them to your customers very successfully." That would be my recommendation.

Then let us believe in farming as a decent, respectable business. That is the first proposition that I would lay down. Now, then, if a man is going to be a farmer, I would first suggest to him that he have a plan and a purpose, and before he makes his investment in the farm, he sits down like a business man and enters into an account as to what he can probably do with it. "I am going to take this farm; it is going to cost me, say, $10,000.00; I am going to use it, finally, when I have developed it, for the following purposes." And after an examination of its possibilities, he makes up his account to see whether he can "get there" or not — whether he can make it pay. Did you ever stop to think that there is no other business but farming where such incompetents could even live? Bankruptcy would follow every single person who engaged in any commercial business who put no more thoroughness and no more skill into it than does the average farmer. Competition compels the merchant and the manufacturer to the very uttermost effort and to the very best methods. His success depends almost wholly upon his skill. Not so with the farmer. He is in partnership with nature. The grass grows spontaneously. The results of his efforts depends upon the rains of heaven, the rays of sunshine, and the productiveness of the soil, and, of course, in another aspect of it, upon his judgment and thoroughness. "But," says some friend, "you mean to say that you do not pity the farmer for having to work so many hours?" Yes, I do, in a certain sense, some of them; but if I stood up before all the farmers in the world, and could say but one thing, it would not be "my dear, overworked agriculturists, I am sorry you have to work so much." I have known more men who did not work ten hours a day, but who ought to have done so in justice to their farms, than I have of men who have worked fifteen or sixteen hours a day when they ought not to. I have known more men who violated God's laws by not working all the six days of the week than I have who violated the Sabbath, and yet when this subject is talked of at all, it is by some poor, timid person who is afraid the Sabbath is going to be used as a day of labor, and who is afraid the laboring men are working too many hours. Are you going to sit down in the legislative halls and by law fix the number of hours that the loving father and husband may work for his wife and his children and his own future. Is that to be measured by law? Is the strength and endurance of each arm to be measured by a rule that is passed in congress?

Now, I say, I have just the profoundest admiration for a young man who has only a few hundred dollars to make his first payment who will go about quietly and carefully and sensibly and hunt up a farm that he can buy on credit, except his first payment; who will then find a good, honest American girl — I do not care whether she is very handsome or not, if she is only very good and sensible and loves the young man, and who has got the sense and courage to lead her to the altar, and then go on to that farm, not to labor at first eight hours a day or ten hours a day, but to labor for himself, for his wife, and for the children who will probably come to them; as many hours as God gives him strength and endurance to labor; who will take that farm and look it over from the north to the south, and from the east to the west, will find where a ditch is needed, where there is a swamp that must be drained, where there is cumbering brush and undergrowth, where weeds need to be plucked out, who will find every field that has been impoverished by unskilful husbandry, and attend to that, who will say to his wife as he sits down by her side at night, "there is an awful job here, wife, but if I live five years from this day, there shall not be a square rod of land on this farm but what will bloom and blossom with productive vegetation. We have got this debt on us; we cannot go into society very much, and we must dress plainly, as our grand parents did, but we will have enough to eat, and every bit of it will be sweetened by hope that the mortgage will be lifted, and we will have a few books and newspapers and magazines, because we must not become intellectually sluggish, but the principle business of our life shall be to pay for this farm, to develop and pay for it; and when it is paid for, then our next business shall be to beautify it and to make it a beautiful home, with good, comfortable buildings, with flowers outside and in; and then, best of all, my dear, we will be a happy family."

Now, isn't that a decent life? Is there anything discouraging about that? But how many young men contemplate the purchase of a farm with that degree of seriousness and with that degree of method that I have recommended? How many young men there are who as they look at their future think that the farm is the last thing that they want. The picture I present to you is one, it seems to me, should be attractive to nine-tenths of the men of this country. Did you ever stop to think that we can have so many lawyers and so many doctors? Most people have got to get their living by work; that is a law of life and nature.

Having purchased his farm and got his plans laid out sensibly, is he going to raise Holsteins? If so, he must go at it methodically to select from the best stock he can get, and take the best care, that he may grow up the best herd of Holsteins that will be creditable. If it is to be a grain-farm, he masters the science of grain-raising, the theory and practice of it, and with the utmost thoroughness he goes ahead to do his business. The next thing I would say to that man would be, promise to do everything when it ought to be done. Have that degree of foresight that amounts almost to genius in this world, so that you will always get there, not like the slack man, but just at the right time, with all your work, so that it will be done when it ought to be. The difference between the thorough farmer and the other is, that one is always just behind and the other is always right on time. After he has got a proper plan, then, clear cut, in his head of what he wants to do, there must be promptness, and then I should say, thoroughness after promptness. What do I mean by that? I mean doing everything in the best and most thorough way. I was born upon a farm, and lived and worked upon one of them. When I became a young man, I had but little to do with farms for some years, and after that I had much to do with the handling of milk from a good many hundred farmers, and for the past several years I have been engaged a good deal in practical farming, with hired help, and it is astonishing what little assistance I can get on practical questions from a farmer. To illustrate, I ask them how shall I put on my manure, and I will get nearly as many answers as I ask men. There is no agreement about it. I ask the amount of wheat I shall sow, and I never asked a farmer one of those questions that I did not get an answer. But there is no agreement among them, and I find that back of their opinions there has been nothing but a little empirical practice. Each one of them has watched two or three crops of his own, and probably has taken from his father the method he has pursued, and has never scientifically investigated it at all.

In reference to fertilizers, one will be a great believer in bone, another in ashes, another in manure, and so on, and when I come to ask the question, what kind of fertilizer do I want for this muck, what do I want for this clayey soil, I get no practical answer from the farmers. These questions have not been thoroughly investigated by them. What I want is thoroughness; not only in execution, but thoroughness in the acquisition of information and knowledge which is so greatly needed to guide the farmer.

Now, I desire to say something in reference to home life. Contrast the farmer's life with the life of a man in business in a city. Go to New York and sit down quietly where you can watch those who pass by, and I declare there is very much in favor of the farmer's life, and I am not so bucolic as some people. I would not like to live where I would always hear the whip-or-will and never the whistle of the trains. I am not so devoted to nature as to always want to listen to the songs of the birds in the trees, and always be looking at the flowers in the fields; but I say there is very much to compensate the farmer for the seclusion of his life for what he looses by not living in villages and cities. In the first place, it is the very paradise for a home. The husband and the wife and the children are by themselves under just such influences as they choose to bring around their children. If a poet of to-day, or of yesterday, or of to-morrow, should sing of a home, it seems to me he must have in his mind a home upon a farm, where one is separated from the anxiety, the fret, and the worry, and eager pursuit for wealth that is found in every city and village of the United States.

Now, what kind of a home do we want? We want a home where, to borrow somewhat from my Bible friends, peace and love are to be found, first of all, and harmony. Of course, Holstein-Friesian men are nice husbands and sons, and, if we are fathers, very nice fathers. But notwithstanding all that, these remarks of mine may possibly reach some who are not members of this Association, and so pardon me for the remark that there is not one of my auditors who would think of being otherwise than extremely polite to his neighbor's wife on all occasions. Now, it does not make much difference to your neighbor's wife whether you are polite to her or not. She can get along very nicely with the politeness and the love of her husband even if her neighbor, Mr. Jones, is rather uncouth, because she is not very much in her neighbor Jones' society. There is one woman on the face of the earth, however, to whom the farmer, like any other gentleman, is under a sacred obligation to be courteous, affectionate, and polite upon all occasions, and that lady is his wife, because she had put into his hands her happiness and her welfare in this world. If there is so much roughness and boisterousness, so much that is not gentle in you that you have got to be offensive to some lady, call upon your neighbor and give his wife a blowing-up. She will not care very much about it, but just spare your own wife. When I was a little boy I lived and worked for my board and clothes in a good many families, and if there is one thing I pride myself upon it is a profound sympathy for the little boy. It seemed to me then that I would be a friend to the poor little boy all my life, and I think I have been so. I would never wound the feelings of a boy. How many men are there who, when they meet their neighbor's little boy, have a sunny smile and a pleasant word for him. Most farmers are full of tenderness to their own children, but some of them are not. There are some men who are pleasant to all children in their neighborhood except their own, but are cross, bearish, and uncomfortable in their own homes, by their own fireside, with their own children. The happiness of the children in the homes about you is not very much in your keeping, and if you must be cross and savage and disturb the happiness of some little boy every day, that is all right, but go to your neighbor's and get Mary and Willie around you and give them a blowing up, and the probability is the father will turn you out doors, as he ought to do, and then you will go to your own children.

The picture I would draw is this: A young man marrying a young girl — a good honest American girl, if possible, for they are the best girls in the world — going out on to a farm and paying for it, planting their characters upon that farm, feeling a sense of pride in its improvement and development, and in the increased productiveness of those acres, so that when the man dies and goes to his grave that farm will be there, a monument to his industry, to his thrift, to his economy, and to his good sense, and that the children he leaves will be a credit to his wisdom as a father, to his affection, and to his sound sense as the head of a family. I would have you men in fact be what you have been in theory, that is, believers in the dignity of actual, honest work; believers in the dignity of the life of a farmer as contrasted with that of any other man on the face of the earth. A farmer, if he is an honest, industrious, intelligent man, should be able to look the kings of the earth in the face, and say, "I am your brother;" the princes of the earth in their eyes, and say, "I am your brother." And if he behaves as well, he is their equal; for I say to you, and I am a believer in aristocracy, but it is an aristocracy of character, an aristocracy of industry, an aristocracy of intelligence, an aristocracy of manhood, and that is the kind of aristocracy that every American citizen should believe in.

THE PRESIDENT: The next address upon the programme is by Mr. E. A. Powell, of Syracuse, N. Y., subject—

THE BREEDING OF DAIRY CATTLE.

Of all the blessings which fall to the lot of any being, there is probably none so rich, so much to be desired, as to be *well-born* — born with ability, with natural powers, which enable the possessor to accomplish great achievements.

This is a rich inheritance, transmitted from one or more ancestors — frequently the concentration of qualities possessed in a lesser degree by numerous progenitors, reaching back through many generations. It is this concentration or happy union of ancestral qualities which places the fortunate possessor far in advance — far above all antecedents — in certain marked characteristics. The stronger any faculty, the more it is developed, and especially if it extends through every ancestral line, the more certain it is to be transmitted in a marked degree.

It is this principle of heredity, assisted by the influence of environment and development, in the human family that has given to the world long family lines of successful financiers, of renowned divines, able jurists, and great leaders.

The same laws of inheritance, the same influence of environment, the same marked effects of development apply with equal force to the animal kingdom.

This force, this power, this law of nature can be guided by the intelligent will of man, and thus become a valuable factor in the development and improvement of our domestic animals, but which is lost by our usual hap-hazard method of breeding.

It is a fixed law of nature that no quality can be transmitted which is not possessed by some ancestor, and hence if the intelligent breeder wishes certain qualities in the offspring, he will surely see that they are possessed by the parents — not only by one, but by both; for otherwise the desired characteristic of one may be counterbalanced by the opposite tendency of the other, and no progress be made.

As the influence of heredity extends through many generations, and is frequently more strongly marked in the second and third, it is exceedingly important that any desired quality which we wish to permanently establish be traced in unbroken lines through many generations. We are seeking for greater power — more force concentrated and exerted in a given direction; in the trotting or running horse, the power which produces speed; in the draft horse, that which moves great weight; in the beef animal, the power which converts food into flesh; in the dairy cow, that which converts the products of the soil into milk.

The intelligent, thinking breeder, by looking back through the history of experiments and results as they are portrayed in a well-established pedigree, discovers the channels whence flow the purest streams, rich in the qualities which he desires; and these with skill he unites, thus combining, accumulating, concentrating the desired forces of nature, and, by guiding them in the right direction, great progress is made.

To leap a high barrier, the experienced athlete goes back to get the additional force of momentum. So must we, to make the greatest progress in breeding, go back to secure the accumulated force of generations.

Not only should each progenitor be the possessor of superior power, but the force of each should be exerted in the direction in which progress is desired.

A thorough knowledge, an intelligent understanding, of the natural powers of each ancestor are essential, yes, indispensable, if we would make the most rapid progress in breeding for specific results. This knowledge can only be obtained from the actual performance of each individual or of its progeny; and therefore, to breed intelligently, we must familiarize ourselves with each ancestor — weigh each in the unerring scale of actual performance, and unite those forces which will give us the greatest accumulated power. Not only should we choose descendants of ancestors which have been tested on account of the unmistakable evidence of their ability which is thus furnished, but because the animal whose natural powers have been developed, expanded, and stimulated by use and exertion is much more certain to transmit those qualities in a marked degree. I wish to emphatically impress this idea. If you wish certain natural qualities in the offspring, develop the ancestors in that direction by actual performance. No more misleading fallacy can be advocated than the excuse which we so often see for not making records — for fear of injuring the vigor and constitution of the offspring. Understand me; I do not advocate, or believe in over-feeding, or forcing, so as to impair or weaken the constitution, but this is not necessary. Action and development means growth and strength; idleness means weakness and decay. The maintenance of perfect health requires the proper exercise and development of every faculty and organ;

this development means growth, an increase of power, which soon becomes so allied to nature as to be transmitted to coming generations. As consistent would it be to advocate the non-development of the human intellect, that our decendants might become intellectual giants. Experience has demonstrated that the descendants of the same ancestors, gotten after judicious development, are superior to those previously produced.

We can more fully appreciate the value of family relationship by glancing back over the history of the various breeds of domestic animals and noting the fact that a large majority of all those which have made themselves illustrious by their performances have descended from a very few families. In reviewing the honored roll of American trotters, how few names we find whose pedigree does not trace to some one of a half dozen great families. Go through the entire list of breeds, and similar facts are presented. No stronger evidence of the value of a good pedigree can be presented.

A few practical illustrations, the result of careful experiments in breeding, will convey a good idea of the great power which highly-bred, prepotent ancestors exert over the natural qualities of their progeny.

Two cows of the same breeding, quality, and production on the side of the dam, but by different sires, one bull being used on account of his superior appearance, the other for his breeding, were tested under like conditions, at about the same age, on the same kind and amount of food. The former cow gave about 10,500 pounds of milk in a year, while the other gave nearly 18,000 pounds; the former made about eleven pounds of butter in a week, while the latter made over twenty-three pounds.

Two heifers from the same dam, but by different sires, one of which was especially noted for the butter qualities of his daughters as well as that of his ancestors, were tested at about the same age, at the same season of the year, on a similar quality and amount of feed, when giving about the same amount of milk, and one actually made over 110 per cent more butter than the other.

Two cows by the same sire, one of them from a superior dam from a rich butter family, the other from a cow whose butter qualities had not been proven, were tested at the same age and under similar conditions. The former made over twenty-five pounds, and the latter eleven pounds per week.

A superior butter cow, from a noted butter family, was bred to her own brother for the express purpose of intensifying the rare butter qualities of a rich butter family. The product was a heifer, which, at twenty-eight months old, made 21 pounds 10¾ ounces of butter in a week, and 80 pounds 6 ounces in thirty days, averaging, for a week, one pound of butter from 13.23 pounds of milk.

A fine three-year-old heifer, from a deep-milking family, made 13 pounds of butter in a week, while her daughter, by a bull from a noted butter family, tested at the same age, has just made 19 pounds ¾ ounce in a week.

These are a few of the many carefully made tests, all from Holstein-Friesian cows, which could be given to illustrate the marvelous results which have been and can be produced by scientific breeding — by breeding with an intelligent understanding of the quality and capacity of the material at our command. In short, these tests convey some idea of what can be accomplished by careful selection and breeding for a purpose. We can hardly realize the progress which has been and can be made in milk and butter productions. No other breed is, in my judgment, capable of making such rapid progress, or of producing such marvelous results.

About seventeen years ago the whole dairy world was astonished at the reported yearly milk records of two Holstein-Friesian cows, which gave respectively 12,681 pounds and 14,027 pounds, which at that time so far surpassed all previous productions as to seem almost incredible. Year by year these records have been advanced until within this short period the standard has been raised for a cow to over 30,000 pounds, and within half that period the highest record for a two-year-old has been raised from 9,000 to over 18,000 pounds. During this entire time Holstein-Friesian cows have continually stood at the front.

The development of the breed in butter production began at a much more recent date, but the progress made has been equally as remarkable. Half a decade has hardly passed since a cow of this breed that would make a pound of butter from twenty-five pounds of milk was considered superior. Now thirteen to fourteen pounds is not unusual, while whole large families will average a pound of butter from sixteen to eighteen pounds of milk. Still greater advancement may be looked for in the future. In the past the breed has suffered by the large number of inferior animals which have been imported and bred without pedigree or family history or authenticated records whereby the superior could be distinguished from the worthless.

These inferior animals have been a great burden — a dead weight — which the better classes have had to carry, and which are still a curse to the breed; but when submitted to the trying ordeal of actual performance, the wheat is separated from the chaff.

The system of advanced registry which has been adopted by this Association, and which, I am glad to see, is meeting with such general favor, is doing much to assist in this sifting, rectifying, and refining process.

With the light and knowledge which is now being disseminated through the various stock journals and other sources, the people are becoming educated. Every breeder can, if he will, breed understandingly and well.

Too little attention is usually paid to the family, for when a large number of animals, all descendent from the same progenitor, have proven their superiority by performance, we are furnished with the best possible evidence of prepotency, and such individuals are vastly superior for breeding purposes to those of equal production which are not backed by such family relationship.

Herein we find the value of PEDIGREE, which should be a continuous history of great performances, extending through an unbroken line of illustrious ancestors.

Pedigree without performance is valueless; so performance without pedigree is robbed of half its worth, as it furnishes no evidence of prepotency. To build up a good herd we must have a solid foundation, laid with the best material. Select not only the best breed, but the best individuals from the best families, all proven by the surest of all tests — that of performance. Breed upwards; not downwards. Go up higher. The summit is still an unoccupied field.

Hereditary force or power is accumulative, increasing, intensifying by judicious breeding, and hence we can, if we will, make vastly greater progress in the future than we have in the past.

As the pure stream which issues from the fountain-head far up the mountain-side, which as it flows on continually widens and deepens by the addition of every rippling rill, every pebbly brook, every crystal spring or rushing stream with which it comes in contact, continually increasing in volume and power as it sweeps on to the great valley below, where, by the intervention of human genius and energy, it is again distributed by irrigation, rendering fertile and fruitful the otherwise barren plain, so the stream of animal life which issues from the royal fountain of pure breeding, wisely guided by an intelligent hand, flows on through successive generations, continually increasing in force and power, diffusing life and energy in its course, purifying every sluggish stream with which it comes in contact, reaching out farther and farther as generations come and go, until the entire species is strengthened, beautified, improved, and enriched by the concentration of those desirable qualities which distinguish the high-bred animal from the worthless mongrel.

THE PRESIDENT: The next address on the programme is by Mr. S. Hoxie, of Whitestown, N. Y., subject —

MILK SIGNS.

Cows in the wild state produce but little milk. Their ability to produce large quantities is acquired in the domesticated state, and is undoubtedly the result of demand, training, and food. It is the general impression that such ability, together with the ability to produce rich milk, may be discovered through outward signs. This has given rise to the science of selecting milch cows, if I may call the teachings on this subject a science. In this paper I simply report upon my own limited observations in this science. The conclusions that I have drawn are by no means established beyond doubt. Personally I hold myself liable to changes of views as investigation goes on.

Under the head of Milk Signs may be included all the outward appearances of cattle, and of their products, that indicate quantity, quality, or healthfulness of milk.

One of the most commonly accepted signs for both quantity and quality is what is called the "milk form." It may be described as a gradual widening of the animal from the front of the shoulders to the hips and setting on of the hind quarters. This widening is sometimes only lateral, and sometimes both lateral and perpendicular. To be perfect, the shoulders should be thin, the forward legs comparatively close together, the quarters without much flesh, and the appearance throughout the whole frame angular.

In the examination of upwards of four hundred Holstein-Friesian cows, I have found very few that have approached the perfect milk form. And in Jersey cattle that have come under my observation, I have found marked departures from this form in those of the highest reputation, especially in the spread of the forward legs and in the thickness of the animal through the heart. The most of these cows have not been angular. Their abdomens have been held well up, and their bodies have been round. The impression has become strongly fixed in my mind that curved lines are as indicative of milk-production as are angular lines.

Another of the commonly accepted signs is "a large udder, drawn up closely to the body, and well rounded at the sides." I think such formed udders are more apt to contain adipose tissue than lower hanging udders. A gentleman conversant with Jersey cattle remarked that he had never seen a remarkable butter cow that had not, as he termed it, "a broken down udder." The size of the udder, even if it could be exactly ascertained, I am persuaded, could not be implicitly relied upon as a measure of the milk-producing ability. There is a quality in the milk glands that must exist in different degrees of intensity in different animals that cannot be discovered by any outward appearances.

Another of the commonly received signs is "very large and very crooked lacteal veins." The lacteal veins carry the blood away from the udder toward the heart. There is no doubt that degrees in the size of these veins, and perhaps their degrees of crookedness, indicate degrees of milking ability. But it is quite clear that they are not exact measures of this ability. I have found, in many instances, cows having very large and very tortuous veins that were excelled in milking ability by cows with veins of less size and less crookedness. In some instances this has been very marked and surprising. And I am inclined to the opinion that these veins become varicose and tortuous from obstructions to the free and rapid flow of blood through them; in some instances from disease, and perhaps in other cases from the disproportion of the size of the orifices in the walls of the abdomen and chest to the amount of blood that is required to be carried away.

Another commonly-accepted sign is the orifices in the abdomen and chest, to which I have just referred. In some animals these orifices are only two in number — one on the right, and the other on the left side of the abdomen. These are called main orifices, and are usually larger than the others. In some cases these orifices are so large that the end of the forefinger may be fairly introduced into them. If I were obliged to choose any one of the so-called milk signs upon which to exclusively rely, it would be these orifices. Yet the impression should not be obtained that these are by any means exact measures or infallible indications of milking ability. I think reliance should be made more on the size than on the number of these orifices. They may be discovered in animals of all ages and both sexes, but of course appear much smaller in young animals. The larger their size, and the more numerous, other things being equal, the greater I should expect the milking ability of a cow to be, and the more would I expect the cow or bull to transmit this ability to their offspring.

Another of the signs quite widely accepted is the escutcheon. Writers and breeders have been arrayed for and against this sign with the intensity of partisans. On the one side it has been studied with the interest and confidence of devotees. On the other side it has been rejected with sneers and scoffs without study or observation. The great errors on the part of its advocates have been in assuming that it was infallible, and in giving mathematical values to various forms and minute tufts of hair. So far as my own observation has extended I have generally found a co-ordination in the comparative size and number of the orifices just described and the size and quality of the escutcheon. And when the mammary glands have been developed, the same co-ordination between them and the escutcheon has been also discovered, although in this there has been more exceptions.

There are two other signs advocated that may have value. It is claimed by many that openness between the spinal processes is an indication of milking ability. It is also claimed that broadness of these processes also indicates this ability. The condition in the chine in these cases is easily discoverable. In the latter case a depression may be felt along the middle of the chine lengthwise of the animal. In the former, depressions crosswise of the chine may be felt, into which one or more of the fingers may be placed. These depressions may have some relation to the size of the spinal cord and the size of the nerves thrown off from it, under which milk production is carried on in the laboratory of the udder.

There is another class of signs for which value is claimed by a limited class of dairymen and cattle-writers. Among these is "the tail reaching to hocks or below," hind legs bent backward at the hocks to an unusual degree, a protuberance under and between the jaws, called the "milk wart," crumpled horns, etc. Quite a noted writer on dairy subjects is reported as saying that he knew no signs of a good milch cow except a large udder and crumpled horns.

Another class of signs are largely relied upon to indicate superior richness of milk. These are oiliness and depth of color, from a pale to a deep orange, in the secretious of the skin. There is not a particle of doubt that the color of these secretions, the color of the fat in the tissues of the body, and the color of the milk often very closely correspond. Hence, as a general rule, the animal that has an abundance of yellow secretions on the skin will produce yellow flesh and tallow, and yellow milk. But as evidences of richness of quality of flesh or of quality of milk, these signs are now being rejected by some of our leading scientists. Prof. Alvord, whom we all know as a scientist and as an especial advocate of the Jersey breed of cattle, says: "It is certain that color is in no respect an indication of the quantity of fat in milk, or of the butter that milk will produce." In his published address before the last convention of the New York State Dairymen's Association this language is italicised. If practical dairymen will reflect upon this statement they will discover that it corresponds with their experience and observation. In the month of June, when our grasses are of a deep emerald-green, the milk of their cows is of a deeper color than in October and November, when the grasses have largely lost such greenness through the action of frosts; yet in the latter months milk is equally rich, and some times much richer. Richness of milk is very largely the result of wise and liberal feeding. I quote from Prof. Stewart's valuable work, entitled, *Feeding Cattle:* "Since certain very partial experiments were made in Germany to test the effect of special feeding upon the composition of milk, dairymen have been told to seek quality of milk in the breed, and not in the food. * * * * *" But since milk is made from the blood at the same degree of elaboration as fits it for assimilation into the tissues, and that what goes to lay on fat or build up flesh in the stall-fed animal goes to the udder in the milch cow, whatever food will do in increasing the aptness of an animal to fatten and in laying on and flavoring flesh, it will do, directed by intelligence, in increasing the secretion and improving the quality of milk. In philosophy and fact the quality and quantity of milk is as perfectly controlled by quality and quantity of food as is the quality and weight of flesh laid upon a stall-fed animal. This principle is widely confirmed by the observations and experiences of thousands of practical dairymen who have no axes to grind in this matter. Prof. Stewart quotes such experiences in proof of this statement.

Hon. Zadock Pratt, of Greene county, N. Y., in a statement made to the New York State Agricultural Society, reports a carefully conducted experiment on fifty cows owned by him during five consecutive years, from 1857 and including 1861, which shows to what a remarkable extent food and care affects the quality of milk: "The first year it required 39.2 pounds of milk for one pound of butter; the second, 33.3 pounds; the third, 29 pounds; the fourth, 23.3 pounds; the fifth, 21 pounds. The amount of butter per cow per year increased in the same proportion. The herd was made up of so-called 'native cows,' and consisted of substantially the same animals, there being only the ordinary changes in such a herd. * *" He was constantly improving his yield of butter by special feeding, and contrary to the German experiments, this increase in butter was not from increased yield of milk, but from an improved quality. It appears that the German experiments were only for very brief periods of feeding, while the experiences of dairymen show that improvement of quality requires long periods. For this reason we conclude that there is nothing really contradictory between the experiments of scientific men and the experiences of practical dairymen.

Passing from this point, I will refer to signs of healthfulness in milk. This is far more important than quality or quantity. Unfortunately this part of my subject has never been studied by scientific men, and what little I can offer must come mainly from my own observations.

Abnormal richness is undoubtedly a sign of chronic diseases in cows and unhealthfulness of milk.

My attention was first called to this about three years ago. A heifer came partially under my observation that had previously been sick from inflammation of the lungs. She recovered; had a calf, and was found to produce very rich milk. She was regarded by her owners as a prize. At length it was discovered that she had a chronic affection of the lungs. She was kept for some time, but, growing worse until there was no hopes of recovery, she was killed. These facts raised a suspicion that diseased conditions, especially of the lungs, might cause abnormal richness of milk. Limited inquiries were made of those who should know, but no positive answer could be obtained. At length a work on midwifery fell into my hands. It was by Cazeaux, a French author of the highest authority. Under the head of Lactation, I found the following language: "*The health of the nurse* is a matter of the highest importance. Chemical analysis shows that in diseases of any kind the proportion of solid constituents increases at the same time that the proportion of water decreases. According to the analysis of M. M. Becquerel and Vernois, this fact is more observable in *chronic diseases* than in acute febrile affections. Now, as M. Bouchut judiciously observes, this increase in the proportion of the solid principles of the milk is an unfortunate alteration, causing the child to be frequently affected with indigestion and consecutive enteritis— inflammation of the bowels. The milk of women suffering from *chronic diseases, phthisis*, for example, *exhibits a great alteration in the milk globules*." If the milk of cows are subject to the same conditions, which cannot be disputed, the inference is unavoidable that abnormal richness in the milk of cows is a sign of unhealthfulness of that milk. And it is a matter of the most vital interest, not only to dairymen and cattle-breeders, but to the general public, to know this fact.

The strongest evidence of cows producing healthy milk is in their dropping strong, healthy calves at birth, and their rapid development and continued health while being fed on the milk of their dams. If I were to advise those who have families of young children in regard to the milk they should purchase and use, I would say get your milk from herds where the calves are healthy and strong. Do not especially worry about its chemical constituents, but look to its pathological conditions. These conditions are of a thousand times more consequence to you and your families than whether milk is yellow, or whether its cream rises rapidly, or whether it has certain proportions of sugar, caseine, and fat. And were I to advise the authorities of our cities in regard to what milk should be sold in their markets, I would say, have inspectors appointed in every district from whence you draw your supply, and have them inspect the cows and their calves, the food they eat and the water they drink, and you will save thousands and thousands of lives and untold anguish of fathers and mothers over the graves of their little ones, slain by unhealthy milk that you admit to your markets, because it has in it the standard amount of solids.

I need not tell Holstein-Friesian breeders what breed of cattle especially produce such calves as I have referred to, or of the special effects of healthy milk on themselves and their children.

THE PRESIDENT: The next address is by Mr. J. N. Muncey, of Jesup, Iowa, subject, "The Practical Value of the Holstein-Friesian Cow."

In the absence of Mr. Muncey, the address will be read by the Secretary.

Secretary Wales read the following address:

THE PRACTICAL VALUE OF THE HOLSTEIN-FRIESIAN COW.

Since the introduction of thoroughbred cattle into North America there has always been two values attached to every animal, viz.: a practical and a theoretical value. These two values are closely associated, and in fact almost inseparable in every animal. Two hundred dollars for a thoroughbred male of good quality may or may not be a theoretical value. It is when the buyer is unable to realize that sum in the enhanced value of the produce, not having good females for a foundation.

Assume that the male produces ninety calves in three years, of that number about one-half will be males. Assume that forty-five steer calves are each only worth fifty cents more than those from an inferior bull — usually a 1700-pound bull will be worth at least $40.00 for beef — the calves cost, therefore, $160.00; the heifers about $3.00 each.

Now, are they worth it? Practically, I think they are. I fail to see any illogical reasoning in the above consideration. If the half-blood heifers are not worth $3.00 more than ordinary heifers, it is very unwise to begin improving your dairy with this breed of cattle, anyway.

The best cow of any breed or breeds for dairy purposes is the one that nets the owner the most money. If you are raising cattle for breeding purposes exclusively, a poor dairy cow sometimes is as profitable as a good one. She may be a fine breeder and a poor milker. The best cow for practical purposes is the one whose milk and calves, selling at the average market prices, brings the greatest return. There are advocates of general-purpose and special-purpose cattle in the field to-day, and I yet fail to see where the exponents of the beef breeds have established any good reason for calling their cattle "dairy cattle." The man who talks beef to me to-day, or beef at four cents per pound, must produce logic that will bear a common-sense inspection.

It is difficult to discuss our subject without mentioning names of breeds. I would prefer to do so.

The question is, will it pay the farmers of this country to feed an ordinary milker and fine breeder for the difference in the price of the beef? I say emphatically *no*. Has not the Ontario Agricultural College demonstrated conclusively that an acre of pasture will produce about twice as many dollars worth of milk as it will beef? The experiment was conducted with only ordinary cows and the finest specimens of the beef breeds. It is more profitable, therefore, do you not think, to produce milk than beef from any breed of cattle.

Suppose a Holstein-Friesian steer sells for only two and one-half cents per pound, and a Short-horn at four and one-half cents per pound, will the extra two cents pay for keeping the typical beef cow?

The following figures will illustrate the idea. I assume that the average profitable life of the average cow in the dairy is six years. Suppose that the milk is sold to the creamery at the average price, say eighty cents per 100 pounds:

Cow No. 1:

Six years, at 9,000 pounds at 80 cents per 100	$432 00
Six years, skim milk at 25 cents per 100 pounds	108 00
Six calves, 80 pounds each, birth-weight, at 2½ cents	12 00
Original cow, 1,200 pounds, at 2 cents	24 00
	$576 00

Cow No. 2:

Six years, at 5,000 pounds at 80 cents per 100	$240 00
Six years, skim milk at 25 cents per 100 pounds	60 00
Six calves, 80 pounds each, birth-weight, at 4½ cents	21 60
Original cow, 1,200 pounds, at 4 cents	48 00
	$369 60

Difference in favor of cow No. 1, $207.00.

A number of considerations in the assumed data are important. I insist that the average eight-year-old Holstein-Friesian cow will sell as quick at two and three-fourths cents per pound as the average Short-horn cow will at four cents per pound. I think the observation of every one will warrant that statement. Further, the advocates of the beef cow may claim a greater profit per pound on the beef produced from the Short-horn cow's calves. All right. Take it that way. It is doubtful if beef can be produced, take the year through, for less than three cents. The cost of a pound on thrifty calves of the different breeds will be approximately, if not exactly, the same. Then, by competing with No. 2, I raise six calves weighing 1,200 pounds each, and lose $72.00, or one cent per pound, by the operation, while No. 2 makes one cent per pound, or $72.00. Deducting, now, $72.00, the assumed loss on the Holstein-Friesian calves produced, from the sum of $432.00, $108.00, and $24.00, there remains $492.00 as the gross receipts for six years; while with cow No. 2, we have increased her proceeds to $420.00. There yet remains $72.00 in favor of No. 1.

Practically the heifers from the Holstein-Friesian cow are worth as much, if not more, for dairy purposes than the Short-horn heifers are for beef, hence only about $36.00, instead of $72.00, should be deducted from the gross proceeds of cow No. 1. There then remains $108.00 for six years in favor of the Holstein-Friesian cow.

There is yet another very important value to be attached to the black and white cow. I refer now to the fecundity of the cattle as a breed. A few figures from my books will point in this direction. From 1884 to January 1st, 1888, seven different registered cows have produced thirty-one calves. Of that number two were twins. Beginning with the dates of the first services, and closing with the dates of the birth of the last calves, thirty-one calves were produced in a total of 10,450 days, or an average of one calf in 348 days. During this time I have intentionally changed the time of "coming in" to fall and winter. This, of course, adds to the general average.

I think that there is no breed of cattle on the market to-day, except perhaps the Jerseys, that may be fed as liberally as the Holstein-Friesians without impairing the organs of reproduction.

Manly Miles, in his valuable work on stock-breeding, gives many reasons why "a remarkable tendency to lay on fat is usually accompanied by a delicacy of constitution, a diminished secretion of milk, and a loss of fecundity." Sterile animals may be found among all breeds of cattle, but it is the general average on which I base my observation and opinion. Prof. Tanner, one of the best authorities on this subject, says: "The non-impregnation of the female may generally be traced to an excessive fatness in one or both of the animals, and an absence of constitutional vigor. The breeding powers are most energetic when the animals are in a moderate condition, uninfluenced either by extreme fatness or leanness."

I insist that the average fertility of the black and white cattle adds much to their practical value for dairy purposes. It is a great loss to have four or five cows in a dairy of twenty that fail to breed. Thirty-eight services produced twenty-six calves, and forty-eight services produced thirty-one calves—an average of 1.4 and 1.6 services per calf, respectively.

I have all along considered myself a liberal feeder, knowing with any cattle it is only the liberal feeding that pays, and though the above figures do not establish a scientific truth, they are in harmony with the foremost theories on breeding. I might add to the numerous milk and butter records of these cattle. I had a two-year-old that gave 9,192 pounds of milk in a year, and five-year-olds that gave over 10,000 pounds of milk a year, and less than a year.

A three-and-one-half-year-old gave fifty pounds and nine ounces of milk in a day, and four per cent unsalted and unworked butter. Three five-year-olds gave 4.43, 5.8, and 5.4 per cent unsalted butter. They gave over fifty and sixty-five pounds of milk in a day.

It may be thought that a breeder cannot give an unbiased consideration to a subject in which he is pecuniarily interested. It has been my aim to do so. My love for the practical value of the black and white cattle was born in a barn where representatives of the different breeds are kept, and before I was financially interested.

I insist that the queen of cows is the one that gives milk and butter, and not the one that converts a part or half of the food into beef. It is milk, and not beef, that pays the greatest profit; and the cow that gives an average of twenty-seven to thirty pounds per day for 300 days is a profitable cow, regardless of the breed she represents.

J. N. MUNCEY.

Mr. F. C. STEVENS: Mr. President, I have a resolution that I would like to introduce.

Mr. Stevens read the following resolution:

"*Resolved*, That we, members of the Holstein-Friesian Association of America, are heartily in sympathy with the bill known as the Palmer senate bill 2083, firmly believing that its passage would greatly aid in the speedy exterpation of all contagious diseases now in this country.

"*It is further resolved*, That the Secretary of this Association be, and is hereby, instructed to send a copy of this resolution to the chairman of the Committee on Agriculture in the house and senate, and also to Mr. Azel Ames, Jr., chairman of the Committee on Legislation appointed by the National Consolidated Cattle-Growers' Association, urging them to use every just and honorable means to secure the speedy passage of said bill."

Mr. DUDLEY MILLER: The bill in itself, Mr. President, I have no doubt is all right — the killing of pleura-pneumonia; but I understand from parties who have been in Washington, and have investigated the matter, that all these persons who are at the bottom of this are working for oleomargarine, and this is simply a stepping-stone to the other. The subject of oleomargarine was brought up in Washington at the time, and an expression of feeling of those assembled was asked. It was remarked by the adherents of this bill that it was no place to bring in oleomargarine — that it was not pertinent to the business before the meeting. Then another resolution was offered, to the effect that they were opposed to oleomargarine, and the thing was tabled like a flash.

Mr. STEVENS: Mr. President and gentleman, in reply to this statement, I desire to say, with all due respect to Mr. Miller and to his informant, that it is false — every word of it. I have been in Washington this winter; I have had the pleasure and the honor of associating myself with these gentlemen, trying to push this matter and secure the proper legislation. So far as these people are concerned, I deny most positively that they have any interest as a committee in this matter. All their labor has been distinctly and directly devoted to securing the passage of the bill named in this resolution. I know all the ins and outs of this matter, and you may take my word for it — so far as it goes; and at the same time, I assure you that Mr. Miller is mistaken.

Mr. MILLER: Mr. President, I would like to ask Mr. Stevens whether he means that my assertions in regard to the bringing forward of this oleomargarine question are false, or what he means by stating that what I said was false.

Mr. STEVENS: The gentleman made the statement as hearsay, and not of his own knowledge. I say that he has been misinformed. I do not mean to say that he has wilfully made a false statement. If he took it that way, I beg his pardon. I say he has been misinformed. I say that the committee who have this matter in charge at Washington have never in any way tried to persuade or suggested to the legislative body the possibility or probability, or anything of the kind, of repealing the oleomargarine law.

Mr. MILLER: Mr. Chairman, that is perfectly proper and right, and does not interfere with my statement at all. I simply made the remark that this subject was brought up and it was utterly tabooed, and they would not listen for a moment or say a thing in favor of or in opposition to oleomargarine, which really showed the animus of the people interested in this bill. Now, I am just as much in earnest in this matter as Mr. Stevens can be, and I want to stamp out pleuro-pneumonia, but I do not want to give the oleomargarine men a chance to repeal the law.

SECRETARY WALES: Mr. President, the committee that is now at Washington working in the interest of the National Cattle-Growers' Association were appointed at the last meeting of said association, in Kansas City. This Association sent delegates to that meeting. Mr. Stevens was there. Mr. Liggett, of Minnesota, was there, our new President was there, and they received every attention. Three members of this Association were put upon the Executive Committee of the National Cattle-Growers' Association, and I am sure I know enough about it to be able to state that that committee will do nothing in the line which Mr. Miller states. First and foremost is the extermination of cattle disease in the United States. It is a question so far ahead of the question of oleomargarine, and the enactment of laws regarding it, that there is, in my opinion, no comparison between them. If our cattle are ruined by pleuro-pneumonia, we certainly will have no butter. We can get along under the present laws governing the sale of oleomargarine; I do not think they will interfere with us a great deal, and I hope this resolution will be adopted by this Association.

Mr. MILLER: I would like to ask Mr. Wales if we have not ample laws on this subject, and are they not being enforced, and vigorously enforced, at the present time under the management of the department of agriculture?

SECRETARY WALES: In reply to Mr. Miller, I will say that I am not entirely conversant with the law as it now stands, but I know that this committee is doing everything in their power to protect the farmers of the United States and their stock, and I think it is our duty to uphold them.

Mr. GOODWIN: Mr. President, as the Acting Secretary of the Consolidated Cattle-Growers' Association of the United States, I would like to make a few statements of fact. The gentleman at my right (Mr. Dudley Miller) has stated as a positive fact that the only man who has been at Washington in the interests of what is now known as the Palmer bill is in favor of the repeal of the oleomargarine law. I believe that was his statement. Allow me to call your attention to the fact that Maj. Henry E. Alvord has been one of the most active advocates of the Palmer bill. The Hon. L. S. Coffin, of Iowa, who is the spokesman of the dairy interest in the west, has also been one of the most active members of the committee at Washington in favor of the Palmer bill. Those are facts that Mr. Stevens can verify if they need verification. One other point. Mr. Miller tells you that the committee refused to express itself on the repeal of the oleomargarine law. I do not doubt that that statement is actually and literally true. The Consolidated Cattle-Growers' Association of the United States has twice declined to commit itself on that question. Why? It came into organization for the sole, express, and explicit object of securing legislation to stamp out contagious animal diseases. For that, and for nothing else; and for that reason it declared, by resolution, that it did not propose to introduce any single object or make any attempt outside of that which would work discord in its ranks.

Mr. MILLER: As regards Professor Alvord, I am informed that he was of that party attempting to carry this bill through, and when he ascertained the true animus of the meeting, that he deserted them, and now no longer supports them.

Mr. STEVENS: I have a letter, dated day before yesterday, from Professor Alvord, urging me to urge this matter in every way.

Mr. MILLER: My informant may have been mistaken, but I give you what he told me.

Mr. E. A. POWELL: I want to make a few remarks in regard to this, Mr. President, and I am sorry to have to plead a great deal of ignorance regarding it. I came here with the feeling that it was very unwise and decidedly wrong for this Association to take any action upon this subject whatever; or if any action, it should be adverse to what is now asked, on several accounts. In the first place, two years ago I attended a meeting of the Consolidated Association at Chicago. I was then a representative of our Association at that convention. At that time it was impossible to get anything through that body that was favorable to the passage of what is called the oleomargarine bill. I myself made an attempt to get some recommendation from that body of men in favor of that measure, and it could not be done. I was told by the parties who were then acting on the committee to go to Washington that it was the most unpopular thing I could say in that body of men, and that I must keep still on the subject; and from what I have recently heard said, which I presume is the same thing that Mr. Miller has alluded to, I was confirmed in my views that it was dangerous for the dairy interests of the country to establish a commission as had been asked for. Since coming here I have talked with Mr. Stevens, and he assures me that while he knew at the time I allude to — two years ago (Mr. Stevens was a member of the committee that went to Washington) — he said he knew that at that time that that committee was opposed to the passage of what is called the oleomargarine bill, but that those men were shelved, as I understand, at the next meeting of the association, and that the committee that was afterwards appointed to go to Washington were entirely different in their views in regard to the oleomargarine question, and that at present the committee as constituted does not favor the repeal of that bill; but that does not correspond with the evidence which has been furnished by a gentleman sent from this state, if I mistake not, by the Dairy Association to look into this matter. His report in regard to Maj. Alvord's position does not conform with the report which we hear from these gentlemen, and I feel now, as I expressed myself to several of these gentlemen a short time ago, that until we had more light on the subject, and understood definitely what we were doing, it was a very prudent thing for us at least to keep still. I do not feel that I myself am competent to act understandingly, or as I should act, on so important a question.

Dr. PATTERSON: Mr. President and gentlemen, I regret to be obliged to make any remarks upon this subject. I regret that the question has come before us in any shape whatever. There probably are not four in this room who thoroughly understand the features of the bill it is proposed to endorse; who have read the bill in any shape or form. They have not even seen or read a synopsis of it. The assertion which is made that it is the only thing to stamp out pleuro-pneumonia in this country is made upon their statement alone, and the statement that the present laws are totally inadequate is also based upon that one statement alone; and when we find that the present department of agriculture and the bureau of animal industry have been working for the last two or three years seemingly to the satisfaction of the public, it would seem that it was best for this Association, unless they can talk intelligently upon the subject, to let the matter rest where it is. Those who have read the journals carefully, and the reports of various meetings throughout the country, will find that quite a large number of associations, particularly in the southwest and far west, have denounced this bill; and it is best for us, and I wish that this association would simply let the thing alone. Were I to carry out my own views upon this subject, I would be glad of an endorsement the other way, because I believe the present law is amply sufficient, for it works through state authorities, and in harmony with them. The gentlemen here, from beginning to end, are absolutely ignorant on the subject, and I would ask that the thing be voted down.

Mr. STEVENS: The doctor is a much better talker than I am, Mr. President, and has the advantage of me in that respect; but he assumes a great deal. He assumes that there are but four men in this room who understand or who have read this bill. Now, I should feel very sorry if that were the case; it is a matter of vital importance to every breeder of cattle in the United States — one of the most interesting things that he has to contemplate, and for him to neglect this matter is very sad. Dr. Patterson says that if he expressed his own opinion he would ask that the bill be carried in the other direction. Perfectly natural. He is to-day an employe of the government. He is here to inspect the stock-yards in Buffalo ostensibly, and it is perfectly natural that he should ask that this matter be carried in that way. The largest association of cattlemen in the United States, made up of representative men throughout the country, have endorsed this bill. Your friend Hatch, of Missouri, the man of whom you can hold up both hands and thank God that he carried the oleomargarine bill through, endorses it to-day, and he says it is the best thing of the kind ever introduced. It is an improvement upon the old bill, which you are familiar with, of last year. As far as the states' right clause is concerned, it is broad enough to satisfy every democrat in the country, and it is conservative enough to be satisfactory to every republican; it is not a question of political issue. I earnestly hope that the bill will receive the endorsement of this Association. Your delegates whom you have sent here and repose your confidence in have worked earnestly for the support of it, and I hope you will not go back on them at this late day.

Mr. LIGGETT: Whatever may be the feelings of the committee at Washington in advocating this bill, I am sure I do not know, but this I do know: I was a delegate representing the Holstein-Friesian Association in Kansas City, and I know that the gentlemen who were with me will bear me out in the assertion that these very gentlemen who were advocating this bill in Washington were the men who were the friends of the dairymen in the convention in Kansas City. There was an effort made there on the part of some stock-yard men in Chicago to get a bill introduced to repeal the oleomargarine bill, and they came their fortified, and were mustering their strength; and Mr. Coffin, Major Alvord, and many others of the men representing the dairy interests of course began to make fight against it, and the very men who are now in Washington upon this committee are the gentlemen who came to us and said, "This is not a matter of oleomargarine at all. It is a matter to suppress pleuro-pneumonia, and we stand heart and hand with the dairymen, and we insist that they should be fairly represented on that committee." Mr. Stevens, of New York, was placed upon that committee, Mr. Wales, of Iowa, and myself, from Minnesota, all representing the dairy interests, and these gentlemen are the very ones who stood by us and saw that we were put there.

Dr. PATTERSON: Mr. Chairman, Mr. Stevens has made a slurring remark, or an intimation that was not quite in accordance with what it should be. He insinuated that there was a doubt in regard to the work that I was sent here to perform, by saying that ostensibly I was sent here for the inspection of the Buffalo stock-yards. When I state to you, Mr. President and gentlemen, that those were my positive orders and written instructions it will be sufficient, I think, and I think sufficient for my friend.

Dr. Patterson, chairman of the Committee on Accounts, made the following report:

Mr. Chairman and Gentlemen: Your committee appointed to examine the accounts of the Secretary, Treasurer, and Superintendent of Advanced Registry would report that they found the accounts of Secretary Wales and Superintendent Hoxie to be correct. On account of sickness in the family of Treasurer Smith's secretary, certain vouchers in connection with his report are not to be found in the bundle, and we have deferred action upon it until they can be sent to us for verification, although we have no doubt that the accounts are strictly correct.

Mr. W. G. Powell moved that the report of the committee be accepted, and that the committee be continued for the purpose of verification of the Treasurer's report.

Seconded and carried.

THE PRESIDENT: We may now resume the consideration of Mr. Stevens' resolution.

The old bill was here read by Dr. Patterson, and the new bill by Mr. W. R. Goodwin, of Chicago.

Mr. BURRELL: I believe this is a wise provision, and that the interest will be in safer hands in this form than as it is now — under the control and direction of the Minister of Agriculture. I am in favor of promoting this bill by a vote of this Association.

PROFESSOR ROBERTS: I hesitate somewhat to say anything upon this discussion because one of my associates is now connected with the Bureau of Animal Industry, but I suppose I still have reserved to me all the rights of an ordinary citizen, although I am connected with a university. As I have watched this work going on, and the progress that has been made, I have been very much gratified as to the success that has been attained under difficulties that it had seemed to me were almost insurmountable. If one comes to know all the difficulties that have arisen as the Bureau of Animal Industry has directed its work in different states, to know that those engaged in it are sometimes in danger of their lives, and yet have quietly and persistently fought this disease, there is confidence in the methods that are now being used to exterminate this terrible disease that is causing so much trouble; and since this is the case, and since, as it appears to me from the evidence I have that six months more of careful work and of operation the same as have been carried on already, will exterminate virtually, if not literally, pleuro-pneumonia from the United States, that it is bad economy to now appoint a new set of officers who are not acquainted with the work, and to change wholly, or partially at least, the present mode of operation. There are some things in the new bill that appear to make it better because it is stronger, but it would seem to me the wiser course to amend the old bill and to go on and see if we cannot rid this country of pleuro-pneumonia. I see nothing to hinder it, and I see much difficulty ahead if we change our present method of operation, although it may be somewhat better. What evidence I have leads me most emphatically to believe that the methods should not be radically changed; that new men should not be put in the place of the old.

Mr. HORR: Mr. President, I never heard of this bill until I came here, so that my opinion upon the question is simply one that comes to me on hearing these two bills read, and hearing a history of the origin of this new bill. Let us see if I give the narrative correctly. There is the National Cattle-Growers' Association of the United States. We sent delegates to that association. Mr. Stevens, Mr. Liggett, and our newly elected President were those delegates. They joined with these gentlemen and appointed a committee that was satisfactory, as I understand, to our agents, satisfactory to Mr. Stevens, and to Mr. Liggett, and to our newly elected President. The committee went to Washington, and after consulting with all the friends of the cattlemen of experience, and men who have the interests of cattle at heart, the result is this very carefully drawn bill. Now, it seems to me that as men interested in the stamping out of these diseases, we can hardly afford to decide in favor of the old, immature, and weak law, when they come and offer us one that is very much more complete in its provisions, and even puts the criminal laws at the disposal of the commission for the enforcement of the enactment. Surely an association of gentlemen who are interested in cattle will not resolve in favor of a weak law and against a strong one.

Mr. Smith moved that Mr. Stevens' resolution be laid upon the table.

Motion seconded.

Question put, and declared lost.

Mr. SMITH: Mr. President, I wish to repeat what I have said before, in one sense, and that is, that I am not well posted on this subject, and I doubt whether many of the members are; but if those who have examined the bill regard it as a better measure than the present law, I have no objections in bidding them God-speed, and I therefore withdraw my motion to table the resolution.

Mr. GOODWIN: I wish to say, Mr. President, that no association of cattlemen west or east, unless perhaps an association of rangemen has adopted a resolution unfavorable to the passage of this bill; but every cattle-growers' association — and I have attended the state organizations throughout the west myself this winter and last winter — have resolved unanimously in favor of this bill. On two occasions I have heard it opposed — on both occasions by the agents of the present Bureau of Animal Industry.

Mr. SWEET: I will say that I think Mr. Roberts expressed the matter fully when he said he thought this bill was much stronger than the other side. I am in favor of this new bill.

Dr. PATTERSON: I should have been glad, Mr. President, for a vote to have been taken, and every member of this Association represented. However, I deem it necessary to say that I regret exceedingly that I have made any remarks whatever upon this floor. I feel that I have already been misconstrued, and I wish to state here positively that whatever I have said or done in this matter has been done from my own individual interest and feeling upon the subject, and outside of my official position as a government officer. I feel that when the remark was made that it is only members or officers of the present government that oppose this bill, it was an insinuation that I was here simply for that purpose. I wish to say that I decidedly decline to discuss the question further with the paid agents of the Live Stock Growers' Association.

A rising vote was taken upon Mr. Stevens' resolution, and it was declared carried.

Mr. E. A. Powell, chairman of the committee appointed upon the question of judges at fairs, presented several names.

Mr. W. G. Powell moved that the matter be referred back to the committee for additional names to be afterwards reported to the Board of Officers for their approval.

Seconded and carried.

Upon motion, the meeting adjourned.

ANNUAL MEETING OF THE BOARD OF OFFICERS,

Held at Buffalo, N. Y., March 21st, 1888.

Present: Messrs. M. L. Sweet, Edgar Huidekoper, W. Brown Smith, F. L. Houghton, William M. Liggett, W. G. Powell, T. G. Yeomans, D. H. Burrell, Thomas B. Wales, and S. Hoxie.

The election of members being the first order of business, the Secretary presented the name of Jeremiah Clark, of Andover, N. Y., recommended by Mr. S. Hoxie.

Upon motion, Mr. Clark was declared elected.

Mr. J. C. Lord having asked a hearing by the Board, spoke as follows:

Those who were members of the Board last year will remember that I appeared before you on a similar case, and I did not at that time receive any encouragement. Perhaps I will not this time. I will say for the benefit of those who never gave the matter any thought last year, that when I went home I found the transfer that my firm were making such a fuss about.

Now, we have a cow two years old that came into our possession when it was a calf. The calf went to Mr. Sexton with some other cattle, but they belonged to us, and within the past week we have sold this heifer, and she is now coming two years old, and is about to drop her calf. The animal stands as bred by Mr. Picton, of Ontario. She has never been transferred to anybody. When this animal went to Sexton's he asked me about the transfer. I wrote him and requested him to send a transfer to Mr. Ellsworth, and ask him to sign and return it. He says in the letter just received that he never received any reply to his letter, and he does not know whether he was at home or what the difficulty was; so I at once did the same thing, and I have not received a reply. The heifer is "Michigan Maid;" we have had possession of the heifer for two years, and she is ready to drop her calf. We have sold her, and we want to give title to the heifer — that is, a transfer; and we want to be in good shape to get her calf registered, and I ask the Board to grant me the transfer. I am ready to make an affidavit to the fact that this heifer has been owned by us for these two years, and that there is no question about her title. I have given the person a legal bill of sale of the heifer.

Mr. W. G. Powell moved that the matter be referred to Secretary Wales, with instructions to make the transfer when he becomes satisfied it should be done.

Seconded and carried.

Mr. HORR: I move that a committee of five be appointed, to consist of three members besides the President and Secretary of this Association, to, by correspondence or subsequent meeting, arrange the special premiums to be offered by our Association, with full authority to hold a meeting for that purpose, or to settle the question by correspondence, as the committee may determine. I offer it as a resolution.

Seconded and carried.

The chair appointed as such committee Messrs. Horr, Liggett, and Burrell.

Upon the request of Mr. Burrell, Mr. S. Hoxie was substituted as a member of the committee in his place.

Upon motion, Messrs. T. G. Yeomans and W. B. Smith were added to the committee.

The committee appointed to recommend judges to act at state fairs, or other like exhibitions, reported a list of names which the Secretary was ordered to furnish all applicants, the list to be sent entire and without comment.

It was voted that should H. D. Warner, of Connecticut, make application for membership, the same be accepted on payment of the usual fee; in which case he is named as one of the Inspectors of the Advanced Registry.

Mr. F. C. Stevens asked to be heard, and spoke as follows:

Mr. President and Gentlemen: I come before you at this time to ask for the consideration of a liberal appropriation for duplicate premiums for our International Fair, to be held in Buffalo, N. Y.

Taking into consideration the magnitude of the concern, and what we are trying to do, we would like to have you give us the same appropriation that you give Columbus for class premiums, and that where we offer premiums for sweepstakes, where Holsteins come into competition with others, we ask you to duplicate the premiums offered by the International Fair Association. The fair will commence September 4th of this year, and continue ten days. It will be our purpose to offer premiums for dairy cows and their products, so that we will get a fair test. Every facility will be offered, and every known device will be there for testing; it will be the greatest exhibition of the kind that has ever been held in this country.

Mr. Huidekoper moved that the request of Mr. Stevens be referred to the committee just appointed, to be acted upon after the receipt of offerings made by the International Exposition.

THE PRESIDENT: Does the gentleman make the motion that it be referred to them with power to act?

Mr. HUIDEKOPER: Certainly. As I understand it, Mr. Stevens asks us to duplicate the premiums without giving us the amount of the premiums or any other information. As quick as he furnishes us with the information our committee has some basis on which to work. The motion is that upon the information furnished by the International Exposition committee to our Secretary, it be referred to this committee, which has been appointed with power to act.

Mr. Huidekoper's motion was seconded and carried.

Upon motion of Mr. Horr, the Board went into executive session.

Mr. Huidekoper moved that Isaac C. Otis, O. P. Chapman, S. Burchard, S. N. Wright, J. C. Poor, and Carey R. Smith be appointed Inspectors of Imported Cattle.

Seconded and carried.

Mr. Huidekoper moved that the members of the committee just appointed as Inspectors of Imported Cattle and Jere Allis, J. N. Muncey, J. L. Stone, Asa R. Sturtevant, A. Bradley, and T. N. Figuers be appointed Inspectors of Advanced Registry.

Seconded and carried.

Upon motion, the meeting adjourned.

Report of Feeding Steers of Different Breeds at the Agricultural College of Michigan.

In March last we published a bulletin (No. 24) which outlined in some degree the proposed experiment of feeding good representatives of some of the best known breeds of cattle from calfhood to maturity, under the same conditions. This bulletin also contained the breeding of the ten animals secured for this purpose — two each of pure-bred Galloways, Short-Horns, Holsteins, and Jerseys; one Hereford, and one Devon — with a complete record of the food consumed, daily ration, monthly weights, and gains up to March 10th, 1887.

The present bulletin gives the results for the seven months ending October 10th, 1887.

Since the date of the last bulletin the steers have been allowed to run in a small field adjoining the experimental barn, in suitable weather, but have been taken up regularly three times a day and fed a meal and hay ration. When kept in stalls they have been watered regularly three times daily, and when outside have had free access to the water-tanks. During the early part of the season they had a fair bite of grass, but in the long continued drouth later they were entirely dependent on the food supplied in the stalls. No account has been made of the pasture, as all had an equal chance in that respect.

In April and May the steers had a small daily ration of ensilage or roots, from five to eight pounds. The meal fed was made up of one-third oats and corn ground half and half, one-third wheat-bran, and one-third oil-meal, from April to August 24th. Since that date the proportions have been fifty pounds corn and oats, ten pounds calf-meal, and thirty pounds wheat-bran.

Some of the animals have made greater gains than were looked for; others have failed to reach weights expected.

It should be remembered that the animals were not selected on account of any phenomenal development, but the object was to get good *average animals* of the various breeds, feed and care for them well, and *exactly alike*, save in amount of food, and see how they would respond in growth and flesh. Their answers are given in the following tables, which I trust will prove of interest to cattle men.

I very greatly regret that we have had but one specimen of the Hereford and Devon breeds, but circumstances beyond our control prevented our securing them for this purpose.

The State Board of Agriculture are in hearty sympathy with this line of work, and we propose to secure another lot of calves during the coming summer for another test. Any parties having well bred and promising calves that they would like to have fed in this way are requested to write me.

While this single test with a limited number of animals does not positively demonstrate the value of the breeds, it is still hoped that the work is in the right direction, and that a number of tests of this sort may lead to a more perfect knowledge of the feeding quality and habits of growth of the different breeds, which will be of real practical value to all breeders of cattle.

Name of Animal.	Breed.	Date of Birth.	Weight October 10, 1887 — pounds.	Gain per day from birth to October 10, 1887 — pounds.	Amount of grain from June 10, 1886, to October 10, 1887 — pounds.	Amount of hay from June 10, 1886, to October 10, 1887 — pounds.	Gain per day from June 10, 1886, to October 10, 1887 — pounds.	Amount of food for every pound gained from June 10, 1886, to October 10, 1887 — pounds.	
								Grain	Hay.
Latitude	Devon	Mar. 23, 1886	820	1.45	2,228	2,413	1.33	3.43	3.71
King Jumbo	Galloway	Feb. 17, 1886	1,050	1.75	2,617	2,937	1.48	3.62	4.07
Judge	Galloway	Jan. 1, 1886	1,266	1.95	3,261	3,862	1.64	4.08	4.84
Hendriks	Hereford	Oct. 27, 1885	1,100	1.54	2,540	3,381	1.12	4.65	6.19
Potter	Jersey	Feb. 25, 1886	925	1.56	2,205	2,771	1.58	2.85	3.57
Roscoe	Jersey	Aug. 27, 1885	1,046	1.35	3,835	3,937	1.16	6.77	6.95
Beltz	Holstein	Nov. 17, 1885	1,406	2.03	4,051	4.122	1.72	4.85	5.29
Nichols	Holstein	Feb. 26, 1886	1,126	1.9	2,972	3,172	1.76	3.47	3.7
Homer	Short-Horn	Nov. 25, 1885	1,310	1.91	3,827	3,983	1.58	4.98	5.17
Holt	Short-Horn	Dec. 17, 1885	1,160	1.75	3,148	3,613	1.56	4.14	4.75

It is our intention to continue the feeding of these steers for another year, when the final results may be compared.

SAMUEL JOHNSON,
Professor of Agriculture.

Months, 1887.	Number of Period.	Daily Ration — pounds.		Total food consumed — pounds.	Weights and Gains — pounds.				Weight March 10, 1888.
		Grain.	Hay.		Weight at beginning of period.	Weight at close of period.	Gain for period.	Gain per day.	
Holstein steer, Beltz —									
March 10 to April 10	11	9.5	10.	990	1,080	1,130	50	1.67	
May 10	12	9.8	12.6	763	1,130	1,170	40	1.34	
June 10	13	8.23	7.4	481	1,170	1,200	30	1.	
July 10	14	9.07	3.2	368	1,200	1,268	68	2.2	
August 10	15	10.67	7.27	538	1,268	1,300	32	1.06	
September 10	16	11.	13.43	733	1,300	1,320	20	.67	
October 10	17	11.02	11.43	679	1,320	1,406	86	2.86	1,600
Holstein, Nicholas —									
March 10 to April 10	13	8.	8.9	927	760	810	50	1.67	
May 10	14	7.3	11.7	662	810	866	56	1.86	
June 10	15	5.87	4.73	334	866	912	46	1.5	
July 10	16	5.47	2.07	226	912	950	38	1.2	
August 10	17	8.23	5.17	402	950	1,000	50	1.67	
September 10	18	9.2	11.43	619	1,000	1,058	58	1.93	
October 10	19	9.47	10.07	586	1,058	1,126	68	2.27	1,350

Months, 1887.	Number of Period.	Daily ration — pounds.		Total food consumed — pounds.	Weights and Gains — pounds.				Weight March 10, 1888.
		Grain.	Hay.		Weight at beginning of period.	Weight at close of period.	Gain for period.	Gain per day.	
Galloway steer, King Jumbo —									
March 10 to April 10	14	7.	7.9	867	746	810	64	2.13	
May 10	15	7.3	9.3	592	810	850	40	1.34	
June 10	16	3.9	2.87	219	850	879	29	.97	
July 10	17	5.53	1.17	201	879	942	63	2.1	
August 10	18	7.7	3.4	333	942	985	43	1.43	
September 10	19	8.63	10.87	584	985	1,040	55	1.83	
October 10	20	7.37	6.07	403	1,040	1,050	10	.34	1,250
Galloway steer, Judge —									
March 10 to April 10	10	8.	8.9	927	960	974	14	.47	
May 10	11	8.8	11.3	697	974	1,040	66	2.2	
June 10	12	4.7	3.87	270	1,040	1,076	36	1.2	
July 10	13	5.6	1.77	221	1,076	1,123	47	1.54	
August 10	14	8.7	4.53	397	1,123	1,140	17	.57	
September 10	15	10.07	13.6	710	1,140	1,208	68	2.27	
October 10	16	10.17	10.43	618	1,208	1,266	58	1.93	1,370
Hereford steer, Hendricks —									
March 10 to April 10	10	7.	8.	870	874	890	16	.5	
May 10	11	7.1	10.2	611	890	920	30	1.	
June 10	12	3.87	4.67	272	920	940	20	.67	
July 10	13	3.9	2.7	198	940	1,010	70	2.34	
August 10	14	5.8	4.6	312	1,010	1,030	20	.67	
September 10	15	7.67	11.87	586	1,030	1,062	32	1.07	
October 10	16	7.93	9.	508	1,062	1,100	38	1.27	1,190
Short-Horn steer, Homer —									
March 10 to April 10	15	8.5	8.9	942	1,052	1,072	20	.67	
May 10	16	8.8	12.2	723	1,072	1,120	48	1.6	
June 10	17	6.6	5.37	389	1,120	1,128	8	.27	
July 10	18	7.34	2.73	302	1,128	1,170	42	1.4	
August 10	19	10.07	5.37	463	1,170	1,209	39	1.3	
September 10	20	10.03	12.03	662	1,209	1,242	33	1.1	
October 10	21	10.47	10.05	629	1,242	1,310	68	2.27	1,488
Short-Horn steer, Holt —									
March 10 to April 10	15	8.	8.9	927	914	920	6	.2	
May 10	16	8.1	11.2	673	920	970	50	1.67	
June 10	17	2.89	3.87	219	970	988	18	.6	
July 10	18	4.27	1.87	184	988	1,060	72	2.4	
August 10	19	7.8	4.7	375	1,060	1,090	30	1.	
September 10	20	8.13	13.3	643	1,090	1,106	16	.53	
October 10	21	8.8	10.4	576	1,106	1,160	54	1.8	1,350
Devon steer, Latitude —									
March 10 to April 10	9	5.5	7.	735	500	550	50	1.67	
May 10	10	5.6	9.	530	550	580	30	1.	
June 10	11	4.97	5.27	339	580	630	50	1.67	
July 10	12	5.77	1.57	220	630	688	58	1.9	
August 10	13	6.7	2.13	277	688	696	8	.27	
September 10	14	7.23	10.	517	696	774	78	2.6	
October 10	15	6.8	7.73	436	774	820	46	1.53	985
Jersey steer, Roscoe —									
March 10 to April 10	14	8.5	8.9	867	870	900	30	1.	
May 10	15	8.5	11.5	690	900	938	38	1.27	
June 10	16	5.53	4.57	307	938	950	12	.4	
July 10	17	5.43	1.93	221	950	1,004	54	1.8	
August 10	18	7.57	4.4	359	1,004	1,010	6	.2	
September 10	19	7.8	9.4	516	1,010	1,004	lost 6	.....	
October 10	20	7.8	8.1	477	1,004	1,046	42	1.4	1,215
Jersey steer, Potter —									
March 10 to April 10	10	5.5	7.	645	588	628	40	1.34	
May 10	11	5.7	8.6	485	628	660	32	1.07	
June 10	12	3.5	3.23	218	660	720	60	2.	
July 10	13	5.4	1.43	205	720	802	82	2.7	
August 10	14	7.17	3.34	315	802	800	lost 2	.....	
September 10	15	7.4	11.07	567	800	860	60	2.	
October 10	16	7.97	9.83	534	860	925	65	2.17	1,070

The above was presented by M. L. Sweet, of Grand Rapids, Michigan.

PROCEEDINGS

OF THE

FOURTH ANNUAL MEETING

OF THE

Holstein-Friesian Association

OF AMERICA,

HELD AT

NEW YORK, N. Y., MARCH 20TH, 1889.

ALSO—

REPORTS OF MEETINGS OF THE BOARD OF OFFICERS,
CHARTER, REVISED BY-LAWS, LIST OF OFFICERS
AND MEMBERS OF THE ASSOCIATION.

Egbert, Fidlar, & Chambers, Printers, Davenport, Iowa.

1889.

OFFICERS OF THE

HOLSTEIN-FRIESIAN ASSOCIATION OF AMERICA,

FOR 1889-90.

President.
EDGAR HUIDEKOPER, ... Meadville, Penn.

First Vice-President,   G. D. WHEELER, ... Deposit, N. Y.
Second Vice-President,   JERE ALLIS, ... , Isinours, Minn.
Third Vice-President,   JOHN A. FRYE, ... Marlboro, Mass.
Fourth Vice-President,   D. H. BURRELL, ... Little Falls, N. Y.

Secretary and Editor.
THOMAS B. WALES, ... Iowa City, Iowa.

Directors.
W. G. POWELL, ... Springboro, Penn.
T. G. YEOMANS, ... Walworth, N. Y.
W. M. SINGERLY, ... Philadelphia, Penn.
MARTIN L. SWEET, ... Grand Rapids, Mich.
C. W. HORR, ... Wellington, Ohio.
C. R. PAYNE, ... Hamilton, N. Y.

Treasurer.
W. BROWN SMITH, ... Syracuse, N. Y.

Superintendent of Advanced Registry.
S. HOXIE, ... Yorkville, N. Y.

Inspectors of Advanced Registry.
S. HOXIE (*Superintendent*), ... Yorkville, N. Y.
O. P. CHAPMAN, ... Wellington, Ohio.
S. BURCHARD, ... Hamilton, N. Y.
S. N. WRIGHT, ... Elgin, Ill.
H. B. DAGGETT, ... Hampton, Iowa.
J. L. STONE, ... Waverly, Penn.
A. R. STURTEVANT, ... Springboro, Penn.
CAREY R. SMITH, ... Santa Ana, Cal.
A. BRADLEY, ... Lee, Mass.
J. C. POOR, ... North Andover, Mass.
H. D. WARNER, ... Lanesville, Conn.
W. A. ROWLEY, ... Mt. Clemens, Mich.
T. N. FIGUERS, ... Spring Hill, Tenn.
J. R. BEUCHLER, ... Leesburg, Va.

MEMBERS

OF THE

HOLSTEIN-FRIESIAN ASSOCIATION OF AMERICA.

AIKEN, M. A.,	Oneida, New York.
ALBAUGH, N. H.,	Tadmor, Ohio.
ALLEN, IRVING W.,	East Syracuse, New York.
ALLEN, WILLIAM H.,	Groton, New York.
ALLIS, JERE,	Isinours, Minnesota.
ANDERSON, MONS,	La Crosse, Wisconsin.
ARCHIBALD, D. H.,	Oxford, Mississippi.
AVERY, T. G.,	Buffalo, New York.
BABCOCK, F. G.,	Hornellsville, New York.
BAKER, RUFUS,	Fairfield, Michigan.
BARNEY, N. C.,	New York, New York.
BARR, W. R.,	New York, New York.
BAXTER, JERE,	Nashville, Tennessee.
BEAL, J. O.,	Rollin, Michigan.
BEAL, W. J.,	Lansing, Michigan.
BEAUCHAMP, E. P.,	Terre Haute, Indiana.
BEAUCHAMP, J. A.,	Nashville, Tennessee.
BELL, JOHN W.,	Shelbyville, Kentucky.
BENT, WILLIAM H.,	Cochituate, Massachusetts.
BEUCHLER, J. R.,	Leesburg, Virginia.
BIDWELL, M. S.,	Monterey, Massachusetts.
BISHOP, W. W.,	Aurora, Illinois.
BLACK, JAMES,	Stanley, New York.
BLESSING, C. L. G.,	Slingerlands, New York.
BLEYKER, J. DEN,	Kalamazoo, Michigan.
BOARDMAN, H. E.,	Rochester, New York.
BORTON, JOB H.,	Carlton, Kansas.
BOWER, B. B.,	Vinita, Indian Territory.
BRACE, H. L.,	West Winfield, New York.
BREUER, H. F. W.,	Charleston, South Carolina.
BRADLEY, A.,	Lee, Massachusetts,
BRAYTON, W. C.,	Syracuse, New York.

BROCKET, C. Z., ... Bonckville, New York.
BROOKS, J. T., ... Salem, Ohio.
BROWN, C. A., ... Portland, Maine.
BROWN, A. W., ... Unadilla Forks, New York.
BROWN, GEORGE E., ... Aurora, Illinois.
BUCHANAN, JAMES N., ... Chicago, Illinois.
BUEL, W. J., ... Hamilton, New York.
BURCH, ROBERT, ... West Schuyler, New York.
BURCHARD, SYLVESTER, ... Hamilton, New York.
BURRELL, DAVID H., ... Little Falls, New York.
BURRELL, E. J., ... Little Falls, New York.

CARLISLE, N. S., ... St. Charles, Illinois.
CARPENTER, G. M., ... Waverly, Pennsylvania.
CARTER, E. D., ... Humbird, Wisconsin.
CHAFFEE, B., ... Springville, New York.
CHAPIN, WILLIAM M., ... Sheffield, Massachusetts.
CHAPMAN, O. P., ... Wellington, Ohio.
CHENERY, W. L., ... Belmont, Massachusetts.
CLARK, W. B., ... Goodlettsville, Tennessee.
CLARK, WILLIAM B., ... Hillsdale, Michigan.
CLARKE, JEREMIAH, ... Andover, New York.
COLE, A. F., ... Pine Woods, New York.
COLE, OGDEN, ... Addison, Michigan.
COLE, O. R., ... Solsville, New York.
COLLINS, J. B., ... Chicago, Illinois.
COMER, J. H., ... New York, New York.
COON, MOREL, ... West Edmeston, New York.
COOPER, IRVING C., ... Theresa, New York.
COY, EDWARD L., ... West Hebron, New York.
CRANDALL, W. D., ... West Edmeston, New York.
CRAPSER, CHARLES, ... Cresco, Iowa.
CRUIKSHANK, J. W., ... Troy, Ohio.
CUMMINGS, JOHN, ... Cummingsville, Massachusetts.
CURTIS, J. M., ... Wilmington, Delaware.
CURTIS, N. B., ... Stockbridge, Massachusetts.

DALE, M. H., ... Scranton, Pennsylvania.
DAMON, ISAAC, ... Cochituate, Massachusetts.
DEAN, JOHN L., ... Westmoreland, New York.
DEGRAAF, G. V., ... Cortland, New York.
DILGER, HUBERT, ... Front Royal, Virginia.
DODGE, THOMAS H., ... Worcester, Massachusetts.
DORWIN, WILLIAM E., ... Owego, New York.
DOWNING, A. S., ... Palmyra, New York.
DUDLEY, HORTENSE, ... Oakville, Kentucky.

DURNALL, EDWIN J., ... Goshenville, Pennsylvania.
DUTCHER, J. B., ... Pawling, New York.
DUTCHER, J. G., ... Pawling, New York.

EASTON, H. S., ... Penn Yan, New York.
EDMUNDS, AMOS, ... Disco, Illinois.
ELLIS, A. V., ... Austin, Minnesota.
ELLIS, J. T., ... Flemington, New Jersey.
ELLWOOD, L., ... Schenectady, New York.
EMERSON, S. B., ... Mountain View, California.
EMRICK, G. M., ... Chicago, Illinois.
EWING, WILLIAM L., ... St. Louis, Missouri.

FARRINGTON, WILLIAM, ... San José, California.
FAY, ELON G., ... Bryan, Ohio.
FERGUSON, T. G., ... Stella, Nebraska.
FIGUERS, T. N., ... Spring Hill, Tennessee.
FINNEGAN, THOMAS, ... Bouckville, New York.
FISK, GEORGE C., ... Springfield, Massachusetts.
FITCH, C. H., ... Boston, Massachusetts.
FLETCHER, GEORGE B., ... Williamsport, Pennsylvania.
FOLGER, B. W., ... Kingston, Ontario.
FOSTER, HENRY, ... Clifton Springs, New York.
FREDERICK, L. S., ... Shelbyville, Kentucky.
FRENCH, ALBERT, ... Hamilton, Ohio.
FROST, RUFUS S., ... Boston, Massachusetts.
FRYE, JOHN A., ... Marlborough, Massachusetts.
FULLERTON, WILLIAM, ... Clifton Station, Virginia.

GALE, H. C., ... Tivoli, New York.
GARDINER, W. L., ... Clarksfield, Ohio.
GEBBIE, ALEXANDER, ... Lowville, New York.
GEDDES, GEORGE, ... Fair Mount, New York.
GIFFORD, W. H., ... Syracuse, New York.
GILBERT, F. M., ... Des Moines, Iowa.
GOODFELLOW, CORNELIUS H., . . . Cato, New York.
GOODPASTURE, A. V., ... St. Bethlehem, Tennessee.
GRACEY, F. P., ... Clarksville, Tennessee.
GREGORY, N. B., ... Unadilla, New York.
GURNEE, W. S., ... New York, New York.

HACK, W. C., ... Orwell, Vermont.
HAGERTY, F. H., ... Aberdeen, Dakota.
HAM, J. M., ... Washington Hollow, New York.
HAMMOND, H. B., ... New York, New York.
HANCOCK, JOHN, ... Barre, Massachusetts.

HANKE, WILLIAM, ... Iowa City, Iowa.
HARVEY, T. W., ... Chicago, Illinois.
HARWOOD, P. M., ... Barre, Massachusetts.
HATCH, H. H., ... Bay City, Michigan.
HAVILAND, JOSEPH, ... Glen's Falls, New York.
HAYES, W. J., ... Ravenna, Ohio.
HEMINGWAY, W. L., ... Jackson, Mississippi.
HENDERSON, JAMES L., ... Washington, Pennsylvania.
HIBBARD, H. G., ... Orwell, Vermont.
HICKS, JOHN H., ... West Chester, Pennsylvania.
HICKS, WILLIAM H., ... Goshenville, Pennsylvania.
HINKLEY, O. B., ... Brookfield, New York.
HINKLEY, D. J., ... Brookfield, New York.
HOFFMAN, A. E., ... Fort Wayne, Indiana.
HORN, HENRY, ... Duquoin, Illinois.
HORR, C. W., ... Wellington, Ohio.
HOUGHTON, CHARLES, ... Boston, Massachusetts.
HOUGHTON, F. L., ... Putney, Vermont.
HOWARD, J. W., ... Aberdeen, Mississippi.
HOWARD, S. P., ... Fairport, New York.
HOWARD, WARREN A., ... Brocton, Massachusetts.
HOWKINS, WILLIAM, ... Newark, New Jersey.
HOXIE, S., ... Whitesboro, New York.
HOXIE, S. L., ... South Edmeston, New York.
HUGHES, W. E., ... Dallas, Texas.
HUIDEKOPER, A. C., ... Meadville, Pennsylvania.
HUIDEKOPER, EDGAR, ... Meadville, Pennsylvania.
HUNT, CHARLES, ... Delphi, New York.
HUNTER, JOHN, ... Sterling Valley, New York.
HUNTINGTON, JOHN, ... Cleveland, Ohio.
HUSH, VALENTINE G., ... Minneapolis, Minnesota.

JACKSON, GEORGE F., ... Minneapolis, Minnesota.
JACKSON, WILLIAM O., ... South Bend, Indiana.
JEWETT, F. J., ... Farmington, New York.
JEWETT, HENRY C., ... Buffalo, New York.
JEWETT, SHERMAN S., ... Willink, New York.
JONES, EDGAR, ... Nashville, Tennessee.
JONES LEANDER, ... Boone Grove, Indiana.

KEMP, EDWARD, ... New York, New York.
KEYES, H. W., ... Newbury, Vermont.
KIEFINGER, HENRY, ... Dayton, Ohio.
KNOWLES, F. B., ... Worcester, Massachusetts.
KOCH, WILLIAM, ... New York, New York.

LAMB, ANTHONY, ... Syracuse, New York.
LANGDON, SAMUEL A., ... Morrison, Illinois.
LANGWORTHY, HOLLUM, ... West Edmeston, New York,
LANGWORTHY, ERWIN, ... South Brookfield, New York.
LANGWORTHY, MORGAN, ... West Edmeston, New York.
LEONARD, H. D., ... Lincoln, Nebraska.
LIGGETT, WILLIAM M., ... Benson, Minnesota.
LIGHTNER, JOHN, ... Iowa, Louisiana.
LORD, B. B., ... Sinclairville, New York.
LORD, C. J., ... Sinclairville, New York.

MCALPIN, D. H., ... New York, New York.
MCGILLIN, E. M., ... Cleveland, Ohio.
MCGRAW, T. H., ... Bay City, Michigan.
MCINTYRE, SAMUEL, ... Salt Lake City, Utah.
MCINTYRE, S. MAXWELL, ... Dresden, New York.
MCNARY, FRANK E., ... West Le Roy, Michigan.
MCPHERSON, J. R., ... Belle Mead, New Jersey.
MACVEAGH, WAYNE, ... Philadelphia, Pennsylvania.
MANN, F. I., ... Gilman, Illinois.
MANN, J. S., ... Elgin, Illinois.
MARTIN, JOSEPH J., ... Philadelphia, Pennsylvania.
MAXWELL, JOSHUA I., ... Geneva, New York.
MAXWELL, T. C., ... Geneva, New York.
MERRITT, M. F., ... Stamford, Connecticut.
MILLER, DUDLEY, ... Oswego, New York.
MILLER, E. P., ... New York, New York.
MILLER, GERRIT S., ... Peterboro, New York.
MOORE, H. C., ... Fond du Lac, Wisconsin.
MOORE, M. F., ... Cameron, Missouri.
MOREHOUSE, GEORGE R., ... Philadelphia, Pennsylvania.
MORSE, L. C., ... Sparta, Wisconsin.
MUNCEY, J. N., ... Jesup, Iowa.
MYER, H. VAN W., ... Madison, New Jersey.
MYERS, M. J., ... Wells, Minnesota.

NAVARRO, J. F., ... New York, New York.
NEILSON, JAMES, ... New Brunswick, New Jersey.
NEWMAN, W. W., ... South Onondaga, New York.
NILES, WILLIAM, ... Los Angeles, California.
NOWELL, T. S., ... North Platte, Nebraska.

OFFICER, THOMAS, ... Council Bluffs, Iowa.
OSTERHOUT, STANTON, ... Cobleskill, New York.
OTIS, ISAAC O., ... Jordan, New York.

PACKARD, B. G.,	Rome, New York.
PATTERSON, F. W.,	Lochearn, Maryland.
PATTERSON, W. H.,	Cresco, Iowa.
PAYNE, C. R.,	Hamilton, New York.
PAYNE, L. H.,	Garrettsville, Ohio.
PERRY, F. S.,	Lenox Furnace, Massachusetts.
PHELON, J. V.,	Wellington, Ohio.
PHELPS, EDWIN,	Pontiac, Michigan.
PHILLIPS, E. R.,	Bay City, Michigan.
PHILLIPS, WILLIAM I.,	Ellington, New York.
PIERCE, GEORGE A.,	Derby Line, Vermont.
POLHEMUS, GEORGE B.,	Coyote, California.
POOR, JAMES C.,	North Andover, Massachusetts.
POPE, DE MOTT E.,	South Edmeston, New York.
POTTER, O. B.,	New York, New York.
POTTER, W. H.,	Alpena, Michigan.
POTTER, W. J.,	Glen's Falls, New York.
POWELL, E A.,	Syracuse, New York.
POWELL, JAMES L.,	Springboro, Pennsylvania.
POWELL, WILL. B.,	Springboro, Pennsylvania.
POWELL, W. G.,	Springboro, Pennsylvania.
PRATT, C.,	Syracuse, New York.
PRATT, W. A.,	Elgin, Illinois.
PROPER, W. W.,	Jefferson, New York.
PUGSLEY, H. V.,	Plattsburg, Missouri.
RADFORD, W. T.,	Pembroke, Kentucky.
RAY, E. K.,	Franklin, Massachusetts.
RAY, JOSEPH, G.,	Franklin, Massachusetts.
REED, WILLIAM W.,	Erie, Pennsylvania.
RILEY, C. T.,	Troy, Ohio.
ROBERTS, CHARLES W.,	West Chester, Pennsylvania.
ROBINS. J. N.,	New York, New York.
ROBINSON, CHARLES,	Barre Plains, Massachusetts.
ROWLAND, LYNFORD,	Cheltenham, Pennsylvania.
ROWLEY, W. A.,	Mt. Clemens, Michigan.
RUMSEY, C. E.,	Pittsburgh, Pennsylvania.
RUSSELL, LUTHER,	Burton, Ohio.
RUSSELL, W. A.,	Lawrence, Massachusetts.
RUST, J.,	North Greenfield, Wisconsin.
SANBORN, J. S.,	Boston, Massachusetts.
SAVAGE, F. B.,	Newburg, New York.
SCHUYLER, R. P.,	West Troy, New York.
SCUDDER, OGDEN H.,	Randolph, New York.

SEABURY, E. K., ... Walpole, New Hampshire.
SEELEY, M. R., ... Farmington, Michigan.
SEVERY, C. A., ... Leland, Illinois.
SEVERY, DEXTER, ... Leland, Illinois.
SEVERY, HENRY A., ... Sandwich, Illinois.
SEXTON, W. K., ... Howell, Michigan.
SHALLCROSS, J. W., JR , ... Louisville, Kentucky.
SHALLCROSS, M. B., ... Louisville, Kentucky.
SHERMAN, D. H., ... Dover Plains, New York.
SHIMER, A. S., ... Redington, Pennsylvania.
SHOLES, N. F., ... Earlville, New York.
SIEDLER, CHARLES, ... Jersey City, New Jersey.
SINGEBLY, W. M., ... : . . . . Philadelphia, Pennsylvania.
SLADE, H. F., ... Oneonta, New York.
SMITH, C. C., ... Meadow Brook, New York.
SMITH, CAREY R., ... Santa Ana, California.
SMITH, ELIZUR, ... Lee, Massachusetts.
SMITH, EUGENE, ... Nashville, Tennessee.
SMITH, EVERETT, ... Waltham, Massachusetts.
SMITH, HARLAN P.. . . . . East Saginaw, Michigan.
SMITH, J. GREGORY, ... St. Albans, Vermont.
SMITH, J. N., ... New York, New York.
SMITH, THOMAS R., ... Lincoln, Virginia.
SMITH, W. BROWN, ... Syracuse, New York.
SMITH, W. H., ... New Carlisle, Ohio.
SMITH, W. J., ... Syracuse, New York.
SMITH, WING R., ... Syracuse, New York.
SPENCER, THEODORE L., ... Madison, New York.
SPOFFORD, T. M., ... Pulaski, Tennessee.
STANFORD, LELAND, ... San Francisco, California.
STANTON, T. G., ... Oxford, New York.
STEELE, E. W., ... San Luis Obispo, California.
STEVENS, F. C., ... Attica, New York.
STEVENS, HENRY, ... Lacona, New York.
STEVENS, R. S., ... Attica, New York.
STILLWELL, J. W., ... Troy, Ohio.
STOCKWELL, B. F., ... Chester Center, Iowa.
STONE, J. L., ... Waverly, Pennsylvania.
STURTEVANT, A. R., ... Springboro, Pennsylvania.
SWEET, MARTIN L., ... Grand Rapids, Michigan.
SWEEZEY, C. F., ... Marion, New York.
SWEEZEY, S. W., ... Marion, New York.

TAFT, E. P., ... Providence, Rhode Island.
TAYLOR, C. C., ... Collins, New York.

TAYLOR, D. H., ... Strawberry Point, Iowa.
TEFFT, E. A., ... South Elgin, Illinois.
THOMPSON, SAMUEL R., ... Stelton, New Jersey.
THOMPSON, M. C., ... Randallsville, New York.
TILTON, W. S., ... Boston, Massachusetts.
TOUSEY, W. H., ... Bay City, Michigan.
TRACY, D. D., ... Erie, Pennsylvania.
TROTTER, HENRY, ... Salem, Ohio.
TRUE, D. W., ... Portland, Maine.
TRULOCK, JAMES H., ... Pine Bluff, Arkansas.
TUCKERMAN, J. B., ... Cassville, New York.

UNDERHILL, F. T., ... New York, New York.
UNDERWOOD, ARTHUR, ... Red Lands, California.
UNDERWOOD, J. M., ... Lake City, Minnesota.

VALE, B. R., ... Bonaparte, Iowa.
VANDEVORT, C. H., ... Amity, New York
VAN DRESER, HENRY, ... Cobleskill, New York.
VAN DRESER, J. W., ... Cobleskill, New York.

WADE, I. C., ... Jamestown, Dakota.
WALES, THOMAS B., ... Iowa City, Iowa.
WALES, THOMAS B., Jr., ... Iowa City, Iowa.
WALWORTH, C. C., ... Boston, Massachusetts.
WARNER, H. D., ... Lanesville, Connecticut.
WARNER, H. O., ... New Milford, Connecticut.
WARNER, S. L., ... New Milford, Connecticut.
WARWICK, GEORGE, ... Dummerstown, Vermont.
WASHBURN, E. M., ... Hillsdale, Michigan.
WATERMAN, HENRY, ... Boston, Massachusetts.
WATERMAN, RUFUS, JR., ... East Greenwich, Rhode Island.
WEBBER, W. L., ... East Saginaw, Michigan.
WELLS, GEORGE L., ... Wethersfield, Connecticut.
WESTOVER, WILLIAM, ... Bay City, Michigan.
WHEELER, C. A., ... Deposit, New York.
WHEELER, G. D, ... Deposit, New York.
WHIPPLE, DALLAS B., ... Cuba, New York.
WHITE, D. M., ... Hudson, Wisconsin.
WHITE, HOWARD G., ... Syracuse, New York.
WHITE, JOSIAH H., ... Lakeville, California.
WHITE, WILLARD, ... Boston, Massachusetts.
WHITING, G. M., ... Torrington, Connecticut.
WHITNEY, H. M., ... Boston, Massachusetts.
WHITWORTH, J. L., ... Nashville, Tennessee.
WILCOX, A. G., ... Minneapolis, Minnesota.

WILLETTS, W. R., ... Skaneateles, New York.
WILLIAMS, GEORGE F., ... Fitchburg, Massachusetts.
WILSON, G. O., ... Baltimore, Maryland.
WILSON, J. B., ... Washington, Pennsylvania.
WILSON, R. R., ... Plymouth, Wisconsin.
WOLCOTT, CHARLES W., ... Dedham, Massachusetts.
WOOD, DON J., ... West Exeter, New York.
WOOLSEY, W. W., ... Aiken, South Carolina.
WRIGHT, ALFRED P., ... Buffalo, New York.
WRIGHT, J. F., ... Shell Rock, Iowa.
WRIGHT, S. N., ... South Elgin, Illinois.

YEOMANS, E. L., ... Walworth, New York.
YEOMANS, L. T., ... Walworth, New York.
YEOMANS, T. G., ... Walworth, New York.

FOURTH ANNUAL MEETING

OF THE

HOLSTEIN-FRIESIAN ASSOCIATION OF AMERICA,

Held at the Fifth Avenue Hotel, New York, N. Y.,
March 20th, 1889.

THE PRESIDENT: Gentlemen, it is now time to commence our proceedings for this meeting, and members will do me a kindness if they will announce their names when they arise to address the chair, as I am unacquainted with a great many here, and it is desirable that the reporter should get all the names of those who speak in the meeting.

The Secretary will now call the roll.

The roll was then called. Sixty-two answered present, and two hundred and twenty-five were represented by proxies.

The next order of business will be my address, and I will ask the Secretary to be kind enough to read it for me.

PRESIDENT'S ADDRESS.

Gentlemen: — At the opening of our fourth annual meeting, I desire to congratulate you on the strength and high standing of our Association, which have been so well maintained during the past year.

In membership we are gradually increasing, and our Treasurer's report shows that as an Association we are well-to-do, and financially sound. Our cattle, as a breed, are still at the front, notwithstanding all efforts to displace them. We have stood well during the year wherever we have entered for competitive tests. Some projected tests which might have aroused great interest among dairymen were not, in fact, made, because they were set down for the summer months, when very few cows are fresh in milk.

We have made a good fight to attain our present position, and now let us keep it, and never back down when competition with other breeds is offered. A generous rivalry will stimulate us to renewed effort, but indifference will tend towards gradual decay.

Owing to the number of Holstein-Friesians now in this country, we have become practically independent of Holland as a source of supply, and importations have almost wholly ceased. It will be well, however, to see that the source of supply is kept as pure as required by our regulations, and to let the Hollanders know that we are still greatly interested in what they are doing.

During the past year the partial failure of crops, and the general downward tendency of all commodities, has materially affected our cattle interests. Let me urge you to a renewal of your aggressive activity, and a general revival of interest in all that pertains to our breed.

Echo, Mercedes, Aaggie, Pietertje, and a few others, have become very prominent names in the dairy world. I am sure that these are not phenomenal, but simply representative of the breed. There is no doubt in my mind that there are many more comparatively unknown cows that are equally good. Bring them out, gentlemen, and show the people the sort of stock we are raising.

Laws now in force are reasonably successful in protecting those who desire to eat bread and butter instead of bread and lard, or bread and tallow.

Butter substitutes put up and sold for what they are, and to a public preferring a substitute to the genuine article, ought not to do us any harm. So long as that business is conducted squarely, we may as well keep silent, and turn the rest of the trouble over to the physicians. Any attempt on the part of the substitute men to change our laws should be promptly met by us.

There is some agitation in our Association over the system of Advanced Registry. It is not generally and extensively used by our members, but those who do use it are entitled to reasonable benefits from it, and are interested in its perpetuation, having already expended considerable time and means in advancing their cattle to this registry. There is nothing compulsory about it, and as it stands, it does not signify except as to the individuals which it describes. The overwhelming majority of our cattle are never offered for advancement. Personally I have not had the time to give the Advanced Registry much attention, and none of my cattle have been offered for advancement, but there is one phase of the question which should furnish an answer to every argument for its abolition.

Most of us will recollect that the institution of the Advanced Registry by the Holstein-Friesian Association was one of the conditions of union of the Holstein and Dutch-Friesian Associations.

Gentlemen, that was a part of our faith with one another when the two associations became one, and should be respected.

To those who object to the so-called aristocracy of advanced cattle, we would say that we do not believe that any of our members will be so short-sighted as to claim that by reason of advanced registry their cattle are any better than those of their neighbors who have not seen fit to have them formally advanced. If the time ever comes when obnoxious comparisons will be drawn, a new question will be presented, which may then be dealt with as the emergency demands.

Among many questions of importance coming up at this meeting will be that of the restriction of pedigree registration of males. There is much to be said for and against such restrictions. Theoretically, it is undoubtedly correct. What its practical working may be among the farmers and small breeders, upon whom we rely for our market, is a matter of great gravity.

As an association we have prospered financially — the surplus has not grown particularly burdensome, but at this time it will be well to reduce the fees for registry and transfer. Of course we can return to a higher scale whenever the necessity for more money arises.

The reduction of these fees may do away with proposed changes or reduction of the fee for membership. When the other fees become merely nominal, the advantage of the member over the non-member will not be greatly apparent.

A good balance in the treasury is advisable at all times, both for current expense money, and for those expenses incident to necessary representation before legislative bodies. We have been able to offer special premiums at public tests and exhibitions, and have aroused the people to the knowledge that the Holstein-Friesians are really very good cattle, after all that their would-be rivals have said against them.

Gentlemen, I have been greatly honored by your choice for President during the year just closed. We have acted in harmony, and are prosperous. Questions may come up at this meeting upon which our opinion may be divided, but we cannot go very far wrong if we have in view always what we believe shall be for the best interest of our association and our breed.

May I bespeak for my successor the same kindly consideration and support which have been accorded to me during my term of office.

The next order of business is the Committee on Proxies.

Mr. T. G. YEOMANS: I move that the chair appoint a committee of two, with the understanding that I shall not be one of the committee.

The motion prevailed, and the President appointed as such committee Anthony Lamb and C. W. Wolcott.

THE PRESIDENT: The Secretary will now read his report:

SECRETARY'S REPORT.

To the Members of the Holstein-Friesian Association of America: GENTLEMEN:— I beg leave to present the following as my report for the past year, which, if carefully examined and compared with reports of other like associations, I feel sure will meet with your general approbation. I take this opportunity, however, to state that I feel positive good results would follow the adoption of the few slight changes in our by-laws proposed to-day which bear upon the business of the Association. I refer, in the first place, to the large volume of correspondence in relation to the naming of animals. A vast number of letters are yearly written on this subject —

mostly to non-members of the Association — the greater part of which could be dispensed with if the proposed addition to Section 5 of Article IV. of the by-laws is agreed upon, as I trust it will be. I also hope that the necessary changes will be made authorizing the Secretary to issue more than one volume of the Herd-Book each year. I would strongly recommend that each volume be closed as soon as a sufficient number of pedigrees have been received, and as the registry of males will undoubtedly relatively decrease, it would be well, as it seems to me, to publish the pedigrees of males and females in one book, and issue as soon as a desirable-sized volume is assured. By a continuance of our present plan we will soon put out a volume of such size as to be inconvenient and altogether unmanagable. By the adoption of the plan I propose we would not only have our volumes uniform, but the work could be done at a considerable saving of labor and expense.

Our membership now numbers three hundred and thirty-two, which will be increased to three hundred and forty-three provided the eleven applications of gentlemen who now desire to join us are accepted. The death of but one member has been reported to me during the year — Mr. John Mitchell, of Vail's Gate, New York. As it may prove of interest to you to know how this membership is distributed among the states, I will say that 119 reside in New York, 32 in Massachusetts, 24 in Pennsylvania, 21 in Michigan, 18 in Illinois, 17 in Ohio, 12 in Iowa, 8 in Minnesota, 8 in Tennessee, 8 in California; Wisconsin and New Jersey have 7 each; Vermont and Connecticut, 6 each; Kentucky, 5; Indiana and Virginia, 4 each; Missouri, Mississippi, and Nebraska, 3 each; Maryland, Rhode Island, South Carolina, Maine, and Dakota, 2 each; New Hampshire, Arkansas, Louisiana, Kansas, Delaware, Indian Territory, and Ontario, 1 each.

The breeders of our cattle, as shown by our books, number about 4,850, and we have now on our records the pedigrees of 17,661 bulls and 27,784 cows — a total of 45,445 animals. Of this number 43,589 have been registered since 1880, when there were but 1,856 animals on record. It is therefore safe to claim that no other breed of cattle can show anywhere near such an increase as ours, and the popularity of the breed has advanced as rapidly as its numbers. I do not recall an instance where, during the past year, our cattle have been defeated at the fairs when competing with other breeds, and in both milk and butter tests made at the leading exhibitions the Holstein-Friesians have nearly always proved the winners.

The special premiums offered by this Association have been awarded and paid as follows:

To the Home Farm Fine Stock Company, of Hampton, Iowa, for best butter cow tested at the Iowa State Fair, $70.00; for third best butter cow at the same fair, $20.00.

To the Friesland Live Stock Company, of Aberdeen, Dakota, for best butter cow tested at the Dakota Territorial Fair, $66.66.

To J. C. Wade, of Jamestown, Dakota, for the second best butter cow, $33.34.

To W. M. Chapin, of Sheffield, Massachusetts, for best butter cow tested at the Bay State Fair, $50.00.

To W. A. Russell, of Lawrence, Massachusetts, for cow producing the largest amount of milk at the Bay State Fair, $50.00.

To B. Waddell, of Marion, Ohio, for duplicate premiums awarded the steer Ohio Champion, at the American Fat-Stock Show, greatest gain per day, $50.00; best Holstein-Friesian steer under one year, $30.00; sweepstakes, $75.00. To Mr. Waddell was also awarded the first prize for cost of production, which will entitle him to $50.00 more.

To F. C. Stevens, of Attica, New York, for duplicates of premiums on butter awarded at the Buffalo International Fair, first on granulated butter, $60.00; second on thirty-pound package, $50.00; second on package of five to ten pounds for delivery unbroken to consumer, $30.00; second on prints, $30.00.

To N. J. Leavitt, of Waseca, Minnesota, for duplicate of special butter prize at Minnesota State Fair, $15.24.

To Frank A. Leavitt, of Waseca, Minnesota, for duplicate of special butter prize at Minnesota State Fair, $14.72.

To Jere Allis, of Isinours, Minnesota, for duplicates of the following premiums awarded at the American Fat-Stock and Dairy Show at Chicago, Illinois: First on Holstein-Friesian butter, $6; second on dairy butter made in Minnesota, $5.

To Ogden Cole, of Addison, Michigan, for duplicates of premiums at same exhibition, first and second on Michigan butter, $15.00.

To the Home Farm Fine Stock Company, of Hampton, Iowa, second premium on dairy butter made in Iowa, $5.00; second premium on Holstein-Friesian butter, $3.00.

Total, $678.96.

During the year which closed March 1st, there have been recorded 56 imported cows, 3,470 American-bred bulls, and 4,392 American-bred cows — a total of 7,918 animals; 5,230 transfers of ownership have been made on our records — 1,934 bulls and 3,296 cows; 101 duplicate certificates have been issued, showing the total number of certificates issued to be 13,293. Volume IV. of the Herd-Book closed with the entry of 3,190 bulls and 4,145 cows; the pedigrees are already printed, and the copy for the tables of transfers and indexes of the volume are well along.

The receipts and expenditures for the year have been as follows:

RECEIPTS.

Received for membership fees	$ 1,275 00
For registry of imported cows	1,120 00
From members for registry of bulls	1,237 50
From non-members for registry of bulls	4,380 00
From members for registry of cows	1,532 00
From non-members for registry of cows	5,867 50
From members for transfer of bulls	303 50
From non-members for transfer of bulls	1,136 50
From members for transfer of cows	636 50

From non-members for transfer of cows	1,742 50	
For duplicate certificates	50 50	
For inspection of imported cattle	260 00	
For Herd-Books	382 72	
		$19,922 82

EXPENDITURES.

For Board of Officers' traveling expenses	$ 463 20	
For clerk hire	2,728 05	
For expenses, including office rent	1,140 24	
For printing report of meeting, index of cattle, certificate books, etc.	1,227 69	
For inspection of imported cattle	44 00	
For special premiums	718 96	
For stamp account, government envelopes, wrappers, etc.	756 34	
For Missouri Agricultural College	176 00	
For sundry personal accounts, fees refunded, drafts returned for endorsement, etc.	212 00	
For cash balance remitted to W. Brown Smith, Treasurer	12,180 65	
For amount due on registry and transfer fees.	275 69	
		$19,922 82

Respectfully submitted,

THOMAS B. WALES,
Secretary.

Mr. W. G. POWELL: I move that the report be received and published in the minutes.

Mr. C. W. HORR: I suggest that the address of the President be included in Mr. Powell's motion.

Mr. W. G. POWELL: I accept that suggestion.

Mr. C. W. HORR: Then I second the motion.

Carried.

THE SECRETARY: I am requested to announce that it will be well at this time to fix upon an hour at which we shall take a recess for luncheon, as the reporters wish to know how to arrange so that they can get out the report of the proceedings speedily.

Mr. J. B. DUTCHER: I move that we take a recess at 1 o'clock, and re-assemble at 2 o'clock again.

Mr. J. L. STONE: I second that motion.

Carried.

THE PRESIDENT: The report of the Treasurer is the next thing in order.

TREASURER'S REPORT.

Mr. President, and Gentlemen of the Holstein-Friesian Association of America: I herewith beg leave to make the following report of the receipts and expenditures of the Association for the fiscal year ending with the date of this meeting:

RECEIPTS.

1888.				
March 21.		Balance on hand, as per last report		$25,413 36
June	5.	Cash from Thomas B. Wales, Secretary, as per quarterly report	$1,471 44	
July	1.	Accrued interest on deposit, Syracuse Savings Bank	60 00	
July	1.	Accrued interest on deposit, Onondaga County Savings Bank	60 00	
July	1.	Accrued interest on deposit, Salt Springs National Bank	342 65	
Sept.	7.	Cash from Thomas B. Wales, Secretary, as per quarterly report	2,132 81	
Dec.	3.	Cash from Thomas B. Wales, Secretary, as per quarterly report	2,632 28	
Dec.	31.	Accrued interest on deposit, Syracuse Savings Bank	60 00	
Dec	31.	Accrued interest on deposit, Onondaga County Savings Bank	60 00	
Dec.	31.	Accrued interest on deposit, Salt Springs National Bank	340 00	
March	4.	Cash from Thomas B. Wales, Secretary, as per quarterly report	5,944 12	
		Total receipts for fiscal year		13,103 30
				$38,516 66

EXPENDITURES.

1888.				
March 23.		S. Burchard, account of Advanced Registry	$ 87 61	
March 23.		Isaac C. Otis, account of Advanced Registry	24 00	
March 23.		Thomas B. Wales, salary, six months to March 1st, 1888.	1,250 00	
March 24.		S. Hoxie, account of Advanced Registry	56 00	
May	1.	J. N. Muncey, account of Advanced Registry	24 00	
May	1.	H. D. Warner, account of Advanced Registry	44 00	
July	31.	Egbert, Fidlar, & Chambers, printing Herd-Book, etc.	3,684 00	
Sept.	15.	Thomas B. Wales, salary, six months to Sept. 1st, 1888.	1,250 00	
Sept.	15.	S. J. Roberts, account of Advanced Registry	16 00	
Oct.	9.	S. Burchard, account of Advanced Registry	40 00	
Oct.	9.	S. Hoxie, salary, six months to Sept. 1st, 1888	500 00	
Nov.	23.	J. N. Muncey, account of Advanced Registry	25 00	
1889.				
Jan.	12.	S. Burchard, account of Advanced Registry	114 00	
Feb.	11.	H. D. Warner, account of Advanced Registry	76 00	
Feb.	23.	S. N. Wright, account of Advanced Registry	16 00	
Feb.	20.	Thomas B. Wales, salary, six months to March 1st, 1889.	1,250 00	
Feb.	20.	W. Brown Smith, salary, one year to March 21st, 1889	250 00	
Feb.	20.	S. Hoxie, salary, six months to March 21st, 1889	500 00	
		Total expenses for fiscal year		$ 9,206 61
		Balance on hand		29,310 05
				$38,516 66

Which is deposited as follows:

In Syracuse Savings Bank	$ 2,940 00
In Onondaga County Savings Bank	2,940 00
In Salt Springs National Bank	23,430 05
	$29,310 05

Respectfully submitted,

W. BROWN SMITH,

Treasurer.

Mr. W. M. LIGGETT: I move that the report be received and published in the minutes.

Mr. S. L. HOXIE: I second that motion.

Carried.

THE PRESIDENT: The next business in order is the report of the Superintendent of Advanced Registry. Mr. Hoxie will read the report:

REPORT OF SUPERINTENDENT OF ADVANCED REGISTRY.

To the President and Members of the Holstein-Friesian Association of America: During the official year closing with this meeting, the second volume of the Advanced Register has been published, bringing the entries of cows to six hundred and eleven, and of bulls to sixty-one. The cost of printing and wrapping in suitable form for mailing has been $477.66. The other expenditures have been as follows:

EXPENDITURES.

Bills for printing rules, blank forms, etc.	$ 53 58
Stationery not included in printing bills	2 68
Four cattle-measures for Inspectors	20 00
Express charges	75
Postage	63 60
Traveling expenses	9 65
Use of telegraph and telephone	1 40
Total expenditures	$629 22

RECEIPTS.

Balance on hand at last annual meeting	$ 18 42
Copy of first volume Advanced Registry sold	1 65
Registry fees received	242 50
Total receipts	$262 57
There is now due the Association for registry fees	$293 00
Due to members for over-payment of registry fees	8 50

S. HOXIE,
Superintendent of Advanced Registry.

Mr. J. D. WHEELER: I move that the report be received and approved, and published in the minutes.

Mr. W. M. LIGGETT: I second that motion.

Carried.

THE PRESIDENT: The next business in order is the report from committees. I suppose that the Committee on Proxies is not yet ready to report. Therefore the proposed amendments to the by-laws will be the first business before the Association. I will ask the Secretary to read the proposed amendments, and the Association can act upon them *seriatim.*

THE SECRETARY: "Article I. of Section 1. By inserting after 'dollars,' in sixth line: 'Also any firm or corporation, owners of Holstein-Friesian cattle in severalty, whose members are all citizens of North America, may apply for membership as a firm or corporation, and deposit the sum of one hundred and fifty dollars. Such firm or corporation, if admitted, shall be entitled to one vote, and one copy of each volume of the Herd-Book published after admission."

Mr. C. W. HORR: Mr. President, I would suggest, if there is no motion in regard to this proposed amendment, that the Secretary proceed to read the next proposed amendment.

THE PRESIDENT: Gentlemen, what will you do with this amendment?

Mr. J. B. DUTCHER: I move to lay it on the table.

Mr. F. L. HOUGHTON: If that course is pursued, Mr. President, I would inquire what I am to do with the proxies that I have been instructed to vote upon. I have been instructed to vote for this amendment by quite a large number of proxies.

Mr. J. B. DUTCHER: Vote with them to lay it on the table, then.

Mr. F. L. HOUGHTON: But I have been instructed to vote for the amendment.

Mr. J. L. STONE: It seems to me, gentlemen, that this proposed amendment touches a matter that has considerable merit in it. There are a great many members that this Association has on its roll who are receiving no benefit whatever from their membership, so far as dollars and cents are concerned, and this proposition will enable them, by the payment of an additional fee, to receive some benefit. I therefore think that the proposition should be considered by this meeting.

Mr. J. B. DUTCHER: Very well, I will withdraw my motion.

Mr. C. W. HORR: Mr. President, whoever framed this proposed amendment has, I think, been unfortunate in the language he has chosen, because he says: "Also any firm or corporation, owners of Holstein-Friesian cattle in severalty." Now, if I understand the meaning of the word "severalty," it is that it means individually. He should have said *jointly*, and so he has not given a notice that is suitable for the accomplishment of the purpose he designed, evidently; he has used a word the meaning of which is directly the opposite of what he intended.

Mr. ———: As the gentleman looks towards me, I suppose he means me, but I did not offer this proposed amendment, and —

Mr. C. W. HORR: (Interposing.) Oh, no; I looked towards you because I like your looks. (Laughter.)

Mr. ———: Well, I would like to say, Mr. President, that that word had attracted my attention. If it is not thought proper, why, I have no objection, so far as I am concerned as a member of this Association, to vote to change it.

THE PRESIDENT: I will ask the Secretary to state to us whether he has had any correspondence in relation to this matter or not?

THE SECRETARY: I will say that a great many persons who have sent me their proxies are members of firms, and they would very much like to have firms admitted to membership. This matter has been brought up at three or four of our meetings, and still there are some thirty or forty firms that are clamoring for admission to this Association. Personally, I do not see any reason why they should not be admitted.

Mr. W. W. PROPER: I have always had to pay a full fee for registry, and I am a member of a firm. I have not had any benefit in that direction at all.

Mr. W. B. CLARK: I will state, Mr. President, that I was a member of a firm for a long time, and paid full fees, and finally had my associate admitted as a member of the Association, and paid the initiation fee of $100.00. Therefore I am opposed to any change in the rule.

Mr. O. P. CHAPMAN: Mr. President, I am in the same boat.

Mr. W. G. POWELL: The serious objection that I see to the addition of the amendment is this: That we have no control over the members of a firm whatever. They may be a corporation of fifty members, and half of them may be scalawags, for all we know, whom we would not admit to membership here under any circumstances. It should be so amended that each member of the firm shall be passed upon by the Board as a suitable person for membership, and also that any violation of our rules by one of the members of the firm shall exclude the whole firm. Then I think it would be all right. Now, persons have been offered here for membership from time to time, and have been rejected. Those same persons may make up a company or firm, and then offer themselves for membership, and if we make no restrictions they may go on and do just what we have prohibited them from doing. While I admit that there are many cases where it seems a hardship, yet if we let down the bars so low as it is proposed, I think it would be exceedingly dangerous. I think our safety as an association should be our first consideration.

Mr. W. M. SINGERLY: I renew the motion, Mr. President, to lay this upon the table.

Mr. J. B. DUTCHER: I second that motion.

Carried.

THE PRESIDENT: The Secretary will read the next proposed amendment.

THE SECRETARY: "Article 2, Section 10: Strike out in last two lines, 'with sureties to the satisfaction of,' and insert, 'of a surety company satisfactory to.'"

Mr. T. G. YEOMANS: I move the adoption of that.

Mr. W. G. POWELL: It looks to me, Mr. President, as though that was an advertisement for the advancement of some surety company. Who is to say whether that company is good or not? The Treasurer has the opportunity now of offering that same kind of security, if the Board will accept it. It seems to me that the privilege of personal security is better, and I think it should be left to the Board to say what security they will accept.

Mr. T. G. YEOMANS: I made the motion simply to get the question up. I now withdraw that motion, and I move to lay the matter upon the table.

Mr. W. G. POWELL: I second that motion.

Carried.

THE PRESIDENT: The Secretary will read the next proposed amendment.

THE SECRETARY: "Article 2, Section 17: By inserting after 'bond,' in last line, the words, 'of a surety company.'"

Mr. W. G. POWELL: I move to lay that upon the table, also.

Mr. W. M. SINGERLY: I second the motion.

Carried.

THE PRESIDENT: The Secretary will read the next proposed amendment.

THE SECRETARY: "Article 3: By inserting Section 2½, to read as follows: 'Members of this corporation cannot vote by proxy at any meeting of this corporation except by addressing a communication to this Association, in which he may discuss the purpose or purposes for which the meeting is called, and state how he will vote on each question which may lawfully come before the meeting, as provided in above section, and such communications, and such votes, shall be read in the meeting at the time when such subject is under discussion to which such communication pertains and refers, and the votes shall be counted and have the same effect as they would if the member was personally present and voted.'"

Mr. W. M. SINGERLY: I move that that be laid upon the table.

Mr. W. G. POWELL: I second the motion.

Carried.

THE PRESIDENT: The Secretary will read the next proposed amendment.

THE SECRETARY: "Article 4, Section 1: Omit in last line, 'at intervals of not less than one year.'"

I wish to say, gentlemen, that this proposition is made by myself, for the reason that I find it quite necessary to issue more than one copy of the Herd-Book each year.

Mr. W. M. LIGGETT: I move that that be adopted.

Mr. T. G. YEOMANS: I second that motion.

Adopted.

THE PRESIDENT: The Secretary will read the next proposed amendment.

THE SECRETARY: "Article 4, Section 2: In ninth line, between the words 'of' and 'bulls,' insert 'three thousand.' Between the words 'of' and 'cows,' insert 'thirty-five hundred.'"

This proposition was also made by me, and I now beg leave to withdraw it, because since I printed the call for this meeting I find that it would not work so well as I had anticipated, for the reason that we shall probably register in the future fewer bulls each year; and I propose to offer in place of this a resolution authorizing me to issue a Herd-Book whenever a certain size shall be reached, the volume to include bulls and cows, and to close whenever the size agreed upon is reached, and then commence another volume. I think this plan will be very satisfactory to every one.

Mr. W. G. POWELL: I second the amendment proposed by the Secretary.

Mr. GERRIT S. MILLER: Would it not be well to state the number of pedigrees?

THE SECRETARY: I think it would be better to provide that each volume shall contain a certain number of pages. Here is a Herd-Book (indicating) that contains eight hundred and forty-one pages. Whether or not the Association thinks this book is about the right size is for them to say.

Mr. GERRIT S. MILLER: How many pedigrees are there in that book?

THE SECRETARY: There are three thousand, five hundred and twelve.

THE PRESIDENT: Well, gentlemen, what will you do with the amendment proposed by the Secretary?

A MEMBER: I would suggest that it be left to the discretion of the Secretary.

Mr. HUIDEKOPER: I hardly think we have had any notice of this proposed amendment, Mr. President, and therefore you cannot put it as an amendment to our by-laws, because there is no such notice. I make that point of order.

THE PRESIDENT: I think that point of order is well taken.

Mr. F. L. HOUGHTON: Mr. President, whenever a by-law is proposed to be amended in any way whatever, the proposed amendment brings the whole by-law in question. That specific amendment is not the only word that we can consider, but we can consider the amendment of any part of that article.

Mr. W. M. SINGERLY: Yes, I agree with the gentleman on that.

Mr. W. G. POWELL: The Secretary's suggestion is that the Herd-Books be published in one volume, both bulls and cows, but in two separate parts.

Mr. W. M. SINGERLY: I move that the matter be laid upon the table.

Mr. GERRIT S. MILLER: I second the motion.

Carried.

THE PRESIDENT: The Secretary will now read the next proposed amendment.

THE SECRETARY: "Add to same section: 'The price to be charged for each volume of the Herd-Book to non-members of this Association shall be its cost price, with postage or expressage added.'"

I will state for the information of the Association that heretofore I have been allowed to charge whatever price I saw fit for the Herd-Book. I desire to be relieved of that discretion, and so I have submitted the change proposed.

Mr. W. M. SINGERLY: I move that that be adopted.

Mr. E. A. POWELL: I second the motion.

Adopted.

THE PRESIDENT: The Secretary will read the next proposed amendment.

THE SECRETARY: "Article 4, Section 3: Strike out the word 'thoroughbred,' and insert in its place 'pure bred.'"

It seems to me, gentlemen, that we have printed the word "thoroughbred" long enough. The correct term is "pure bred."

Mr. E. A. POWELL: I move the adoption of that.

Mr. W. M. SINGERLY: I second the motion.

Adopted.

THE PRESIDENT: The Secretary will read the next proposed amendment.

THE SECRETARY: "Article 4, Section 4: Strike out the word 'thoroughbred,' and insert in its place 'pure bred.'"

Mr. W. M. SINGERLY: I move the adoption of that.

Mr. E. A. POWELL: I second the motion.

Adopted.

THE PRESIDENT: The Secretary will read the next proposed amendment.

THE SECRETARY: "Article 4, Section 5: Strike out of the second line the words, 'or following the form,' and insert 'forms.'"

That will oblige applicants for registry and transfer to make their applications on our forms, which will be much more convenient for us.

Mr. W. M. SINGERLY: I move the adoption of that.

Mr. E. A. POWELL: I second the motion.

Adopted.

THE PRESIDENT: The Secretary will read the next proposed amendment.

THE SECRETARY: "Add to this section: 'In case the name given in the application for the registry of an animal is in use, or cannot be allowed for any reason, the Secretary will furnish a name; and if, upon receipt of the certificate of registry, the name should not be satisfactory to the applicant, the certificate must be returned *at once* for correction, accompanied by a list of names in order of preference.'"

Mr. W. G. POWELL: I think, Mr. President, that every breeder would prefer to name his own cattle, and the adoption of a rule of that kind might lead to dissatisfaction in many cases. I think it would give greater satisfaction to let every breeder name his own cattle.

Mr. W. H. SMITH: I move that that be laid on the table.

Mr. W. G. POWELL: I second the motion.

Carried.

THE PRESIDENT: The Secretary will read the next proposed amendment.

THE SECRETARY: "No name of an animal shall be accepted for entry if containing more than thirty letters, not including the numeral affixed. The name of an animal once printed in the Herd-Book shall not be changed."

Mr. W. G. POWELL: I would inquire if there are any names in the book which contain more than thirty letters, or which contain as many as thirty letters?

THE SECRETARY: Yes, sir; some contain forty letters, and even more. The Jersey Cattle Club have gotten down to twenty letters, and I have suggested here that we restrict it to thirty.

Mr. W. M. SINGERLY: I move that we divide that proposed amendment into two parts. I suggest that we make the first sentence one proposed amendment, and the second sentence another proposed amendment. Therefore, I move the adoption of the first sentence, as read by the Secretary.

Mr. A. LANGWORTHY: I second that motion.

Adopted.

Mr. W. M. SINGERLY: Now, Mr. President, as to the second sentence read by the Secretary, I move that it be laid on the table.

Mr. J. B. DUTCHER: I move, as an amendment, that it be rejected.

Mr. W. M. SINGERLY: I accept that—or, rather, I will second that amendment, that it be rejected.

Rejected.

THE PRESIDENT: The Secretary will now read the next proposed amendment.

THE SECRETARY: "Article IV., Section 6. Strike out of second line the words, 'shipped from Europe after March 18th, 1885.'" The reason for this proposition is, to do away with the printing of this two or three times a year, over and over again, when it really means nothing.

Mr. W. G. POWELL: I move the adoption of that.

Mr. C. R. PAYNE: I second that.

Adopted.

THE PRESIDENT: The Secretary will read the next proposed amendment.

THE SECRETARY: "Strike out of the fourth and fifth lines, 'or following the form for such certificates,' and insert 'forms.'"

Mr. O. B. POTTER: Mr. President, there are a multitude of papers and circulars that I get during the year, and it is very difficult for me always to keep them so that I can put my hand upon them. Now, if I was called upon to make out an entry according to the exact form prescribed by this Association, it would be very difficult for me to do so unless I copied a previous form that I had. If you mean a printed circular that has been sent to us by the Secretary, I think it might lead either to inconvenience or to preventing people from registering too many cattle.

THE SECRETARY: I think if the gentleman had to take care of as many papers as I, and keep every letter, name, and number in order for five thousand people, he would wish to have his papers all so uniform that they could be filed properly and referred to easily. That is the only reason why I desire this change. The forms are furnished by me in any quantity desired, free of cost.

Mr. A. LANGWORTHY: I move the adoption of that proposed amendment.

Mr. W. M. SINGERLY: I second it.

Adopted.

THE PRESIDENT: The Secretary will now read the next proposed amendment.

THE SECRETARY: "Article IV., Section 8. Strike out of lines seven to ten inclusive: 'The importer's name to be inserted in breeder's certificate before shipment, and after June 10th, until July 1st, 1885, it shall be verified by list from American Consul, on and after July 1st, 1885.' Omit from line twenty-five: 'Shipped from Europe after March 18th, 1885.' Omit from line thirty-six: 'Shipped from Europe after March 18th, 1885.'"

This is simply made, as the previous proposition was, to avoid printing over and over again.

Mr. T. G. YEOMANS: I move its adoption.

Mr. W. G. POWELL: The words "the importer's name to be inserted in breeder's certificate before shipment," I would not strike out, and neither would I strike out the provision that the list shall be verified by the American Consul; and I would strike out "on and after July 1st, 1885." I would also strike out the next two clauses: "Shipped from Europe after March 18th, 1885," and "shipped from Europe after March 18th, 1885," in line thirty-six. I make that motion.

A MEMBER: I second that motion.

THE SECRETARY: I would state to the Association that we have never had a case yet where the services of the American Consul were required, and when applications for these breeder's certificates are sent to me, I am obliged, under our by-laws, to insert the name of the importer, and keep a record of the blanks that are sent out, and attach to each one the seal of the Association. I only made the proposition to save useless printing.

THE PRESIDENT: The question is now upon the amendment as proposed by Mr. W. G. Powell. We will take a vote upon that.

Adopted.

THE PRESIDENT: The question now recurs upon the adoption of the whole clause as amended.

Adopted.

THE PRESIDENT: The Secretary will read the next proposed amendment.

THE SECRETARY: "Article IV., Section 10. Strike out 'and payment of fifty cents by members of the corporation, and one dollar by all other persons,' and insert 'free of charge, if made within thirty days of date of sale; if after that, one dollar will be charged for each transfer.'" This virtually does away with the transfer fee, both for members and non-members.

Mr. C. PRATT: I would amend that amendment, and make it read: "Free for members," without any reference to date. I want to make it so that it is a benefit to belong to this Association. If you are going to make these things free for non-members, why they are going to hold out for it.

Mr. W. M. SINGERLY: From an amendment passed by the Board of Officers yesterday in regard to the registration of bulls, by which the fees of this Association would probably be reduced very considerably, I move the rejection of that whole amendment, so as not in any way to impair our receipts for the coming year.

Mr. T. G. YEOMANS: If we reject this, we have nothing to build upon.

Mr. W. M. SINGERLY: My object is not to reduce our receipts.

Mr. T. G. YEOMANS: If we reject this, then we have no opportunity to-day to reduce our transfer fees, or to reduce our registrations; but the registration of bulls comes up later, not of cows.

Mr. E. A. POWELL: It will be remembered, perhaps, that two years ago a motion was made to reduce one-half the registry fee, and transfers were free. That was made for one year. At the expiration of that one year the matter was entirely overlooked. It was not brought up before this Association at all, and consequently it went back to the old registration fee. That has produced more dissatisfaction than any one omission that I remember to have taken place in a long time. The feeling among breeders generally is that the present time has been a hard one to tide over for all breeders, and that we are carrying a large surplus in the treasury. The breeders generally seem to feel — and it was a very universal feeling of regret — that they had to go back to that old fee at these times; and I think it will be a great disappointment to breeders generally if there is not some action taken in regard to this registration fee at the present time, especially when we consider the balance we have in the treasury. At the present time we have more money on hand than we need. I therefore move, as an amendment, that we make the registry fee the same as it was two years ago.

Mr. ——— : I second that motion.

Mr. EDWARD P. TAFT: I would rise to the point of order that this is simply the registry of transfers. Section 5 provides for the registry fee, which is a different thing entirely.

THE PRESIDENT: I think that point of order is well taken.

Mr. E. A. POWELL: Then I move to amend this in the same way — that the transfer fee be the same as it was two years ago.

THE SECRETARY: If the fees are to be changed, it is necessary to change the by-laws, and make some stated fee. That fee was fifty cents for registry by members of the Association, and $2.00 for non-members.

Mr. EDWARD P. TAFT: If we pass this amendment, it makes transfer fees entirely free to everybody, and the registration fee stands exactly as it is provided for in Section 5, Article IV.— "$1.00 for members, and $2.00 for non-members."

THE SECRETARY: The reason I proposed that we make the transfers free was that it is very important that we get the transfers in as soon as possible. There is not a great deal of work to be done to complete a transfer of ownership, and I thought it would be well to abolish the fee. Of course I shall not press it.

Mr. E. A. POWELL: The time, "thirty days," is too short, and I would suggest making the time longer. We all know that quite frequently, in selling stock, persons will come and make a selection, and possibly pay a small deposit, and then go home and make further arrangements. I think it would be very foolish to adopt that for thirty days, and I certainly would not make it less than ninety days.

Mr. J. B. DUTCHER: There is one question that I would like to ask the Secretary: A member of the Association selling an animal to a nonmember and giving him an application for transfer, whether that would be chargeable to the member or non-member; whether the non-member would have to pay, or the member would have a right to transfer without payment?

THE SECRETARY: I was ordered by the Board, provided an application for a transfer came from a member, to charge the member's fee; if it came from a non member, to charge him the non-member's fee.

Mr. W. H. SMITH: I move an amendment to the amendment: To charge non-members fifty cents for transfer, and to charge members nothing at all.

Mr. W. G. POWELL: I move to make it ninety days instead of thirty days.

Mr. E. A. POWELL: I second that.

Mr. W. M. SINGERLY: Then I withdraw my motion, and that will make Mr. Powell's the original motion before the Association.

Mr. J. B. DUTCHER: Then, at the expiration of ninety days, if this amendment is adopted, all the members or non-members will have to pay the one dollar?

THE SECRETARY: Yes.

THE PRESIDENT: The question now before the Association is on the motion of Mr. Powell. A vote will be taken now upon that.

Adopted.

THE PRESIDENT: The Secretary will now read the next proposed amendment.

THE SECRETARY: "Add to this section: 'Extended pedigrees of registered animals, bearing the seal of the Association, will be furnished, upons application, for one dollar each.'"

This change is proposed by myself. It takes quite a long time to write extended pedigrees, and I think we should not give that to anybody unless they pay a fair price for it.

Mr. E. A. POWELL: I think that should be adopted.

Mr. A. LANGWORTHY: I second the adoption of that.

Adopted.

THE SECRETARY: I have been instructed to give notice that it will be proposed to reduce the registration and transfer fees for members and non-members, and also to abolish any or all fees at present charged to members. The application for this change has come from many people, and in many forms.

Mr. C. W. HORR: I move you, Mr. President, inasmuch as we have practically disposed of that question, that we pass it for the present, until we have discussed the all-important bull question. If the suggestion of the committee on the bull question is adopted, it may have a very serious bearing upon this. I therefore suggest that we pass this for the present.

Mr. W. M. SINGERLY: I move that we lay it upon the table.

Mr. E. A. POWELL: We cannot take it up again from the table at this session if that course is pursued.

Mr. W. M. SINGERLY: Then I will withdraw my motion to lay it on table.

THE PRESIDENT: Very well. Then it will be passed for the present. What is the next business in order, Mr. Secretary?

THE SECRETARY: The next business in order is to hear the report of the committee appointed to report a plan for the restriction of the registration of males. This committee consisted of the entire Board of Officers, and was appointed at the last annual meeting to report at this.

THE PRESIDENT: This matter was up in special meeting yesterday, and I think the Secretary can inform the Association better than I can what was done about it.

THE SECRETARY: As I understand it, the committee agreed to recommend to the Association that the registry fee for bulls be increased to $5.00. Also that the Association agree to pay $5.00 for each and every male calf slaughtered or castrated while in good health between the ages of five and forty days, upon proper proof furnished to the Secretary, which must include the affidavit of the owner.

Mr. D. H. BURRELL: Gentlemen, before proceeding to discuss this subject, I wish to call the attention of the Association to a very pleasant fact. We have the pleasure of having here at this moment the Hon. Warner Miller, and I call upon Mr. Horr, of Ohio, to present to Senator Miller our welcome in a formal manner. [Applause].

Mr. C. W. HORR: Mr. President and Members of the Holstein-Friesian Association of America: There are many things in this country that we are proud of; there are many things in New York State to be proud of, of its great cities, and of its great commercial activity; but, more than all this, New York State has a right to be proud of its four millions of intelligent, happy, and patriotic citizens, and especially proud of the fact that included among those persons, living and dead, are such names as Alexander Hamilton, Roscoe Conkling, and Warner Miller. [Applause]. I suppose my friend, Mr. Burrell, after consultation with your President, accorded to me the pleasure of saying a few words of welcome to Mr. Miller upon this occasion, for the purpose of letting him know that he is as well known to the citizens of Ohio as he is to the citizens of his own state. His honorable career is well known to every boy, and especially to every boy who has a Republican father; that he left one of your best colleges to enter the army as a private, and that he came out from the war with eagles on his shoulders. It is well known that he went into the assembly and made a record that he may well be proud of; that he was then elected to congress, and filled a position in the lower house with such dignity and ability that the legislature of the state of New York, in their wisdom, called upon him to assume the duties of a Senator representing this great state, and that in that honorable position he stood the friend of the laboring men, particularly the friend of the farmer, and that the same degree of intelligence and patriotism that had characterized his previous career was conspicuously displayed in that national arena. It is also well known to us in Ohio, as well as to the citizens of your own state, that when we sought legislation in this country to protect us against oleomargarine, that it was Senator Miller who stood forth our friend. [Applause]. It is as well known to us as it is to you that Senator Miller has identified himself with the best interests of his state and with the nation upon all the great questions of finance and statesmanship; and we know, too, that Senator Miller has a home of his own, and that he is in favor of legislation that protects homes; and we thank God that he had the courage to be in favor of temperance. [Applause]. It is not, perhaps, known to every citizen of Ohio, however, that Senator Miller has a farm, and that the same intelligence that characterized him as a politician stood by him when he came to select stock for that farm, and that he had the sagacity to discover that among the various great breeds of cattle that are seeking favor the Holstein-Friesians were the best. [Laughter and applause]. Then we welcome on this occasion, and will sit with pleasure so long as he wishes to address us, Senator Warner Miller, not of New York State alone, but Senator Warner Miller of the whole United States of America. [Applause].

Mr. Miller arose amid great applause, and addressed the Association as follows:

Mr. President, and Gentlemen of the Holstein-Friesian Association: I certainly am very glad to be here this morning, and I am more than pleased with the hearty reception you have given me. I thought to come in here simply as one of you, and to listen and be benefited by your proceedings, and profit by them. Mr. Horr has been kind enough to refer to myself as a brother farmer, and to the wisdom which I displayed in selecting for the stock upon my farm the Holstein-Friesian breed. I cannot, however, take to myself any credit for that selection. Whatever of credit there is belongs to my friend and neighbor, Mr. Burrell. Several years ago, when he first began importing this stock, he suggested to me that I should put them on my farm, believing they would be best adapted to dairy purposes. Knowing that Mr. Burrell was a much better farmer than myself, and knowing that he had made his own farm very successful, even during the hard times, I accepted his judgment as that of an expert, and so he imported for me a few cattle, with which I began. I have not been as successful a breeder as Mr. Burrell, or as my friend Mr. Powell, of Syracuse, because, to tell you the truth, instead of being able to look after my farm for the past ten years, my time has been principally passed in Washington. Still I have been enough of a farmer not to let my farm run me in debt. I have followed along very quietly in the practice of those gentlemen farmers who have expended a great deal of money, but I have followed so far in the rear that I have maintained a balance on the right side, though I am free to confess the balance is small. Mr. Horr has spoken of some things that I did, or attempted to do, while a member of the United States Senate. It needs no comment on my part, but simply to assert that whatever I did in that direction I did it as a work of love — not because I was a farmer myself, but because my memories ran back entirely into the line of farming from the very beginning, and because I knew something of the hardships of a farmer boy's life, and something of the difficulties which surround this great industry in this country; and, therefore, whatever I did I did it as a work of love. [Applause]. If I was fortunate in doing anything which in my career has in any way benefited the agricultural classes, it is certainly a very great pleasure to me. It was a hard-fought battle, and it may not be entirely over yet. I have no doubt that much has to be done yet, and I am very sure that much remains to be done in the matter of protecting our whole country against the ravages of pleuro-pneumonia. I did succeed in passing through the Senate a bill, which, if the House had passed it, would have resulted, within five years, I think, of entirely ridding this country of that terrible pest. These things still require much attention, and I know that it is through such organizations as this that much aid and comfort is to be given to a man in public life who undertakes this sort of work. When I had in charge the pleuro-pneumonia bill I know that I received my most effective aid from the cattle-men of the great west, men representing the great cattle interests out there, who came to Washington, and, through their powerful arguments, gave me great aid in that matter. So I think I can say to this Association, that organizations such as this will have, and have had in the past, great influence upon national legislation in the way of arousing interest in the members of both Houses, and in finally affecting public opinion — and public opinion, when aroused, is the final maker of the laws in this country. I am very sure, gentlemen, that I can say nothing here to-day that would be either interesting or profitable in the matter of breeding cattle. Notwithstanding that I have a dairy farm and some cattle upon it, if I want to know anything about this business myself, I go and see Mr. Burrell, or Mr. Powell, or I go down to the farm of my friend, Mr. Dutcher, at Pawling, and take my lesson, and then go back and practice it in a weak way; but these fine farms which are scattered throughout New York, and throughout Ohio, and still further west in our grand farming country, are to my mind experimental schools which can be visited by large numbers of farmers, and which are visited yearly by large numbers of farmers, and I think they are doing a grand and great work in the way of educating our farmers in the care of stock, and in the methods of breeding, and in everything that pertains to this great industry; and I hope that the members of this Association are all so successful that, wherever they come from, whether it be Ohio, Iowa, Minnesota, or any other great farming state, that they are able to set up these fine farms of theirs and show the people the benefits that come from raising good cattle. I believe that any one can by a little vigor show to the people of this country that the improvement of stock of all kinds is bringing to our people the greatest value for their farms. It costs little more to raise well bred cattle than it does to bring up poor stock, and the surplus over the expenditure in the raising of fine-bred cattle more than pays for the experiment.

Gentlemen, I will not take up your time any longer. I thank you for the great honor you have done me in thus presenting me to the members of this Association. [Applause].

Mr. E. A. POWELL: Mr. President, I move you that this Association tender a vote of thanks to Senator Miller for his address, and that we extend to him an earnest invitation to visit us at our annual meetings — not as a visitor, but as an active member of this Association.

Mr. C. W. HORR: I second the motion.

Carried.

THE PRESIDENT: The next business in order is the report of the committee.

Mr. W. M. SINGERLY: I move the adoption of the report of the committee. The object of this thing is, that last year there were 3,400 bulls registered and 4,300 cows. The object of this Association is to reduce the registration of bulls.

Mr. C. W. HORR: I second the motion.

Mr. H. LANGWORTHY: I would like to inquire when this is to take effect.

THE PRESIDENT: The time has not been fixed.

Mr. EDWARD P. TAFT: I am sorry to rise to a point of order again, but it seems to me if we are going to pass that, we should do it as an amendment to Section 5, of Article 4, of the by-laws. That provides that "American-bred animals," etc. That article standing as it does, I don't see how this resolution can be passed without amending that.

Mr. J. B. DUTCHER: I think it should be understood and stated distinctly that the females should be charged $1.00 and bulls $5.00.

Mr. E. A. POWELL: I would suggest that this be acted upon independently of the females.

Mr. J. B. DUTCHER: I would like to withdraw that amendment in regard to females.

THE PRESIDENT: We will consider that withdrawn.

Mr. O. B. POTTER: It seems to me, Mr. President, that if we raise the registration, whether it be $5.00 or $10.00, upon bulls, that it is hardly worth our while to offer a reward for castrating full-blooded animals which may not be registered. If they are kept simply as grades, they will benefit, so far as they are kept, the general breed. They will not be registered if the fee is sufficiently high unless they are pure bred, and unless they are believed by their owners to be worthy of registration. I think it frequently happens that a calf that is not very promising becomes a very excellent and superior animal. Whether you offer a reward for castrating that animal in advance, or for killing it, when it is a pure bred animal, it seems to me is worth while to consider. What we want is to build up this breed of cattle as much as we can. It seems to me that you will accomplish all we need to accomplish in this direction by simply raising the price of the registration of bulls to a sufficient figure, whatever that may be. It seems to me the butchering part we had better leave out.

Mr. C. W. HORR: I was influenced myself in voting in the meeting of the officers that had this matter under consideration for this plan by the following considerations: First. Suppose the gentleman who just spoke was the owner of ten good bulls. He is interested, therefore, in having ten poor ones killed. The man who kills them looses their entire value, except what they would be worth when killed. Suppose, as a business proposition, we could control this whole matter here to-day, and there were two thousand bulls. Now, I would give more for one thousand of them with the other one thousand castrated; that is, I would give more for a half interest, because then I would have that much less competition. One-third of the Holstein bulls saved each year can be sold for more money than they all can. Let me illustrate. Take, for instance, onions. I know something about them, for I have raised them. Now they are worth about twelve cents a bushel, and they cost from twenty-five to thirty-five cents a bushel to raise them. If there were only half as many raised, therefore, the farmer would receive three times as much. There is a surplus, and the surplus of bulls is a pretty tough surplus. Then we accomplish, first, the object of having left only the good ones, and the law of supply and demand fixes the price. A number of gentlemen wanted to charge $10.00 for registration and pay $10.00 for killing, and others thought that would not do, and so we finally worked down to this plan. If I was to do this myself, my plan would be to have the knife stuck either at one end or the other of two-thirds of our calves. Now, I would simply say that, having given a good deal of thought to this matter, I believe that we had better try this plan. It seems to be the most practical and the best worthy of a trial, and in a year from now we will know whether it is a wise plan or not. Again, we thought you ought to make the premium that we pay from persons who have the bulls that are not killed. So you see this plan seems to be founded upon divine justice and equity. [Laughter]. We are all fond of equity, you know. I hope, for the sake of the good bulls, and to dispose of the poor ones properly, that this plan will be adopted, and that in another year we will just double it, and make it $10.00 for registration and $10.00 for killing.

Mr. HUIDEKOPER: Some one has asked to have this take effect the 1st of May, or at some future time. It seems to me that it does not make any difference to us whether the bull is already born, or whether we wait until the 1st of May. I think it may as well take effect at once, and get rid of a certain number of the bulls already born, as to wait. It would take some time for the Secretary to get out the proper form, so that perhaps forty days would be too short a time to limit those calves that are already born, or will be born within a few days; but it seems to me that it should take effect upon all calves already born.

Mr. J. B. DUTCHER: I was going to raise that question about getting the forms ready. I take it for granted that it is a very easy matter to get those done. When you get one, you have ten thousand if you want them. It is not necessary to extend the time for that purpose. Now, another question in connection with this matter in regard to these bulls. It is not the value of the bull calf so much, but it is the fact that every Holstein breeder has an interest not only in perpetuating the breed, but in improving the breed. Every man who is a breeder knows that he has some animals that are not near as good as others. Every man knows that. I have got them, and Mr. Powell has got them, and probably every other member of this Association has them. A great many people don't like to kill their bulls, but I have been killing my bulls this winter which I did not consider first-class animals. I believe it is to the interest of the Holstein breeder to try to excel in the class of the animals he has; and if we are to make a success of the Holstein cattle in this country, we have got to do it. It is in the value of the animal rather than the number that our profits lie.

Mr. E. A. POWELL: We all understand very well that every breed, in comparison with other breeds, is known by its average — that half of each breed is below that average, and the other half is above that average line. Whenever you breed below that average line you are reducing the standard of that breed of cattle. Now, what we want to do is to increase the value of this breed of cattle. We will suppose that our standard is fifty per cent. If we take off the lower half, it increases the standard to seventy-five per cent. I wish there was some way of doing it, not only with males, but with females. I wish the whole lower half could be wiped out of existence, and then the breed would stand higher. We approach to it, in a certain measure, in this way, and the nearer we get to it the better we are off. Now, in regard to Mr. Potter's suggestion that these grade bulls would be circulated through the country, and would not be well cared for and used on the best kind of cows, and the tendency would be to lower our standard, I would say, induce these owners to castrate those bulls, and thus raise the standard by keeping fewer bulls, and those only the good ones.

Mr. EDWARD P. TAFT: Mr. President, in order that we may have the matter intelligently before us, I have prepared this amendment: I move to strike out all after the words "payment of a fee of," and insert the following: "Payment of a fee of $1.00 for the registry of females, and $5.00 for males, by members of the corporation, and of $2.00 for females, and $5.00 for males, by persons not members of the corporation, and that the sum of $5.00 be paid for each male slaughtered or castrated between the ages of five and forty days; such change to take effect May 1st."

Mr. ———: It has been stated that the evidence of the castration shall be the affidavit of the owner. What shall be the other evidence? We ought to know exactly what we have to do.

Mr. HUIDEKOPER: As was talked in the committee, every man who wishes to castrate a bull or kill it shall fill out a blank which has been furnished him previously by the Secretary, certifying that this bull calf was born on a certain day, and shall give his proof of the identity of the calf just as he does for registering, and shall also certify that the cow was bred to a certain bull on such a date, and that the calf was born on such another date, about nine months after that, so that the Secretary sees that there is a calf born from that cow, and from service to a certain bull. That stops any calf being registered from that cow in that year.

Mr. C. R. PAYNE: The details could be worked out by the Board.

Mr. E. A. POWELL: I move, as an amendment, that this shall take effect immediately.

Mr. W. H. SMITH: I second that.

Mr. EDWARD P. TAFT: I will accept that amendment.

Mr. H. LANGWORTHY: I suggest that we divide this, and consider the fee on bulls first.

Mr. EDWARD P. TAFT: I accept that.

Mr. E. A. POWELL: I think the report made reads "on bulls." It should say "American-bred," because a person might import bulls younger than forty days of age and have them entered at $5.00. The present rule makes it $25.00 on imported bulls.

Mr. HUIDEKOPER: What objection is there to having it take effect with all bulls after this date?

Mr. W. G. POWELL: None at all.

Mr. H. LANGWORTHY: In reply to that question, I would say that I would not consider it justice to the breeders to have it apply to calves already born.

Mr. HARWOOD: I agree with what the gentleman says, because in my own case I have two calves born within the last thirty days, and I have not sent in an application for registry for those calves, but they have been sold, and it is possible that I might want to dispose of them in another way if the registry fee had been raised, or if I had known that it was to be raised at this meeting. There is one point which has been brought up by Mr. Potter, and that is in reference to disposing of bulls in some other way. It does not seem to me that this proposed amendment interferes with that at all; that is, if a person has bulls that he wishes to dispose of without registration, there is nothing in this that interferes with that. But still I think there is an objection to doing a great deal of that kind of work, for it opens the question which has been brought up here about putting in other animals as being the progeny of these cows where the record of the Association does not show the calves to have been registered during the past year.

Mr. CLARK: I would like to make one suggestion in regard to this amendment as to the age. The state of Tennessee prohibits us from selling veal which is less than six weeks old. Now, I would suggest that the time be extended to fifty days instead of forty.

Mr. C. PRATT: I would make this fee $1.00 for registry and $10.00 for castration. Three-quarters of my calves have been bulls. Last year I sold a bull calf for $30, and when I went to deliver the animal the man had bought one from somebody else a good deal cheaper. I cannot afford to sell a bull and have it raised as a breeder for anything less than $25, if it is a week old, but I want to make the fee high enough so it would be an inducement to kill it.

Mr. E. P. TAFT: I have re-written this original amendment, and I will withdraw the first one, and strike out the fourth, fifth, and half of the sixth line, of Article 4, Section 5, and insert: "$1.00 for the registry of females and $5.00 for males, by members of the corporation, and $2.00 for the registry of females and $5.00 for the registry of males, by persons not members of the corporation, which must accompany the application, and that the sum of $5.00 be paid for each American-bred bull slaughtered or castrated between the ages of five and fifty days, on evidence satisfactory to the Board of Officers. Such change to take effect on April 1st."

Mr. J. B. DUTCHER: I think a serious objection to that is extending the time from forty days. Every man knows that they can castrate these calves easily enough. You castrate it when it is first born, and it makes better veal.

Mr. E. A. POWELL: I second Mr. Taft's amendment, with the provision that it takes effect immediately, also with the condition that Mr. Miller makes to divide the question.

Mr. ——————: In order that this thing may be done exactly right, I suggest that the chairman appoint a committee of five, with Mr. Taft as chairman, to consider this matter and report at our afternoon session.

Mr. C. W. HORR: I think that is a good idea.

Mr. W. M. SINGERLY: No, no; let us fix it up now. We will have the same discussion after dinner.

Mr. E. A. POWELL: I think we could get it right now if we try.

Mr. J. B. DUTCHER: I would like to have the date changed from birth to five days. I want to knock my calves in the head the first day.

Mr. O. B. POTTER: Is this limited to members of the corporation, or is the premium offered to everybody outside?

Mr. E. A. POWELL: Everybody.

Mr. C. R. PAYNE: I think, as the resolution reads now, that we shall have a good many aborted calves to pay for.

Mr. C. W. HORR: Then I suggest that you put in: "Alive and in good health." [Laughter.]

Mr. ——————: Mr. President, we shall never arrive at any understanding about this thing, going on as we are now. The only way to do is to have a committee appointed to consider this.

Mr. CHAPMAN: I think that we can get at this thing better by having a committee appointed and let them come in and report this afternoon.

Mr. PRATT: Is that with the understanding that their report shall not be final?

Mr. CHAPMAN: Oh, yes. They will report to us here in meeting, and then we will take what action we see fit.

Mr. E. P. TAFT: I think myself we could get this right in committee.

THE SECRETARY: I am very much interested in this matter; I want it perfectly straight, and I want it down in black and white. I think that the suggestion that a committee be appointed is a good one.

Mr. CHAPMAN: I move that the President appoint a committee of five to consider this matter, and report at 2 o'clock.

THE SECRETARY: I second that motion.

Carried.

THE PRESIDENT: I will appoint as such committee, Mr. Taft, Mr. Horr, Mr. E. A. Powell, Mr. Clark, and Gerrit S. Miller. Now, gentlemen, I understand that the Committee on Proxies is ready to report, and we will hear their report.

Mr. C. W. WOLCOTT: Mr. Lamb has the report. He will read it.

Mr. ANTHONY LAMB: Your Committee on Proxies beg leave to report as follows: Whole number of proxies received, 225; of which Thomas B. Wales is entitled to 79; F. L. Houghton, 47; Wing R. Smith, 26; S. Burchard, 12; Martin L. Sweet, 9; H. Langworthy, 7; W. B. Clark, 6; Dallas B. Whipple, 4; T. G. Yeomans, 4; S. Hoxie, 4; C. R. Payne, 4; S. L. Hoxie, 3; Watkin G. Powell, 3; W. M. Liggett, 2; Charles Robinson, 2; Thomas W. Wales, Jr., 1; Thomas B. Wales, Jr., 1; Isaac C. Otis, 1; J. B. Dutcher, 1; S. W. Sweezey, 1; H. D. Warner, 1; J. L. Stone, 1; John L. Stone, 1; O. P. Chapman, 1; F. C. Stevens, 1; Blank, 1; Thomas B. Wales, Jr., by W. H. Smith & Son, 1; Thomas B. Wales, by Alexander R. Gebbie, 1.

This report is signed: "Respectfully submitted, Anthony Lamb, Charles W. Wolcott."

Mr. E. A. POWELL: I move that the report be received.

Mr. S. L. HOXIE: I second the motion.

Carried.

Mr. E. A. POWELL: Mr. President, there was no committee appointed to audit the Treasurer's report. That should have been done.

THE PRESIDENT: Yes, I omitted to do that. I will appoint as such committee Mr. Langworthy, Mr. Chapman, and Mr. Huidekoper, who will also examine the reports of the Secretary and Superintendent of Advanced Registry.

The time has now arrived when we agreed to take a recess for lunch. Gentlemen, we will re-assemble promptly at 2 o'clock.

Recess.

AFTERNOON SESSION.

THE PRESIDENT: Gentlemen, we will now come to order. If the committee are ready to report, we will hear them.

Mr. E. P. TAFT: The committee to whom the subject of revision of Section 5 of Article IV. was referred, report as follows, and I will say that it is unanimously recommended:

Strike out the fourth and fifth line and half of the sixth line in Article IV., Section 5, and insert the following (at the request of one of the members, Mr. Taft then read the section as amended):

"American-bred animals shall only be registered in the Herd-Book upon application made upon forms furnished by the corporation, and the payment of a fee of fifty cents for the registry of females, and $5.00 for the registry of males, born after March 20th, 1889, by members of the corporation, and of $1.00 for the registry of females, and $6.00 for the registry of males born after March 20th, 1889, by persons not members, which payment must accompany the application. And the sum of $5.00 shall be paid by the Association for each American-bred male eligible for registration born after March 20th, 1889, that is killed or castrated while in good health after it is five days old, and before it is fifty days old, on application and affidavit of the owner of the dam, on forms furnished by the Secretary and approved by the Board of Officers, stating the date of service and birth, name of sire and dam, date of slaughter or castration, and by whom performed." And then it goes on as before—"no two animals shall have the same name."

Mr. W. M. SINGERLY: Mr. President, I move the adoption of the report.

Motion seconded.

THE PRESIDENT: Gentlemen, you have heard the motion; those in favor will please say aye; opposed, nay.

Motion carried.

Mr. W. M. SINGERLY. We want to turn our attention to the production of the dams of calves as a test of registry, so as to make a standard-bred animal only eligible to registry. This matter has nothing to do with this meeting. I only want to throw out the hint, so that you, gentlemen, can think of it for the next year. I think, for the purpose of raising the character of the Holstein cattle, that some of these days we have got to make a standard that no bull calves whose dams or grand dams do not produce twelve thousand pounds of milk per year shall be eligible.

Mr. J. B. DUTCHER: I think every breeder ought to be in favor of that.

If we are going to improve our breed of cattle, we should have a standard that we shall register by. I think it is to the interest of every breeder to do it. I am in favor of it.

THE SECRETARY: The next thing before us, gentlemen, is "an appropriation for special premiums for the ensuing year."

Mr. W. M. SINGERLY: I move that that matter be referred to the Board of Officers, the same as it was last year.

THE PRESIDENT: The appropriation was $4,000.00 last year; that includes all the special premiums.

Mr. W. M. SINGERLY: The way it was done last year, it was referred to the Board of Officers.

Motion seconded by Mr. Powell.

THE PRESIDENT: It is moved and seconded that this matter be referred to the Board of Officers.

Mr. W. M. SINGERLY: With the limitation that they shall not spend over $4,000.00.

THE PRESIDENT: Yes. All those in favor will say aye; opposed, nay.

Motion carried.

Mr. T. G. YEOMANS: I would move that the Board of Officers be permitted to make a plan for the restriction, next year, of males.

Motion seconded.

THE PRESIDENT: Gentlemen, you have heard the motion; all those in favor will say aye; opposed, nay.

Motion carried.

THE SECRETARY: There is also "an appropriation asked for to aid in the circulation of the *Holstein-Friesian Register*." I would like to state that a citizen of New York made this proposition, and asked me to bring it up.

THE PRESIDENT: Gentlemen, what do you wish to do with the proposition?

There being no response, the President directed the Secretary to pass it over for the present.

THE SECRETARY: There is also a request for appropriations for other purposes. The only thing that I know of that we need an appropriation for is to pay the assessment of last year of the "Consolidated Cattle-Growers Association of the United States." I was asked to pay this some time ago, but I did not feel authorized, and the matter was laid over until to-day for your action.

Mr. W. M. SINGERLY: How much is it?

The Secretary: Two hundred and fifty dollars, I think the assessment is.

Mr. W. M. Singerly: What advantage is it to the Association?

The Secretary: Excuse me; it is $160.00. We are members of this Association, and these are the dues assessed to us.

Mr. W. M. Singerly: We are members of it?

The Secretary: We are.

Mr. W. M. Singerly: I move that the amount be paid.

Mr. E. A. Powell: One moment, I happened to be one of the delegates to its last meeting, and I learned something. I found that we were assessed according to the number of delegates we sent, and every association seemed to be aware of that, and they only sent one or two, while we sent a good many. The consequence was that we were assessed a great deal higher. I am in favor of paying what we have to pay, but next time we want to be more careful.

The Secretary: I desire to state further, that I wrote to the Treasurer of the "Consolidated Cattle-Growers Association," and stated to him the fact that Mr. Powell has just stated, and asked for a reduction of our assessment, requesting the Treasurer to reply to me here. I have not received his letter. That is the way it stands at present.

Mr. E. A. Powell: I move that it be referred to the Secretary, with instructions to settle it as best he can.

Mr. W. M. Singerly: I second the motion.

The President: Mr. Powell's motion is that it be left to the Secretary to settle as best he can; all those in favor will please say aye; opposed, nay.

Motion carried.

The Secretary: I have a letter here which I would like to read to the Association; it will take but a moment. It is from Dr. Collier, Director of the New York Agricultural Experiment Station, at Geneva, N. Y.:

"Geneva, N. Y., June 13th, 1888.
"*T. B. Wales, Esq., Secretary of the Holstein-Friesian Association:*

"My Dear Sir:— At a regular meeting of the Board of Control of the New York Agricultural Experiment Station, held in Geneva on the 5th inst., the following resolution was passed unanimously, and ordered to be sent to the Holstein-Friesian Association:

"'The Board of Control of the New York Agricultural Experiment Station thank the Holstein-Friesian Association for their liberal offer to aid this Station in their experiments with different breeds of cattle.'

"Sincerely yours,
"Peter Collier, *Director.*"

Mr. W. G. POWELL: *The Holstein-Friesian Register* question was passed over; it may be brought up now. If it is in order, I move that the matter be referred to the Board of Officers, with instructions to do as they see fit in the matter.

Mr. W. M. SINGERLY: I second the motion.

THE PRESIDENT: Gentlemen, you have heard the question. All those who are in favor will please say aye; contrary, nay.

Motion carried.

THE SECRETARY: Mr. President, I should like to ask if the Board of Officers think it desirable to render any assistance, in order to increase its circulation, whether the money is to come from the fund which is appropriated for special premiums, or from some other source?

Mr. W. M. SINGERLY: Mr. President, are we through with all the business before the Association now?

THE SECRETARY: I would like to ask again where we will get this money from, if we see fit to aid this paper. Shall we take it out of the appropriation made for special premiums?

Mr. W. G. POWELL: My idea was that if the Board of Officers see fit on investigation, to use some of the funds belonging to the Association to increase the circulation of the paper, they have a right to do so.

Mr. T. G. YEOMANS: Any unappropriated funds?

Mr. W. G. POWELL: This is a separate matter—a different matter from the appropriation for special premiums. We had separate action on that.

Mr. W. M. SINGERLY: Is there any business now before the meeting?

Mr. W. B. SMITH: Mr. President, it isn't understood here what funds we are speaking of. We don't know what this proposition is; what are you going to help or aid?

Mr. W. G. POWELL: It is a question that rests with the Board of Officers whether we do anything or not.

Mr. W. B. SMITH: What are you talking about?

Mr. W. G. POWELL: It is left to the Board.

THE SECRETARY: It is to aid *The Holstein-Friesian Register*.

Mr. W. W. PROPER: Mr. President, I have a little matter that I would like to bring before the meeting.

Mr. W. G. POWELL: I made the motion, and it was put and carried.

Mr. W. BROWN SMITH: From what I hear said about me, the majority of the people in this part of the room didn't know what the vote was taken upon; they don't know what it was.

THE PRESIDENT: I supposed it was generally understood before I put the question, or I should have stated what it was. Mr. Powell, will you please get up and state your motion over again, so that they can all understand?

Mr. W. G. POWELL: I move that the matter of rendering assistance, or anything else, to *The Holstein-Friesian Register* be left to the discretion of the Board of Officers, to give such assistance, in such manner and to such extent as they see fit, and that the money shall come from the treasury of the Association.

Mr. T. G. YEOMANS: It seems to me that we have been getting along very nicely with our business; it has almost been disposed of — everything on the list. I think it is better for this Association here assembled to settle this question for themselves. For one, if I were to be a member of the Board, as I at present am, I would rather they would give expression of their views than to depend on me. It is their money which is to be appropriated, and they are all interested one way or the other.

Mr. J. B. DUTCHER: Mr. President, it seems to me that inasmuch as this question has been decided, and the motion has been carried, we are "firing" blank cartridges. The way to do would be to make a motion to reconsider this, and then it will be open for discussion.

THE PRESIDENT: Did you vote for it?

Mr. J. B. DUTCHER: Yes, sir. I will move to reconsider the vote.

Mr. W. G. POWELL: Second the motion.

THE PRESIDENT: It is moved and seconded that we reconsider the vote just cast. Those in favor will please say aye; opposed, nay.

Motion carried.

Mr. W. G. POWELL: I now renew my motion.

Mr. PRATT: I think, Mr. Chairman, you ought to place some limit on this appropriation. You say not to exceed $4,000.00 for premiums on our cattle. You don't want to put this resolution through without any limit whatever.

THE PRESIDENT: This is an outside matter. It has nothing to do with the appropriation for premiums.

Mr. W. M. SINGERLY: They are not an extravagant Board.

THE PRESIDENT: If the gentlemen desire to take it into their own hands, it is better for them to do it.

Mr. W. G. POWELL: Mr. President, I think this Board is perfectly competent — we hope to have a Board of that kind. Out of an appropriation of $4,000.00 that was authorized last year, we didn't spend a quarter of it. It is a matter of discretion in this matter.

Mr. C. G. BLESSING: What do they desire — how much? I would ask for that information, if the Secretary has it.

Mr. J. B. DUTCHER: A gentleman at my right, who seems to be connected with the *Register*, requests me to state that what they would like to have done is this: He says they are circulating about five thousand copies, for four thousand of which they get no pay. One thousand is paid subscriptions and the other four thousand are sent all over creation, and I judge they are pretty well circulated, for I have had a great many letters from all over the country saying they got my name from the paper. They want the Holstein-Friesian Association to take from them three thousand papers at $1.00 a paper, and circulate those papers wherever they choose, which is equivalent to $3,000.00. That I understand to be the proposition. He says now not three thousand necessarily, but he did think three thousand. Any number that you see fit will be what they wish. I want you to understand that I have done this at the request of the gentleman here.

THE SECRETARY: I have been unable to answer Mr. Blessing, because I was not here when he commenced his request. What would Mr. Blessing like to have me inform him on?

Mr. C. G. BLESSING: Inasmuch as you stated that they desired assistance from the Association, I thought perhaps you had some knowledge as to the amount that they expected or desired help for.

THE SECRETARY: No, sir. The gentleman who wrote to me did not make any statement whatever, except that they wanted us to increase the circulation. He did suggest that twenty copies be sent to each member of the Association, to be paid for by the Association. He thought it would be a good plan. The gentleman was Dr. Miller. I don't know whether he is here or not.

Mr. W. M. SINGERLY: As I understand the question, it is whether this should be referred to the Board of Officers or not, to see what they should do.

DR. MILLER: I am a comparatively new member of your organization, and I have the misfortune to be so hard of hearing that I cannot hear all that is said during your deliberations, but I have taken a deep interest in the Holstein breed of cattle. As I understand, this organization is for the purpose of letting the people know of the merits of the Holstein-Friesian cattle, and to educate the people somewhat in regard to them. It seems to me that there is no more effective way of accomplishing this than by the distribution of a paper that is devoted expressly to the breed of that particular kind of cattle. Of course I have no interest in the matter, except to do what I can to make the people of this country familiar with the merits of the breed, and my idea is that a little paper like the *Holstein-Friesian Register*, if it is published every fortnight, or every month, and if the members of this Association are instrumental in buying it and putting it in the hands of the people who do not know anything about the breed, it will do more toward making them familiar with the merits of the breed than anything else that can be done. I know there are other stock papers that do a great deal in the way of educating the people, but there are none that are devoted expressly to the use the *Holstein-Friesian Register* is, and as I understand there is quite a large fund in the treasury of the Association, it seems to me that it would be a good plan to appropriate a certain amount of that fund for the support of the *Register*, and then let each member of the Association furnish a certain number of names to the publisher, of men who they are familiar with, or farmers in the locality in which they live, and have the *Register* sent to them for, say, a half a dozen issues, and half a dozen issues to another set of names, and so on through the year, and in that way you place in the hands of those who don't know anything about the breed the very best kind of information to educate them in regard to it. I think it would be the means of getting orders from a great many, and cattle would be sold to parties who would read the journal in that way. I don't know of any more effective means of getting at the people than putting a document of that kind in their hands. I think that the publishers of the *Register* are making it a readable journal, and are putting in a great deal of very valuable information in regard to the breed, and I believe that the most you have got to do now is to let the people know the merits of this breed of cattle, and a great majority of the farmers will want to get them. I think the Holsteins are the very best breed of cattle for farmers in general to raise, and the dairy interest in particular is being increased all over the country. We find there are creameries starting in western states and in nearly all our large cities. There are a large number of cows required for the supply of milk in these cities; it takes sixty thousand to supply New York City alone, and we have to add a great number every year to supply the increase of population. Now, if a paper of that kind was generally distributed among the people, it would do an immense amount of good, and I believe it would do the Association more good than anything they could do in the way of educating the people in regard to the breed.

THE PRESIDENT: Gentlemen, the motion is that this matter be left to the incoming Board, to do as they see fit in this matter. Those in favor will please say, aye; opposed, nay.

' Motion a

THE SECRETARY: Mr. President, I have been requested by a member of this Association, who is present — Mr. C. C. Smith, of Vail's Gate, New York — to read the following:

"*Mr. President and Gentlemen:* Those of you who reside in this state are well aware of the excellent work that Dairy Commissioner J. K. Brown and his able assistants have accomplished in purifying the milk supply of our cities and towns, in the total eradication of imitation butter, in the manufacture of better cheese, and in the general advancement of agriculture, and all to the marked benefit of both producer and consumer.

"And, whereas, it is a well known fact that in consequence of the famous ceiling business at Albany, there is a strong feeling among our legislators toward retrenchment.

"Therefore I ask that we, as a body of agriculturists, pass a unanimous resolution urging upon the Assembly of this state the great importance of granting to the dairy department an appropriation that will increase the usefulness of the commission, and carry the good work forward."

THE PRESIDENT: What disposition will you make, gentlemen, of this paper?

Mr. PRATT: I suppose that resolution should be adopted.

Mr. W. BROWN SMITH: Mr. President, I should be in favor of some such resolution as that. The work done by this commissioner has been very effective, and he is working at it every day. I think we should do what we can to sustain him.

Mr. C. W. HORR: I move that we authorize our Secretary to write a letter embodying the sentiments as expressed in the letter received by him as the unanimous expression of this Association.

Motion seconded.

THE PRESIDENT: Gentlemen, you have heard the motion. Those in favor will please say aye; opposed, nay.

Motion carried.

The resolution is as follows:

"*Resolved*, That this Association, realizing the great importance of the work that has been accomplished by Dairy Commissioner J. K. Brown, of New York, and his assistants, in purifying the milk supply of the cities and towns of the state, as well as the eradication of imitation butter, desire to urge upon the General Assembly of New York the great importance of granting to the dairy department an appropriation sufficient to sustain and increase the usefulness of the Dairy Commissioner."

Mr. W. W. PROPER: I have a little matter that I would like to bring before the Board. When I began to breed this stock my father in-law was a partner with me; that was some eight years ago. A year ago last June he died. His share of that stock was left to my wife, and I, being executor of his estate, did not transfer it to her. It stands on the books as stock of H. B. Vaughn and myself; it is so registered in the Herd-Books. Last October we had the final accounting, and settled up all matters. Now, what I want to do is to get that stock in my own name. Mr. Wales and I have been corresponding, and he understands this, and it is perhaps right that I should bring it before the Board and have it decided.

Mr. W. M. SINGERLY: Doesn't our by-laws provide for such cases?

The Secretary: If this gentleman owned a part of them, he should sign an application for their transfer. If he is the executor of the estate of a former owner, he should sign as executor also.

Mr. W. W. Proper: I have the power to do that yet, Mr. Wales, have I?

The Secretary: Certainly.

Mr. W. W. Proper: Could I transfer them from him to myself, or would it have to go to my wife, she being the heir to that property, and then have it transferred back to me?

The Secretary: If you are the executor of his estate, you have the right to transfer them to whoever you please. Supposing you should sell them, then you would have to transfer them.

Mr. C. W. Horr: It would depend upon whether his wife consents to his being an owner or not.

Mr. W. M. Singerly: I move, as there is no business before the meeting, that we proceed to the election of officers for the ensuing year.

Motion seconded.

The President: Gentlemen, you have heard the motion; those in favor will say aye; opposed, nay.

Motion carried.

Mr. T. G. Yeomans: As a means of facilitating the business of this meeting, I would move that after the candidates have been nominated, if there is but one name for a given office, the Secretary be authorized to cast a ballot for that office for the person nominated; it will save, in many instances, a large amount of balloting.

Motion seconded.

The President: It is moved and seconded that the Secretary be instructed to cast the vote if there is but one candidate for an office. Those in favor will please say aye; contrary, nay.

Motion carried.

Mr. W. M. Singerly: I move that we proceed to the nomination of candidates.

Mr. Thomas B. Wales: Mr. President, I believe I have never yet presented the name of a gentleman for office, except that of Mr. E. A. Powell, which was many years ago. I take pleasure to-day in nominating an old member of this Association, and one who has done a great deal for it. I nominate Mr. Edgar Huidekoper, of Meadville, Pennsylvania, for President.

The Secretary was then instructed to cast the vote for Mr. Huidekoper, and he was declared elected.

THE SECRETARY: The next office is First Vice-President.

Mr. T. G. YEOMANS: I will nominate for First Vice-President Mr. George D. Wheeler, of Deposit, N. Y. He has been with us on all occasions that I have, and is in the habit of attending our meetings, and seems to take an active interest in them.

There being no other nominations, the Secretary was instructed to cast the vote for Mr. Wheeler, and he was declared elected.

Mr. SMITH: I will nominate Jere Allis, of Isinours, Minnesota, as Second Vice-President. He is a fine breeder.

There being no other nominations, the Secretary was instructed to cast the vote for Mr. Allis, and he was declared elected.

Mr. S. HOXIE: I would nominate John A. Frye, of Marlboro, Massachusetts for Third Vice-President.

There being no other nominations, the Secretary was instructed to cast the vote for Mr. Frye, and he was declared elected.

Mr. D. H. Burrell, of Little Falls, N. Y., having been nominated for Fourth Vice-President, the Secretary was instructed to cast the vote for him, and he was declared elected.

THE SECRETARY: The next is three Directors for two years.

Mr. W. M. SINGERLY: I nominate Mr. Martin L. Sweet for a Director.

Mr. PRATT: I will second that.

The Secretary then cast the vote for Mr. Martin L. Sweet, of Grand Rapids, Mich.

Mr. T. G. YEOMANS: I nominate Mr. C. W. Horr, of Wellington, Ohio, as a Director.

The Secretary was then directed to cast the vote for Mr. C. W. Horr, of Wellington, Ohio.

Mr. BURRELL: I nominate Mr. C. R. Payne, of Hamilton, N. Y.

The Secretary was then directed to cast the vote for Mr. C. R. Payne, of Hamilton, N. Y.

THE SECRETARY: Gentlemen, the next office to be filled is Treasurer.

Mr. O. P. CHAPMAN: I would nominate W. Brown Smith, of Syracuse, N. Y., as Treasurer.

The Secretary was then directed to cast the vote for Mr. Smith, of Syracuse, N. Y.

Mr. W. G. POWELL: I believe it is characteristic of most of the successful corporations, that when they find a good man for a place they keep him in it, and I move and nominate that our present Secretary and Editor, Mr. Thomas B. Wales, be elected for another year.

The President then cast the vote for Mr. Wales, and he was declared elected.

THE SECRETARY: The next is Superintendent of the Advanced Registry.

MR. HORR: I take great pleasure in nominating Mr. S. Hoxie, our present Superintendent.

The Secretary then cast the vote for Mr. S. Hoxie, of Yorkville, New York, and he was declared elected.

THE PRESIDENT: The next thing in order, gentlemen, will be the reading of papers, and I take great pleasure in introducing to you Professor Johnson, of Lansing, Michigan.

Mr. Johnson then read the following paper:

THE RELATION OF BREED TO MILK AND BEEF PRODUCTION.

Breed is the term in common use by which we designate a group of animals distinguished by qualities not common to other groups of the same species. Breed characteristics may be few or many. To illustrate, color, alone, is the one characteristic that distinguishes the Essex from the Suffolk breed of swine. In all other respects the two breeds are identical. The Sussex breed of cattle differ from the Devon only in being of larger size, according to our best authorities, and I believe there are examples where the distinction between breeds has been, in fact, in name only. Usually, however, these points of difference are more numerous and pronounced, embracing color, form, size, temperament, and uses. Indeed, a trained observer will, in comparing two animals of distinct breeds, note points of difference in almost every external characteristic. To his eye these externals indicate differences of internal organism that have to do with the amount of food consumed, the ability to assimilate and digest such amount as shall return most profit in a certain line of products. In short, the utilization of food in production.

These breed characteristics are sometimes the product of natural causes. More frequently man's agency is apparent in the changes observed, and these are in line with the universally admitted law in all animal life — the tendency to adapt itself to its environment.

The habitat of animals has much to do with their peculiarities of development.

Upon soil conditions depends the kind and amount of food produced, and so soils indirectly have much to do with the developing and establishing of breed characteristics. Fertile lands, level or moderately rolling, develop our larger, early maturing breeds. Rich pastures, with full food supply, without much effort develops large animals. On the other hand, sparse pastures, on uneven, hilly, or mountainous land, tends to decrease size; and so we find most of our small breeds have had their origin on lands of uneven or barren character.

Climate, too, plays no unimportant part in producing breed characteristics. Those breeds most highly prized for their economic values are natives of the temperate zones. These are all natural conditions, and affect animals prior to, as well as after their domestication. And yet, while each and all of these factors have had great influence in molding into form our numerous breeds, and have more or less to do with the improvement or deterioration of their peculiar characteristics, it must be admitted that to skillful breeding and feeding we are indebted most largely for those breeds whose value for practical uses are most positively decided.

The practical breeder, versed not alone in the best theories of his profession, but uniting with them the knowledge which has been gained by years of practical experience and observation, may, very often does, by the judicious application of his knowledge, modify very largely the characteristics which have been produced through the agency of the natural causes named.

It is only, however, when development secured by the most perfect utilization of these natural forces is supplemented by man's endeavor to intensify and improve those qualities which have brought a breed into recognition for its economic value that the greatest success is assured.

It then follows that the relation of breeds to milk or beef production, or to any line of development, is not a fixed, but under certain limitations a variable one, dependent upon the continuance of the causes that have contributed, by intensifying its distinguishing characteristics, to its individuality.

With these brief references to breeds and the agencies by which they have been developed, let me allude to the history of the breed of cattle in which you are most directly interested, and see how far these references apply.

The home of the Holstein-Friesian breed, so far as we can trace its origin, was on the flats of North Holland and Friesland, noted for their fertility from a very early period — every condition of soil and climate calculated to develop a large, hardy breed of cattle. And when we remember that the sturdy Hollanders were the pioneers in dairy husbandry, and that their dairy products in amount and quality have never been equalled by any other people on the same area, we have the reason of their zeal and effort to perfect a breed of cattle suited to their special industry. A soil of great natural fertility, especially adapted to the production of the most valuable grasses and forage crops, has been made more fertile, sure, and productive by the added benefits of irrigation and heavy manuring. It is to their credit that as early, if not before any other people, the Hollanders identified themselves with the cultivation of the tame grasses and the clovers which have proved potent agents in the developing of this breed of cattle which has been famous for dairy qualities for centuries.

In short, the Holstein-Friesian breed of cattle are the product of most favorable natural conditions. Soil and climate have contributed to the furtherest limit in their development, and the Dutch farmers, with more far-reaching ken, perhaps, than of any other nationality, have weighed the advantages of dairying in maintaining fertility and returning adequate rewards for capital and labor invested. To them the typical dairy cow has been the image of profit. To develop in her offspring those qualities that should add to her value for this particular purpose has been their study, not for one, but many centuries. Can we doubt the strength of heredity thus acquired; and intensified through successive generations, under natural conditions so favorable, coupled with the studious efforts of the breeders, by careful selections, to attain their ideal of perfection? That ideal being the animal that could transmute the product of their fields into the largest amount of milk and its products.

I think there can be no question of the dairy characteristics of the Holstein-Friesian breed, as thus evolved in the land to whose fame and wealth they have so largely contributed. It has remained for American skill, however, to take the choicest specimens that could be found in Holland, and not only to equal, but eclipse the largest recorded production in the home country on American soil, and under American management; but bear in mind that these results have only been realized when the American breeder has taken for his ideal that which has enabled his over-the-sea-contemporary to achieve success, viz.: the development of the dairy cow, the intensifying of qualities valuable for this special purpose. By these successive generations of breeding for a particular purpose, the dairy characteristics have been improved and intensified to a remarkable degree. Heredity is potent, and these qualities are transmitted with increased power and intensity to offspring, and we conclude that the relation of the breed characteristics of the Holstein-Friesians are very largely in the line of dairy production.

But what of the future? Breeds of cattle under natural or artifical conditions do not stand still. The unalterable law of advance or retrograde applies here as forcibly as in any other domain of man's effort. And so the question is a pertinent one. While we congratulate ourselves on the present status of the breed, "what of its future?"

Breed characteristics, while they may not be entirely eliminated, may be very greatly modified by change of conditions and management, by the endeavor to utilize the animal in other directions than those in which it has been improved and developed. To illustrate, we may secure delicacy, fineness of bone, and low per cent of offal at the expense of size, vigor, and roughness. We may breed so as to sacrifice milking qualities for beef production. We may disperse, weaken, and modify those characteristics that have become hereditary only as the product of years of persistent and wisely-directed effort on the part of the breeder. It takes a long time to establish breed characteristics so that we can depend on their being transmitted to offspring. A very short time, in a course of opposite or antagonistic procedure, will vitiate very greatly, almost destroy, these characteristics.

And so, to my mind, the future success of the breed, the holding of its present place and achieving greater victories, depends on your working on the same line to secure in more perfect degree the realization of the ideal of your Dutch predecessors, viz: the best dairy breed of cattle. If you have it to-day, be thankful; but remember that eternal vigilance and a continuance in the same line, with the same object kept ever in view that has brought the breed to its present position can maintain, perpetuate, and add to its excellence. Do not be distracted by any clamor that the breed is wanting in beef quality. That is a matter of very little consequence when compared with its value for the dairy. Don't be persuaded to displace your ideal cow for the dairy for a myth, an uncertainty. Don't follow in the lead of some unthinking enthusiasts who are full of wild theories which invariably side-track them a good distance from the home station where practical results are realized. Your ideal cow has not sprung up in a night; nor come forth full panoplied, in her most valuable qualities, from airy nothingness. Avail yourselves of all the knowledge and science of this ultra-scientific age. It may help you in methods and management in your efforts to improve the ideal, but if any success is attained it will be because you study and plod along the same lines of practice adopted by your predecessors over the sea — because you have the same object in view for a guiding star, an inspiration.

What is science in breeding cattle but the application of those principles that long years of observation and experience in actual breeding have demonstrated to be of general application? It is the right use of what is known on this subject. Not the counterfeit wisdom which is too often apparent in the advocacy of unknown, if not unknowable, theories. With a profound respect for every ray of light, for every grain of knowledge that modern science can contribute to us in our labors as breeders, we must not forget that success will only crown our efforts when we utilize our knowledge by applying it in common-sense ways along the same lines where the best practice of the wisest doers in the past have marked the lines of real advance in breeding.

An English writer has recently said, with much truth, "That great dairy properties may be present where there is also a tendency to rapid and abundant flesh-making; that you have, for instance, an excellent dairy cow which, when fed off, at least makes a profitable return to the grazier and pleases the butcher and his customers besides. Such animals, indeed, are common enough in districts where breeding for general purposes is skillfully practiced, but they do not supply evidence contradictory of the necessity of sticking to one object if you want perfection in any one property. They rather suggest what may be done by repeated blendings of properties which can not permanently co-exist without more or less impairing one another. They are not, it is here suggested, examples of permanent results, but of results which may be obtained in perpetuity by fresh combinations"

So far as the Holstein-Friesian breed is considered for beef productions, we should not forget that this quality has been secondary in importance ever since the breed had a history. I have no hesitancy in saying that in my opinion the future success of the breed depends upon keeping this quality in subjection to the dairy qualities.

It will not be forgotten by those conversant with the history of the early Short-Horns, that the Teeswater breed, as they were called in an early day in Yorkshire, England, were noted for dairy qualities, and while some of the descendants of this old stock have been so wisely bred that this quality of milk-production has not been lost, in far too many cases the desire for symmetry, beef quality, and early maturity, have led to a course of breeding that has sacrificed this quality in good part. That Short-Horn breeders realize that such action has not been altogether wise, is evident from the official action of the state and national organizations on this subject.

There is no question of the quick-growing qualities of the Holstein-Friesian breed. I have had some opportunity of comparing their growth with the so-called beef breeds, under exactly the same conditions, and I think that they will make as many pounds in the same time as any other breed. They lack the early maturing qualities, the large development in the places where our highest-priced cuts are secured, the early ripeness and finish which are prime characteristics of the beef breeds — characteristics, remember, that have been secured through generations of breeding for this particular development, and at a corresponding loss, invariably, of dairy qualities.

And, while I am forced to the conclusion that while they are quick growers they lack in the qualities that will enable them to compete in beef rings with the earlier maturing beef breeds, I must say in all honesty that I believe that the standing of the breed in our beef markets to-day is not what its actual merits entitle it to, and I beg your indulgence while I suggest what seems to me to have contributed largely to this prejudice, and what I would suggest in the way of a remedy. Prejudice is very likely to be the child of ignorance. It is the lack of the facts that very often leads to erroneous impressions, to false conclusions.

There has been such a demand for your pure bred cattle that only a few have found their way to the shambles, hardly enough to enable the dealers in our principal markets to grade them in value properly; and without knowing how or why, dealers invariably class them as very unsatisfactory animals for the markets.

Would it not be wise for Holstein-Friesian breeders to weed out more of the animals that are not up to the standard in their herds? More or less calves in all herds should be culled out. Sold as breeders, they impair the reputation of the breed. Such a course lowers the breed standard and the price of individuals. It is not good policy from a financial stand point. It does not add to the prestige of a breed. I think at your last meeting your President suggested that it might be wise to adopt a rule providing that no bull calf should be eligible to registration except from a dam eligible to the advanced registry list. He thought it would be of advantage to the individual breeder, as well as the Association, to largely cut down the registry of bulls.

If such a course of procedure were followed in every herd, we could soon place so many animals on the market that whatever of merit they have as meat-producers would be known; and I am confident that much of this prejudice would be dissipated by a better knowledge of the edible qualities of the beef of this breed. In addition, by such a course the higher and more valuable qualities of the breed as dairy animals would be strengthened.

This Association is to be congratulated on its action in establishing a system of advanced registry. You have been the first to take this action, the wisdom of which in thus uniting well-vouched and recorded performance with pedigree commends itself to every thoughtful breeder. That your laudable example, with more or less modification, will sooner or later be followed by other cattle breeders organizations I cannot doubt.

This is a questioning age. We scan traditions and claims in stock, as well as other matters, very closely, and unless they are girt about with the facts that appeal to our practical sense, we reject them. We do not have as many pedigree worshippers as formerly, or at least wiser ones, and it is a good omen when breeders insist upon a standard of performance as the truest measure of value.

Pedigree is only the prophecy, the promise of value in a certain direction. Performance is the prophecy fulfilled — the most isdisputable evidence of the ability of the animal to pay, in current coin of the realm, what is promised in its pedigree.

Mr. E. A. POWELL: Professor Johnson has given us, in his paper, some of the most valuable suggestions I have ever heard in a paper of the kind. I think that we want to thank Professor Johnson for having come here among us, and for having prepared and given us this able paper. I presume every member of this Association will respond to that sentiment, and I move, sir, that a hearty vote of thanks be extended to Professor Johnson.

Mr. MILLER: I will second that.

THE PRESIDENT: It is moved and seconded that a vote of thanks be extended to Professor Johnson; all those in favor will please say aye; contrary, nay.

Motion carried.

Mr. C. L. G. BLESSING: I suppose this will all be printed.

Mr. W. G. POWELL: I move, right here, that the Secretary be authorized to publish five thousand copies of the proceedings, including the addresses, and mail one copy to each member, and distribute the others as he sees fit.

Motion seconded.

Mr. W. G. POWELL: Including the members of the Association, and also the constitution and by-laws, so as to have them to refer to.

Motion carried.

Mr. C. L. G. BLESSING: I would like to inquire of the Secretary if he knows about how many breeders of Holstein cattle there are in the United States.

THE SECRETARY: Yes, sir; there are about four thousand, eight hundred.

Mr. C. L. G. BLESSING: The point was to get enough printed to cover sending one to each breeder. That was my object in asking the question.

THE PRESIDENT: The next thing in order, gentlemen, is the reading of a paper by Professor Collier.

Professor Collier then read the following paper:

THE DAIRY INDUSTRY.

Gentlemen: — In announcing to your Secretary the subject of the paper which I was kindly invited to present to you, I accepted for myself a somewhat roving commission, as you see, and deliberately, as I was really uncertain as to the line I should choose. What I have to say will be almost entirely statistical, and yet I hope not necessarily uninteresting, for after all it is the ultimate results in quarts and pounds, in dollars and cents, which chiefly concern us; and if in what I may say there is anything which may help in the future to have the accounts of our dairymen and stock-breeders show a balance upon the right rather than the wrong side of the ledger, it cannot be other than acceptable.

I believe my statistics will help in this direction, if the lessons they present are carefully considered. In taking at first a general view of the dairy industry of this country, I desire to call attention to the facts set forth in the following table, in which I have represented the aggregate number and value of dairy cattle in the several sections, viz.: In the New England, Middle, Atlantic and Gulf, Central, Western, and Pacific, and West West States:

DAIRY CATTLE IN UNITED STATES OF AMERICA.

Six New England States — Maine, New Hampshire, Vermont, Massachusetts, Connecticut, Rhode Island.

Five Middle States — New York, New Jersey, Pennsylvania, Maryland, Delaware.

Nine Atlantic and Gulf States — Virginia, North Carolina, South Carolina, Georgia, Florida, Alabama, Mississippi, Texas, Louisiana.

Six Central States — Ohio, Indiana, Illinois, Kentucky, Tennessee, West Virginia.

Eight Western States — Michigan, Wisconsin, Minnesota, Iowa, Missouri, Arkansas, Kansas, Nebraska.

AVERAGE VALUE OF CATTLE IN THE UNITED STATES.

	Number.	Value.	Average Value	Cows Per Cent.	Average Value
6 New England States	822,435	$ 25,617,081	31.15	5.5	100.0
5 Middle States	2,811,242	84,624,316	30.11	18.9	96.6
9 Atlantic and Gulf States	2,556,227	41,461,762	16.22	17.2	52.1
6 Central States	3,102,716	81,634,573	26.31	20.9	84.5
8 Western States	4,713,869	108,139,368	22.94	31.7	73.6
12 Pac. and W. West States	849,925	24,775,073	29.15	5.7	93.6
Average	14,856,414	$ 366,252,173	24.65	100.0	

Fifty-one per cent average 43.3 per cent more in value per cow than 49 per cent.

NUMBER OF COWS TO POPULATION AND AREA.

	Persons to One Cow.	Acres Hay per Cow.	Number Cows to Square Mile.	Acres of Cultivated Land per Cow.
6 New England States	4.88	5.22	12.6	6.4
5 Middle States	4.12	3.08	24.5	7.3
9 Atlantic and Gulf States	4.16	.26	4.2	16.8
6 Central States	3.89	3.01	13.0	16.5
8 Western States	2.08	2.32	9.0	14.0
12 Pacific and W. West States	2.01	3.02	.68	16.0

Average of New England and Middle States 7.1
Average of all other states 15.5

Eighty-one per cent of cultivated land in the New England States is in hay; 42.2 per cent in Middle States; 1.5 per cent in Atlantic and Gulf; 18.2 per cent in Central; 16.6 in Western; 18.9 in West West and Pacific.

I have also shown the average value, the per cent of dairy cows in the several sections, and their average percentage value in these several sections.

It will be seen that the average value of 51 per cent of the cows is 43.3 per cent greater than the average value of the remaining 49 per cent, the highest average value being in the New England states, and the lowest being in the Atlantic and Gulf states.

There is also shown the number of cows to population, to the square mile, to acres of cultivated land, and to acres in hay in the several sections.

It will be seen that west of the Mississippi there is on the average one cow to two inhabitants, while the average for the eastern portion of the country is about one cow to every four of population, being less in the New England states, where the average is one cow to 4.88 persons.

The number of cows to the square mile varies greatly, averaging two-thirds of a cow to the square mile in the Pacific and West West as a minimum, and 24½ cows to the square mile in the Middle states, being the maximum.

The acres of cultivated land to a cow averages, for the New England and Middle states, 7.1, and for all the others 15.5, there being a remarkable uniformity shown in this relation of number of cows to acres of cultivated land.

An interesting fact is shown when we compare the average number of acres in hay to each cow, there being about a quarter of an acre of hay to each cow in the Atlantic and Gulf states, and twenty times as much, 5.22 acres, to each cow in the New England states. The other sections average about three acres of hay to each cow.

In connection with this subject of the hay crop, and its immense importance in relation to agriculture, and particularly in connection with the dairy industry, it is interesting to observe that of all the cultivated land in these several sections devoted to the leading crops, viz., the cereals, cotton, tobacco, potatoes, and hay, 81 per cent in the New England states is in hay, 42.2 per cent in the Middle states, 18.2 per cent in the Central states, 16.6 per cent in the Western states, 18.9 per cent in the Pacific and far west states, and but 1.5 per cent in the Atlantic and Gulf states.

None need to be reminded of the fact, which thousands of practical illustrations abundantly confirm, that profitable agriculture and productive lands are closely connected with flocks and herds, and these in turn with the extended cultivation of the hay and forage crops.

Of course every one is familiar with the general fact of the enormous increase in the dairy industry, which, during the past half century, has kept pace with the general development of the material interests of the country; but there are certain features in this development which are worthy of consideration:

INCREASE OF THE DAIRY INDUSTRY EAST AND WEST.

States.	1869.	1879.	1889.
New York,	1,459,866	1,446,200	1,552,373
Pennsylvania,	663,935	828,400	929,371
Ohio,	747,250	714,100	783,481
	2,871,051	2,988,700	3,265,225
	100	104	109
		100	109
Iowa,	417,448	676,200	1,293,095
Kansas,	109,142	321,900	652,883
Nebraska,	42,071	127,600	400,066
Minnesota,	151,242	278,900	455,664
Missouri,	349,440	516,200	737,259
	1,069,343	1,920,800	3,538,967
	100	180	
		100	184

CATTLE IN TEN STATES.

States.	No. Cows.	Value.
New York,	1,552,373	$ 45,950,241
Iowa,	1,293,095	28,861,880
Illinois,	974,975	24,569,370
Pennsylvania,	929,371	25,613,465
Texas,	826,806	11,302,438
Ohio,	783,481	22,525,079
Missouri,	737,259	14,229,099
Kansas,	652,883	13,292,698
Indiana,	573,670	14,628,585
Michigan,	441,676	12,698,185
	8,765,589	213,671,040
	57 per cent of total.	58 per cent of total.

In this table I have selected for comparison the three states of New York, Pennsylvania, and Ohio, and the five western states, Iowa, Kansas, Nebraska, Minnesota, and Missouri, because the statistics of this year show an aggregate of dairy cattle in these three eastern states approximately the same as in the five western states.

If, now, we consider the last two decades, we find that from 1869 to 1879 the increase in dairy cattle in the three eastern states was 4 per cent. But from 1869 to 1879 the five western states increased in the number of dairy cattle 80 per cent; and from 1879 to 1889, 84 per cent.

It appears that in ten states there is 57 per cent of the total number of dairy cattle in the United States, and 58 per cent of the total value of the dairy cattle of the country.

DEVELOPMENT OF GENERAL CATTLE INDUSTRY EAST AND WEST OF MISSISSIPPI RIVER.

In 1869, 82.2 per cent of the number of milch cows, and 87.3 per cent of the aggregate value of the milch cows of the United States was east of the Mississippi.

In 1879, 68.2 per cent of number, and 71 per cent of value.

In 1889, 58.5 per cent of number, and 62.9 per cent of value.

	East of Mississippi River.	West of Mississippi River.	Per Cent West.
1840	14,026,314	1,041,958	6.9
1850	15,341,358	2,990,958	16.3
1860	19,796,059	8,959,256	31.2
1870	16,125,100	9,359,000	36.7
1880	17,610,000	15,648,000	47.1
1889	21,211,151	29,119,891	57.9

East of Mississippi river increased 51 per cent. West of Mississippi river 2,795 per cent in fifty years.

As further evidence of the wonderful development of the west, it appears from the above table that in 1869 82.2 per cent of the entire number of milch cows was east of the Mississippi river, and 87.3 per cent of the aggregate value of those in the United States. In 1879 there was 68.2 per cent of the number and 71 per cent of the value; in 1889, 58.5 per cent of the number, and 62.9 per cent of the value.

Or, if we consider the entire number of neat cattle for the past fifty years, we find that in 1840 but 6.9 per cent were west of the Mississippi; while in 1889 57.9 per cent are now beyond the Mississippi river. Further, that while there has been, during the past fifty years, an increase in the number of neat cattle east of the Mississippi river of 51 per cent, the increase west of that river is nearly 3,000 per cent, or 2,795 per cent.

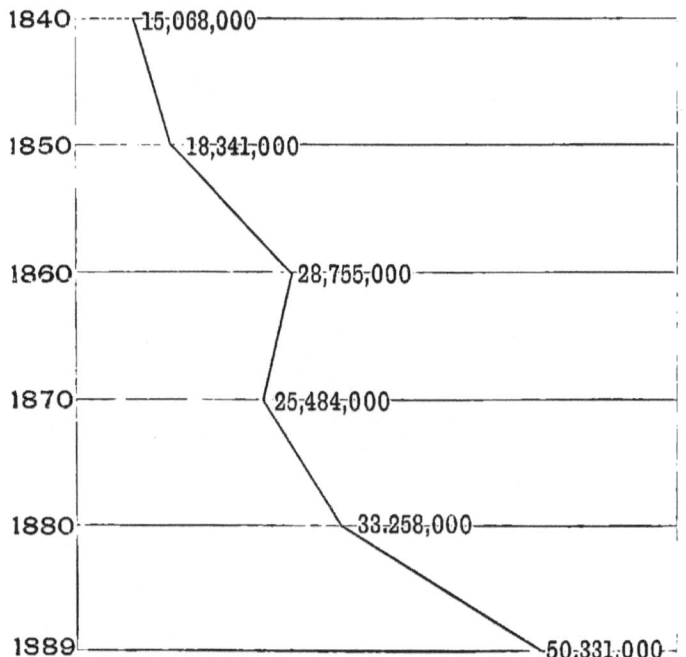

INCREASE OF NEAT CATTLE IN U. S. A. IN 50 YEARS.

During the first decade (see chart A), from 1840 to 1850, the increase in neat cattle in the United States was 22 per cent; from 1850 to 1860, 57 per cent; from 1860 to 1870, 31 per cent; and from 1880 to 1889, an increase of 51 per cent.

In this connection I desire to call attention to chart No. 1, where you will see that during the past twenty years there has been an uninterrupted

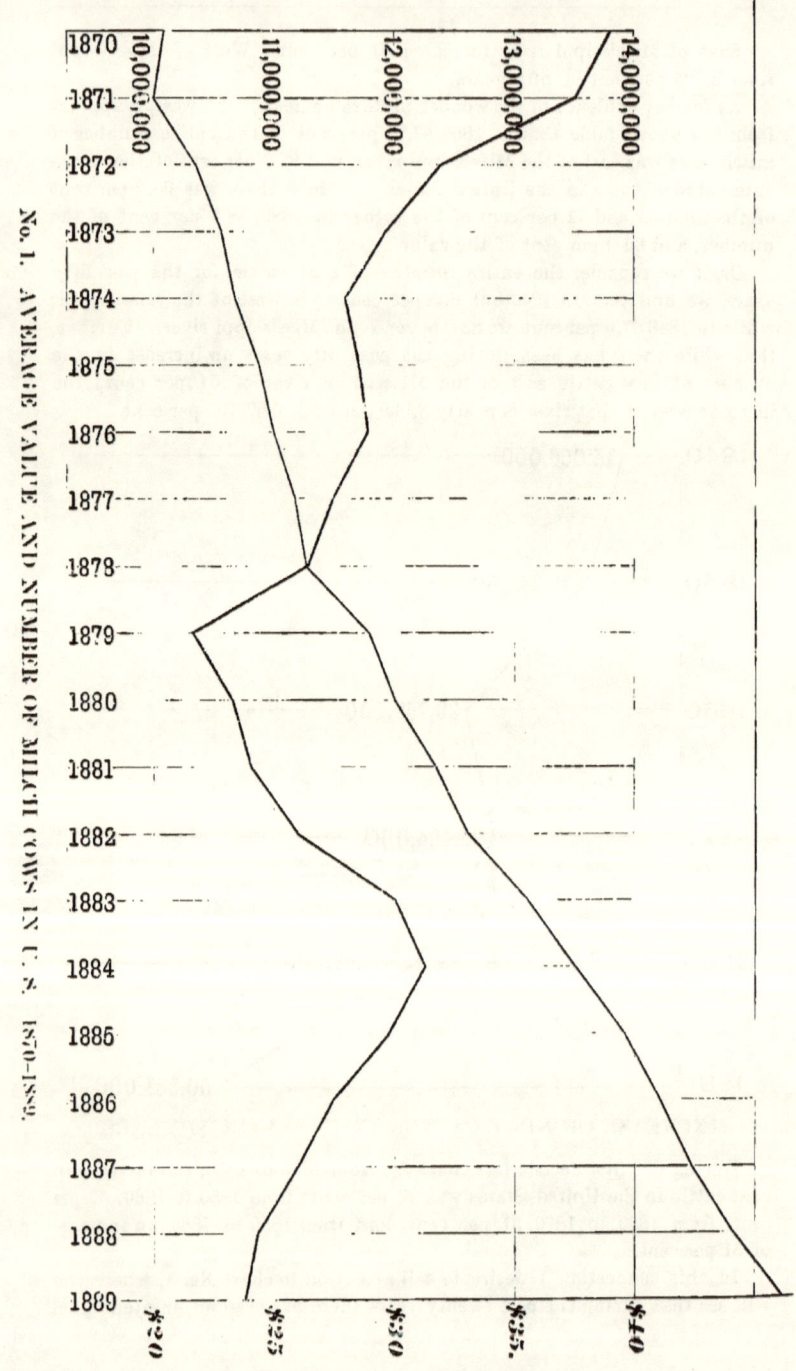

No. 1. AVERAGE VALUE AND NUMBER OF MILCH COWS IN U. S. 1870-1889.

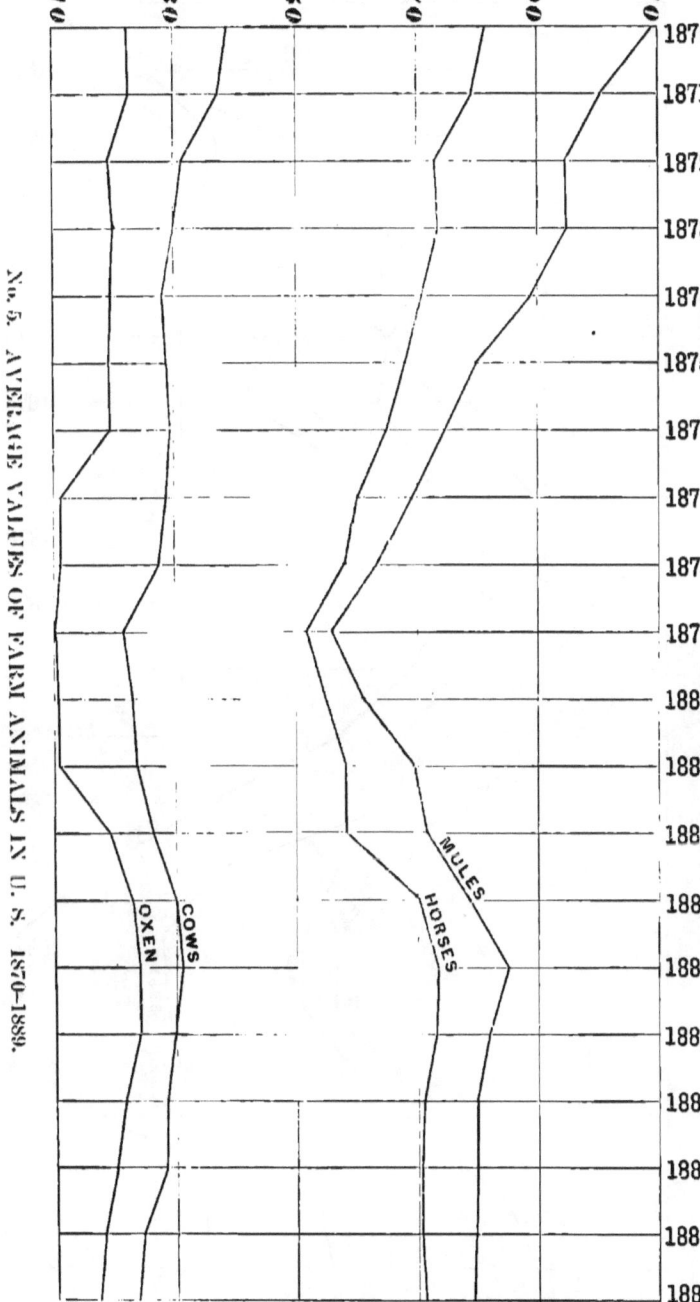

No. 5. AVERAGE VALUES OF FARM ANIMALS IN U. S. 1870–1889.

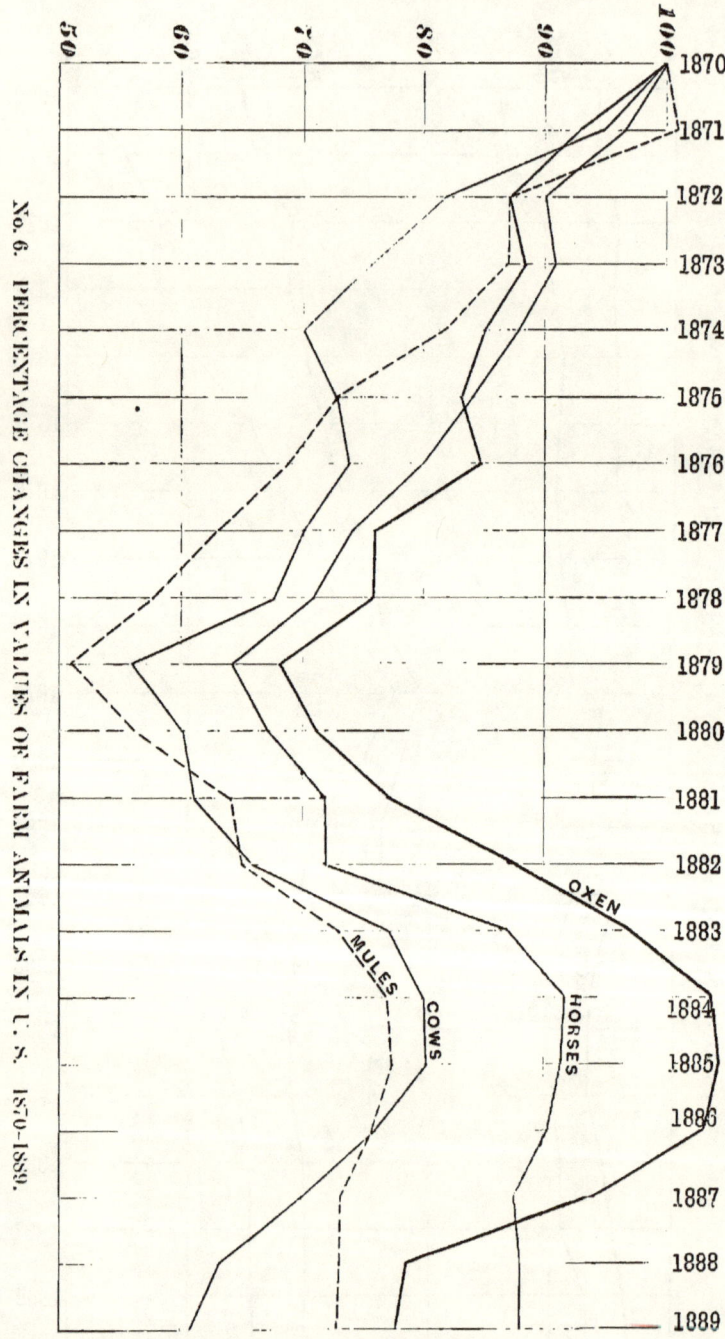

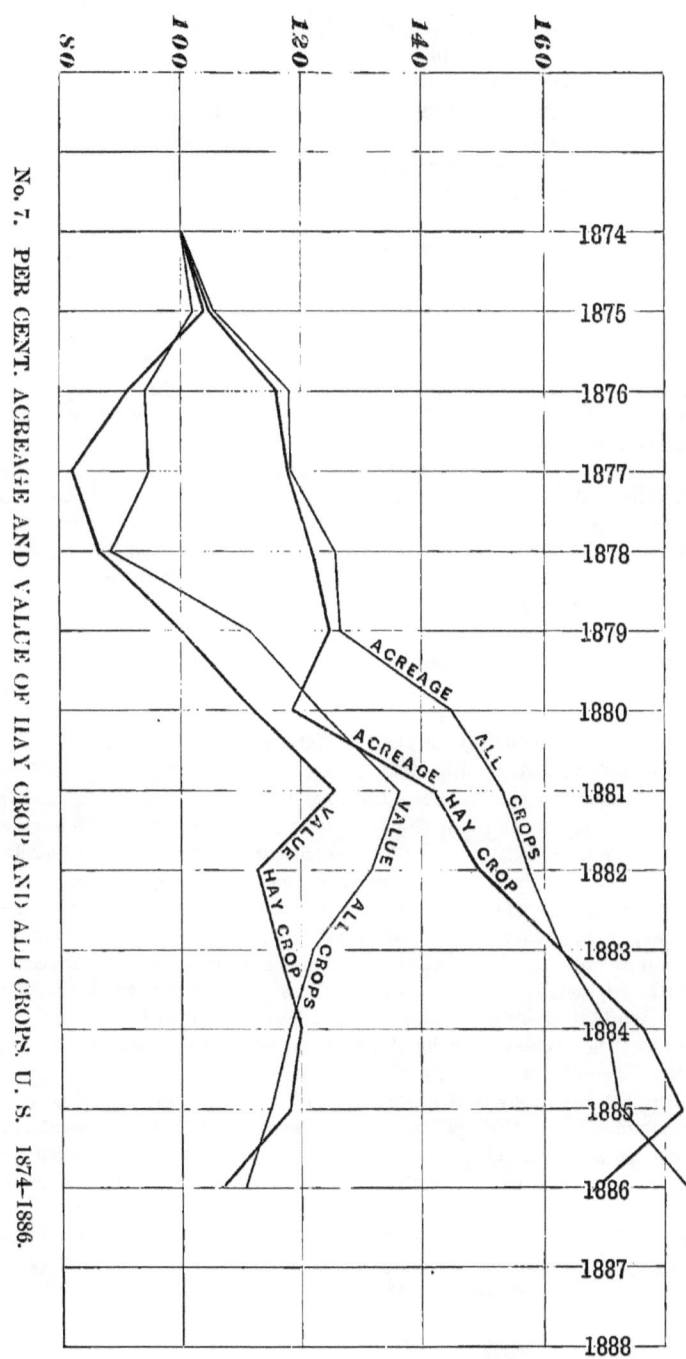

and steady increase in the number of dairy cattle in the United States, as is shown by the diagonal and nearly straight line. It will be seen that the line which represents graphically the fluctuations in average value of the cattle descends gradually from a maximum of $39.20 in 1870 to a minimum of depression in 1879, when the average price was but $21.60, again increasing to 1884, since which time the price has steadily fallen away, being given for January 1st, 1889, at about $24.00.

These facts would appear to demonstrate that there was no relation existing between the increase in cattle and their value, and that they shared the ordinary fluctuations in the values of farm products, whether of crops or animals.

That this latter view is probably the correct one is shown by charts Nos. 5 and 6, which show the fluctuations in price of the leading farm animals since 1870, which fluctuations are seen to be practically the same, as is more clearly shown in chart No. 6, in which the lines of the diagram show the changes which have taken place by percentages; the prices in 1870 being taken as $100. It will be seen that in 1879 the average price of oxen had fallen off 32 per cent; horses, 36 per cent; cows, 44 per cent, and mules, 49 per cent. In 1884 and 1885 the price of oxen had advanced to 104 per cent; horses, 92 per cent; cows, 80 per cent, and mules, to 77 per cent of the prices of 1870; and again had fallen off down to the present year, although the decrease in milch cows and oxen has been more marked than in the case of horses and mules. It is, however, noticeable that the legislation which has been carried forward for the benefit of our dairy interests has not apparently strengthened the prices of either the dairy cattle or their products.

Through the courtesy of Mr. C. W. Jennings, of Belleville, N. Y., I have been furnished with the data collected by him in what he termed the "Cow Census" of the town of Ellisburg, Jefferson county, N. Y. Jefferson county stands third of the sixty counties of the state in the number of its milch cows, Oneida and St. Lawrence alone surpassing it; but five counties, St. Lawrence, Chautauqua, Chenango, Delaware, and Otsego, surpass it in the amount of butter made upon the farm; and but five counties, Oneida, St. Lawrence, Cattaraugus, Herkimer, and Orange, surpass it in the amount of milk sold or sent to butter and cheese factories. The results ascertained, therefore, by this census of Mr. Jennings' are in the highest degree important to our dairy interests, and being, so far as I know, unique, I have thought them worthy of the extended consideration I have given them, the results of which I desire to submit to you.

And I desire to say that while I shall have no hesitation in giving what appears to me to be the legitimate conclusions which these facts establish, I am disposed, rather, to submit the facts themselves, as I have classified and collated them, leaving you gentlemen to draw your own conclusions therefrom.

The following exhibit shows the character of the data placed in my hands by Mr. Jennings. It comprises in all 370 different herds of dairy cattle, with an aggregate of 5,594 cows:

GRADES AND NATIVES.

Full blood, 3.5 per cent; grades, 63.9 per cent; natives, 32.5 per cent.

Average Earnings.	Grades.		Natives.		Per Cent Natives of No. Cows.
	No. Herds.	No. Cows.	No. Herds.	No. Cows.	
Below $20	5	41	7	93	69
$20 to 25	15	255	20	254	50
25 to 30	58	929	56	626	40
30 to 35	60	1,226	43	544	31
35 to 40	47	854	20	236	22
40 to 45	18	287	5	47	14
45 to 50	4	21	3	17	45
Over 50	9	164	..	..	..
	216	3,777	154	1,817	

(Many cows returned as grades no doubt should have taken their places among the natives, as they were evidently of that denomination. I noted them as given, lower even. Nearly all the farmers use grade sires. Their progeny are called grades. They are grades, it is true, having been graded down and not upward).

The above table gives the per cent of full bloods, grades, and natives, and owing to the small number of thoroughbreds, they have by me been classed as grades. I have given the number of herds and cows of both grades and natives of which the average total earnings per cow were below $25; from $25 to $30; $30 to $35; $35 to $40; $40 to $45; $45 to $50, and over $50.

The first noticeable result in this table, after the general fact that the average earnings are so low with the great majority of the animals, is, that from the first the per cent of natives rapidly diminishes as the rate of average earnings increases, from 69 per cent of the cows the average earnings of which are below $20. To 14 per cent of those the average earnings of which are from $40 to $45, and none among the cows the average earnings of which are above $50.

The total number of cattle is, 216 herds of grades, containing 3,777 cows, and 154 herds of natives, containing 1,817 cows.

EFFECT OF GRAIN ON EARNINGS.

No. Herds.	No. Cows.	Value Grain per Cow.	Average Earnings per Cow.
8	86	$ 2.08	$18.26
27	402	3.19	23.24
89	1,307	3.14	27.84
87	1,599	3.47	32.25
60	983	3.54	37.08
20	290	4.09	41.91
6	34	5.44	47.37
4	117	8.18	51.81
4	42	7.31	57.45
1	5	15.00	81.00
306	4,865		

VARIATION WITH NO GRAIN FED.

No. Herds.	No. Cows.	Average Earnings per Cow.
4	48	$19.26
8	107	24.05
25	248	27.67
16	171	32.27
6	90	36.78
2	26	41.64
1	4	46.50
62	694	

Average earnings of all with grain, ... $ 32.48
Average earnings of all without grain, ...   29.47
The value of all grain fed, ... 17,301.45
Increase value, $3.01 x 4,865 = ... 14,643.65

I next endeavored to determine the effects of grain fed upon the total earnings; and to this I desire to call your especial attention, since in this feature of the discussion of the data I came upon results which somewhat surprised me.

I selected all the herds, whether grades or natives, 306 in all, containing 4,865 cows, to which grain was fed, and then these into groups, where the earnings, as before, were below $20, between $20 and $25, $25 and $30, $30 and $35, and so on. I then determined the average value of grain fed to each cow in these several groups, and found, as perhaps we should have expected, that as the average earnings per cow increased, the amount of grain fed per cow also increased in regular order, though not in proportion.

But I found of the remaining herds, 62 in all, containing 694 cows to whom no grain was fed, that there was a similar variation in average earnings, although the maximum earnings without grain were not so large as with grain; still, while none of these herds without grain reached an average earning of $50.00, there was of those cows which received grain only 3.4 per cent the average earnings of which surpassed $50.00. Moreover, I found that the average earnings of all those cows which received grain was but $3.01 per cow above the average of earnings of those cows receiving no grain; and that the increased value of the aggregate earnings of those cows which were fed grain was $14,643.65, while the grain fed them was valued at $17,301.45, or $2,657.80 in excess of the increased earnings.

To still further determine, if possible, the effect of grain fed, I grouped the returns in accordance to the value of grain fed per cow, *i. e.* all those receiving less than $1.00 worth of grain per cow; from $1.00 to $2.00; $2.00 to $3.00, and so on, and then averaged the returns, both by herds and by cows. By herds, in the hope that any result due to difference in treatment, care, and other conditions which would alone be the cause of difference in results might affect the result as little as possible; and by cows, in order to determine the general average.

This was done separately for grades and natives, and the results are presented in the following tables:

AVERAGE EARNINGS TO VALUE OF GRAIN FED.
By Herds.

Grades.		Natives.	
32.84	.73	28.39	.93
30.00	1.63	29.28	1.63
33.69	2.56	30.06	2.65
33.30	3.57	30 30	3.49
34.40	4.53	32.67	4.52
33.89	5.51	31.40	6.00
36.63	6.47	40.40	6.42
40.32	7.51	29.60	7.75
35.44	8.44	40.09	8.33
25.65	9.96	27.75	11.50
32.77	10.31		
47.12	11.46		
41.52	13.59		
81 00	15.00		

AVERAGE EARNINGS TO VALUE OF GRAIN FED. — BY COWS.

NATIVES.				GRADES			
Number of Herds.	Number of Cows.	Value of Grain.	Average Earnings.	Number of Herds.	Number of Cows.	Value of Grain.	Average Earnings.
7	97	$ .91	$26.75	10	233	$ .64	$32.06
31	397	1.53	29.28	42	689	1.61	30.09
42	501	2.62	30.30	44	671	2.49	32.17
18	200	3.44	29.78	33	635	3.49	33.61
10	78	4.44	30.95	22	400	4.44	34.21
1	12	6.00	31.40	13	283	5.49	34.49
3	47	6.38	37.23	6	146	6.60	34.93
2	29	7.93	27.13	8	146	7.50	36.88
1	9	8.33	40.09	4	82	8.41	34.78
1	4	11.50	27.75	1	26	9.96	25.65
				1	65	10.31	32.77
116	1374			3	78	11.55	44.88
				2	23	13.78	37.03
				1	5	15.00	81.00
				190	3482		

It will be seen that while there is a general tendency towards increased earnings with an increase in the grain fed, there is no approach towards regularity in increase, whether we consider the results by herds or cows, by grades or natives.

I desire to call your particular attention to this, inasmuch as a less exhaustive discussion of very limited data appeared to me, and to all those to whom the results have been submitted, as conclusively establishing the economy and profit in feeding grain (and with grain is included bran), and even determining the extent of profit.

Of course I shall not be understood as maintaining that the feeding of grain is not both wise and profitable; but only in these cases it is difficult, if not impossible, to determine the degree of wisdom or extent of profit in such a course.

I gladly avail myself, therefore, of this opportunity to correct, not the conclusion reached, but the reasoning by which it appeared to have been clearly established. Thus far in my discussion of the results of this "Cow Census" the benefits from feeding grain are not proven as clearly as might be expected.

There is another matter vitally connected with the success of the dairy industry of the country to which I desire to call your earnest attention. I find that I am reported as having said, at the recent meeting of the Dairymen's Association of New York State, that if the angel of destruction should pass over the herds of our milch cows with some intelligent discrimination and sweep off to-night three-fourths of a million, or fifty per cent of them, next fall the profit from our dairies would be vastly increased over that of last season, notwithstanding the enormous loss of about $24,000,000 worth of cows.

One nowadays is more brave than discreet who questions the notes of the professional stenographer. I shall not do it, for I suspect I said that; and I confess it sounds like me. I believe it to be true, moreover, and I believe that the data furnished in this "Cow Census" will fully establish its truth; and on account of its immense practical importance, I ask you to critically follow in the next point I present, viz.: the cost of keeping the cows of the dairy. During the past twenty-five years the average acreage value of the hay crop in the state of New York has been $16.05. It hardly appears that in the county of Jefferson it can be less, but rather more than the average of the state. Certainly the cost of feeding out the hay upon the farm would add somewhat to its value when sold in bulk.

The grain, the fodder corn, the rough fodder, are all products costing either money in their purchase or the full cost of their production. The average taxes amount to about $2.50 per cow; and since the chief income of the farmer in these cases is from the dairy, it appears only proper that the taxes be added to the items of cost. Pasturage is variously estimated at from $8 to $12 per cow. Either sum appears to me to be too large. The interest upon investment, it would appear, should be paid before one could begin to estimate his profits. The necessary repairs of the farm in buildings, fences, and wear and tear of the implements used; the care of the cattle; the manufacture and marketing of the products of the dairy; all these items must go to swell the list of expenses which each for himself may make.

COST OF FEEDS PER COW, GRADES AND NATIVES, AT VARIOUS EARNINGS.

Total Earnings	Grain.		Fodder Corn.		Meadow.		Roughage.		Taxes.	
	Grades.	Natives.	Grades.	Natives.	Grades.	Natives.	Grades.	Natives.	Grades.	Natives.
Below $25	$3.37	$1.43	$2.24	$1.94	$25.38	$24.30	$1.96	$2.10	$2.66	$2.45
$25 to 30	2.73	2.50	1.78	1.36	23.15	22.59	1.75	1.42	2.66	2.22
30 to 35	3.50	2.47	1.81	1.73	21.78	25.29	1.61	1.31	2.63	2.52
35 to 40	3.49	2.28	1.75	1.81	22.21	20.00	1.38	1.66	2.37	2.14
40 to 45	3.64	4.40	1.73	2.02	22.34	24.93	1.31	1.38	3.07	2.21
45 to 50	5.48	4.12	3.57	.88	26.41	19.83	2.53	2.00	3.81	1.46
Above 50	8.08		4.15		15.62		1.47		3.19	

PROFIT OR LOSS PER COW AT DIFFERENT EARNINGS.

Total Earnings.	Number of Cows.		Average Total Earnings.		Average Sale of Calves.		Average Product Besides Calves.		Average Product Besides Calves.		Average Cost Keeping less Pasture.		Gain or Loss per Cow.	
	Grades.	Natives.	Grades.	Natives.	Grades.	Natives.	Grades.	Natives.	Grades.	Natives.	Grades.	Natives.	Grades.	Natives.
Below $25	296	347	$22.54	$22.24	$ 2.52	$ 5.67	$20.02	$16.57	$35.51	$32.22	$12.97—	$ 9.98—
$25 to 30	929	626	26.98	27.40	4.92	6.66	22.04	20.74	32.07	30.09	5.09—	2.69—
30 to 35	1,226	544	32.54	32.22	4.01	6.60	28.53	25.62	31.33	33.32	1.21+	1.10—
35 to 40	854	236	37.22	36.94	6.16	4.25	31.06	32.69	31.20	27.89	6.02+	9.05+
40 to 45	287	47	42.12	40.53	5.70	4.47	36.42	36.06	32.09	34.91	10.03+	5.59+
45 to 50	21	17	47.38	47.17	5.79	4.38	41.59	42.79	41.80	28.29	5.58+	18.88+
Above 50	164		53.14		12.35		40.79		32.51		20.63+	

In the table showing cost of feeds per cow, grades and natives, at various earnings, I have tabulated for both grades and natives; and according to their average earnings, the actual cost per cow for grain, fodder corn, meadow, roughage, and taxes, the meadow being the only thing estimated, and that, as has been previously explained, at $16.05 per acre, it will be seen that with the sole exception of cost of grain fed there is little difference in the several items of expense, whatever the average earnings.

In the table showing profit or loss per cow at different earnings, I have tabulated the total earnings, the product from sale of calves, the cost of keeping, including grain, fodder corn, hay, roughage, and taxes only, but not including cost of pasture, and the other necessary items of expense already enumerated.

I have also determined the net profit or loss per cow at different average earnings for both grades and natives. It will be seen that the average product from sale of calves in the case of the grades increase with the total earnings per cow; while with the natives, as a rule, the greater the product from the sale of calves, the less the earnings. This fact would appear to indicate that the raising of calves for veal was hardly profitable, and also that a portion of the increased average earnings of grades was derived from the sale of higher priced calves, which, in the case of the pure thoroughbred herds, is obviously true.

It appears that there were 1,225 grades and 1,517 natives which fell far short in their earnings of paying for their feed alone, even not including their pasturage; and that there were 32.4 per cent of the grades and 53.6 per cent of the natives the average earnings of which were below $30.00; 87.5 per cent of the grades and 96.5 per cent of the natives the average earnings of which were below $40.00; or 39.3 per cent of all the cows with average earnings below $30.00, and 90.4 per cent of all the cows with average earnings below $40.00. The average cost of food, excluding pasturage, was $31.83.

There remains, therefore, with over 90 per cent of the dairy cattle in these 370 herds, with a total of 5,594 cows, the narrow balance of $8.17 per cow, which must pay for pasturage, for care, for milking, manufacture and marketing of products, the needed repairs of buildings and fences, the wear and tear of implements needed in carrying on the work, and the numberless incidentals with which you are more familiar than I; and when these (and you will observe that I have not included the interest upon the capital) items are deducted from $8.17, the balance may be set aside as the actual profit per cow realized by the owners of 5,058 of the 5,594 cows, the returns from which we have been considering.

Gentlemen, I need hardly assure you that even the desire to be found correct in my calculations in the discussion of this important matter — a laudable desire, truly — still even this is not so great but that I should rejoice to find that I was in error, and that this industry was not upon the whole conducted so disastrously as the statements I have submitted for your consideration appear to me to prove.

But the recent report of the Dairy Commissioner, Mr. Brown, gives very strong confirmatory testimony, since he shows that 37 counties of New York State (1,183 factories reporting — receiving milk from 407,810 cows, owned by 30,746 farmers), give an average milk yield per cow of only 3,034 pounds, and the Commissioner has personally assured me that in his deliberate opinion this is rather too large than too small. At an average price of 85 cents per 100 pounds this equals an average annual earning per cow of $25.79.

In his report I find that of the 37 counties reporting, 18 counties fall below, giving only 74 per cent of this general average, or 2,245 pounds of milk, worth $19.08; while 17 counties are above, and average 3,914 pounds of milk per cow, worth $33.27.

Nearly three-fifths, 57.4 per cent, of all these cows, over a quarter of the milch cows of the state, give an average return of only $18.17 per cow.

Three counties, Oswego, Cattaragus, and Herkimer, containing 251 factories, receiving milk from 89,323 cows, give an average return per cow of $17.60. Here are two lots of cows, nearly 100,000 in each, the average returns per cow from one being about 120 per cent greater than from the other

I have not in this discussion forgotten, nor do I wish lightly to pass over, a most important matter in connection with this subject, and this is the valuable product of manure incident to this industry. If only this product is carefully husbanded, and returned to the fields whence the several food products for the dairy cattle are obtained, it will largely diminish the net cost of the feed, which should be charged for such material if sold off the farm. The sum to be carried to the credit side of the dairy industry by the economical saving of the manure will depend wholly upon the intelligent appreciation of its value by the individual dairyman; and there can be no doubt that this single item will alone in far too many cases be the factor which shall determine the degree of profit or extent of loss which results.

Since preparing this paper I have received Bulletin No. 32 of the Massachusetts Agricultural Experiment Station, which presents in detail the "Record of Twelve Cows which Served at the Station for Experiments to ascertain the Cost of Feed for the Production of Milk;" and this is so entirely in accord with what I have already presented, that I know you will be pleased to have a summary of the results obtained by Dr. Goessmann.

This herd of twelve included five Ayrshire grades, two Durham grades, two Jersey grades, one Devon grade, one Dutch grade, and one native.

The average age of the twelve was seven years, and they had averaged three and one-half calves each.

The average days in milk during the experiment were 402; maximum, 599; minimum, 261.

The average yield of milk per day for entire period was 11.14 quarts, or 24.14 pounds.

The average yield of milk per cow for 300 days, averaging the beginning and ninth month of lactation, was 3,870 quarts, or 8,385 pounds.

The average gain in weight of ten of the cows during the trial was 87.6 pounds, and the average loss of the other two was 42 pounds.

According to the report of the Dairy Commissioner, the best 22 per cent of the cows reported by him averaged 4,538 pounds of milk per cow, or 46 per cent less than the average of this herd of twelve grades reported by Dr. Goessmann.

The Doctor concludes his report as follows: "It is evident that the most serious attention ought to be bestowed on collecting and preserving the manurial refuse obtained in connection with the production of milk; for it depends largely on a judicious management of this matter how much of the stated manurial value will be actually secured." He estimates the value of the manure secured by him in his experiments as equal to 40.45 per cent of the value of the feed used; and he continues: "The liability of a loss in the manurial value of the refuse matter renders it advisable, for financial reasons, not to depend on too close a margin of cash returns. Although it will be concluded that the dairy cow, aside from the special service, is a most important factor in a mixed farm management, as far as an economical disposition of home-raised fodder crops and a liberal production of home-made manure is concerned, yet when reduced to a mere manure-producing machine, this value may well be questioned from a financial standpoint." And he concludes that a "cow whose total milk record averages not more than eight quarts per day, judging from our own condition, promises to prove a better investment when prepared for the meat market than when constituting a liberal proportion of the stock kept for supplying the general milk market at stated prices."

Eight quarts per day, or the butchers' block, is the conclusion of Dr. Goessmann, judging from the conditions at Amherst, Mass. Let us, then, consider those conditions as compared with those of New York State, for example.

Three cents per quart is the market value placed upon the milk produced by his herd — but 3 cents per quart is a price 63 per cent higher than is 85 cents per 100 pounds, the average price, as I will assume, paid by the cheese factories of New York, which would bring the cheese produced at 9 cents per pound. On the other hand, the average acreage value of the cereal and hay crop of Massachusetts during the past three years has been 32 per cent higher than in New York.

Eight quarts per day is 5,200 pounds in 300 days, and but a single one of the 1,183 factories reported by Mr. Brown surpassed such a record, while 101 factories came next, with a record of 4,702 pounds of milk per cow, or 10 per cent below the point of profit fixed by Dr. Goessmann.

Fifty-two hundred pounds of milk at 85 cents is $44.20, and yet there were but seven herds, containing 81 cows, among the 370 herds, containing 5,594 cows, reported by Mr. Jennings, the average earnings of which, in milk, butter, or cheese, surpassed this limit.

Barely 81 cows, or less than 1½ per cent, averaged, for milk, butter, and cheese, $17.83 earnings.

I am aware, gentlemen, that while this is, as I believe, a truthful, it is also a very gloomy statement of the present condition of the dairy industry.

It would be indeed disheartening were it inevitable and necessary. It is unnecessary.

Very briefly let me indicate the conditions of success which, if intelligently considered, may render the dairy industry one of the most pleasant and profitable branches of agriculture.

I will give, as an illustration, a case in point which has fallen within my own experience, which I have no reason to believe to be unique, which, however, we must admit is exceptional.

Not many years ago I was going back and forth over the hills and valleys of Vermont holding farmers' institutes, and frequently in company with members of our Board of Agriculture, one of whom was, as now he is, a leading dairyman of the state. During those journeys to and fro he often spoke of his work and plans for the future, and especially do I recall his confident declaration that he should within a few years double the annual product of his herd of cattle, which even then was far in advance of the average dairies of the state.

He was getting 150 pounds of butter per cow, fully 25 pounds beyond the general average then, as I believe it to be now. He declared his intention to secure at least 300 pounds, and detailed his plan for accomplishing it.

I have his statement with one of his results last season. The average of his 34 cows was 302 pounds of butter per cow. The cost of keeping averaged $43.50 per cow. The receipts per cow, less cost of keeping, were $53.61. Cost of packing and marketing butter, $6.00 per cow. Average net receipts per cow, $47.61. Total net receipts of herd, $1,618.76. Total value of product of herd, $3,301.66.

At the recent Dairymen's convention held at Burlington his butter received 98 points out of a possible 100 — evidence enough as to its quality. The average price per pound of his butter, packed in tubs, was $28\frac{1}{2}$ cents.

The gentleman is Hon. Francis D Douglass, of Whiting, Vt., President of the Vermont Dairymen's Association.

Mr. Douglass declares with truth and emphasi that there is absolutely nothing to prevent the dairymen of his state, and of the country, from doing the same thing, if only they will.

On motion, duly seconded, a vote of thanks was extended to Professor Collier.

Mr. E. A. POWELL: I beg your pardon for taking up time, but I wish to state something that I think will be of interest. Messrs. Wood & Son, of Exeter, New York, reported to us a short time ago the result of thirty cows, nearly all of them high grades — a few thoroughbreds; nine of them were three-year-old heifers. They sold to the milk factory this season 183,000 pounds of milk; they made 1,500 pounds of butter, taking 37,000 pounds more, and they gave the items of milk, making nearly 9,000 pounds per cow, nearly all of them being three-year-olds. Those were kept for profit. Mr. Henry Jerome, who sells his milk to the Orange County Milk

Association, commenced a great many years ago by crossing on the best Holstein-Friesian bulls. At the time he commenced he was making 4,000 or 5,000 pounds of milk, which he sold to this association. This season he sold over 9,000 pounds to that association, three of his cows being only two-year-olds. Mr. Schuyler, the next neighbor to him, sold this season 10,448 pounds on an average, and that was the milk he got his pay for from the association, and he stood all the waste and everything of that kind, besides using milk in his family. The first gentleman was paid about $90.00 per cow, and Mr. Schuyler was paid $107.55, by the association.

THE PRESIDENT: Gentlemen, the next thing before us is the reading of a paper by Professor Morrow. He is unable to be present, but has sent his paper, and I will ask Mr. Goodwin, of Chicago, Illinois, to read it.

Mr. Goodwin then read Professor Morrow's paper, as follows:

THE BASIS OF VALUE IN CATTLE.

The final measure of value of farm animals is, adaptation to the wants of man. The final basis of price is, the actual and relative numbers of animals of different grades and adaptations. Beauty of form or color, personal attachment to individual animals, or good reputation of the ancestry may increase the estimate of value of a few animals. Prices may be controlled for a time or permanently for animals with rare characteristics, but the permanent estimate of the value of any class of animals produced in large numbers, and the prices at which they can be disposed of, depends on its demonstrated fitness to meet the practical wants of man.

The cattle breeding and feeding interests in the United States are unusually depressed. All classes show this depression — the best and the poorest, pure bred and grade, fat cattle and milch cows, all sell at lower prices and find a less ready demand than was the case a few years ago. It is well worth while for individual cattle-breeders and the representatives of any breed to ask whether it be possible to secure a more general belief in the superior merit or wider adaptation of their cattle.

The working ox has so largely disappeared in this country that the fitness of any breed for the production of working cattle cuts no figure in the popular estimate of value. Practically the estimate of value of almost all the good cattle of the country depends upon their supposed merit as producers of meat or dairy products, or of both of these.

The owners of, perhaps, one-third of the nearly fifty million cattle in the United States care little or nothing for the milk-giving ability of their cows, so long as they are able to supply the needs of the calves. By far the largest number of the cattle of this class are in the herds of the far western states and territories. Any breed of cattle the cows of which are inferior as milkers, or are believed to be so, will work against odds in attaining or maintaining wide-spread popularity in any district of considerable size east of the Missouri river.

The owners of, perhaps, one-tenth of the cattle in the country care little or nothing for the beef-making capability of their cows, valuing them only because of ability to give a large quantity or an excellent quality of milk. Many dairy farmers think the possession by either bulls or cows of the size and form best fitting them for beef-making a serious objection. This is also true of many village or town residents.

The owners of more than half of the cattle in the country attach importance to both the beef and dairy qualities in placing an estimate on the value of a cow or a breed of cattle. Some attach much more importance to one than to the other, but many nearly equal importance to each. The seven great corn-producing states — Ohio, Indiana, Illinois, Iowa, Missouri, Kansas, and Nebraska — have nearly one-third of the cattle of the country. In these states are reared and fed vast numbers of fine beef cattle. The special dairy interests of some of these states are important. But more than half the cattle in these states are kept in comparatively small herds by farmers who do not believe they can wisely ignore either beef-making or milk-giving in their cows — farmers who are not special dairymen, yet are not content to keep a cow simply to suckle a calf.

As affecting the bearing of these facts, it should be borne in mind that it is practically inevitable that the relative number of dairy cows will increase in the older states, except, possibly, in the south; and that in the opinion of many, the rearing of beef-cattle is to be more and more confined to what we now call the far west.

For the present, the largest demand for cattle is for those believed to be good both for beef-making and milk-giving; the next largest, for cattle believed especially good as beef-producers; the next, for cattle believed to be especially valuable as dairy cattle, with little or no reference to other qualities.

Is it possible, or practicable, to meet the preferences of this largest number of cattle-owners? If so, is it wise to attempt to so do?

It is a well established principle in breeding, that it is difficult, often practically impossible, to combine the highest degree of excellence in two or more directions in one animal or one breed. The requirement that there shall be uniformity in color, size, or any distinguishing mark greatly increases the difficulty in developing or maintaining the highest degree of excellence in any breed. Adding an additional " fancy " or unimportant point to the standard of excellence for any breed usually does harm.

There is overwhelming evidence, however, that we may have a symmetrical development of the whole animal, giving fitness for every natural function. We must choose between unusual or extraordinary devolpment of one quality and fair development of two or more. Special development in the domestic animals, as in man, attracts most attention, commands the highest price, and, in many situations, is by far the most valuable. Fair ability to do more than one kind of work in the domestic animals, as in man, is less showy, usually lower priced, but meets a larger demand.

The most widely-popular breeds of chickens are those which combine good size and form with good egg-producing ability. The most sought for breeds of sheep are those combining mutton and wool production in the greatest degree. The most generally popular breeds of hogs are those for which both early maturity and good size are claimed. Along side the demand, at high prices, for horses of great speed and horses of great strength, there is an increasing popular demand for horses combining speed, size, beauty of form, and activity in good degree.

Milk-giving and flesh-making are equally natural functions of every cow in natural conditions. Milk and flesh alike come from the food eaten, digested, and assimilated. The quantity and quality of either product will be affected by individual peculiarities, acquired or inherited, by the quantity and quality of food, and by good or bad care. Full work can not be done in both directions at the same time. The maximum product in both is not to be expected from the same animal, even at different times. There are thousands of cows, however, representing a half dozen breeds, or various crosses, which are conclusive proofs of the possibility of combining in one animal a merit above the average, both for the dairy and for beef making — a combination making animals more valuable for a multitude of our farmers than would be those in which there was a special development in either direction with corresponding weakness in the other. It is well worth an effort to supply the best possible of these double-purpose cows.

The number of pure bred cattle of each of the more popular breeds is large — so large that high average prices are not to be expected in the future. Very high prices may be expected for cattle which are, or are believed to be, exceptionally good, but with increasing numbers of technically pure bred animals, the average of prices for such will more nearly approach those for good cattle not eligible to record. Attempting to increase the demand by demonstrating adaptation to the wants of a large number of possible purchasers is a wiser policy than is any attempt to restrict production, except by discouraging the use of inferior animals.

The supply of pure bred cattle equals the present demand at any satisfactory range of prices. But the possible demand is far in excess of the supply. All the registered cattle of all the improved breeds in the United States would not, in number, replace the herds of any state or territory in the union, save only Rhode Island and Delaware. It is the exception, not the rule, to find herds the chief purpose of which is the production of dairy products or steers composed of pure bred animals. The large majority of the bulls used throughout the country, as a whole, are not pure bred. Improvement of most of the herds of the country has been only indirectly, if at all, by the use of pure bred sires and dams.

The least demand for improved cattle is usually found in regions where there is most need of improvement; the best demand from regions in which are already found a goodly number of fairly good cattle. Improving the average merit ordinarily increases the desire and ability to secure cattle of the highest excellence.

Experience has shown that records of phenomenal results, either in milk-production or in beef-making, are not more effective in securing favorable regard for any breed by farmers generally than is accumulation of evidence of comparatively moderate results under conditions closely approximating those under which the better class of cattle-men must place their stock.

It would be exceedingly unwise for the breeders of any class of cattle which has deservedly won reputation as possessing superior excellence for either one of the two great purposes for which we keep cattle, to purposely or carelessly suffer any loss in this regard.

The highest prices, and perhaps the largest profits, will be secured by those who can produce animals or families which naturally or by skillful development are able to show the largest yields of milk or butter, or the most or best beef.

It would be equally unwise for the friends of any breed of cattle to fail to magnify the fact, if it be a fact, that its merits are not all in one direction. To fail to do this, is to fail to invite appreciation by very many cattle-breeders, who insist that they are so situated that they most need cattle with symmetrical, rather than special, development.

The special friends of the most numerous and widely-distributed breed of improved cattle in the United States are now officially and privately announcing their belief that the former policy of giving attention to the development of this breed for one purpose only was a mistaken one, and are officially encouraging the opposite policy.

It has been preferred in this paper to state principles, and leave their application to intelligent cattle-breeders. Comparison of breeds is not necessary here. The breed of cattle to the interests of which this Association is devoted stands in the front rank as regards milk production. Cows belonging to it have extraordinary records as butter producers. Clearly it should be ranked among the dairy breeds. It has characteristics which commend it to many farmers who are not distinctively dairymen. Its large size and the rapid growth of the calves are greatly in its favor. Rarely has any breed of farm animals long maintained wide-spread popularity among farmers unless it was above medium size. An honorable record has been made in beef production in a comparatively small number of cases. Grades and crosses of this breed have given large gains for food consumed, and very large weights for age, in many trials.

Inspection of noted herds, or the animals exhibited at leading fairs, shows that there is a considerable difference in the type preferred by leading breeders. Some evidently attach much more importance to the supposed typical milk form than do others. Plentiful illustrations are to be found of finely-bred bulls and cows of this breed which would show creditably in any collection of beef-cattle.

Is it wise to admit that this breed, which has grown in popularity so rapidly, which has so many friends among the most intelligent of cattle-breeders, is and can be adapted only to the needs of one division of the smallest of three great classes into which the cattle-owners of the United States are to be divided?

Mr. W. G. POWELL: Through Mr. Goodwin, I would like to have conveyed to Professor Morrow our thanks, and those of this Association, and warm appreciation of his paper, regretting that he is not here personally.

Motion carried.

THE PRESIDENT: Gentlemen, the next paper is from Benjamin C. Sears, Superintendent of the New Jersey State Agricultural College Farm. The subject is "The Milk Supply of Large Cities."

Paper read by Mr. Sears as follows:

THE MILK SUPPLY OF LARGE CITIES.

In the early settlement of any country it is the first care to provide for the actual necessities of the family, and everything which they need must be produced on the farm. As the country grows older, its inhabitants acquire wealth and gather themselves into cities. Civilization becomes more and more complicated; the demands of consumers become more and more exacting, until they can only be met by those who make an especial study of the production of some one article.

The farm loses its virgin fertility; land advances in value; taxes increase. The expenses of our home-life grow greater. The farmer ceases to believe that what others enjoy of home conveniences and home adornment, of culture and education for their children, he and his are not also entitled to and *must* have, all of which makes a larger income necessary, and renewed exertion is needed to meet these just and growing demands. He finds that his neighbors in the city are willing to pay him for articles of food and luxury, and his attention is turned to supplying their wants. Others living about him are as quick as he in seeing this demand, and all are anxious to supply it.

One of the first wants felt by cities in their growth is a supply of perishable articles — fruit, vegetables, and fresh milk. The milk supply is one of the first wants felt as soon as land becomes too valuable for pasturage. This want is first supplied by those living near enough to drive in and deliver with the same conveyance. Soon the town outgrows this supply. Farmers at a distance send in milk by rail and river, adding freight charges to the cost of producing the milk, and also increasing very much the cost of delivery; increasing the cost of milk to the consumer, and taking off a share of the profit to the producer, as it is always incumbent upon him to place his product within reach of the consumer. But adding another class of consumers to the many which go to make the large cities a market for all kinds of produce.

I propose to treat this subject by a brief history of the growth of the milk supply of New York City, as probably what will apply to that will apply to most other cities in proportion to their growth.

At an early date in the history of New York City, the milkmaid was driven from the pastures bordering on Maiden Lane, up the Bowery, to and beyond the old homesteads which bordered the East and North rivers, making a stand for a time at Morrisania and the fertile plains of Harlem, then on into Westchester, and, by means of ferries, drawing also from Long Island and the adjacent shores of New Jersey. The opening of the Harlem railroad extended the field of supply into Westchester, Putnam, and later into Duchess counties.

In the year 1844 the Erie railroad was opened to Goshen, and milk was shipped from Orange county to help fill the demand in New York City. At first it was shipped in all sorts of vessels, but soon the regular tin can came into use, at first of different sizes, holding twenty, thirty, forty, fifty, and sixty quarts, then gradually getting down to forty quarts, or ten gallons each, and now a can of milk in Orange and adjoining counties means forty quarts.

At first the cows were milked at a very early hour, the milk, imperfectly cooled, shipped at 6 o'clock in the morning, taken by the way of Piermont and the connecting river line to New York, reaching there in the heat of the day, delivered, in many cases, by dealers interested in near-by dairies, and, with water added, sold as Orange county milk, at a lower price than the pure article, sold as their own production, thus injuring for a time the reputation of Orange county milk. The natural advantages, sweet pastures, pure water, and greater care of the milk, not sending it away until thoroughly cooled, the greater convenience of night trains leaving in the cool of the day and arriving in the city in time for the early morning delivery, all these gradually overcame the early prejudices against these new sources of supply, and "Orange County," "Putnam," and "Duchess County Milk" was painted in large letters upon the delivery wagons, sometimes, perhaps, without a strict regard to the facts in the case.

We then thought that the Shawangunk mountains of Orange and the end of the Harlem railroad were the natural limits of the milk supply of New York City, and that it was one of the natural and inherent rights of the farmers within those limits to supply that demand; but those living just outside of this charmed circle became desirous of helping to supply this demand. Railroad companies recognized in *the milk freight* a steady and *every-day* income, and used all their efforts to work up this business by putting on refrigerator cars for long distances, and charging no more freight for "long hauls" than shorter ones, thus practically bringing the farms situated one hundred and fifty miles distant as near the great metropolis as those only fifty miles away. The Hudson River Railroad reached out into Herkimer county — until ten years ago the centre of its milk traffic was one hundred miles from New York. The Housatonic drew from all Western New England. The Erie shoved its milk train over the Shawangunk range into the rugged valley of the Delaware. The Ontario & Western tunnelled the same range, and now draws from Delaware and adjoining counties, while the Walkill Valley, Ulster & Delaware, Susquehanna & Western, New Jersey Central, Long Island, and Northern Railroad of New

Jersey and New York add their quota, so that there is no night so dark that there are not very many "milky-ways," with long lines of lighted trains, bearing their supplies of milk food to New York City and its suburbs. And what is true of New York, is true, no doubt, of Boston, Philadelphia, and Chicago, and all other large cities of this and other countries, to a greater or less degree.

The dairies of all these regions were naturally summer dairies, and the natural food for milk had always been the fertile pastures, for which these regions had become famous. The result of this was a flow of milk during the summer months, and during the winter season it was very difficult to supply even a moderate demand. Out of this state of the market grew the modern creameries, located at some point convenient to a large number of dairies, equipped with all modern machinery, with facilities for handling large quantities of milk, with separators for taking off the cream, with steam power for churning when the cream cannot be sold, with large quantities of ice for storing and keeping the cream until it can find a market, thus using up some of the surplus when the production is too great, and having on hand milk which can be shipped as received, or cream in storage to supply a sudden demand. By this aid a large demand for cream has been created and supplied, and this article, long considered a luxury, has become with many a necessity for table use, while a very large proportion of the product is made into ice-cream, and the various forms of desserts and confections which tempt the appetite of the wealthy customer, and add largely to the consumption of the products of our dairies.

Stimulated by higher winter prices, the farmers of the older milk-producing districts have built comfortable barns, have made their dairies largely winter dairies, and by a careful study of feeds, and the most improved methods of preparing and feeding them, have succeeded in supplying the market as well in the winter, when our great cities are full and the demand is largest, as in the summer months. So that now there is no great flood followed by a great scarcity, but the city of New York and its suburbs receive with great regularity their daily quota of about 700,000 quarts of milk each and every day of the year — the time of our "late blizzard" being the only exception.

In order that the great amount of milk which now reaches the market may meet with a ready sale, and in order that the demand may grow with the growing population of our cities, it is necessary to sell it at moderate prices, that it may compete with the other food products.

The quality must be maintained, so that the physician may know that his patient is getting the right quantity and quality of food in the "milk diet," which seems to be a cure for many diseases and a needful food to many invalids; the mother and nurse must be sure that the infant is getting the proper amount and quality of nourishment, and that it comes from healthy cows.

Our milk laws, requiring twelve per cent of solids, as judiciously enforced by our Dairy Commissioners, have done much to give pure milk to the poor, and the active competition which prevails in this branch of trade, as much, if not more than in any other, insures to the rich the same boon; also putting upon the market milk in glass bottles has added to its consumption, by making it more attractive for table purposes, by being in convenient vessels for the sick room, for the boarder, for placing on the ice for a cool drink, convenient to take upon board the steamer when sailing for Europe, or upon shorter voyages, picnics, and in many other ways in which bottled wines and beers are used. All these things help not only to hold, but also to create, a market for this primitive, natural, healthy food.

To keep and satisfy this demand, the milk must be clean, free from stable odor, perfectly sweet, and must keep sweet at least twenty-four hours after delivery; should be made from good, sound food; should be well up to the standard of solids, and the fat should be held in solution by the milk, in order that it may reach the consumer after a long journey in the form of *milk, not partially churned butter*. It should come from healthy cows, so that no cry of tuberculosis or pulmonary disease may alarm the nervous consumer. The cows should have pure water and healthy surroundings, in order that any outbreak of typhoid fever may not be attributed to the milk supply, by your showing to all inquirers that your cows have a purer water supply than most cities have. In short, whatever can make our product better and give the consumer greater confidence in the purity of our milk should be our study. Whatever will deceive, or even disappoint, our customer, and all unnecessary excitement which may alarm, should be carefully avoided.

A year or two since I learned from a representative of the Anglo-Swiss Milk Condensing Company that the price which they paid for milk varied very little either in Orange county, New York, in England, or in one or two other points on the Continent, but was a little cheaper in Switzerland. Taking this fact in connection with the other, that it must compete with other articles of food, in price, to invite a large consumption, it appears that we cannot look for any higher price from the consumer, and as long as the present freight rates and very heavy expenses of delivery continue, to not much larger prices to the producer. Any larger profits, therefore, must come from improved production, to accomplish which we must have well equipped farms and good buildings. We must make a careful study of our feeds. We must see that our daily ration is properly balanced, that there is no waste; but above all, our dairy must be made up of the best specimens of a good milk-producing breed, and as far as possible, of a good family of that breed. *Natives of the soil*, the owners' pride, the *owners' peculiar care*, well worthy the slightly changed words of Whittier:

> "In our good dairy, so sleek and fair,
> No bones of leanness rattle;
> No tottering hide-bound ghosts are there,
> Or Pharaoh's evil cattle.
> Each stately cow bespeaks the hand
> That fed her unrepining;
> The fatness of a goodly land
> In each sleek hide is shining."

Mr. HORR: Mr. President, it is with pleasure that I move that a vote of thanks be extended to Benjamin C. Sears for the address which he has just given, and I would ask that we have it published in the minutes. It is certainly worthy of a place with the rest.

Motion carried.

THE PRESIDENT: The next thing in order, gentlemen, will be the report of the Auditing Committee.

Mr. H. LANGWORTY: Mr. Chairman and gentlemen, the Auditing Committee have the pleasure of reporting that they have found the accounts surrendered by our Secretary and Treasurer, as also the Superintendent of Advanced Registry, correct, with the exception of $1.00 in the Association's favor.

On motion, duly seconded, the report was adopted.

THE PRESIDENT: The next thing in order is the reading of a paper by Prof. Thorne.

Prof. Thorne then read his paper:

THE COMPARATIVE TESTING OF THE DAIRY BREEDS.

Whether dealing with the soil, with the plants that grow upon the soil, or with the animals that feed upon these plants, the first question that confronts the professional experimenter is that of variety.

Do the soils that are the product of decomposed sandstones require the same treatment as those which result from the weathering of the harder limestones, in order to maintain their fertility? Which variety of grain, fruit, or vegetable will give the largest return, and which breed of horses, cattle, sheep, or swine is best adapted to certain specific purposes? These are questions of perennial interest.

Indeed, this question of variety lies at the very foundation of scientific progress in rural industry; for, whether we look at it from the evolutionist or the creatist standpoint, we must admit that the differentiation of species into varieties has for its direct object a better adaptation to environment, and thus ultimately, in the case of cultivated plants and domestic animals, a greater suitableness to the wants of man.

There is abundant justification, therefore, for the lively interest which the intelligent farmer manifests in the question of breed, and for the earnestness with which he demands information that shall be a reliable guide to him in the selection of such a breed as shall be best adapted to his peculiar condition and surroundings.

But it is not possible, in the present state of our knowledge, to give a response to this demand which shall be founded upon incontestable facts. We say, in general terms, that certain breeds are better adapted to the production of beef, and certain others to the production of milk; but we are not prepared to say that any one of the beef breeds will produce a pound of flesh at less cost than another, nor can we yet assert, and support our assertion with scientific demonstration, that either of the dairy breeds, as a breed, is superior to all others for the production of milk.

I wish to be distinctly understood on this point: I am not here to disparage any breed of cattle, nor to cast doubts upon the claims made for it; and especially is this true of the magnificent breed in whose interest this convention is held. Standing, as I do, without pecuniary or other interest in any breed whatever, except the desire to arrive at the truth, I have to say that I firmly believe that there is a very large place for the Holstein-Friesian breed in the dairy industry of America; but if I were called upon to give a scientific basis for this belief, I should be compelled to admit that it is as yet simply founded upon hypothesis, although these hypotheses lack but the clinching of their nails, as it were, to become parts of the fixed record of the breed. What I say of the Holstein-Friesians applies equally to each of the other breeds; each has its own peculiar field, large or small, but the boundaries of these separate fields are very indefinite.

The desire to locate these boundaries is being constantly manifested in innumerable competitive tests at our fairs, and in countless private tests, designed to arrive at some rule by which the capacity of this or that breed might be estimated.

No one will be more ready than the gentlemen who have been personally interested in either of the methods indicated to admit that such tests are wholly unsatisfactory. The very nature of the competition at the fair precludes the possibility of arriving at any exact truth, even were judges or awarding committees thoroughly competent, and entirely beyond the reach of bribery; while in the private test the temptation to over-estimate is so strong, and average human nature so weak, and withal so distrustful, that such tests have very little weight either among breeders or with the general public.

Nor has the official test made under the auspices of the breeders association proved a solution of the problem. The great difficulty with all these tests is that they only give us the performance of phenomenal animals, and leave us entirely in the dark with respect to the capacity of the breed as a breed. But this is just the point on which the farmer and dairyman want more light. They do not care for the enormous yields made by a few cows under exceptional treatment, unless these yields be an index of the capacity of the breed in general; for they know that it is possible to select individual cows among natives, grades, or even among the beef breeds, whose performance, under similar conditions, would far exceed what the breed in general is capable of doing.

Hence I say that the question which the general public — and I apprehend the majority of breeders, as well — desire to have answered is, not what can this or that individual cow do, but

WHAT CAN THE BREED DO?

This, I repeat, is the question that we are called upon to answer to-day. This is the problem toward whose solution we must steadily direct our investigations if we would meet the demands of the times. But it is often easier to point out a prominent landmark in the distance than to indicate the route by which it may be reached. The distant mountain seems easy to climb; it is only when we actually begin the ascent that we realize the difficulties of our undertaking, and this is emphatically true of the subject in hand.

Although this work is not included in the long list of subjects for investigation given in the act of congress establishing experiment stations in the several states and territories, yet there is abundant evidence that it is a work which the people expect the stations to undertake, and already several stations have moved in the matter. Some of the stations have been urged to join in a co-operative movement of this character, the plan of which, briefly stated, is for each station to purchase a few animals, supposed to be fair representatives of each of several breeds, and subject them to comparative tests, in which the feeding and treatment shall be similar, beginning at calfhood, or later, as the judgment of the station may dictate.

The objection to this method is that it will be impossible to select out of any breed a limited number of animals which will be accepted generally as a fair representative of the breed, especially if this selection fails to come out ahead in the competitive test. It is urged in opposition to this objection, that if a number of stations join in the test, the errors arising from such selection will be largely eliminated by the number of animals under test; but this does not necessarily follow. Two guesses may or may not give a better average than one, but they remain nothing but guesses. Moreover, the resources of the stations will not permit the purchase of phenomenal animals, or members of fancy families of any of the breeds; and unless some of these are included, the test will not be accepted as a fair measure of any breed's capacity. As a modification of this plan, a circular proposing the following method was issued some months ago by the Ohio station, and submitted to prominent breeders for criticism and suggestions:

"I. In the case of the beef breeds, let the respective state associations select each year a certain number of steer calves — say six of each breed — these to be purchased at their market value by the station, and subjected to the same treatment throughout until they arrive at maturity; an accurate account being kept of the food eaten by each, and of the monthly increase in weight.

"II. In the case of the dairy breeds, let the state associations select annually — say three representative cows of each breed — these to be removed to the station, and there subjected to the same treatment for a year (or during their flow of milk), and then returned to their owners in unimpaired health and condition. In order to avoid disputes respecting the health and condition of the animals, the following rules are proposed:

"(1) No cow will be accepted for test until the veterinarian of the station, or other officer appointed for the purpose, shall have examined her and pronounced her sound.

"(2) Upon each cow offered for test a valuation shall be placed, and if this valuation be deemed excessive, the station shall have the privilege of rejecting the cow.

"(3) The station shall not be held responsible for injuries to cattle caused by fire, lightning, or storms.

"(4) In no case shall the station be held responsible for injury to any cow in a greater sum than the valuation placed upon the cow when accepted for test.

"(5) In case of any dispute respecting the condition of a cow on her delivery to the owner, the matter shall be submitted to a board of arbitration, consisting of the veterinarian of the station, or other officer appointed for the purpose, the president of the breeders' association of the breed to which the cow belongs, or other person appointed by him, and a third person, chosen by these two, and the decision of this board shall be accepted as final."

It will be seen that there are several weak points in this plan. The first is, that under it only exceptional animals will be offered for test; another is, that it involves the moving of the cow to be tested and placing her under new and strange conditions and surroundings, and this will in many cases cause her to fail to do her best; a third is, that however careful the station might be, cases would be continually arising in which the owners of the cattle would feel that they had not been properly cared for, and however the boards of arbitration might decide, there would be dissatisfaction which would work to the disadvantage of the stations.

In the correspondence growing out of this circular, the following plan was suggested by Mr. B. B. Herrick, of Wellington, Ohio, which, while it leaves much to be desired, yet it seems to me to cover more of the essential points of such a test than any other yet proposed:

"Let the station send a competent man to such herds of pure-bred cattle as may be offered for test; this man to weigh accurately all food consumed by the cattle; to take samples of the same, and send to the station for examination and analysis; to weigh the milk produced by each cow, and determine its quality, both by chemical analysis and by the churn; to determine by actual working test the amount of caseine or curd in the milk, and to determine the weight of the animals under test by daily weighings. It is proposed that the test continue one or two weeks, and that it be repeated once each quarter, at least, throughout the year. By this method six herds at least may be kept under observation at the same time, and as will be shown further on, the herds may contain any number of individuals up to a hundred or more each."

It will be seen that this method proposes to deal with aggregations, whereas other methods deal with individuals only. It is true that individual tests will be included in this method, but the aggregate result will be the grand object of the work.

It may be objected to this plan that breeders will not care to have the records of their poorer animals published. But the stations have nothing to do with the commercial side of this question; their object will be simply to arrive at a scientific answer to the question, "what is in the breed?" and it will be no part of their duty to publish such details as may interfere with the business of those who furnish the cattle for test. The range of variation and the aggregate result, the details of care and management, and such facts as may be required to show the relation between food and product, are all the points in which the stations will have any interest. To the owner of the herd, and to those interested in building up a breed upon the solid foundation of actual merit alone, such tests will have great value, because they will point out the animals that are living on the reputation of the breed alone, and in so doing are loading it with so much dead weight.

The objection may be raised that the methods of management of different breeders will vary so greatly that no comparable data can be obtained by this method; and but for the light which modern science has thrown, and is throwing, upon the relation of food to animal nutrition, this would be true. As it is, however, the chemist can now reduce the various feeding stuffs to their dry matter, and this dry matter to its constituents of protein, carbhydrates, and fat, in such a manner that the variations in method between different feeders will be but a slight impediment to the direct comparison of results.

It has been objected to any method involving the handling of large numbers of cattle, that it would be practically impossible to analyze their milk separately; and under the old systems of analysis this objection was a valid one. But a new method of milk-analysis has recently been devised by Prof. F. G. Short, of the Wisconsin Experiment Station, by which any man of intelligence, and that without any previous knowledge of chemistry, may accurately determine the fat in a very large number — one hundred or more — samples of milk daily. This method has been thoroughly tested, and proven equal in its results to the best methods of the chemical laboratory.

It may be objected that breeders will feed their herds lavishly in anticipation of the quarterly test, and then reduce the feed while the test is in progress. Possibly this trick may be attempted in some cases. There are comparatively few breeders who will stoop to such trickery, however, and when there is reason to suspect that it has been attempted, it may be exposed at once by continuing the test for two weeks, as the falling weight will show that the feed has been changed.

These are the chief objections which occur to me as likely to be brought against this method. They are objections of weight; but, as I have already intimated, there seems to me to be a greater possibility of overcoming these and of successfully solving the problem before us by this method than by any other yet proposed. My object in coming before this convention, however, is to get the judgment of the practical breeders here assembled, and therefore I invite your criticism and suggestions.

On motion, duly seconded, a vote of thanks was extended to Prof. Thorne.

Mr. G. D. WHEELER: I am very sorry that we have not time to discuss some of these questions that are brought up in these papers. This question of testing the different kinds of cattle is very interesting to us, and as far as I have ever known, we have never been challenged to any contest whatever in this way but what we have accepted it, and we would be glad now to accept any challenge from any breed of cattle, and let the tests be made by persons who are disinterested; and I am glad that this subject has been brought up. We love to have tests made of our stock.

Mr. C. W. HORR: I also regret that we cannot spare the time to go into discussion on these subjects. I think we have struck a point that we ought to talk about; I think we should say something about this paper of Prof. Thorne's. The experiment that he narrated which took place on the Ohio Experimental Farm was not quite satisfactory, because a milk that will make cheese is just as good to us as one that will make butter. My understanding of the Jersey cow's milk is that while it is extremely rich in butter, it is not so rich in cheese. In other words, Jersey skim-milk is the poorest stuff that was ever put into a stomach; Holstein milk is rich in caseine. I got this information from one of the United States agricultural reports. In my early reading of the Holstein breed I found that the milk was rich in caseine. An experiment that did not touch the cheese qualities of the milk, as well as butter, would not be satisfactory to me, that is certain; but the value of a cow is not fixed simply by finding that if you furnish to her so much feed it will go to so many cents worth of milk; it is one of cheese and butter. Suppose that a Jersey would produce one-half as much butter and cheese on an average as a Holstein, you would have to have a barn twice as large, but it would not take twice as long to milk twenty Jerseys giving twenty pounds a day as it would ten Holsteins giving forty-five pounds; it would take more time to clean the stables and care for the cows, and it would be a larger investment in every way, so that the whole question would not be decided in that way. Again, you can not get at the value of a horse by weighing him, and saying that he can go so many miles in a minute, or a mile in so many minutes, and then that the horse is capable of going so many miles in an hour. Why, the disposition of a horse, his agreeableness, and many other things are taken into account before you get his real value. Now I claim for the Holstein cattle that if you enter into a comparison of qualities in that way, the verdict must be in their favor over any other cow. I never had but one cow — Holstein cow — upon my premises that would kick. I sold her cheap because she kicked, and she never kicked after the man had had her a week. Now such a record as that, so far as my knowledge, information, and belief goes, is not to be compared with any breed. Not a single kicker; there is no trouble in my barn in breaking in my heifers; there is no difficulty whatever in milking my two-year-old heifers when they first calve. Now I am only making this as a suggestion. It would not be told by this test. I would like to ask the professor whether the same method of testing will reveal the amount of caseine as well as the amount of butter?

Prof. THORNE: It is proposed that there should be a curd test at the same time.

THE PRESIDENT: Before we adjourn, I wish to give notice that the incoming Board will meet right away, here in this room.

Mr. HORR: Where will we meet next?

Mr. E. A. POWELL: I was going to say in regard to that same matter — where shall we meet? We have had here one of the most interesting and one of the best-attended meetings that we have had for years, and I think there is only one New York. New York is a splendid place; therefore I move that the next annual meeting be held at this place.

Mr. LIGGETT: I second that.

Mr. HORR: One moment. We have come willingly from the west this time, but I don't believe that the western men will be quite so willing next time.

Mr. LIGGETT: Yes, they will.

Mr. HORR: I have been congratulating myself that I was going home at ten o'clock — going to leave this city with its many temptations. I move that the next annual meeting be held in Syracuse.

Motion seconded.

Mr. J. B. DUTCHER: My friend, Mr. Powell, lives in Syracuse, and that is why he favors that place. If it is in order, I would renew the original motion. I have conversed with a great many gentlemen here, to-day, and the universal expression seems to be — even if Mr. Powell is a resident of Syracuse — that New York City is the place to hold these meetings; it is accessible, and as much so as any place we can go; a great many want to come to New York once a year. The state of New York has the largest membership. I hope that the amendment will be voted down.

Mr. E. A. POWELL: I move, as an amendment to the amendment, that the next meeting be held in the city of New York.

Motion seconded.

THE PRESIDENT: Gentlemen, you have heard the motion, that the next annual meeting be held in New York. Those in favor will please say aye; contrary, nay.

Motion carried.

Mr. J. B. DUTCHER: I have been requested to bring up the time of meeting. I have no particular feeling about it myself, but I have always understood that this time was rather a bad time to hold these meetings. While I have no feeling in the matter, still I have been requested to bring this matter before the meeting.

Mr. E. A. POWELL: It is fixed by the charter.

Mr. G. D. WHEELER: The last vote in regard to place of meeting was taken on the amendment, but we have not passed the original motion yet.

THE PRESIDENT: I supposed it was pretty well settled by the vote.

Mr. C. W. HORR: Mr. Chairman, I move that a committee of three citizens of New York be appointed to prepare a modification of our charter, so that we can have the annual meeting at any time during the months of February and March that may be fixed by the chair — even any time during the year. I don't care whether it is the first of May or the first of February. I wouldn't want it changed simply to suit us, but we are greatly inconvenienced. If you are inconvenienced as we are, I think the time should be changed, even if we have to get our charter amended.

THE SECRETARY: Mr. President, the charter reads in this way: "Said offiers shall be elected by ballot from and by its members at its first meeting, and thereafter at its annual meeting, to be held on the third Wednesday of March of each and every year, in the city of Buffalo, at its place of business, or other convenient time and place fixed by the by-laws and duly designated by the Secretary in his notice by mail to members of such meeting."

Mr. J. B. DUTCHER: I would like to ask another question while I am on my feet. Do the hotel proprietors charge for the use of the room here?

THE SECRETARY: They do not.

Mr. LIGGETT: I move that a vote of thanks be extended to the proprietors of the hotel for their kindness in furnishing us with acommodations.

Motion seconded and carried.

Mr. E. A. POWELL: There is one more matter that I want to speak of. It is very seldom that you can get the men present at our meetings that are here now. It is the fact that Holstein men are noted for their silence. They make large records; have remarkable cows; make large butter yields, but the public never know anything about it; I have noticed in some of the leading agricultural papers, which I presume are read all over, for instance: *Country Gentlemen*, *Rural New Yorker*, and *Breeders' Gazette*. I know that they are read. Yet you will see a dozen records of Jersey cows to one of this breed, because this breed of cattle usually belong to men who are busy. There isn't any greater service that we can do for the benefit of this breed of cattle and for the benefit of the community, than to let the people know about it. Any cow that will make fifteen pounds of butter in a week ought to be reported, so that the community may know what is being done and what can be done. I feel anxious, and will urge that from this time forth every member of the Association take special pains to test the cows and have their records published. The *Holstein Register* has urged everybody to send every item of news of that character, and it hasn't been done, as it should be. I know of several cows that have made from twenty to twenty-one pounds of butter in a week, and have never appeared in print at all. This is neglect on our part.

Mr. J. B. DUTCHER: I wish to state, Mr. chairman, that so far as making butter is concerned, I never have made any except for a short time. I have just started testing my cows for butter. I have tested one cow; she closed a seven days' test last week. Before she was five years old she made twenty-nine pounds of butter in seven days. That cow is five years old to-day; I expect to do better with her.

Dr. E. P. MILLER: It seems to me that this Association ought to do something to facilitate the process of making these records of the cows, both butter and milk. There are a great many persons who are beginning new in the Holstein breed, and they do not know how to keep these records, and this is true, particularly of a great many farmers. I believe that if the general dairymen of this country were to keep a record of the milk and butter that their cows give it would not be a great while before there would be a great increase in the demand for Holstein cattle, because they would find that the cows they were keeping did not actually pay for their keeping. I think that the evidences which have been brought forward show that a great many cows in this state do not pay for their keeping. Now, if this Association would get up blanks and give directions about how it is done, especially those who have had experience, it would encourage beginners in the field to keep these records. They would be doing a great deal for the Association, and Holstein cattle in particular.

Mr. HORR: It seems to me that we have consumed all the time we can, in justice to the new Board. They want to leave on the ten o'clock train to-night, and we are giving them limited time to transact the business before them. I therefore move to adjourn.

Motion seconded.

THE PRESIDENT: Gentlemen, you have heard the motion to adjourn; those in favor please say aye; opposed, nay.

Motion carried.

The meeting thereupon adjourned.

MEETING OF THE BOARD OF OFFICERS

OF THE

HOLSTEIN-FRIESIAN ASSOCIATION OF AMERICA,

Held at the Fifth Avenue Hotel, New York, N. Y.,
March 19th, 1889.

Roll call showed the following members to be present: Messrs. M. L. Sweet, W. M. Liggett, Edgar Huidekoper, F. L. Houghton, W. Brown Smith, D. H. Burrell, W. G. Powell, T. G. Yeomans, W. M. Singerly, S. Hoxie, C. R. Payne, and Thomas B. Wales.

The President, M. L. Sweet, presided.

The following gentlemen were admitted to membership:

GEORGE B. POLHEMUS, ... Coyote, California.
SAMUEL MCINTYRE, ... Salt Lake City, Utah.
F. P. GRACEY, ... Clarksville, Tennessee.
W. J. HAYES, ... Ravenna, Ohio.
T. G. FERGUSON, ... Stella, Nebraska.
JOHN HUNTINGTON, ... Cleveland, Ohio.
J. L. WHITWORTH, ... Nashville, Tennessee.
J. M. HAM, ... Washington Hollow, New York.
E. P. MILLER, ... New York, New York.
W. E. HUGHES, ... Dallas, Texas
C. H. VANDEVORT, ... Amity, New York.

It was moved by Mr. W. M. Singerly that a meeting of the Inspectors of Advanced Registry be authorized, for comparing methods of examination and securing uniformity of work; that the necessary expenses of such meeting and the traveling expenses of the members be paid by the Association, but that no payment be made for time. They are also to revise the scale of points, and to formulate amendments to the rules of advanced registry, all of which are to be submitted by the Superintendent, by letter, to each member of the Board of Officers.

Motion seconded.

Mr. W. Brown Smith offered, as an amendment to Mr. Singerly's motion, that the Superintendent be authorized to call such meeting at such time and place as he deemed best, and to invite such Inspectors as he pleased.

Amendment accepted, and motion carried.

It was voted to allow the request of Dr. E. P. Miller to change the name of the bull "Milla's Netherland" to "Pietertje 3d's Netherland," and re-register the animal for the usual fee; also to change the name of the cow "Young Zanke" to "Piersma 3d," provided it does not conflict with the by-laws, the animal to be re-registered for the usual fee.

The application for the registry of an imported animal tracing to colored ancestry was rejected.

The application for the refunding of transfer fees which had been paid under protest was refused.

The request of the University of Tennessee for a set of Herd-Books was granted, and books ordered sent free of charge; also set of Advance Registry.

The salaries of all officers were paid for the ensuing year at same rate as for the past year.

A set of Herd-Books was also voted to the Agricultural College of Minnesota.

Mr. S. Burchard, who had been appointed to select six calves for the New York Experiment Station, at Geneva, submitted his report, which, on motion, was referred to a committee of three, which committee was to report to an adjourned meeting of the Board. The chair appointed Messrs. Horr, Liggett, and Burrell.

It was moved and carried that the subject of the registration of bulls be next considered.

Mr. Smith introduced a suggestion for the consideration of the committee appointed at the last annual meeting of the Association (which committee was the Board of Officers), as follows: "That the Association charge a registry fee of $5.00 for each bull recorded in the Herd-Book; and also, that the Association offer a premium of $5.00 for each male calf killed or castrated, payable upon proper proof."

Many other plans were suggested, but the above proved to be the most acceptable, and it was agreed to recommend to the Association that the registry fee for bulls be $5.00; that the Association agree to pay $5.00 for each and every male calf slaughtered or castrated while in good health, between the age of five to forty days, upon proper proof furnished to the Secretary, which must include the affidavit of the owner.

Adjourned at 6 o'clock to meet at 8:30 A. M., Wednesday, March 20th, 1889.

THOMAS B. WALES,
Secretary.

ADJOURNED MEETING OF THE BOARD OF OFFICERS.

Held March 20th, 1889, at 8:30 a. m.

Present: Messrs. Sweet, Powell, Huidekoper, Yeomans, Payne, Houghton, Hoxie, Wales.

It was moved by Mr. Huidekoper that further consideration of the question of the registration of bulls be laid on the table, which motion was seconded and carried.

The committee appointed to consider the report of Mr. S. Burchard on calves for the New York Experiment Station reported as follows: "That after talking with the owners of said calves selected and approved by S. Burchard, it is recommended that the Association accept and pay for the animals at prices set forth in Mr. Burchard's report."

It was moved and seconded that the report of the committee be accepted, and that the calves be received and paid for.

THOMAS B. WALES,
Secretary.

ANNUAL MEETING OF THE BOARD OF OFFICERS

OF THE

HOLSTEIN-FRIESIAN ASSOCIATION OF AMERICA,

Held at the Fifth Avenue Hotel, New York, N. Y.,
March 20th, 1889.

The members present were: Messrs. Huidekoper, Wheeler, Frye, Burrell, Horr, Payne, Sweet, Powell, Yeomans, Smith, Hoxie, and Wales. President Huidekoper was in the chair.

The following persons were admitted to membership:

HORTENSE DUDLEY, ... Oakville, Kentucky.
WILLIAM H. BENT, ... Cochituate, Massachusetts.
ISAAC DAMON, ... Cochituate, Massachusetts.
JOSEPH J. MARTIN, ... Philadelphia, Pennsylvania.

Messrs. James Neilson and H. D. Warner, the committee appointed to select cows for the New Jersey Experiment Station, reported progress, and requested to be allowed to lease animals, instead of purchasing, if it was found by them to be desirable. This request was granted, and the sum of $1,500.00 was voted the committee, to be used for the purchase or lease, as seemed most desirable.

The subject of arranging the special premiums for the present year was discussed, and referred to a committee of five, to consist of the President and Secretary and three other members of the Board, to be named by the President. The committee to meet at the call of the Secretary.

The matter of assisting the circulation of the *Holstein-Friesian Register*, referred by the Association to the Board, was next taken up, and after thorough consideration, on motion of Mr. Horr, the chair appointed a committee consisting of Messrs. Horr, Burrell, and Powell to consult with the editor of said journal.

The committee agreed upon the following report, which was adopted by the Board:

Your committee would recommend the acceptance of Mr. F. L. Houghton's proposition to mail a copy of the *Holstein-Friesian Register* for one year to as many subscribers as are furnished by the Association in the following manner, to-wit:

Each member of the Association to be asked in a circular-letter, to be issued by the Secretary, to forward to Mr. Houghton the names of twenty-our persons to whom the member wishes the *Register* sent for a period of three months; Mr. Houghton to divide this list into four sets of six names each, and to mail copies of his paper to each member of each set for a period of three months. The Association are to pay Mr. Houghton for each copy furnished for an entire year the sum of eighty cents. Mr. Houghton is to forward all letters and the lists to the Secretary, accompanied by a certificate of the number of papers furnished, and the Secretary is to give Mr. Houghton, at the end of each quarter, an order upon the Treasurer of the Association for one-fourth of the money due him for papers furnished under this arrangement.

Respectfully submitted,
C. W. HORR, *Chairman*.

Mr. Hoxie was appointed a committee to inspect a steer calf offered by Mr. Burchard for the New York Experiment Station, with authority to purchase same for as little money as possible, but in any event not to exceed $100.00.

The Inspectors of the Advanced Registry were then elected as follows:

O. P. CHAPMAN,	Wellington, Ohio.
S. BURCHARD,	Hamilton, New York.
S. N. WRIGHT,	Elgin, Ill.
H. B. DAGGETT,	Hampton, Iowa.
J. L. STONE,	Waverly, Pennsylvania.
A. R. STURTEVANT,	Springboro, Pennsylvania.
CAREY R. SMITH,	Santa Ana, California.
A. BRADLEY,	Lee, Massachusetts.
J. C. POOR,	North Andover, Massachusetts.
H. D. WARNER,	Lanesville, Connecticut.
W. A. ROWLEY,	Mt. Clemens, Michigan.
T. N. FIGUERS,	Spring Hill, Tennessee.
J. R. BEUCHLER,	Leesburg, Virginia.

The Board then adjourned.

THOMAS B. WALES,
Secretary.

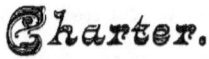

CHAPTER 333.

AN ACT TO INCORPORATE THE HOLSTEIN-FRIESIAN ASSOCIATION OF AMERICA.

PASSED May 25, 1885; three-fifths being present.

The People of the State of New York, represented in Senate and Assembly, do enact as follows:

SECTION 1. Theron G. Yeomans, William M. Singerly, William C. Brayton, Thomas B. Wales, Jr., Gerrit S. Miller, Frederick C. Stevens, Wing R. Smith, J. D. Guthrie, Frederick L. Houghton, Francis W. Patterson, Wayne MacVeagh, G. M. Emrick, George F. Jackson, H. H. Hatch, William H. Hemingway, Daniel D. Durnall, Irwin Langworthy, John B. Tuckerman, Charles R. Payne, Robert Burch, E. R. Phillips, Solomon Hoxie, and all other members of the present "Holstein Breeders Association of America," and "The Dutch-Friesian Herd-Book Association of America," and all other persons at any time hereafter duly associated as provided by the By-Laws with or succeeding them, under and for the purposes of this Charter and Act of Incorporation are hereby organized and constituted a body corporate, and are a corporation under and by the name of the "Holstein-Friesian Association of America," for the purpose of improving the breed of Holstein-Friesian cattle; ascertaining, preserving, and disseminating, as provided by its By-Laws, all useful information and facts as to their pedigrees and desirable qualities, and the distinguishing characteristics of the best specimens, and preparing, publishing, and supplying all necessary volumes of the Holstein-Friesian Herd-Book; and generally for promoting and securing the best interest of the importers, breeders, and owners of said cattle, and thereby the public generally; and for the purposes and to attain the objects aforesaid, said corporation is hereby given all necessary power, authority, and rights, including the powers, and subject to the liabilities prescribed by title three, chapter eighteen, part one of the Revised Statutes.

Sec. 2. The officers of said association shall be a President and four Vice-Presidents — to be designated as first, second, third, and fourth; one Secretary and Editor, six Directors, and such other officers as may be provided for by the By-Laws of this association; and said officers shall respectively perform the duties imposed upon them by the By-Laws. Said officers shall be elected by ballot from and by its members at its first meeting, and thereafter at its annual meeting, to be held on the third Wednesday of March of each and every year, in the city of Buffalo, at its place of business, or other convenient time and place fixed by the By-Laws and duly designated by the Secretary in his notice by mail to members of such meeting.

Sec. 3. Said corporation shall issue its certificate of membership, signed by its President and Secretary, and sealed with its corporate seal, to each of its lawful members; which certificate shall not be transferable, and shall be evidence of membership, and shall entitle its owner, while a member in good standing, to vote personally or by proxy at its meetings, and to all the privileges and advantages of such membership. But said corporation may cancel any certificate and forfeit and terminate any membership, and all rights and privileges arising therefrom, for his wilful disobedience or evasion of its By-Laws or other rules and regulations, and for any wrongs committed by him against said corporation or its property, interests, or rights; which forfeiture and eviction shall be cumulative to any other legal remedy said corporation may have against such evicted member.

Sec. 4. Said corporation may hold such other meetings in addition to said annual meeting, and said annual meetings may be held at such other places than Buffalo, as provided by its By-Laws.

Sec. 5. The By-Laws of said corporation shall be made and adopted by a majority of its members voting personally or by proxy at the first regular meeting held under the provisions of this act. Said By-Laws may be altered, amended, or repealed at any annual meeting by a like vote of its members.

SEC. 6. At the first regular meeting of said corporation, its members shall agree upon and adopt its corporate seal.

SEC. 7. All property, rights, and interests of said "Holstein Breeders Association of America," and "The Dutch-Friesian Herd-Book Association of America," of every name or nature, shall, by virtue of this act, vest in and become the property of this corporation.

SEC. 8. No debts or pecuniary obligations shall be incurred by this corporation except duly authorized by a previous two-thirds vote of all its members.

SEC. 9. Upon the organization of this association, and election of its officers in pursuance of this act, the associations formed under chapters four hundred and forty-seven of the laws of 1880 and two hundred and seven of the laws of 1882 shall cease to exist.

SEC. 10. This act shall take effect immediately.

STATE OF NEW YORK, } ss.
OFFICE OF THE SECRETARY OF STATE,

I have compared the preceding with the original law on file in this office, and do hereby certify that the same is a correct transcript therefrom, and of the whole of said original law.

JOSEPH B. CARR,
Secretary of State.

BY-LAWS

OF THE

Holstein-Friesian Association of America.

Adopted at its first meeting, held at Buffalo, New York, May 26th, 1885.

Amended March 20th, 1889.

Article 1.

OF MEMBERSHIP.

SECTION 1. Any person of good character who is a citizen of North America, interested in the breeding of Holstein-Friesian cattle, and the owner of such, may apply for membership in this corporation by filing a written or printed application, in such form as the Board of Officers may prescribe, with the Secretary, with the membership fee of one hundred dollars. The form of application for membership shall give the applicant's name in full, his residence and post-office address, and such other particulars as the Board of Officers may require.

SEC. 2. Every application for membership shall be submitted to the consideration of the Board of Officers, and if in their judgment the applicant is eligible for membership, and ought to be admitted as a member of this corporation, and a unanimous vote of the Board of Officers present to that effect is passed, his name shall be entered on the records as a member, and the Secretary shall issue a certificate of membership.

SEC. 3. Any member of the corporation may at any time withdraw and terminate his membership by returning his certificate of membership to the Secretary, with a letter expressing his wish and intention to terminate his membership.

SEC. 4. Any member of this corporation who shall be found guilty of any misrepresentation, deception, or fraud in relation to the registry of animals in the Holstein-Friesian Herd-Book shall forfeit his membership in the corporation.

SEC. 5. Each member of the corporation shall be entitled to one copy of each volume of the Herd-Book published after his admission, which shall be forwarded to his address as soon as convenient after its publication.

Article 2.

OF THE OFFICERS.

SECTION 1. The officers of this corporation shall consist of a President and four Vice-Presidents — to be designated as first, second, third, and fourth; one Secretary and Editor, one Treasurer, six Directors, and one Superintendent of Advanced Registry, who shall constitute the Board of Officers of this corporation. There shall be three Directors elected at the first meeting for the term of one year, and three for the term of two years. Thereafter, at each annual meeting, there shall be elected three Directors to serve for the term of two years. In the event of the death or resignation of the Secretary or Treasurer, the Board of Officers shall have power to fill such vacancies until the next general election. The Board of Officers shall appoint Inspectors of Imported Cattle, with power to remove for cause and to fill vacancies.

SEC. 2. The Board of Officers of this corporation, as a Board, shall have and take the entire control and management of its affairs and business, with full power and authority to do what they deem proper and best for its interest, but nothing contrary to the expressed wish of the Association; and they shall have no authority to contract a debt against the corporation beyond its current expenses — and in no case, beyond the amount of cash in the treasury. And nothing shall be done which is not in accordance with the purpose and spirit of the Charter and By-Laws; but shall in all cases execute every expressed will of the Association as expressed at any regular meeting.

Sec. 3. At any meeting of the Board of Officers which is duly called, a majority of its members shall constitute a quorum for business.

Sec. 4. A legal meeting of the Board of Officers of this corporation may be held at any time and place when and where all the members of the Board are present together and agree to hold a meeting, and all votes and acts done at such meeting shall have the same validity and effect as they could have if passed and done at a regularly called meeting.

Sec. 5. A meeting of the Board of Officers shall be held on the day of the annual meeting of the members, and a meeting may be called by the President or Secretary, or by a majority of the Directors, when in his or their judgment the affairs or business of the corporation make it necessary for the Board of Officers to hold a meeting.

Sec. 6. Notice calling special meetings of the Board of Officers shall be given by the person calling the meeting, in writing, setting forth the date and place of meeting, and the purpose or purposes for which the meeting is to be held; and no other business than that specified in the notice shall be acted on, unless all the members of the Board of Officers are present.

Sec. 7. Members of the Board of Officers cannot vote by proxy at meetings of the Board, but any member of the Board who cannot attend a duly called meeting may address a letter to the Board of Officers, in which he may discuss the purpose or purposes for which the meeting is called, and state how he will vote on the question or questions which may come before the meeting under the notice, and such letter and such votes shall be read in the meeting, and the votes shall be counted and have the same effect as they would if the member was personally present and voted.

Sec 8. All notices or calls for meetings of the Board of Officers shall be recorded at length in the record-book of the corporation, and the substance of all letters from members of the Board containing votes on matters set forth in the notice calling the meeting shall also be recorded, and such letters shall be kept on file, and all proceedings had and votes passed at meetings of the Board of Officers shall be fully set forth and recorded in the record-book.

SEC. 9. The President shall preside at all meetings of the members of the corporation, and all meetings of the Board of Officers, when he is present; and when he is absent or unable to perform the duties of the office, a Vice-President shall act in his stead. The President shall sign all certificates of membership which may be issued.

SEC. 10. The Treasurer shall be the custodian of cash funds and securities belonging to the corporation, and shall deposit, invest, or otherwise dispose of the same as the Board of Officers may direct. He shall give a bond with sureties to the satisfaction of the Board of Officers.

SEC. 11. The Secretary shall be the corresponding and recording officer of the corporation, and shall receive and attend to and dispose of, as the Charter and By-Laws require, all applications for membership in the corporation, all applications for registry of animals in the Herd-Book, and all applications for transfer-registry of animals in the Herd-Book; and shall sign and issue all certificates of membership and registry, and of transfer-registry; and shall keep a record of all such certificates issued. He is authorized to expend such sums as he may find necessary for the carrying on of the business of the association.

SEC. 12. He shall edit and publish the Herd-Book at such times and in such form as the Board of Officers may direct.

SEC. 13. He shall issue notices of the time and place of the annual meeting of the corporation, and of special meetings which the Board of Officers may order to be called; but no amendments to the Charter or By-Laws shall be made at any meeting, either annual or special, unless thirty days notice of the substance of such proposed amendments has been given by the Secretary in the call for such meeting.

SEC. 14. He shall issue notices of meetings of the Board of Officers when requested to do so by the President or by a majority of the Directors.

SEC. 15. He shall record all notices of meetings in the record-book of the corporation, and certify therein that they were issued and sent in accordance with the provisions of the By-Laws.

SEC. 16. He shall keep full and accurate records of all the meetings of the corporation, and of the Board of Officers, at which he is present; and when he is absent, a Secretary *pro tempore* shall be chosen to attend to and perform the duties of the Secretary.

SEC. 17. He shall keep an accurate account in detail of all moneys received and paid out by him in the performance of his duties, a copy of which he shall transmit to the Treasurer once in each quarter year — during the first month of the quarter. And shall give a bond satisfactory to the Board of Officers.

SEC. 18. The Board of Officers shall hereafter, at their last meeting prior to the annual election of officers, fix the salaries of all salaried officers for the next ensuing year.

SEC. 19. The Board of Officers shall take cognizance of any and all specific charges made under oath and presented to them in writing against any member of this corporation, for violation of his obligation to this corporation or to any of its members, and shall appoint a committee of two members of the corporation, which said committee shall notify the alleged offending member, at his last known place of residence, of the specific charges fully set forth in writing, and designate a place and day when and where he may have a hearing before said committee, who shall hear the parties and take proof relevant to the charges, in writing and under oath, and report the same in full, with their opinion of the matter, in writing, to the Board of Officers. All notices of such hearing shall be given to the alleged offending members not less than sixty days before the time set for such hearings. In case of a wilful failure of the alleged offending member to appear and answer the charges made, at the time and place named, the Board of Officers shall be hereby empowered to act the same as though said charges were true, and take such measure in regard to the same as they may deem proper and advisable under the Charter.

SEC. 20. The accusers and accused shall then, if they desire it, be heard before the Board of Officers, or a majority of them; and after such hearing, or opportunity afforded by the Board to the parties to have such hearing, they shall determine whether the charges made have been proved, and if so, whether the accused ought to forfeit his membership in the corporation, and take such action in the matter as they may deem advisable.

Article 3.

OF MEETINGS.

SECTION 1. Notice of all meetings of the corporation and of the Board of Officers shall be mailed at least fourteen days before the time named for the meeting.

SEC. 2. All notices of meetings shall be served by sending a written or printed copy by mail to the post-office address of each member entitled to such notice, and shall fully set forth the matters to be acted on at such meeting.

SEC. 3. If the Board of Officers deem it advisable to hold the annual meeting, or any special meeting of the corporation, or any meeting of the Board of Officers, at any other place than Buffalo, N. Y., and so order, the Secretary shall make the notices calling the meeting in accordance with the order of the Board.

SEC. 4. Special meetings of the members of the corporation shall be called when a majority of the members of the Board of Officers join in a request or direction to the Secretary to call such meeting.

SEC. 5. The traveling expenses of the Board of Officers, when called together for the transaction of business of the association, shall be paid out of the funds of the association.

SEC. 6. One-third of all the members of the corporation shall constitute a quorum for business at the annual meeting and at any special meeting duly called.

Article 4.

OF THE HERD-BOOK.

SECTION 1. This corporation shall publish the Holstein-Friesian Herd-Book.

SEC. 2. Each volume of the Holstein-Friesian Herd-Book shall contain the Charter and By-Laws, and a list of members of the corporation, the record of the proceedings at all meetings held since the publication of the last volume of the Herd-Book, the reports of the officers, and any other matter of general interest which the Board of Directors may deem advisable to publish, and an accurate registry of all the animals accepted for registry in it, which shall be divided into two parts, one part containing the registry of bulls, and the other the registry of cows. Such registry shall set forth the number, the name, the date of birth, the name and residence of the breeder and owner, and if imported, the name of the importer, the markings of the animal sufficient for its identification, and the names and numbers of both sire and dam in the Herd-Book. It shall contain the record of pedigrees, but no plates, engravings, or publication of any records of animals. The price to be charged for each volume of the Herd-Book to non-members of this Association shall be its cost price with postage or expressage added.

SEC. 3. In the Herd-Book there shall be registered only such animals as are determined under the rules and regulations of this corporation to be "pure bred"

SEC. 4. Pure bred Holstein-Friesian shall be held to mean and refer to only those large, improved black and white cattle already registered in the Holstein and Dutch-Friesian Herd-Books, and such as are descended from them in direct line, both as to sire and dam, and such imported animals, or their descendants, as are registered in the Netherlands, Friesian, or North Holland Herd-Books, proved by the affirmation of the breeder of the animal satisfactory to the Inspector.

SEC. 5. American-bred animals shall only be registered in the Herd-Book upon application made upon forms furnished by the corporation, and the payment of a fee of fifty cents for the registry of females, and five dollars for the registry of males born after March 20, 1889, by members of the corporation, and one dollar for the registry of females, and six dollars for the registry of males born after March 20, 1889, by persons not members, which payment must accompany the application; and the sum of five dollars shall be paid by the Association for each American-bred male eligible for registration born after March 20, 1889, that is killed or castrated while in good health, after it is five days old and before it is fifty days old, on application and affidavit of the owner of dam, on forms furnished by the Secretary and approved by the Board of Officers, stating the date of birth, date of service of dam, name of sire and dam, date of slaughter or castration and by whom performed. No two animals shall have the same name. Only direct descendants of an animal shall be entitled to the family name with numbers prefixed or added, and after the first generation, the family name only in combination. Males shall only be entitled to the family name in combination, in which the family name shall be first. In all combinations, the name of the sire or dam, in part or in full, may be used as desired by the applicant. All titles of distinction, nobility, military, or honorary, and all first or given names not in use as *family* names, shall be free for use in combination. No name of an animal shall be accepted for entry if containing more than thirty letters, not including the numeral affix.

SEC. 6. Only members of this association may register imported animals. When application for registry of imported animals is made, the certificate of the breeder of the animal, made upon forms furnished by this corporation, is required.

SEC. 7. Animals *must* be transferred to owners *before their offspring are registered.*

SEC. 8. Application for registry of imported animals shall be made to the Secretary, and by him referred to the Inspector, who shall visit and separately examine each imported animal proposed for registry, and the certificate of the breeder relating to such animal; and the Inspector shall make his report of the result of such examination in writing on or annexed to the breeder's certificate. The importer's name to be inserted in breeder's certificate before shipment; and after June 10th, until

July 1st, 1885, it shall be verified by list from American Consul. All breeders' certificates must be numbered by the Secretary, who shall fill in the name and address of importer. The certificates shall bear the official seal of the association. The Secretary shall keep a record of the number of certificates and to whom issued. No imported animal under one year of age shall be examined or accepted for registry. All imported animals shall be registered in the name of the importer. The application for registry of animals imported in dam must be signed by the importer. All applications for registry of animals which are not filed with the Secretary within one year from date of birth or importation shall be charged three times the usual registry fee. All animals bred in America shall be registered in the name of the owner, in which case a certificate of service is required from the owner of the bull, and the signature of the breeder to the application. No imported animal shall be eligible to registry in the Herd-Book unless the animal or its dam and sire are registered in the Netherlands, Friesian, or North Holland Herd-Books. In recording such imported animal, if it be recorded in the Netherlands, Friesian, or North Holland Herd-Books, its name and number shall be spread upon the records; if not recorded there, its breeding, as it appears in the Netherlands, Friesian, or North Holland Herd-Books, with the names and numbers by which its sire and dam are registered in such Herd-Book, shall be spread upon the register of this association. Any person applying to the Secretary for the inspection of imported animals shall pay to the Secretary of the association five dollars for each animal to be inspected *before such inspection is ordered;* and after such payment, the Secretary shall be authorized to order such inspection, the inspection to be made at quarantine or upon the farm of the importer. The registry fee of each imported animal shall be twenty dollars. Inspectors shall receive from the association, as compensation, eight dollars for each day occupied in inspecting cattle and in going to and from places of inspection. All necessary and reasonable traveling expenses shall be paid by the association. No imported animal shall be accepted for registration until it has been passed by an

Inspector; and the Inspector shall be instructed that no animal be accepted for registry in the Herd-Book except those of superior excellence, that might fairly be ranked as strictly first-class.

SEC. 9. When an animal is accepted for registry, the Secretary shall issue a certificate of the fact to the owner, giving the number, and name, and description the animal will take in the Herd-Book.

SEC. 10. A register of transfer of ownership of any animal registered in the Herd-Book will be made on application of the owner; if made by members of the corporation, no charge will be made, and if made by a non-member the fee for each transfer will be fifty cents, provided the application is made within ninety days of date of sale; if after that, the charge will be one dollar for each transfer; a certificate of each transfer will be made by the Secretary. A charge of fifty cents will be made for each duplicate certificate of registry or transfer. Extended pedigrees of registered animals, bearing the seal of the association, will be furnished, upon application, for one dollar each.

SEC. 11. Every application for the registry of an animal in the Herd-Book shall be taken as the guarantee of the owner that the animal is pure bred, and that all the matters stated in the application are true. No application for registry or transfer will receive attention unless accompanied with the required fee.

SEC. 12. If after registry of an animal in the Herd-Book anything shall be learned which raises a doubt as to the propriety of such registration, the Board of Officers shall cause the matter to be investigated; and if it shall be found that an animal has been improperly registered, they shall cause the registry to be expunged, and take such other steps or measures as the nature of the case in their judgment may require.

Article 5.

In accordance with the provisions of the Charter, a system of advanced registry shall be provided for by the Board of Officers. It shall be under the management of a Superintendent to be elected by the members of the association, and to be a member of the Board of Officers. Said registry to be published in a separate volume.

Article 6.

The seal of the corporation shall be a circular-faced die with the name of the corporation, the date of Charter, and the head of a Holstein-Friesian animal so cut on the face of it that the whole can be embossed on paper by pressure, and the minutes of this meeting shall be sealed with it.

NOTE.— Firms or corporations whose members or stockholders are not all members of the Holstein-Friesian Association will be charged full fees. The executor of the estate of a member may register and transfer animals for members' fees.

PROCEEDINGS

OF THE

FIFTH ANNUAL MEETING

OF THE

Holstein-Friesian Association

OF AMERICA,

HELD AT

NEW YORK, N. Y., MARCH 19TH, 1890.

--- ALSO ---

REPORTS OF MEETINGS OF THE BOARD OF OFFICERS.

Egbert, Fidlar, & Chambers, Printers, Davenport, Iowa.

1890.

OFFICERS OF THE

HOLSTEIN-FRIESIAN ASSOCIATION OF AMERICA,

FOR 1890-91.

President.

DAVID H. BURRELL, ... Little Falls, N. Y.

First Vice-President,	GEORGE D. WHEELER,	. . . Deposit, N. Y.
Second Vice-President,	WILLIAM M. LIGGETT,	. . Benson, Minn.
Third Vice-President,	JOHN A. FRYE,	. . . . Marlboro, Mass.
Fourth Vice-President,	JOHN B. DUTCHER,	. . . . . Pawling, N. Y.

Secretary and Editor.

THOMAS B. WALES, ... Iowa City, Iowa.

Directors.

MARTIN L. SWEET, ... Grand Rapids, Mich.
C. W. HORR, ... Wellington, Ohio.
C. R. PAYNE, ... Hamilton, N. Y.
W. G. POWELL, ... Springboro, Penn.
L. T. YEOMANS, ... Walworth, N. Y.
W. M. SINGERLY, ... Philadelphia, Penn.

Treasurer.

W. BROWN SMITH, ... Syracuse, N. Y.

Superintendent of Advanced Registry.

S. HOXIE, ... Yorkville, N. Y.

Inspectors of Advanced Registry.

S. HOXIE (*Superintendent*), ... Yorkville, N. Y.
O. P. CHAPMAN, ... Wellington, Ohio.
S. BURCHARD, ... Hamilton, N. Y.
S. N. WRIGHT, ... Elgin, Ill.
J. C. POOR, ... North Andover, Mass.
CAREY R. SMITH, ... Santa Ana, Cal.
H. B. DAGGETT, ... Hampton, Iowa.
J. R. BEUCHLER, ... Leesburg, Va.
J. L. STONE, ... Waverly, Penn.
A. R. STURTEVANT, ... Springboro, Penn.
A. BRADLEY, ... Lee, Mass.
H. D. WARNER, ... Lanesville, Conn.
W. A. ROWLEY, ... Mt. Clemens, Mich.
T. N. FIGUERS, ... Spring Hill, Tenn.
W. M. LIGGETT, ... Benson, Minn.

FIFTH ANNUAL MEETING

OF THE

HOLSTEIN-FRIESIAN ASSOCIATION OF AMERICA,

Held at the Fifth Avenue Hotel, New York, N. Y.,
March 19th, 1890.

THE PRESIDENT: Gentlemen, it is time for us to come to order. The chair requests that any member addressing the meeting will be particular to give his name, so that the Secretary may know who speaks, in order to give full credit in the report of our proceedings. The first order of business will be the calling of the roll. Members will please answer to their names as called, and also answer to the names of those members for whom they hold proxies.

The Secretary then called the roll. Forty-three answered present, and one hundred and eighty-six were represented by proxies. Those who were present were:

  BENT, WILLIAM H., ... Cochituate, Massachusetts.
  BEUCHLER, J. R., ... Leesburg, Virginia.
  BIDWELL, M. S., ... Monterey, Massachusetts.
  BURCHARD, SYLVESTER, ... Hamilton, New York.
  BURRELL, DAVID H., ... Little Falls, New York.

  DAMON, ISAAC, ... Cochituate, Massachusetts.
  DUTCHER, J. B., ... Pawling, New York.
  DUTCHER, J. G., ... Pawling, New York.

  FRYE, JOHN A., ... Marlboro, Massachusetts.

  GREGORY, N. B., ... Unadilla, New York.

  HAM, J. M., ... Washington Hollow, New York.
  HAVILAND, JOSEPH, ... Glen's Falls, New York.
  HINCKLEY, D. J., ... Brookfield, New York.
  HOUGHTON, F. L., ... Putney, Vermont.
  HOXIE, S., ... Yorkville, New York.
  HOXIE, S. L., ... Leonardsville, New York.
  HUIDEKOPER, EDGAR, ... Meadville, Pennsylvania.

  KEYES, H. W., ... Newbury, Vermont.

LANGWORTHY, HOLLUM,	West Edmeston, New York.
MILLER, DUDLEY,	Oswego, New York.
MILLER, E. P.,	New York, New York.
NEILSON, JAMES,	New Brunswick, New Jersey.
OSTERHOUT, STANTON,	Cobleskill, New York.
PAYNE, C. R.,	Hamilton, New York.
POTTER, O. B.,	New York, New York.
POWELL, E. A.,	Syracuse, New York.
POWELL, W. G.,	Springboro, Pennsylvania.
ROBINSON, CHARLES,	Barre Plains, Massachusetts.
RUMSEY, C. E.,	Pittsburg, Pennsylvania.
SMITH, W. BROWN,	Syracuse, New York.
SMITH, W. J.,	Syracuse, New York.
SWEET, MARTIN L.,	Grand Rapids, Michigan.
SWEEZEY, C. F.,	Marion, New York.
TAFT, E. P.,	Providence, Rhode Island.
WALES, THOMAS B.,	Iowa City, Iowa.
WARNER, H. D.,	Lanesville, Connecticut.
WARNER, H. O.,	New Milford, Connecticut.
WELLS, GEORGE L,	Wethersfield, Connecticut.
WHEELER, G. D.,	Deposit, New York.
WILLIAMS, GEORGE S.,	Fitchburg, Massachusetts.
WRIGHT, S. N.,	South Elgin, Illinois.
YEOMANS, L. T.,	Walworth, New York.
YEOMANS, T. G.,	Walworth, New York.

THE PRESIDENT: Is there any gentleman here whose name has not been called? There is a quorum present. The minutes of the last meeting have been printed, and unless there are objections we will dispense with the reading of them, and they will stand approved. There being no objections, they are approved.

The next business in order is the consideration of the proxies. Unless there is some motion, the chair will appoint a committee to examine the proxies. The chair will appoint as such committee, H. Langworthy, D. H. Burrell, and C. F. Sweezey. Gentlemen having proxies will please give them to that committee, that they may examine them. The President's annual address is next in order, and that I will read:

PRESIDENT'S ADDRESS.

Members of the Holstein-Friesian Association of America. GENTLEMEN:—It gives me pleasure to meet the members who have heretofore attended our annual meeting, and in your behalf it gives me pleasure to welcome those who are among us for the first time.

The number of members of our Association when it was chartered, in 1885, was 284. Since then there has been an increase averaging about fourteen per year. To-day we have 352 members.

During the year 1889 one bull and thirty-four cows were imported from Holland. Since we last met a herd consisting of one bull, one steer, and four females has been furnished by us to the New York Experimental Station. Three cows have been furnished to the New Jersey Experimental Station — one was purchased, one was leased for three years, and one was presented by Senator McPherson.

Gentlemen representing these stations are with us to-day, and will no doubt be happy to give us information concerning them.

Our committee appointed to offer premiums met at Cleveland and offered premiums as reported in the circular issued by our Secretary. In compliance therewith the Secretary has paid $4,365.00. The result is a grand showing of butter and milk cows and creditable herds in public competition.

At home many cows have attained a high place of honor. We have met the enemy, and defeated him in almost every point. Our Association is to be congratulated upon its victory. While our cows have taken the foremost place in the world as dairy cows, we must not be satisfied to rest here. With watchful care, intelligence, activity, and perseverance on our part, there is still a higher place to be attained for our wonderful cattle. We must not only attain it, but must hold it.

We must keep in the procession, and we must, and will, march at the head, where the music plays.

I congratulate you that our organization is so complete and our constitution and by-laws so satisfactory that but few amendments are offered for your consideration here to-day. I may inform you that it has not been necessary to call the Board of Directors together during the past year. Our Association business is practically managed by our very efficient Secretary, and his report for the year covers the ground so thoroughly that there is little left for the President to mention.

The President takes pleasure in referring you to the reports of the Secretary, Treasurer, and Superintendent of Advanced Registry. They are full of interesting information, and contain valuable thoughts for your consideration.

Mr. W. G. POWELL: Mr. Secretary, I move that the President's address be received and published in the minutes.

Mr. E. A. POWELL: I second that motion.

(The Secretary put the motion, and the same was carried.)

THE PRESIDENT: The next business in order is the report of the Secretary.

Secretary Wales then read his report, as follows:

SECRETARY'S REPORT.

Mr. President and Members of the Holstein-Friesian Association: The year that has just closed certainly has been the red-letter year of our existence, and no one can possibly feel greater satisfaction than myself in being able to make such a statement.

Never in the history of Holstein-Friesian cattle have such grand victories been won — carrying with them, as they do, positive proof to the world of the great capabilities of our breed — as during the year 1889. The splendid showing of the past year is no doubt partly owing to our large offerings of premiums for herds, as well as for public tests for milk and butter, which were open to all other dairy breeds. I have included in my report a statement of these premiums and to whom awarded, wishing them to go on record.

It is not likely that the National Butter-Test Premium would again find favor, for the reason that it is quite impossible for the tests to be uniform. With this possible exception, the result of our offerings have been most satisfactory. It may be considered an open question, after the general success we have for years met with in public butter tests with other breeds, whether any further expenditure in this direction is necessary.

THE SPECIAL PREMIUMS OFFERED BY THE ASSOCIATION AT STATE AND OTHER FAIRS AND EXPOSITIONS WERE AWARDED AS FOLLOWS:

Alabama. — Butter-test prize to J. W. Howard, Bonham, Texas, $50.00; milk-test prize to J. W. Howard, Bonham, Texas, $50.00.

American Fat Stock and Dairy Show, at Chicago, Ill. — First herd prize to Stanton Bros., Greenwood, Ind., $150.00; second herd prize to Thomas B. Wales, Iowa City, Iowa, $75.00; third herd prize to Stevenson Bros., Bulger, Penn., $50.00; first prize, steer two years old, to B. Waddel, Marion, Ohio, $25.00; first prize, steer one year old, to B. Waddel, Marion, Ohio, $25.00; second best two-year-old steer, to M. L. Sweet, Grand Rapids, Mich., $15.00; second best steer under one year old, to B. Waddel, Marion, Ohio, $15.00; sweepstakes, Holstein-Friesian, to B. Waddel, Marion, Ohio, $50.00; first butter-test prize to F. C. Stevens, Attica, N. Y., $50.00; second butter-test prize to Stevenson Bros., Bulger, Penn., $25.00.

Bay State Fair. — Herd premium to William H. Bent, Cochituate, Mass., $100.00.

Buffalo International Exposition. — The following premiums were awarded to Smiths, Powell & Lamb, Syracuse, N. Y.: First aged herd premium, $200.00; second young herd premium, $75.00; first for bull and produce, $200.00; first for bull three years and over, $60.00; first for bull one year old, $25.00; second for bull one year old, $10.00; second for bull calf, $5.00; sweepstakes, bull, $50.00; second for cow three years old and over, $30.00; first for heifer two years old, $40.00; second for heifer one year old, $10.00; second for heifer calf, $5.00. The following premiums were awarded to F. C. Stevens, Attica, N. Y.: Second best herd, $100.00; best young herd, $100.00; second best bull and produce, $100.00; Second best bull three years and over, $30.00; best bull two years old, $40.00; second best bull two years old, $20.00; best bull calf, $15.00; best cow three years and over, $60.00; second best heifer two years old, $20.00; best heifer one year old, $25.00; best heifer calf, $15.00; sweepstakes, female, $50.00.

California.— Herd premium to George B. Polhemus, Coyote, Cal., $50.00.

Georgia.— Butter-test prize to O. A. Bowen, Pendleton, S. C., $50.00; milk-test prize to O. A. Bowen, Pendleton, S. C., $50.00.

Illinois.— Herd premium to Home Farm Fine Stock Company, Hampton, Iowa, $100.00.

Iowa.— Herd premium, $100.00, also butter-test prize, $50.00, and milk-test-prize, $50.00, to Home Farm Fine Stock Company, Hampton, Iowa.

Kansas.— Herd premium, $100.00, also butter-test prize, $50.00, and milk-test prize, $50.00, to M. E. Moore, Cameron, Mo.

Maine.— Milk-test prize, $50.00, to D. L. Brett, Otisfield, Maine.

Michigan.— Herd prize, $100.00, to T. D. Seeley & Co., Bay City, Mich.

Minnesota.— Herd premium, $100.00, to I. C. Wade, Jamestown, S. D.; butter-test prize, $50.00, and milk-test prize, $50.00, to N. J. Leavitt, Waseca, Minn.

Mississippi.— Butter-test prize, $50.00, and milk-test prize, $50.00, to J. W. Howard, Bonham, Texas.

Nebraska.— Butter-test prize, $50.00, and milk-test prize, $50.00, to Home Farm Fine Stock Company, Hampton, Iowa.

New England.— Milk-test prize, $50.00, to Charles Robinson, Barre Plains, Mass.

New York.— Herd premium, $100.00. to Smiths, Powell & Lamb, Syracuse, N. Y.

Ohio.— Herd premium, $100.00, to Stevenson Bros., Bulger, Penn.; butter-test prize, $50.00, to W. H. S. Foster, Fostoria, Ohio; milk-test prize, $50.00, to C. W. Horr, Wellington, Ohio.

Rhode Island.— Herd premium, $50.00, to William H. Bent, Cochituate, Mass.

South Dakota.— Butter-test prize, $50.00, to I. C. Wade, Jamestown, S. D.

Texas.— Herd premium, $100.00, to Henson & Rathbone, Council Grove, Kas.

Western Michigan State Fair.— Herd premium, $100.00, to Martin L. Sweet, Grand Rapids, Mich.

West Virginia.— Milk-test prize, $50.00, to W. C. Munson, Vienna, Ohio.

Wisconsin.— Herd premium, $100.00, to H. Rust & Bros., North Greenfield, Wis.

National Sweepstakes Tests.— First for butter-test, gold medal and $100.00, second for butter-test, $50.00, and first for milk-test, gold medal and $100.00, to F. C. Stevens, Attica, N. Y.; second for milk-test, $50.00, to Charles Robinson & Sons, Barre Plains, Mass.

Total amount of premiums awarded to Holstein-Friesian breeders, $4,365.00.

The receipts and expenditures for the fiscal year ending March 1st, 1890, have been as follows:

RECEIPTS.

For membership fees	$ 1,500 00
For herd-books	335 94
For registry of imported bulls	20 00
For registry of imported cows	2,040 00
For registry of bulls from members	2,543 00
For registry of bulls from non-members	5,019 00
For registry of cows from members	1,532 00
For registry of cows from non-members	4,935 50
For transfers of bulls from members	78 00
For transfers of bulls from non-members	757 50
For transfers of cows from members	148 00
For transfers of cows from non-members	1,482 50
For inspection of imported cattle	195 00
For extended pedigrees	27 00
For duplicate certificates	84 00
From W. Brown Smith, Treasurer, to pay premiums	2,000 00
Balance suspense account	5 00
Total	$22,702 44

EXPENDITURES.

For special premiums ($533.00 being for 1888 premiums)		$ 4,898 00
For bounties paid for bulls castrated	$1,690 00	
For bounties paid for bulls slaughtered	1,290 00	2,980 00
For Experimental Station account for cattle furnished New Jersey Experiment Station	751 98	
For expenses of selection committee for New York and New Jersey stations	585 74	1,337 72
For inspection of imported animals		264 95
For expense account		1,490 70
For printing account		1,525 03
For clerk hire		2,854 52
For stamp account		724 81
For sundry personal accounts, overpaid fees, drafts returned for endorsement, etc.		306 97
For Board of Officers		636 09
For W. Brown Smith, Treasurer		5,615 20
Due on registry and transfer fees		68 45
Total		$22,702 44

An interesting feature shown by the above figures is the amount of money called for to pay bounties on slaughtered and castrated bulls. The $2,980.00 thus paid represents five hundred and ninety-six of probably our poorest bulls wiped out of existence. If the present plan is continued, I fully expect another years' crop will count up at least a thousand head. The paying of bounties by the Association is highly appreciated by breeders everywhere, and I think is one of the wisest moves ever made by a Herd-Record Association.

In close connection with this, is the question of fees charged for the registry of bulls. It was feared by some that the five dollar fee would prove a burden to many breeders. Very few complaints have been received. The greatest have come from breeders in Canada. It is a fact that the bounty and increased registry fee has been the means of very materially reducing the number of bulls recorded during the year, as we find but 2,618 have been registered in 1889, against 3,470 in 1888, while in the natural course of increase, providing all bulls that were entitled to record had been registered, the number for 1889 must have reached at least 4,000 head.

It seems to me we are now on the right track with the bull business. Of course we should like to reduce the registry fee if it were possible, and this question should be carefully considered. Our expenditures show a large amount of money paid to breeders for special premiums and bounties, not less than $7,300.00, besides about $3,000.00 for Experiment Stations. If we cannot afford to be as liberal another year, let us be as liberal as our best judgment and business principles will allow.

Since we last met Volume IV. of our Herd-Book has been issued. Volume V. has been published, the manuscript for Volume VI. is completed and is now being printed. The plan recently adopted of closing a volume of the Herd-Book as soon as a sufficient number of pedigrees are received works well, avoiding the great rush of applications when the date of closing a volume was advertised.

During the year which closed March 1st, 1890, there have been recorded one imported bull, 2,617 American-bred bulls, 94 imported cows (of which only 34 were imported during the year) and 4,323 American-bred cows. Total number of animals registered, 7,040. Total number of animals transferred 6,208 — 1985 bulls, and 4,223 cows. 168 duplicate certificates have been issued; total number of certificates issued 13,284. The total number of animals recorded to March 1st, 1890, is 52,385 — bulls 20,279; cows 32,106.

During the year I have been advised of the death of the following members: William B. Clark, Hillsdale, Mich.; Elizur Smith, Lee, Mass.; Dr. E. A. Teft, Elgin, Ill.; Gen. Wm. S. Tilton, Boston, Mass.

Twelve new members have been admitted, and our membership now numbers three hundred and fifty-two.

      Respectfully submitted,
        THOMAS B. WALES, *Secretary.*

THE PRESIDENT: Gentlemen, you have heard the report of the Secretary. What is your pleasure?

Mr. C. W. HORR: I move that it be accepted, and published in the minutes.

Mr. W. G. POWELL: I second the motion. Carried.

THE PRESIDENT: The next business in order is the report of the Treasurer.

Mr. W. J. SMITH: At the request of the Treasurer, I will read the Treasurer's report:

TREASURER'S REPORT.

Mr. President and Gentlemen of the Holstein-Friesian Association of America: I herewith present the following report of the receipts and expenditures of the Association for the fiscal year ending with the date of this meeting:

RECEIPTS.

1889.				
March 20.	Balance on hand as per last report			$29,310 05
June	5.	Cash from Thomas B. Wales, Secretary, as per quarterly report	$ 177 02	
July	1.	Received interest on deposit, Syracuse Savings Bank	58 80	
July	1.	Received interest on deposit, Onondaga County Savings Bank	58 80	
July	1.	Received interest on deposit, Salt Springs National Bank,	400 00	
Sept.	9.	Cash from Thomas B. Wales, Secretary, as per quarterly report	1,250 1	
Dec.	9.	Cash from Thomas B. Wales, Secretary, as per quarterly report	1,000 00	
1890.				
Jan.	1.	Received interest on deposit, Syracuse Savings Bank	58 76	
Jan.	1.	Received interest on deposit, Onondaga County Savings Bank	58 76	
Jan.	1.	Received interest on deposit, Salt Springs National Bank,	329 02	
March	8.	Cash from Thomas B. Wales, Secretary, as per quarterly report	2,887 97	
		Total receipts for fiscal year		$ 6,579.34
				$35,889 39

EXPENDITURES.

1889.			
Feb.	23.	T. N Figuers, account of Advanced Registry	$ 16 00
April	4.	O. P. Chapman, account of Advanced Registry	32 00
April	4.	S. Hoxie, account of Advanced Registry	238 94
April	5.	Henry Stevens, account Experimental Station	300 00
April	6.	S. Burchard, account Experimental Station	50 00
April	6.	Dallas B. Whipple, account Experimental Station	200 00
April	11.	Smiths, Powell & Lamb, account Experimental Station	800 00
April	20.	O. P. Chapman, account Advanced Registry	26 70
April	20.	H. D. Warner, account Advanced Registry	20 60
April	20.	W. A. Rowley, account Advanced Registry	29 22
May	1.	Carey R. Smith, account Advanced Registry	57 00
May	8.	H. B. Daggett, account Advanced Registry	81 31
May	10.	J. L. Stone, account Advanced Registry	11 00
May	13.	Gerrit S. Miller, account Experimental Station	300 00
July	27.	Subscription to Holstein-Friesian Register	255 43
Aug.	3.	H. B. Daggett, account Advanced Registry	32 00
Aug.	11.	Egbert, Fidlar, & Chambers, Herd-Book	3,288 30
Aug.	11.	H. D. Warner, account Advanced Registry	36 00
Aug.	11.	H. D. Warner, account Advanced Registry	32 00
Sept.	4.	S. N. Wright, account Advanced Registry	72 00
Sept.	9.	Thomas B. Wales, salary six months, to September 1st, 1889	1,250 00
Sept.	30.	S. Hoxie, salary six months, to September 20th, 1889	500 00

Oct.	4.	S. Burchard, account Advanced Registry	48 00
Oct.	7.	Thomas B. Wales, for expenses	2,000 00
Oct.	25.	Subscription to Holstein-Friesian Register	348 00
Nov.	16.	S. N. Wright, account Advanced Registry	64 00
Dec.	9.	J. R. Beuchler, account Advanced Registry	33 50
Dec.	20.	Egbert, Fidlar, & Chambers, Herd-Book	1,461 60
1890.			
Jan.	16.	A. Bradley, account Advanced Registry	48 39
Feb.	11.	S. N. Wright, account Advanced Registry	96 00
Feb.	24.	Subscription to Holstein-Friesian Register	735 00
March	8.	S. Hoxie, account Advanced Registry	29 78
March	8.	Thomas B. Wales, salary six months, to March 1st, 1890.	1,250 00
March	12.	S. Burchard, account Advanced Registry	56 49
March	17.	H. B. Daggett, account Advanced Registry	8 00
March	17.	A. R. Sturtevant, account Advanced Registry	50 00
March	19.	S. Hoxie, salary six months, to March 19th, 1890	500 00
March	19.	W. Brown Smith, salary one year, to September 19th, 1890	250 00
		Total expenses for fiscal year	$14,606 96
		Balance on hand	21,282 43
			$35,889 39

Deposited as follows:

In Syracuse Savings Bank	$ 2,998 80	
In Onondaga County Savings Bank	2,998 80	
In Salt Springs National Bank	15,284 83	
	$21,282 43	

Repectfully submitted,

W. BROWN SMITH, *Treasurer*.

THE PRESIDENT: Gentlemen, you have heard the Treasurer's report read. What is your pleasure concerning it?

Mr. MARTIN L. SWEET: I move that it be accepted and placed on file.

Mr. C. W. HORR: I second the motion.

Carried.

THE PRESIDENT: The next business in order is the report of the Superintendent of Advanced Registry.

Mr. S. HOXIE: Mr. President and gentlemen, I submit the following report:

REPORT OF SUPERINTENDENT OF ADVANCED REGISTRY.

To the President and Members of the Holstein-Friesian Association of America: During the official year closing with this meeting there has been an increase of interest in our system of Advanced Registry. The third volume is now going through the press. The time for receiving entries to this volume has been extended to the date of this meeting, or until the printing is advanced beyond the pages devoted to such entry. This volume will probably show as many entries during the thirteen months that it is expected to thus cover as were made during the previous two years, or to the second volume.

The Board of Officers at their last annual meeting authorized the calling of a meeting of the inspectors to revise the rules and scale of points, and for instruction in the work of inspection. This meeting was held at Syracuse, New York, on the 10th and 11th of April. The rules and scale were carefully revised in a conservative manner; only such changes were made as past experience suggested to increase the efficiency of the original system. This meeting also devised a method of applying the scale that promises to revolutionize the ordinary method of judging cattle in contests for prizes, as well as in the work of this Registry. The reason for every step in the judgment is shown with clearness. It thus has the advantage of disarming suspicion of partiality. The revised rules and scale were submitted to the members of the Board of Officers by letter, and adopted by them without a dissenting voice. Three thousand copies of the revised scale and four thousand copies of the revised rule, with instructions to owners and inspectors, were then published, nearly all of which have been distributed to breeders and others making inquiries.

The steady growth of this system in public estimation thus indicated, and the absence of criticism, seem to show that its principles are settled, and that experiments in other associations will finally settle upon the same general basis. In this fact our Association is to be congratulated as the pioneer and leader in Advanced Registry.

The receipts and expenditures of my office for the year are as follows, viz.:

RECEIPTS.

Receipts of registry fees	$ 416 00
Receipts for books sold	29 67
Receipt of balance on first quarterly report from Treasurer	238 94
	$ 684 61

EXPENDITURES.

Balance at last annual meeting	$ 366 65
For printing bills rendered	92 11
For stationery (other than in printing bills)	1 40
For express charges	2 25
For traveling expenses	2 80
For postage	42 06
For clerk hire, copying, etc	26 13
For returning over-pay for books	1 50
For returning over-pay for registry fees	11 00
	545 90
Balance to credit of Association	$ 138 71

S. HOXIE,
Superintendent Advanced Registry.

THE PRESIDENT: What shall be done with this report?

Mr. STANTON OSTERHOUT: I move that it be received and placed on file.

Mr. GEORGE F. WILLIAMS: I second the motion.

Carried.

The President: The next business is the appointment of a committee to audit the accounts of the Treasurer, the Superintendent of Advanced Registry, and the Secretary. What is your pleasure about this, gentlemen?

Mr. C. W. Horr: I suggest that the chair appoint a committee of three.

The President: Do you make that as a motion?

Mr. C. W. Horr: Yes, sir.

Motion seconded.

The President: Gentlemen, you have heard the motion, that the chair appoint a committee of three to audit the accounts of the Secretary, the Treasurer, and the Superintendent of Advanced Registry. All in favor of the motion will say aye.

Carried.

Mr. C. W. Horr: I ask the President not to appoint me on that committee, as I have something else to do.

The President: The chair will appoint as that committee, J. B. Dutcher, L. T. Yeomans, and William H. Bent.

Mr. T. G. Yeomans: I would suggest, for the relief of any committee to have such a matter in charge, that I understand it is a laborious task, and keeps them out of the meeting a good while, and I would therefore suggest whether it would not be wise to appoint another committee to take charge of a part of that work. Here are three distinct accounts to be taken in charge, and I think it is putting more than a reasonable amount of labor upon one committee to have them do the whole of the work.

The President: Does the gentleman make any motion to that effect?

Mr. C. W. Horr: The accounts are so mixed together, one with another, that they all ought to go through one committee.

The President: No, I think not. I think each of these officers has the vouchers for his own account.

Mr. C. E. Rumsey: I move that the accounts of the Secretary be referred to one committee, and those of the Treasurer and the Superintendent of Advanced Registry be referred to another committee.

Mr. C. W. Horr: I second the motion, with the understanding that the present committee already appointed take charge of the Secretary's account.

The President: The question is first on the amendment. Are there any remarks? The question, then, is upon the amendment, that the accounts of the Treasurer and the Superintendent of Advanced Registry be referred to a committee yet to be appointed, and that the accounts of the

Secretary be referred to the committee already appointed. Those in favor of that will vote aye.

Carried.

THE PRESIDENT: The chair will appoint as the committee to audit the accounts of the Treasurer and Superintendent of Advanced Registry, C. E. Rumsey, Frederick L. Houghton, and E. P. Taft.

Mr. E. P. TAFT: I ask the chair to excuse me, as I have to leave shortly.

Mr. C. E. RUMSEY: Mr. President, I came five hundred miles to listen to what is going on in this meeting. My head is full of figures all the rest of the year, and I would not give up what is going on in this meeting for a good deal, and I prefer not to serve on any committee.

Mr. F. L. HOUGHTON: I would also ask to be excused from serving on the committee.

Mr. E. P. TAFT: I think these committees should attend these matters during our recess at lunch time.

Mr. W. J. SMITH: It strikes me that this is a piece of business very annoying to the committee, and I don't see why the trouble cannot be obviated as Mr. Taft suggests. People have come a great many hundred miles to attend this meeting, and naturally they want to be present all the time. I would therefore suggest that the committees make their reports and have them published in our printed proceedings, and that the Secretary send out those proceedings after the meeting, and that the committees report at our next meeting. Later in this meeting I propose to suggest the appointment of a committee of seven, three of whom shall constitute a quorum, which shall examine the accounts previous to the annual meeting each year, and report at the next annual meeting. In fact, I will make that motion now.

Mr. S. BURCHARD: I second that motion.

THE PRESIDENT: Gentlemen, you have heard the motion. Are there any remarks? All in favor of that motion will please say aye.

Carried.

THE PRESIDENT: The committees, then, will stand as appointed. Your attention is next called to the call of the Secretary, who submits proposed amendments to the by-laws. The Secretary will please read them.

THE SECRETARY: Article IV., Section 5. "So that no affidavit be required in order to secure the bounty offered by the Association for castrated or slaughtered bull calves."

Mr. C. W. HORR: I move to lay that suggestion on the table.

Mr. W. H. BENT: I second that motion.

THE PRESIDENT: All in favor of laying the proposed amendment to the by-laws on the table will vote aye.

Carried.

THE PRESIDENT: The Secretary will read the next proposed amendment to the by-laws.

THE SECRETARY: Article IV., Section 5. "So far as it relates to the amount of bounty to be paid by the Association for bull calves castrated or slaughtered.

Mr. W. G. POWELL: I would move to lay that upon the table, except that possibly some one might think it was cutting off discussion a little too short. However, if no one cares to speak on it, I will move to lay it upon the table.

Mr. C. W. HORR: I second the motion.

THE PRESIDENT: Shall this be laid upon the table?

Carried.

THE SECRETARY: It is proposed to amend any or all by-laws regulating the fees charged for the registering or transfer of animals. That subject is before the meeting.

Mr. E. A. POWELL: I would ask the Secretary to state what the different fees are now.

THE SECRETARY: Mr. President, The fee for the registry of bulls, at present, under one year of age, for members of the Association, is five dollars, and for non-members six dollars. The fee to register cows under one year is fifty cents to members of the Association, and one dollar for non-members. The transfers are free to members of the Association, provided the application for transfer is received within ninety days from the date of sale; otherwise it is one dollar. The transfer fee for non-members of the Association is fifty cents, provided the application is received within ninety days from the date of sale; otherwise it is one dollar. The registry fee for imported animals remains as it has been for three years.

Mr. JAMES NEILSON: I would ask if the Board of Officers have any recommendation to make in regard to fees? The report of the Treasurer showed that the Association has during the past year run behind seven or eight thousand dollars, reducing its surplus from thirty thousand to a trifle over twenty thousand dollars.

THE SECRETARY: Mr. President, In reply to the suggestion of Mr. Neilson, I will say that yesterday the Board of Officers held a meeting, the minutes of which I have here. There was a resolution passed in regard to fees: "The Board unanimously agreed to recommend to the Association that all fees for the registry and transfer of animals in the Herd-Book remain as now called for in our by-laws; also that the bounty for the slaughter and castration of bull calves remain the same as at present."

Mr. JAMES NEILSON: I would like to ask, then, whether the Board have considered any means for preventing a similar deficit next year? Because, if that goes on each year it will be rather serious in time. I did not know anything about the accounts until this moment. I think perhaps they have some recommendation for preventing so large an outgo next year. I think something could be done.

Mr. C. W. HORR: I believe the Board did not cover the gentleman's point by a formal resolution, but I think by the consent of every member it was agreed that we would have over twenty thousand dollars income, and all we had to do in order not to have a deficit was not to spend over that amount. Last year we spent too much. In the judgment of the Board we had ample funds. We have been a little extravagant — wisely extravagant, I think. This year we will be wisely economical.

Mr. W. G. POWELL: In other words, you made an investment last year.

Mr. C. W. HORR: Yes, a wise investment.

Mr. C. E. RUMSEY: This is not a money-making institution, but an institution to consider the good of these cattle. That is the way I understand it. I think the money expended last year was well spent. I think it was a good work. The only question is, shall you raise fees so as to be able to spend more, or shall you let the fees stand where they are and spend less? Those are the two questions to face. I would like to see the money spent.

THE PRESIDENT: Gentlemen, you have heard the Secretary read the proposed amendment, and the recommendation of the Board of Directors. What is your pleasure concerning it?

Mr. W. J. SMITH: I would like to ask the Secretary what information he has.

THE PRESIDENT: It is not properly before the house now, as there is no motion.

Mr. W. J. SMITH: Well, this is an informal discussion, as I understand it, and I want to ask the Secretary what effect the $5.00 registry fee for bulls has had upon not having bulls registered. Does he think that there are any number of bulls that have not been registered, or castrated, or killed because of the fee?

THE SECRETARY: Yes, sir.

Mr. W. J. SMITH: What is the effect of that?

THE SECRETARY: The effect I cannot tell; but there are many bulls that have not been registered and are still living.

Mr. E. A. POWELL: I want to ask the Secretary the comparative effect upon the finances from the fee that we pay for castration and the additional fee for registry — whether one hand washes the other?

THE SECRETARY: Yes, sir; there is about $4,000.00 on the credit side.

Mr. C. W. HORR: Isn't it $4,800.00?

THE SECRETARY: Yes, sir; about that.

Mr. C. W. HORR: It was suggested to the Board yesterday that there would be a pretty free recording of bulls immediately after this meeting. A good many gentlemen have been waiting, thinking the fee would be reduced. Now, we have paid this bounty, and we have between $4,800.00 and $4,900.00 left from the registration of bulls.

Mr. E. A. POWELL: It seems to me, as it has been suggested, that last year we incurred extraordinary expenses from the fact that it was at a time when it seemed necessary for us to show for our breed of cattle what it was capable of doing; we paid out a large amount of money to secure what we got, and the result was most satisfactory, certainly to all interested in this breed of cattle; it seems to me that it will not be necessary this year to repeat that in order to convince the world that no other breed will equal this as a butter-producing breed of cows. Therefore we can curtail our expenses the coming season to correspond to our income, and perhaps have an accumulation.

Mr. C. W. HORR: Unless there are others who wish to take part in this informal discussion, I move that the matter be laid upon the table.

Mr. C. E. RUMSEY: I second the motion.

THE PRESIDENT: Gentlemen, you have heard the motion to lay this matter upon the table. Are there any further remarks? If not, all in favor will vote aye.

Carried.

THE PRESIDENT: We will now hear the committee on proxies.

Mr. H. LANGWORTHY: Mr. President, and gentlemen: The committee on proxies report that the following gentlemen are entitled to vote, on proxies, as follows: Thomas B. Wales, 71; W. J. Smith, 57; H. Langworthy, 12; S. Burchard 10; M. L. Sweet, 10; Charles Robinson, 7; S. Hoxie, 4; W. G. Powell, 3; C. W. Horr, 2; T. G. Yeomans, 2; C. R. Payne, 2; 'C. E. Rumsey, 1; S. L. Hoxie, 1; C. F. Sweezey, 1; S. N. Wright, 1; D. J. Hinkley, 1; J. R. Beuchler, 1. Total, 186.

Mr. JAMES NEILSON: I move that the report of the committee be received, and the committee discharged.

Mr. S. HOXIE: I second the motion.

Carried.

THE PRESIDENT: The next business in order is: "An appropriation will be asked for Special Premiums for 1890." What is your pleasure concerning this subject?

Mr. JAMES NEILSON: I would like to hear some suggestions in regard to that. What suggestions have the Board to make in regard to it?

Mr. C. E. RUMSEY: Could not this safely be left to the judgment of the Board, with instructions that it should not reduce its surplus?

THE PRESIDENT: Oh, it could be, undoubtedly; but the Board always prefers some expression of opinion from the Association. It is also necessary that any appropriation shall be made by the Association, so that the Association may give instructions to the Board and make an appropriation beyond which the Board shall not offer premiums. It is necessary for all appropriations to be made by the Association.

Mr. T. G. YEOMANS: Mr. President, I don't know whether the Association would be in favor of appropriating any premiums this year or not. I think, in view of what we have done last year to convince the world that our cattle are at the front, it is hardly necessary for us to incur much of an expenditure this year in the same direction. My own idea would be that we had better save our money until the World's Fair, in 1892, when we shall probably have the largest exhibit of live stock ever seen in this country, and it would be perhaps more important for this Association to save its money for that fair rather than to be putting it out piece-meal before that time. My idea would be to reserve our money, and be liberal with our premiums at that fair.

THE PRESIDENT: Are there any further remarks? Last year you challenged the country to meet you in open competition, and you have won. Will you challenge again, or will you rest upon your laurels, and let some one else challenge you?

Mr. T. G. YEOMANS: We have got the belt now. [Laughter].

Mr. W. G. POWELL: Unless we have some money left at the discretion of the Board, we might be challenged with our hands tied, unless we saw fit to accept otherwise. On that account I would move that one-half of the amount of last year's premiums be left at the discretion of the Board.

THE PRESIDENT: Please name the amount.

Mr. W. G. POWELL: It was $4,000.00 last year, and my motion is that it be $2,000.00 this year.

Mr. C. W. HORR: I second the motion.

Mr. JAMES NEILSON: That would not bring us within the surplus yet.

Mr. C. W. HORR: Even if we should spend this $2,000.00, we have plenty of other places in which to get the balance of the $8,000.00. Then, if there wasn't, the Board would not have to spend this $2,000.00 if they did not want to spend it.

Mr. T. G. YEOMANS: My idea would be that if we are challenged, that we accept that challenge, the duel to occur in the year of the World's Fair.

Mr. W. J. SMITH: I think Mr. Yeomans has hit the right key. I question very seriously whether we have derived a benefit from duplicating premiums. While it has been a very nice thing for the exhibitors, I doubt whether it has brought out anything more than the regular premiums where they are shown. While I do not believe in tying the Board down where they might be embarrassed, yet I think we should express to them as the sentiment of this meeting, that we should offer no premiums the coming year, and limit them to $2,000.00 as the extreme limit. I don't know whether I make myself clear, but I want to put it in such a way that if any unusual emergency should arrive they shall have the power to meet it.

Mr. T. G. YEOMANS: Perhaps the gentleman's idea, then, would be to amend the motion: That it is the sentiment of this Association that it is not wise to offer any premiums for butter or milk during the coming year, but we will appropriate $2,000.00 to be used at the discretion of the Board.

Mr. W. G. POWELL: That was my motion.

Mr. T. G. YEOMANS: I add to that motion, that it is the sense of this Association that it is not wise to expend anything in premiums this year.

Mr. W. G. POWELL: I will accept that.

Mr. T. G. YEOMANS: I would give more for $5,000.00 put into premiums in one year than for $20,000.00 expended in premiums during a series of many years. If we dribble along a little money each year we do not induce the breeders generally to make an exhibit.

Mr. E. A. POWELL: I am sorry to disagree with any gentleman who has spoken on this subject, but it occurs to me that just at the present time we are on the tide, and with a little assistance we are floating further in advance, and there is no time, probably, when a small amount of money would do as much to settle the question, which in the minds of nearly all parties is settled now, but which is disputed by some, as at present — to make something of such a record as we have made the last year. If we drop out entirely for the year to come it will enable others to come to the front, and it will require a special effort for us to regain the ground we have lost. While I am not in favor of spending money as we have for the last year, yet I would be in favor of leaving that matter in the hands of the Board, so that under any circumstances that might arise they would feel justified in meeting the emergency and paying such prices as in their judgment would be best the coming year. The suggestion of reserving our forces for the exposition year is, in one sense, a good one; but then all eyes will be turned in one direction, and supposing we succeed at that time in making a very large exhibit, it is only made at one point. This last year we have met our opponents in all the states, at every large fair, and it is the number of prizes in the number of localities that we have won, and not any one single contest, that has given us the victory. Therefore I would amend these motions that have been made, and say that this be left in the hands of the committee to act at their discretion, but to see that during the coming year the entire expenses shall not exceed the income — or at least not to any extent.

Mr. C. W. HORR: If Mr. Powell offers that as an amendment, I will second it. I beg the Association either to trust its Board, or not to trust it. The resolution first says that we will trust $2,000.00 to the Board, and then in the next breath it says that they must not spend it. Now I would do either one thing or the other. I do not believe in individuals spending more than their income, nor a state, nor this Association, and so far as I have influence we will not spend more than our income. Now, two years ago, at the state fair in Ohio, there was only a small display of Holstein cattle, but last year, owing to the encouragement of this Association, there was a very large display. I had never attended any of their exhibitions, but I felt that the Association having made an appropriation to encourage the exhibit of Holsteins, that I must respond myself, and I knew I should be ashamed of myself if I didn't go. So I went, and took nearly twenty head of cattle with me, but I did not get all of the prizes; I went there with a bull that I thought could beat anybody else's in the state, but I found there were half a dozen other fellows there with animals that they thought could beat anything else — all weighing over two thousand pounds. Now, when we get to that great centennial blow-out, why, we have a reserve fund that we can fall back upon.

Mr. L. T. YEOMANS: The remarks of the last gentleman seem to call for a reply. We have heard once or twice here that the Board of Officers would like to know the sense of this meeting. This resolution expresses to them the sense of the meeting, but gives them the freedom to use their judgment, and fixes a limit to which they can spend the money. We have just answered their request that they shall have the sense of the meeting. If we are an Association, and we are electing a Board of Officers to transact this business the coming year, I think it is proper and right that we should express to that Board of Officers — before we elect them, if you please — what the sense of this Association is upon anything in which the finances are concerned. I do not think it is a reflection at all upon the Board of Officers. If I were a member of the Board I should want to know the wishes of my constituents. I would like to ask these gentlemen who have said so much in favor of the large premiums last year: Do they candidly think that if we should appropriate one-quarter of the premiums at any fair this year that we did last year that we should have as good a display of Black and Whites as we did last year? If they say yes, then I have nothing more to say. If they say no, then they have nothing more to say. I say that one-quarter will not bring out such a display. We should save our money for the World's Fair. That will be the grand occasion, and if we filter our money away now, when it comes to that fair we will be unable to make a great display there.

Mr. C. E. RUMSEY: The gentleman has spoken of saving our money until 1892. I think he forgets the great reserve fund there is in this Association. Why should we cramp ourselves for a fair that is not yet to come off? I think the reserve fund is the interest which the breeders of this cattle take in the Association, and if there is a fair held in 1892 there will be money enough. The Secretary can put me down for $250.00 for a fund to be offered outside of the Association for premiums in 1892. [Applause.]

Mr. C. W. HORR: My friend, Mr. Yeomans, so entirely misapprehended the spirit of my remark that I must be indulged for a moment. In the first place, I did not suppose I was mad, and the interpretation that the gentleman from New York State makes upon the spirit of friendliness that prevails all through Ohio; we don't call that getting angry in Ohio, we just call it earnest. In the next place, I ask for more specific instructions, and as a reply he charges that I don't want any instructions. What I asked was that you speak in no uncertain sound; that if you say at the very commencement of the resolution, "We trust $2,000.00 to the Board" — having made it apparent that you don't want any of us to expend so much money — that you do not in the very next part of the resolution paralyze us by saying that you don't think we had better spend it. I must say that that seems to me queer. Again, the gentleman said that if you should offer only one-fourth as much next year as we did last year, you would not get the same exhibit. Now there is more versatility among the Board than that. The Board would find some way of getting a good exhibit. I again say that I would not object to not allowing any premiums next year, but would much prefer that you did that; or else, having indicated by this discussion clearly that we are all in favor of economy, that if in the judgment of the Board they choose to do so, they may expend not to exceed $2,000.00.

Mr. C. E. RUMSEY: Is all this talk about economy going to be published for the benefit of these fellows that we have licked? If I lick a fellow I never tell him what it costs. [Laughter.] I do not like this kind of talk at all. I have been astonished since I became a member of this Association to read all the little by-talk which a couple of gentlemen have had in the meeting. The Chinese have a proverb that economy is saving and spending, and my experience is that the spending is the biggest economy. I have tried an experiment with two cows, feeding them five pounds of grain more than the rest of the herd got, and they gave me milk enough on the extra five pounds of feed to pay for all the hay the other cows ate. Now are we sorry we have whipped them because it cost so much? If we are sorry, don't let us tell about it.

Mr. W. G. POWELL: If we publish to the world that we are going to be weak the next year, why they will bluster a good deal on the other side. I am perfectly willing, if it meets the views of my seconds, to leave it in the hands of the Board to say what we shall spend. I am perfectly willing not to make any limit, and leave it in the hands of the Board to make an appropriation.

Mr. C. E. RUMSEY: I move to amend the whole matter by leaving it all to the discretion of the Board, and if any one of these other gentlemen think we are weak they won't find it out from the record.

Mr. E. A. POWELL: It is a question whether there is any time that we can spend a little money to as good advantage, perhaps, as the coming year. It has been suggested here, by the President, that we should keep at the front. What does that mean? It means we have got to keep going on; we cannot stand still. All other breeds are being advanced, and it will not answer for us to stand still even for a single year. We were at the front last year, and we must be at the front in the year to come. Now, to do this some encouragement from our Association is necessary. The amount need not be large. The Board will understand that in the sense of the Association our fund should not be largely reduced; but I think in their hands we are safe, and we can leave it to them to expend what is necessary judiciously. I cannot help but feel that the best way to do is to leave this matter so that the Board can offer some prizes. This Association is not poor. We have $20,000.00 in the treasury. I therefore renew my amendment, that this matter be referred to the Board with instructions that the total expenses of the Association for the coming year shall not exceed, to any large amount, the income for that time, and leave it to them to say where that money shall be expended.

THE PRESIDENT: The last part of your amendment is covered by the by-laws, which expresses exactly the same thing.

Mr. JAMES NEILSON: The whole matter seems to narrow itself down to this: That we have exceeded our income last year. Now, then, the question is, how much money we shall spend next year, and if business discretion calls for expending as much this year, how shall we raise it. And if it is thought best not to raise it, then we must cut down somewhere. I think in future the Board ought to give a general recommendation about things, because they have these matters all before them.

Mr. C. E. RUMSEY: The reason I wanted to leave this to the Board is because those gentlemen know the income of the Association.

THE SECRETARY (interposing): If the gentleman will allow me, I would say that it seems to me that our income for the coming year will exceed considerably that of last year, and it would be unwise not to appropriate money for special premiums. I think the matter could well be left to the judgment of the Board. Of course the Board would like an expression of opinion from the Association, but I would like to have the Board allowed at least as much as they had last year; not, of course, expecting that they will spend it unless in their judgment it is necessary to do so. I think our members all over the country who are not personally present to-day would feel very badly indeed if no money should be appropriated for this purpose. There can be money saved in some other direction. For instance, the experiment stations, for which we have spent three or four thousand dollars last year, will not call on us again. The bounty business is taking care of itself, and proving an income for us — that is, in connection with the increased registry for bulls.

THE PRESIDENT: Gentlemen, are there any further remarks upon this subject? If not, the question is upon the amendment as proposed by Mr. E. A. Powell, namely: That this matter be left to the members of the Board, but that the Board be instructed, as the sense of this meeting, not to exceed in the total expense the income to any large amount.

Mr. E. A. POWELL: I won't make it definitely in that form, because they may not be able to tell definitely at the time they make the appropriation, but they will know very nearly. Therefore I make the amendment in this way: That they be instructed for the coming year that the total expense of the Association shall not exceed, to any large amount, its income.

THE PRESIDENT: Those in favor of the amendment will say aye.

Carried.

THE PRESIDENT: Now the question recurs upon the original motion as made by Mr. W. G. Powell. Are you ready for the question?

Mr. L. T. YEOMANS: I would inquire where my amendment has gone to. Mr. Powell's was an amendment to my amendment.

THE PRESIDENT: I understood that you two gentlemen had agreed, having made practically the same amendment.

Mr. E. A. POWELL: I accepted Mr. Yeomans' motion.

Mr. L. T. YEOMANS: Oh, all right.

THE PRESIDENT: The question now is upon the original motion as amended.

Mr. J. B. DUTCHER: This seems to be somewhat mixed, and I would move as a substitute that the whole matter be referred to the Board with power.

Mr. E. A. POWELL: Virtually the suggestion of Mr. Dutcher covers my amendment, only that with certain portions, in regard to the views of the Association that our expenses next season shall not exceed our income. Aside from that it covers the ground exactly. It seems to me that it is due to the gentlemen who have made these motions that we should take a vote upon it.

Mr. S. L. HOXIE: I understand that our by-laws cover this point.

THE PRESIDENT: That is correct.

Mr. S. L. HOXIE: Then the amendment just passed is not strictly in order.

Mr. C. W. HORR: When we come to make up this record, you will find that it is in a very awkward shape, I imagine; while if you substitute it as my friend Mr. Dutcher suggests, the Secretary will have a pleasanter job of it.

Mr. W. J. SMITH: I rise for information. I always supposed that it was necessary to pass a resolution authorizing the expenditure of a definite amount, beyond which we could not go. Can the Board offer any money for premiums unless the Association passes a resolution authorizing it.

THE PRESIDENT: The Association must authorize the appropriations.

Mr. J. B. DUTCHER: I would like to inquire if the Association did it last year?

THE PRESIDENT: Yes, sir; naming the amount, $4,000.00.

Mr. J. B. DUTCHER: But did it exceed that?

THE PRESIDENT: Yes, sir.

Mr. J. B. DUTCHER: Then what does that direction amount to?

Mr. C. W. HORR: Well, I must defend the Board. We had no idea that these black and white cattle would win such a universal victory, and so the aggregate of winnings exceeded our utmost expectations.

Mr. C. E. RUMSEY: The way the Association can control this is by not putting up their best cattle.

THE SECRETARY: I would like to read a by-law of the Association. I think the Board of Officers has power to go on and do anything they please. I read Section 2, Article II.: "The Board of Officers of this corporation, as a Board, shall have and take the entire control and management of its affairs and business, with full power and authority to do what they deem proper and best for its interest, but nothing contrary to the expressed wish of the Association; and they shall have no authority to contract a debt against the corporation beyond its current expenses — and in no case, beyond the amount of cash in the treasury. And nothing shall be done which is not in accordance with the purpose and spirit of the charter and by laws, but shall in all cases execute every expressed will of the Association as expressed at any regular meeting." I understand that the Board has authority to go on and spend anything they like under their by-laws, unless they are forbidden at a meeting of the Association.

Mr. JAMES NEILSON: I understand that they were forbidden to expend more than the expenses.

Mr. W. J. SMITH: I move that this whole matter be laid on the table. That will give the Board full power to do as they see fit.

Mr. C. E. RUMSEY: And that no report of this discussion be made public.

Mr. W. J. SMITH: No; I don't include that. I don't see anything wrong about having people know that we propose to be economical.

Mr. C. E. RUMSEY: Well, I don't think all this talk ought to go down in the record.

THE PRESIDENT: Gentlemen, this motion is not debatable.

Mr. C. E. RUMSEY: The motion has not been seconded, and I move that no record of this discussion be made.

Mr. W. J. SMITH: Why, what harm will it do? I do not see any objection whatever to letting people know that we intend to be economical.

THE PRESIDENT: Gentlemen, the question is not debatable. Is the motion of Mr. Smith to lay the whole matter on the table seconded?

Mr. C. W. HORR: I second it.

THE PRESIDENT: Those in favor of laying the whole matter on the table will vote aye.

Carried.

Mr. C. E. RUMSEY: I move that this discussion be left out of the record of our proceedings.

Mr. J. B. DUTCHER: I hope that motion will not prevail. I do not want to see any part of our discussion expunged from the record. This is not a Star Chamber meeting, by any means.

Mr. JAMES NEILSON: I agree with Mr. Dutcher. There is nothing to be ashamed of on our part at all.

THE PRESIDENT: Well, the motion is not seconded.

Mr. C. E. RUMSEY: I would like to have an expression from the chair in regard to just what position that leaves the Board in after all this discussion.

THE PRESIDENT: The Board has authority now to offer any premium it sees fit, as I understand it, or conduct this whole matter of premiums subject to the current income and expenditures of the year.

Mr. C. E. RUMSEY: Then do we understand that they have no right to touch the accumulative surplus of the Association? How can they tell before the end of the year what the income is?

THE PRESIDENT: They will probably be careful to come within the income of the year. The new Board cannot draw upon the funds of the

Association without direct authority from the Association. They can spend the income of the year.

Mr. JAMES NEILSON : The officers now have the opinions of the different members of the Association, and from what has been read from the by-laws I think the matter can properly be left in the hands of the Board.

THE PRESIDENT : Gentlemen, the next order of business is : "An appropriation will be asked to aid the *Holstein-Friesian Register*."

Mr. L. T. YEOMANS : I offer the same motion that I made previously.

Mr. J. B. DUTCHER : This is a matter in which the members of the Association have as much interest as in any other thing connected with the Association. While I have no personal feeling in the matter at all, I believe it is to the interest of every man here to bring these cattle before the dairy interests of this country, and that is not being done under the present system. I believe this *Holstein-Friesian Register* should be put into the hands of every dairyman in the United States. It is a fact which can be demonstrated, and which every man knows who has made the test as between the different breeds of cattle, that one Holstein cow is worth two native cows to any dairyman in this country. I have in my dairy 150 native cows, the best I can buy in this country — and I appeal to the gentlemen here who have seen them — and I say of my Holstein cows, one of them is worth two native cows. Now the dairymen of this country do not know that, and we should take measures to bring before them in some way the fact that the Holstein is the cow for the dairyman to own, and make them understand that instead of the cows averaging 3,000 pounds of milk a year they will be keeping cows that will average 10,000 pounds a year. I believe it is to our interests to take this *Holstein-Friesian Register* and make a dairy paper of it. We have other agricultural papers all over the land which are devoted to agriculture generally. "*The Country Gentleman*" goes into the hands of everybody engaged in agriculture, but it is not devoted entirely to the interests of this breed of cattle, and I believe that this Association cannot spend money any more judiciously than by the means I have suggested. I look upon it as one of the most important of all subjects for us to consider — far better than these special premiums that you are offering at county fairs. I would like to make a dairy paper of this, and I contend that it will do more than anything else to advance the interests of the Holstein breed of cattle. These are simply my own ideas, and I would like to have an expression of views from others on it.

THE PRESIDENT : Does the gentleman make any motion ?

Mr. J. B. DUTCHER : No, sir ; I simply make this as a suggestion.

Mr. C. W. HORR : I move that the matter be referred to the Board, and authorize them to appropriate such a sum as they deem wise, not to exceed $1,250.00.

Mr. CHARLES ROBINSON: I offer an amendment, that the Board be authorized to appropriate $4,000.00.

THE PRESIDENT: Gentlemen, you have heard the motion of Mr. Horr, that the Board expend not to exceed $1,250.00 in aiding the *Holstein-Friesian Register*. Then Mr. Robinson made an amendment that the amount be fixed at not to exceed $4,000.00. That amendment was not seconded. Then the motion is that this matter be referred to the Board, and they be authorized not to expend more than $1,250.00 to assist the *Holstein-Friesian Register*. Are there any remarks on the subject?

Mr. J. B. DUTCHER: Yes. The gentlemen seem to have the impression that this is a donation to Mr. Houghton. I take an entirely different view of it. It is to place before the public a knowledge of the merits of these cattle. I don't believe in spending money injudiciously, and I don't believe in taking measures particularly to get rid of a surplus. I am more in favor of a surplus than a deficiency. But instead of spending $4,000.00 in special premiums at fairs, I would put this into something that would bring before the farmers of this country the merits of the Holstein breed of cattle. You may go to a fair and award a special premium, but it don't do half the good that the money will do if used in this way. I am in favor of doing both, but I would make a judicious expenditure of the money to the support of the *Holstein-Friesian Register*. I would make a liberal expenditure to it, and see that it is put before the people extensively.

Mr. JAMES NEILSON: Mr. President, some such paper, where everything connected with the Holsteins can be readily referred to, is very necessary — some place where the files are preserved. And such paper should have an index, so that it could be easily gotten at, because it is constantly necessary to refer to information connected with the Holsteins. For instance, the other day, after a paper had been read referring to the great records of the Holsteins, at once several gentlemen turned to the speaker and said: "Where can you get affidavits pointing to those matters?" I must say that I have been careless; I was going to refer them to Mr. Powell, or Mr. Dutcher —

Mr. J. B. DUTCHER: (Interposing). You can have the affidavits.

Mr. JAMES NEILSON: Matters of that kind should be indexed, and it should be a store-house of all that kind of information. We should preserve that paper, and file and bind it. Then, beyond that, we should support it by writing to it — send it our ordinary every-day records. My people have kept a record for ten years of every cow's milk. I don't make butter, but if I did I should have had a record kept of that. I don't know how much it is requisite to give the paper, but it should have a fair amount, certainly. I have called attention once or twice to the fact that there was only a certain amount of money in the treasury. Therefore I should not expend everything for one thing. It is all very well to put enough money in a thing to amount to something. It is impossible for us to give the exact amount for everything, but I am heartily in favor of the spirit of Mr. Dutcher's resolution.

Mr. T. G. YEOMANS: I move to strike out of the motion the limit to $1,250.00. That I know will meet the views of the gentlemen who made the motion, because that leaves the matter entirely with the Board. The same argument that he applied to the butter premium applies to this exactly.

Mr. W. J. SMITH: I second that amendment.

Mr. T. G. YEOMANS: If the Board is to do one part of the business, let them do it all.

THE PRESIDENT: The amendment is that the amount of $1,250.00 be stricken out of the original motion. Are there any remarks?

Mr. C. W. HORR: I hope that will not prevail. This is a question about which there are wide differences of opinion among members of the Board, and no doubt would be in the Association. We all feel very friendly toward this paper, and we join in congratulations to the gentleman who edits it. He appeared before the Board and made a very favorable impression, and after a discussion we decided to recommend exactly the resolution that I have offered here to-day. That was a larger sum than some members desired to appropriate; it was smaller than other members wanted to appropriate. But as a compromise, and in view of the fact that we have got to cut down expenses this year, it was the final unanimous opinion of the Board that that was the wisest course. I hope the Association will not precipitate that discussion upon us again to-day.

Mr. E. A. POWELL: I would like to make a few remarks on that subject, because I consider it one of the most important that has come before this Association. The remarks of Mr. Dutcher in regard to familiarizing the country with our breed of cattle is important. One of the principal duties of this Association is to show these gentlemen — not only breeders, but dairymen — that we have a breed of cattle that are capable of doubling the products of their herd when introduced. We believe that ourselves, and if we can convince others of it we will have found a market for all our surplus stock. To show you that we have reason for that, I will mention the records of three herds that were graded up at a very small expense merely by the introduction of bulls into two herds and the introduction of two females into the third. Mr. Jerome, near Syracuse, who sells his milk to the Onondaga County Milk Association, sold last year his entire product and received pay from the association, aside from what he used in his own family, for over 9,000 pounds apiece for his entire herd. A near neighbor of his, Mr. Schuyler, received pay for 10,419 pounds per cow, netting him an income of $127.00 a cow. Messrs. Wood & Co., of Exeter, started a few years ago by buying two females and one bull, and last year their entire herd of thirty head sold milk enough to amount to 9,000 pounds per cow. The average product of the cows of the state of New York is only 3,034 pounds, according to the report of the State Dairy Commission. If this is a fact, and we can show the people that the yearly products of their dairies can be doubled, there will be no trouble in selling our stock. I know of no means by which that can be done as well as through the public press. And while all the agricultural papers, both east and west, have been glad to publish anything that has been sent them on this subject, there is only one paper that is working entirely for the interests of this breed of cattle, and that is the *Holstein-Friesian Register*. It is not the organ of an individual, but of this Association. Two years ago I opposed any appropriation being made for this purpose, from the fact that the paper had recently gone into new hands and we did not know what the future of it was going to be. It then had not been sufficiently established for this Association to spend money upon it as an Association, but as individuals I recommended that we take hold of it and contribute to its support. That was done quite largely by several of the breeders, and so far as the breeders subscribed, it was done liberally; but it was not done in a general way. Last year there was an appropriation made by another method, which indirectly achieved the same result, but it was made on conditions which I believe reduced the income below what was expected to have been realized. Now, it seems to me there is not any means by which we can spend a portion of our funds to so good an advantage as by increasing the circulation of this paper, and I hope the members will look at this matter in the light of an investment.

Mr. C. E. RUMSEY: Mr. President, I think it is proper for me to say just what this paper did for me. I was allowed a certain number of those papers to distribute. I had some bull calves which I had sold from two hundred to five hundred miles away from my farm, but it hurt my pride that I could not sell them to the dairymen right around near me. I got those papers, and sent them around to the dairymen within a radius of ten miles of my farm. This spring I sold two bull calves to those dairymen. I don't know whether it was my continued example of breeding these cattle, or the constant pounding away at them with these papers that finally persuaded them that the Holsteins were the only breed of cattle worth raising, but I sold two bull calves anyway. Now, the firm I am in expends from eight thousand to ten thousand dollars a year in advertising, and I believe that my hammering away on that dairyman finally caused the fact to get through his skin, and made him come and buy those bull calves of me. I took clover hay for one of them, but I took a good lot of it.

Mr. E. A. POWELL: I would like Mr. Houghton to make a statement of the number of papers he issued last year.

Mr. HOUGHTON: I received last year from the Association about $1,250.00. That represented some 1,500 subscriptions at 80 cents per year. But, mind you, each subscription was divided into four parts; it went three months to each man. So that the total number who received the paper during the year was probably nearly 7,000.

Mr. C. W. HORR: I hope it will not be necessary to go into a general discussion of the reasons which actuated the various members of the Board on this question. I want to state exactly what we are appropriating it for. Mr. Houghton's paper has a circulation, as I understand from him, of 1,700 outside of that furnished by the Association. In the arrangement that the Board made — and it was my privilege to help make that a year ago with Mr. Houghton — we aimed to get the worth of our money, and then we aimed to let the papers be disposed of by the members according to their respective appropriations, so that no one could claim that his money was used by the Board to obtain 6,000 copies without his getting his proportion. We hoped that that would lead to an increased circulation. Mr. Houghton tells us that so far as he can judge up to the present time the increase has only been about one per cent. Now, so far as getting subscriptions for his paper is concerned, it seems to me all folly. I should suppose there could be some other course devised by the Board. Greeley said that the way to resume was to resume; the way to go west was to go west. Now, I think it would be the sober second thought of this Association that if we set about last year's appropriation — in view of the fact that we spent so much more money than we received last year — it is all you can ask. So I hope the $1,250.00 will be stood by.

Mr. W. J. SMITH: I think if Mr. Horr insists upon the Board being instructed about this matter, I don't see why we should trust them so fully in regard to the premium question. I have great confidence in the Board, and I am perfectly willing to trust the entire matter to them; and, although the result of subscription may not appear as satisfactory as it ought to, still I think we can look at the results behind them. A great many men think when they get a paper for nothing that there is no use subscribing for it, and that is the way it has been with this, I imagine.

Mr. J. B. DUTCHER: I think one reason of the circulation of the paper not increasing is the fact that it treats almost exclusively — instead of being a dairy paper — to the breeding of the Holstein cattle. I believe we should make it more of a dairy paper, and have the dairy interests discussed in it; then the dairymen will readily subscribe for it. I know lots of people that are breeding beef cattle who have had this paper. Why you might as well throw it in the fire. I certainly hope that this Association will appropriate more than $1,250.00 to the support of that paper. I believe it is to the interest of every member of this Association to do that, and I think it is one of the most important things in connection with our Association.

Mr. O. B. POTTER: I rise to corroborate the expression of Mr. Dutcher, that this paper should discuss something besides the breeding of Holstein cattle. I take all the agricultural papers published in the country, I believe, and yet I find that my farmer only preserves a few of them on files. He does not consider this paper on the Holstein breed of cattle as sufficiently interesting to him to keep it on the files, and he doesn't read it very much. My own opinion is clearly that if you ever expect this paper to have a large circulation, and to exercise an important influence in the direction you wish, it has got to contain something more than facts about the Holstein cattle.

Mr. E. P. MILLER: It seems to me that this Association cannot afford to do more for this paper than it has the past year. I know it is an uphill business trying to make any money out of publishing a paper devoted to some special interests, as this paper is. Here is a paper devoted expressly to the interests of the Holstein-Friesian, and every man who is breeding those cattle is interested in a paper of that kind, and if the paper is properly managed it can be of great interest to every man, particularly in advancing this breed of cattle. We have in this country over 15,000,000 cows, and it is calculated that they do not average 3,000 pounds of milk a year, and not 150 pounds of butter. There are men here who have Holstein cows that have records of 30,000 pounds of milk a year. Now, what the breeders of this kind of cattle want to do is to bring the subject before the dairymen of this country of the importance of getting a breed of cattle that will give them from five to ten or fifteen thousand pounds of milk a year more than they are getting now. The experiments that have been made at our stations go to prove very clearly that a man can keep on his farm a dairy cow that will net him $50.00 to $75.00 a year as cheap as he can keep a steer that won't net him a cent. The farmers improve their farms by keeping dairies, and I think it would not be a hard matter to make the farmers of this country understand that they can almost double the profits on their farms by keeping cows; creameries are being established all over the land now, and it won't be a difficult matter for the publisher of the *Holstein-Friesian Register* to get the names of the patrons of those creameries all over the United States, and to see that this paper is put into their hands. It ought to be devoted more extensively to the dairy interests. I certainly think every breeder of Holstein cattle is personally interested in circulating a paper of this kind. If the publisher can make any money out of it, the larger the circulation the better it will be for him. It costs just as much to set the type for 1,000 subscribers as it does for 100,000. All it costs extra is the paper, the press-work, and the mailing. Consequently, if the publisher can get the cost of the paper and press-work, it is a great deal better for him to receive aid in distributing the paper in that way than it is to not have it increased; and he can make more money on his advertising if he has a large circulation. I would suggest that the Association keep up the appropriation for this paper, and also that every member make it a point to contribute articles on dairy subjects to the paper.

Mr. G. D. WHEELER: The discussion here seems to turn upon the fact that we really own the paper. If the gentlemen say that, we will give unlimited support to this paper, and make it our paper, then it is our paper; but if we are to contribute something to aid the editor of the paper in the individual work which he has undertaken, the question arises how far that liberality should go. Last year we gave $1,250.00, and this paper was sent to one thousand five hundred new dairymen. The result was that it increased the editor's subscription list fifteen members. If we should double that amount this year we would assist him to thirty new subscribers perhaps for the next year. Now, we might perhaps consult with the editor and get him to change the character of the paper, and make it a dairy paper. But if we are to do what has been proposed to us now, it seems to me that the $1,250.00 might answer for the purpose.

Mr. HOUGHTON: One word of explanation seems necessary. My friends, Mr. Wheeler and Mr. Miller, seem to be laboring under the impression that they have been kind of supporting me. Every dollar has been laid out in spreading the paper before the people of the country. The direct results from your subscription last year, so far as my book-keeper could trace them, were about one per cent. Mr. Wheeler seems to think that was the entire gain in the circulation of the paper for the year. Nothing of the kind. The gain last year was nearly seven hundred copies. When I started out I had one hundred and twenty-five paid subscribers. And in two year's time I have raised it to one thousand seven hundred paid subscribers. I think it has progressed on its own merits. What you have done is not fostering the paper. You have only expended your money for the distribution of these copies among those to whom you wanted to bring the merits of these cattle. Our friend, Mr. Rumsey, of Pittsburg, has given a practical illustration of how it worked in his own neighborhood, and I have many people all over the country telling me the same thing.

Mr. E. A POWELL: I understood Mr. Houghton to say that this expenditure had resulted in putting this paper before some seven thousand people for three months.

Mr. HOUGHTON: Yes, sir; that is what you paid for.

Mr. E. A. POWELL: I think that is good advertising. I think it is a pretty good investment.

Mr. HOUGHTON: I have issued twenty thousand copies, and sent them everywhere, and have been using these lists of dairymen to bring this subject before them. The paper has nearly supported itself the past year.

Mr. E. P. TAFT: I move that we substitute the sum of $2,000.00 instead of $1,250.00.

Mr. T. G. YEOMANS: I second that motion.

Mr. J. B. DUTCHER: I don't know how the members of this Board all feel, but this looks to me very much like a conviction before trial. They all seem to be opposed to spending money. I would put it in a little different shape. I would say that they are instructed to expend upon that paper $2,000.00 for the next year.

Mr. E. P. TAFT: I adopt that.

Mr. C. E. RUMSEY: It looks to me as if they made a pretty sharp bargain with Mr. Houghton last year. If they got those papers distributed at 80 cents a year, it must have been very close to cost; there could not have been any profit in it to the gentleman who runs the paper. If you appropriate $2,000.00, does that carry with it that the gentleman shall go on and furnish more papers at cost, or below it, if you can pinch him that hard, or does it mean that you want him to make a little profit out of it this year?

Mr. C. W. HORR: I will consent to adopt the amendment that Mr. Dutcher made, to leave the whole matter to the discretion of the Board.

Mr. J. B. DUTCHER: I have only made one amendment.

Mr. C. W. HORR: Well, Mr. Yeomans seconded some amendment, and that is the one I refer to.

Mr. T. G. YEOMANS: I seconded Mr. Taft's amendment.

Mr. C. W. HORR: Well, I accept that.

THE PRESIDENT: As the chair understands it, the original motion was made by Mr. Horr and seconded by Mr. Yeomans. There is now an amendment made by Mr. Taft and accepted by Mr. Horr, and it stands in this shape: That the *Holstein-Friesian Register* be subsidized not to exceed $2,000.00, and that the matter be placed in the hands of the Board to complete.

Mr. E. P. TAFT: My motion was to make it $2,000.00 instead of $1,250.00.

Mr. C. W. HORR: Then it was Mr. Yeoman's motion that I accepted, which was to strike out the $1,250.00 and leave it to the discretion of the Board.

Mr. J. B. DUTCHER: Mr. President, was the substitute I offered in order?

THE PRESIDENT: No, sir.

Mr. J. B. DUTCHER: Why not?

THE PRESIDENT: Because there was a motion before the meeting, an amendment, and a substitute, I believe, and a second substitute which was not seconded.

Mr. J. B. DUTCHER: There was a substitute, and an amendment which was not seconded, and then Mr. Taft offered an amendment, and then I made this motion as a substitute for the whole thing. It appears to me that that is in order; that this Board of Officers be authorized to expend upon the *Holstein-Friesian Register* for the next year $2,000.00, and that they do it in such manner as they deem best, and if they do not do it to the satisfaction of this Association, why, next year we will haul them up.

THE PRESIDENT: Gentlemen, you have heard the motion, that this whole matter be referred to the Board with power to act.

Mr. J. B. DUTCHER: No, sir. The substitute I offered was this: That the Board of Officers be instructed to expend upon the *Holstein-Friesian Register* for the next year $2,000.00. They are not authorized to do it in their discretion. They are instructed to do it.

Mr. C. R. PAYNE: It seems to me that in that event we will give the editor $2,000.00.

Mr. W. G. POWELL: The substitute has not been seconded.

SEVERAL MEMBERS: I second it.

Mr. J. B. DUTCHER: It is seconded now, two or three times.

Mr. W. G. POWELL: I have favored this appropriation, but I would simply say, as a business matter, that I will have to object to Mr. Dutcher's substitute. I certainly would not put myself in his hands and he would not put himself in mine in that way, as a business transaction. I know he is too shrewd a business man to do it, and I claim to be something of a business man myself.

Mr. J. B. DUTCHER: I was about to offer an addition to that resolution — and I will offer it now so that you can discuss it — that this money be expended upon a similar basis to that of last year.

Mr. D. H. BURRELL: I hope this motion will prevail, for the reason that it will be a delicate matter for the Board to deal with the question if you do not define the amount. I am of the opinion that we better make the amount $2,000.00. If we had $50,000.00 in the treasury, I should be in favor of expending twice as much money. This Association ought to have a balance sheet each year a little in excess of the preceding year. For my part, I am not at all satisfied. I think we ought to go back and have in our treasury $28,000.00, because some time or other an emergency will arise when we may want to expend that money in a profitable way.

THE PRESIDENT: The question now before the meeting is on the substitute to take the place of the original motion: That the Board of Officers be instructed to expend $2,000.00 upon the *Holstein-Friesian Register* upon a similar basis to that of last year. All in favor of that will say aye.

Carried.

The President: The question is now on the adoption of the motion as amended. All in favor will say aye.

Carried.

Mr. C. W. Horr: Mr. President, as this is as good a time as any other, I desire to submit to the Association the following resolution:

"*Resolved*, That a committee of five be appointed by the President to obtain information in reference to the laws that have been enacted by the United States, and the several states, for the protection of the dairy interests against the manufacture and fraudulent sale of butter and cheese that are not made wholly from cream or milk; that after said committee has obtained said information they shall visit Washington, and use every honorable endeavor to procure the passage by congress of as wise and effective an enactment as can be devised for prohibiting, restraining, and regulating the shipment from one state into another of butter and cheese that are not the sole product of cream or milk; that said committee shall be instructed, if possible, to have embraced in said enactment a clause that shall prohibit the shipment from one state to another of cheese that is not made in whole or in part from skim-milk, except in packages that are so branded as to clearly and fully disclose the character of the goods.

"*Resolved*, That the Secretary of our Association and the chairman of said committee be instructed to solicit in procuring said enactment the advice, assistance, and co-operation of all the leading dairy associations of the United States.

"*Resolved*, That the Secretary be authorized to pay the expenses of said committee while discharging the duties assigned to them by this resolution."

Now, Mr. President, what has suggested this resolution to me is this: Probably some gentlemen may not be aware that I am largely interested in the manufacture of cheese and butter in Ohio. We have a law there which is satisfactory to our farmers in reference to the manufacture of cream cheese. We have laws in reference to the manufacture and sale of butter that is made partly from fat. But we meet with this difficulty, that while we can enforce these laws against the citizens of Ohio, parties living in adjoining states can ship in packages of cheese or butter which do not conform to our laws, and we are powerless. And it seems to me that the dairy interests of the United States are going to be so large and important that we have got to have national legislation before we can protect ourselves against cheese that is partially made from other substances than milk and butter that is made from fat. I apprehend that if this Association takes hold of this matter and appoints a committee which shall inform itself of the legislation that has been enacted in the various states, and get a clear, general knowledge of the whole field of legislation, and then lays the matter before congress, we shall get, in the course of a year or a year and a half, the legislation that we need. I hope the Association will adopt this or some similar plan. Some men may wonder why it is so limited to the simple matter of regulating so far as the shipment from one state to another is concerned. If I am correctly informed, that is the only way the national government can get at this thing.

Mr. JAMES NEILSON: While the gentleman is stopping up all these ratholes, there is another thing wherein they are still more sly, perhaps — perhaps not more wicked — than in Ohio. They tell of mixing a skim-milk cheese with what they call butter-fat in Wisconsin, and it has very much interfered with the price of butter. They avoid the law, because they do not use matter which is foreign; they use altogether the product of the cow. I think, while he is about it, he should include that. I second Mr. Horr's resolution.

Mr. J. B. DUTCHER: It seems to me as if this Association was taking upon itself a pretty big contract to revolutionize the dairy interests of this country, and when we were talking a little while ago about appropriating a few dollars to bring the objects of this Association before the dairymen, my friend Mr. Horr was very eccnomical. Now, this is too big a question to take up and bring before congress. It belongs properly to the dairy interests of the country. I am decidedly opposed to selling anything for what it is not, whether it is oleomargarine or skim-milk cheese. Let the New York State Dairy Commissioner take up the matter; I believe there is one somewhere; I never have seen him, and I don't think very much of him. But don't let us bring that matter up here. It is not a subject for this Association to consider.

Mr. N. B. GREGORY: I endorse the remarks of Mr. Dutcher, all excepting his slur upon the President of our Board of Milk Trade. Mr. Brown, I think, has been a very good officer. I think Mr. Horr has been a little precipitate in foisting upon this Association the question of regulating the dairy interests.

Mr. J. B. DUTCHER: I move to lay the whole matter upon the table.

Mr. N. B. GREGORY: I second the motion.

Mr. C. W. HORR: Well, I was going to make that motion myself (laughter), but I wanted to make a few remarks first.

Mr. J. B. DUTCHER: Then I will withdraw my motion in order to permit you to make the remarks.

Mr. C. W. HORR: I was going to say that I would move to lay it upon the table for one year. This is an old subject, about which this Association has not interested itself, I know; but if you will notice one little clause in my resolution, you will see that the Secretary was directed to solicit the advice and assistance of all the dairy associations of the United States. It was not intended that we should take the whole work upon our shoulders. That is all I have to say.

Mr. J. B. DUTCHER: I now renew the motion.

Mr. O. B. POTTER: Mr. President—

THE PRESIDENT: (Interposing.) The motion to lay upon the table is not debatable.

A MEMBER: I think we ought to hear Mr. Potter.

Mr. O. B. POTTER: If the matter is not debatable, I think I had better not say anything.

THE PRESIDENT: We should like very much to listen to what the gentleman has to say.

Mr. O. B. POTTER: I simply desired to say that this oleomargarine matter has not been definitely settled by the courts, and if we should make a precedent in regard to this product, I am afraid it will be a precedent that will necessarily lead us from the ground of state control in domestic matters, which, in my judgment, is at the very foundation of all the prosperity, progress, and greatness of our country. I think it should lay upon the table a year, and believe it will lay there much longer. We have existed under the form of government that we have, and under which we have given our general government no power except the power to make citizenship within the states greater and broader than before, to enlarge the liberties of the citizens within the states — not a power is given in the constitution but it is given directly for the purpose and to the end, and it has secured the purposes and the ends, of enlarging the liberty of citizenship within the states. We have achieved a progress that no nation on earth has equalled during the last hundred years, and we shall continue to progress so long as we leave our states to control their own business in obedience to the laws of the country and within the powers that have been delegated to the general government, and the general government keeping equally within its powers. We shall continue in that line, I believe, to advance the fortunes of this nation, and through it the fortunes of mankind, as we can do under no other system. All the advances that have been made — and I do not hesitate to say that nobody who examines the subject will fail to come to this same conclusion — in law and liberty which now affect the citizens of all the states of the Union have been made by the states themselves. Our system of common school education sprang from it in the colonies of Massachusetts and Connecticut — that there must exist somewhere a right to tax property to educate children in a common school. Connecticut first adopted it, although Massachusetts claims the honor; but it was first put into her constitution and was then adopted by Massachusetts, and it has gone on from state to state until it has become a household right of every child born and reared upon the soil of the country, and it has come to stay for all future generations. Now, I wish to say the time has never existed, and it is doubtful if it now exists, when you could have discussed that question in the halls of congress with any prospect whatever of having it supported, and so you will find with all the rights that have been achieved under the state governments. Let me say, do not belittle our state government. This very question, as it seems to me, Ohio can control. The general government can control what may be carried from state to state. Ohio can make it a crime and punish anybody within that state who sells anything which they ought not by law to sell. And upon that line, and within the rights of the states, I believe all can be accomplished that is sought to be accomplished here, and without any evasion or change in the grandest system of government this world has ever seen.

Mr. J. B. DUTCHER: Now, Mr. President, I renew the motion to lay the matter upon the table.

THE PRESIDENT: Those in favor of laying the resolutions offered by Mr. Horr upon the table say aye.

Carried.

THE PRESIDENT: The business now in order is the election of officers.

Mr. T. G. YEOMANS: As it is now 1 o'clock, I move that we take a recess until 2 o'clock for dinner.

Mr. J. B. DUTCHER: I second that motion.

THE PRESIDENT: The Secretary informs me that dinner is not served until 2 o'clock.

Mr. W. C. POWELL: Well, lunch commences at 1 o'clock, and we can get lunch between now and 2 o'clock and then go on and finish our business.

THE PRESIDENT: Those in favor of taking a recess until 2 o'clock will say aye.

Carried.

Recess until 2 o'clock.

AFTERNOON SESSION.

The President: Gentlemen, have you any other business before proceeding to the election of officers?

Mr. W. Brown Smith: Mr. Chairman, there is one matter of business that I think was not fully understood. I apprehend that the people generally understood that the Auditing Committee here this morning was to serve for the next year; our President does not so understand it. I therefore offer a resolution that a committee be appointed to audit the accounts for the ensuing year, so that they may be audited before the meeting organizes next year.

Mr. T. G. Yeomans: Mr. President, I offer a suggestion that we authorize the Board of Officers to appoint a committee at their first meeting, which is the day preceding the annual meeting next year. If the Board of Officers had authority to appoint such a committee next year, they would be sure to appoint gentlemen who are in the city, while if they are appointed now there may not be more than one or two here on the day preceding the day of the meeting to perform their work.

Mr. W. Brown Smith: That will be entirely satisfactory if the convention are satisfied with that way of doing business. The thought was, yesterday afternoon, that the members of the Board would hardly be willing for the officers to make the accounts and then make a committee to audit them, but I will accept that as an amendment. Mr. Judson Smith suggested that a committee of seven be appointed, of which four should be a quorum, and he was intending to make that as a motion.

Mr. J. B. Dutcher: I think our Treasurer is right, upon general principles. While there is nobody here but would have entire confidence in the officers appointing a committee to audit their own accounts, I think it a very wise suggestion; and I think Mr. Judson Smith's motion, that an auditing committee of seven be appointed, of which four should be a quorum, would be acceptable. I think there would be no difficulty in appointing seven men of whom there would probably be four here.

Mr. L. T. Yeomans: I think Mr. Smith's suggestion was a good one.

Mr. W. J. Smith: I would like to explain. My idea was to have the President appoint a committee of seven, three of which would be a quorum, and they could have the accounts all ready for the next annual meeting. That is the reason of my motion. I like that idea better than to leave the whole matter in the hands of the Board.

Mr. W. G. Wheeler: Mr. President, why not make a committee of five and have two a quorum?

Mr. T. G. YEOMANS: To obviate any possible objection, I would like to make this addition, that if there is not a quorum that the Board of Officers may add enough to that committee to make a quorum.

Mr. E. A. POWELL: In the first place, it is not the accounts of the Board that would be audited; it is only the accounts of certain members of the Board, for instance, the Treasurer, Secretary, and Superintendent of Advanced Registry. If you have not confidence enough in the Board to allow them to appoint an auditing committee, why not ask the President to appoint that committee previous to the date of the next meeting? The President can appoint it then as well as he can now; therefore I move that the President be instructed previous to each meeting to appoint a committee of three to audit the accounts. I move that as a substitute. He can appoint them the first day before or the second day before the next meeting. It would be well enough when the Board meets next year.

The motion was seconded, and carried.

Mr. W. Brown Smith moved to proceed to the election of officers.

Motion seconded by Mr. E. A. Powell, and carried.

It is moved that when there is but one nomination made, the Secretary be instructed to cast the vote in the usual way; and when there are more than one, that we proceed to ballot in the usual way.

Motion seconded, and carried.

Mr. Powell moved that two tellers be appointed by the President.

Motion put, and carried.

The President appointed H. Langworthy and C. E. Rumsey.

Mr. Yeomans nominated Mr. David H. Burrell as President.

Mr. Dudley Miller nominated Mr. John B. Dutcher.

Mr. Dutcher declined.

There being no other nominations for the office of President, the Secretary was directed by the President to cast the vote of the Association, whereupon Mr. D. H. Burrell was declared duly elected President of the Association for the ensuing year.

Mr. M. L. Sweet nominated Mr. George D. Wheeler for First Vice-President of the Association. There being no further nominations, the Secretary cast the vote, and Mr. George D. Wheeler was declared elected First Vice-President.

Mr. S. Burchard nominated Mr. W. M. Liggett, of Benson, Minn., for Second Vice-President. There being no further nominations, the Secretary cast the ballot, and he was declared duly elected.

Mr. John A. Frye, of Marlboro, Mass., was nominated for Third Vice-President. There being no other nominations, the Secretary cast the ballot, and he was declared duly elected.

Mr. W. Brown Smith nominated Mr. John B. Dutcher for Fourth Vice-President. There being no further nominations, the Secretary cast the ballot, and Mr. Dutcher was declared duly elected.

The President having stated that nominations were open for three Directors, to hold office for two years, Mr. Smith nominated Mr. W. G. Powell, Mr. C. W. Horr nominated Mr. L. T. Yeomans, and Mr. William M. Singerly, of Philadelphia, was also nominated. There being no further nominations, the Secretary cast the ballot of the Association, and Messrs. W. G. Powell, L. T. Yeomans, and William M. Singerly were declared duly elected for two years.

Mr. C. W. Horr nominated Mr. Thomas B. Wales, the present incumbent, as Secretary and Editor.

It was moved that this election be made unanimous, and that the President cast the ballot.

Carried.

The President having cast the vote of the Association, Mr. Thomas B. Wales was declared duly elected.

Mr. Sweezey nominated Mr. W. Brown Smith, of Syracuse, N. Y., as Treasurer of the Association, and the Secretary having cast the ballot, he was declared duly elected.

Mr. S. Hoxie was nominated as Superintendent of Advanced Registry, and the Secretary having cast the vote of the Association, he was declared duly elected.

THE PRESIDENT: This, I think, constitutes the full election. There is one thing more which the chair wishes to call the attention of the meeting to, and that is to determine the place of meeting for 1891.

Mr. Yeomans moved that the next meeting be at Syracuse.

Motion seconded.

THE SECRETARY: I feel obliged to state for a member from Illinois, Mr. Amos Edmunds, who sent his proxy, that he wished me to propose that the meeting be held at Buffalo, as being farther west than New York or Syracuse. I make that as a motion.

The Secretary's motion not having been seconded, the motion to hold the next meeting at Syracuse was put by the chair, and declared duly carried.

THE PRESIDENT: The next meeting will be held at Syracuse. The chair now takes pleasure in introducing Mr. D. H. Burrell as President of the Association:

Mr. BURRELL: Gentlemen of the Holstein-Friesian Association, in accepting this position for the ensuing year I have consented with much reluctance, and should have been very happy if Mr. Dutcher had accepted the nomination, and I should have done all I could to have persuaded you to vote for him. I could not for one moment have accepted the position if it were not for the fact that we have a Secretary who is the best one we ever had; and I can trust myself safely to him to take care of me during the next year, and I shall call upon him for instructions and directions to keep me from making mistakes. I would like to say a good deal of what the Holstein-Friesian Association has accomplished in the past and what work it has before it in the future — how valuable the Holstein-Friesian cow has become; what an impression it has made in the country and how superior the milk which it furnishes to the children. But I will desist, because there are other gentlemen who are to address you, and I know that a business meeting made of such an audience as are here present will not exchange and interchange compliments, and I therefore beg to ask what is your pleasure?

Mr. Powell moved that a vote of thanks be presented to the retiring President and Board of Officers, and the motion was unanimously carried.

THE PRESIDENT: The next order of business is an address by Dr. Peter Collier, of the New York Experiment Station. Subject: "How to Make Dairying Profitable." I take pleasure in introducing Dr. Collier.

DR. COLLIER'S ADDRESS.

THE DAIRY INDUSTRY — HOW IT MAY BE MADE MORE PROFITABLE.

Mr. President, Gentlemen and Members of the Holstein-Friesian Association of America: I assure you that I fully appreciate the honor in having been again invited by your Secretary to address you, and I hope I may be able to say something which may not only be of interest, but of practical value in advancing the great interest which has again brought us together.

I will not weary you with an array of statistics, since those can be published and can be then considered at your leisure; but I will informally present the general conclusions which these statistics appear to justify and give the results of what I regard as very important experiments which we have recently concluded at the Experiment Station at Geneva.

THE EXTENT OF THE DAIRY INDUSTRY.

The estimated number of cows in the United States, January 1st, 1890, was, approximately, 16,000,000 (15,952,883), an increase from January 1st, 1889, of 654,258 — 4.3 per cent increase.

New York leads with 1,552,373, having nearly 10 per cent of the total and about twice as many as all New England, valued at $45,750,241.00. Iowa is a close second, with 1,331,888; while Illinois comes third, with 1,072,473.

The average price of milch cows is now lower than at any time for the past ten years, but it is well to observe that this is not exceptional, since cattle generally have fallen off much more, and swine a little more, than have milch cows.

If we take the highest average prices of cows, cattle, and swine attained any time during the past ten years and compare them with the prices on January 1st, 1890, we find that cattle are worth only 65 per cent, swine 70 per cent, and milch cows 71 per cent, so that cows have not suffered unusual depression.

If we compare the three states of New York, Illinois, and Iowa, which alone have almost exactly one quarter of all the cows in the whole United States and territories, which states also surpass all others in the aggregate value of their leading farm crops, Illinois and Iowa alone exceeding New York in this respect, owing to their larger acreage, as will appear when we consider that the average acreage value of the leading farm crops of New York was in 1886 $12.60, while in Illinois it was $8.30, and in Iowa $7.30 (differences due mainly to distance from market); a ratio of 100, 65.9, and 57.9, while the average value of cows in January, 1890, was: New York, $28.11; Ohio, $24.80; Iowa, $19.79, or in the ratio of 100, 88.2, and 70.4, so that relatively it would appear that the value of cows in Ohio and Iowa was more than kept up.

WHAT HAS SCIENCE DONE FOR AGRICULTURE?

Let us take a hasty retrospective glance and see what science has already done for agriculture, and watch me close, lest I claim too much, since upon this basis of accomplished facts I rest my claim that these are really but the first fruits — promises only of the abundant blessings yet in store for agriculture.

Consider that agricultural science has, we might almost say, had its birth within the lives of most of us; certainly its development during the past twenty-five years surpasses all that had been accomplished for as many centuries. Why, fifty years ago, even, a prize problem of the Gottingen academy was whether mineral matter was neccessary to the life and development of the plant. Consider, if you can, the condition of agricultural science while such a fundamental question was a matter of doubt? And what followed the solution of that question? At the least $100,000,000.00 worth of this mineral matter is manufactured and sold annually, the direct result of a positive answer to that question. In New York state alone fully $4,000,000.00 worth of these so-called commercial fertilizers are annually sold. Every isle of the sea, every corner of the earth has been ransacked; the bleaching bones on the plains of the west have been gathered up; the catacombs of Egypt have been rifled, of their mummies; the very dung of reptiles extinct million of years ago, preserved as fossils in the rocks of the earth, all have contributed to supply the enormous and steadily increasing demand for this plant food.

But more than this. If to-day a chemist should carefully burn a sample of wheat grown, whether in Dakota or New York, England or the Crimea, India or Australia, and should find very much more or less than a fiftieth of its weight in ash or mineral matter, he would instantly review his work, confident that an error had been made; more, even, than this, should he find this ash to contain very much more or less than 31 per cent of potash or 46 per cent of phosphoric acid, he would be a bold man who would venture to publish such analysis without very careful revision. And what is true of wheat has been found true of the other products of the farm.

AGRICULTURAL EXPERIMENT STATIONS.

You are doubtless aware that the first agricultural experiment station was established at Moeckern, in Saxony, in 1851, and that since that time, so valuable have they proved themselves to be, that they have been multiplied with great rapidity in nearly every state of Europe, and in the German empire alone there are reported 184, devoting themselves to the investigation of every branch of agriculture.

The first established in this country was in Connecticut, in 1875.

What have they done of value, do you ask? Let me recall to your memory Liebig, to whom agricultural science is, perhaps, more indebted than to all who preceded him. You may some of you remember how, in 1840, he said that "guano contains not only the mineral elements of food, but serves to quicken their action and shorten the time required for their assimilation;" and it was in that same year that he suggested the manufacture of super-phosphates by the use of sulphuric acid. Now mark the date, for that very year, 1840, twenty casks of guano were imported into England, and within five years nearly 300,000 tons of this most valuable fertilizer were imported into Great Britain alone. And yet remember that this man was pre-eminently a book farmer, blessing the world by his researches in the laboratory and the practical conclusions which he drew from chemical analysis.

What else have the experiment stations done for agriculture, do you ask? In reply, I would say, without danger of contradiction, that there is hardly a quarter of a column in any of the agricultural papers of this or any other country of practical or scientific value to agriculture which is not based directly or indirectly upon the results which have been worked out in the experiment stations, either public or private. To-day the intelligent farmer and dairyman, and there are thousands of them, discuss the matters in which they are engaged in a language which was but a few years since an unknown tongue to them. Carbohydrates and albuminoids, German standards and nutritive ratio, close and open rations, digestion and nutrition — why, the ordinary discussions of to-day at any one of our institutes, dairy associations, farmers' clubs, and granges would have been wholly unintelligible twenty, or even ten, years ago, except to a very limited number.

But has science exhausted itself? Far from it. Take, as has been well said, that art which is to-day nearest perfection, and you will select the one which has fellowshipped most closely with science.

But I propose to speak upon the subject, "How Dairying May be Made More Profitable." Suppose some modern Croesus should to-day, and annually thereafter, go through the agricultural districts of our state and distribute $50,000,000.00 among the farmers of this state. That would be $132.00 to each of our farmers. Would we hear much about hard times among our farmers in such a case? One hundred and thirty-two dollars would pay taxes, buy a suit of clothes, and in very many cases turn depression into gladness. The difference between nothing and something is vastly greater than between something and a great deal. Well, we have these Croesuses here in this city, but they will not do this, and 'tis vastly better that they should not, even if they would. Our farmers should know, and they cannot too soon learn, that the remedy is within their own hands.

Let us take the dairy industry, which chiefly concerns us. The only statistics we have in this state, and they, upon examination, appear reliable, show that 1,284 cheese factories gave an average of 3,034 pounds of milk per cow. These factories received this milk from 407,810 cows, owned by 30,746 farmers, and it is doubtless true that these cows were upon the whole better than the average of cows in the state, since there would naturally be more or less intelligent rivalry among the patrons of a factory to secure the best results. But here are over one quarter of all the cows of the state giving only 3,034 pounds of milk per cow per annum.

Again, the Dairy Association of this state held thirty-nine conferences, where butter was made from the cream of seventy of the best dairies of the state. The average pounds of milk to a pound of butter was 21.17, while Dairy Commissioner Brown found in twenty-eight butter factories the average to be something over twenty-five pounds of milk for a pound of butter. Over 26 per cent of our cows, therefore, do not yield, upon an average, an annual amount of butter over 121 pounds, or 143 pounds if we assume the milk to have been as good as was supplied at these conferences, an assumption quite unwarranted.

Gentlemen, we will not here speak of the phenomenal yield which has recently been announced of 320 pounds of butter in ninety days, or assertion of 196 pounds 13 ounces in ninety days, other than to mention these as possibilities with some; but what shall we say of 121 pounds as an average for an entire year?

There are scores of herds scattered over the country which average fully 300 pounds of butter per cow. Of ten New York dairymen who have furnished me with the details of their work, there were three who turn their attention to the production of butter, and these three averaged per cow 363 pounds per annum — from 150 to 200 per cent more than the average of the state. I have but recently been looking over some records sent me, and find that one dairyman reports an average for three years, of his entire herd, which averaged ten cows each year, of 6,017 pounds of milk per annum per cow, an average of just twenty pounds of milk per day, and averaging 303 days in milk; another, for ten years, averaging thirteen and one-half cows per year, averages 6,310 pounds of milk per cow; while another, for ten years, averaging eight cows a year, receives an average of 6,986 pounds of milk per cow. While such results are gratifying as evidence of what is being done right along year after year, we all know that these results are by no means rare, although attained by a very small fraction of our dairymen.

First. Then, as to how dairying may be made more profitable, I would say, improve the quality of the cows. Weed out, by careful selection, the thousands, yes, hundreds of thousands, even in this state of New York, of worthless cows; yes, worse than worthless cows. "I cannot afford to keep a cow which will not give more than 200 pounds of butter a year," writes an intelligent and prosperous dairyman to me. Well, who can, we may ask? And yet at least 25 per cent of the cows of New York are averaging 121 pounds of butter, or its equivalent, per year.

"Well, how do you tell which are the good cows?" finally was asked me by a gentleman with whom I had been riding two hours in the cars, engaged in discussing this important matter, and this gentleman was Vice-President of one of the leading dairy associations of the country, but this was several years ago. He knows now, and for years has known, how to learn the relative value of the members of his herd. I have already given you his carefully ascertained statistics. No merchant or banker now more carefully conducts his business, and his results prove that it has paid him.

Now this first point is one of very great importance, gentlemen, as we all know. As evidence, let me give you some recent results as ascertained at our station. In our herd we have two cows, both recently in milk, and I question whether at auction the one would bring $5.00 more than the other. They are both beautiful animals.

These cows are side by side in their stalls, receiving the same good care, the same food, and the same quantities of food, but one gave during a week's trial 55.4 per cent more milk and 44.8 per cent more butter than did the other. Upon a second trial, with a change of ration, the one gave 65.6 per cent more milk and 72.1 per cent more butter than the other; and upon still a third trial, one gave 73.9 per cent more milk and 66.7 per cent more butter than did the other.

Upon a fourth trial the one gave 71.8 per cent more milk and 84 per cent more butter, and, finally, upon the fifth and last trial, the one gave 64.2 per cent more milk and 74.5 per cent more butter.

The average of the five trials shows that one gave 66.2 per cent more milk and 68.4 per cent more butter than did the other.

Now you may ask why, then, do we keep this poorer cow? and I would say that I am not as yet certain that she is not a source of profit. But if only the lesson she has taught us could be impressed upon all our dairymen, that cow has been worth her weight in gold, and may be well kept to a good old age as a "horrible example."

Granting that the poorer of these cows barely pays her cost of keeping, it needs no argument to prove that as a source of profit the other is a thousand times more valuable. But can anybody doubt that every herd of cows in the state, whether of one breed or another, or of no breed, will show even greater difference than those found by us in these two cows?

These facts must be impressed upon our dairymen, and when they are fully understood it will result in an increase of millions and millions of dollars annually to the products of our dairy industry, and revolutionize the agriculture of the state.

Second. How may dairying become more profitable? I have already referred to the ten leading dairymen, whose results are most gratifying; but, as will be seen, they are mainly turning their attention to the securing of large returns with less care as to the economy of production. That will receive their attention later, let us hope.

Well, now, one of these ten feeds his cows a daily ration costing 28 cents per cow; while another, getting practically as good results, feeds a ration costing 14 cents per cow per day — the feed of one costing exactly 100 per cent more than the feed of the other. But a saving of 1 cent a day upon the dairy cows of New York is over $15,000.00 daily, nearly $6,000,-000.00 a year. But here is a difference between our most intelligent dairymen of 14 cents a day. Still another feeds a ration costing $31\frac{1}{2}$ cents a day, or 125 per cent greater.

Gentlemen, I will not stop long to emphasize the importance of this matter. Each for himself may estimate the enormous saving which may be effected without any reduction in the amount of products simply by careful attention to the compounding of well-balanced rations of those foods which may be fed with the greatest economy. It is no exaggeration, but literal truth, to say that there are millions in it — millions!

Third. How may dairying be made more profitable? Avoid, so far as we may, an over-stocked and glutted market, first, by ceasing to make a product which nobody wants at any season of the year — and that fairly describes about three-fifths of our dairy products.

Why, to-day there is being served upon the tables of this city butter of such varied quality that, to any one who in the dark could tell a bunch of roses from a jimson weed, there is a difference of a thousand, yes, of ten thousand, per cent in quality alone.

I was dining at one of the hotels in Boston with a friend during the last Bay State Fair, when my attention was called to the exceeding excellence of the butter upon the table; and when an hour later I was looking over the dairy exhibit at the fair, I found that this peculiar excellence which arrested my friend's attention was by the judges allowed, as I remember, fifty points out of a possible one hundred.

Having, then, improved the quality of your products, place them upon the market when the best product brings the best prices. All are not going into winter dairying, and there is room for many thousand dairymen to enter this field without much crowding.

The silo continues to grow in favor, but still has doubting Thomases, whom apparently nothing will convince. Well, in explanation it may be said that there is even now ensilage and ensilage; and I doubt not you will be interested to learn of our experience at the experiment station at Geneva, and I think I may safely say that the work of the station has established beyond question the immense practical value of the silo. During the past season careful digestion experiments were made with orchard grass, and it was found that the animals digested an average of 314 pounds of each 2,000 pounds of fresh orchard grass fed them; and a recently concluded experiment has shown that of the corn ensilage which is now being fed at the station the animals digest of each 2,000 pounds fed them 296 pounds, or a fraction less than 95 per cent of the amount obtained from orchard grass, and that the amounts of nitrogeneous matter, fats, and carbohydrates in both ensilage, as made at the station, and fresh orchard grass are practically the same, so that our dairymen may, if they will, carry their animals through the winter upon rations which are practically the same as those of summer, when our meadows and pastures are at the best.

This is so important a matter that I venture to give somewhat in detail the results of the actual digestion experiments with the cows in the experiment with fresh orchard grass and our corn ensilage.

The corn was King Phillip, and it was planted and cultivated precisely as though intended as a grain crop, and was cut up for the silo at the time when ordinarily it would have been cut up and placed in shocks for future husking. At present, by actually weighing out one hundred pounds of the ensilage and carefully picking out the half inch pieces of ears and any loose kernels, it is found that thirty pounds of the one hundred consists of grain and cob.

The following percentage analyses give the composition of the fresh orchard grass and of corn ensilage as now fed at the station at Geneva:

	Water.	Ash.	Albuminoids.	Fiber.	Carbohydrates	Fats.	Total Dry Matter.
Orchard grass	71.48	2.14	2.65	10.23	12.29	1.21	28.52
Corn ensilage	77.85	1.16	1.88	5.73	12.46	.92	22.15

The following gives the percentages of the above constituents which were actually digested by the animals:

	Albuminoids.	Fiber.	Carbohydrates.	Fats.	Total Dry Matter.
Orchard grass	60.5	63.4	56.3	56.4	58.8
Corn ensilage	58.7	69.0	71.9	86.5	69.7

The following gives the pounds of each of the nutritive constituents actually digested by the animals in two thousand pounds of each food:

	Albuminoids.	Fiber.	Carbohydrates.	Fats.	Total.	Nutritive Ratio.
Orchard grass	32.0	129.8	138.4	13.6	313.8	1: 9.4
Corn ensilage	22.1	79.0	179.2	16.0	296.3	1:13.6

It will be seen that there was 94.4 per cent as much digested food in one ton of the ensilage as in the same amount of fresh orchard grass.

Fourth. What can be done to make dairying more profitable? We may greatly increase the fertility of our soils, and increase the production of our meadows and pastures, thus furnishing to our stock more abundant and more nutritious food. Now we need, certainly in New York state, feel no alarm about the exhaustion of our arable lands, for the statistics do not show it to be as yet appreciably great. Agricultural depression is rather due to the great fall in the prices of farm products rather than in diminished yield.

The following statistics, taken from a recent publication of the Geneva station, clearly set this forth so far as New York is concerned, and the same is true over larger areas of the country:

CHANGES IN YIELD AND VALUE OF FARM CROPS IN NEW YORK.

In the following tables I have given the average acreage yield in bushels or pounds of our leading crops in the state for the several periods, 1862 to 1870, inclusive, 1871 to 1879, inclusive, and 1880 to 1887, inclusive; also the average market value of these crops for the same period:

Average Acreage Yield of Leading Crops.

YEARS.	Corn.	Wheat.	Rye.	Oats.	Barley.	Buckwheat.	Potatoes.	Hay.	Tobacco.
1862–70,	30.20	14.93	15.15	30.32	22.33	19.77	103.1	2516.	918
1871–79,	32.94	14.87	13.91	32.96	22.14	18.42	81.7	2404.4	919
1880–87,	29.60	14.91	12.00	28.83	22.79	13.26	77.4	2225.	1383

Average Market Value of Leading Crops.

1862–70,	1.088	1.917	1.182	.652	1.240	.889	.63	15.211	.159
1871–79,	.698	1.364	.810	.428	.856	.708	.552	13.46	.11
1880–87,	.644	1.028	.718	.40	.746	.638	.52	12.495	.12

The following table shows the percentage changes which have taken place during these same periods in yield and market value:

Percentage Changes in Yield.

YEARS.	Corn.	Wheat.	Rye.	Oats.	Barley.	Buckwheat.	Potatoes.	Hay.	Tobacco.
1862–70,	100	100	100	100	100	100	100	100	100
1871–79,	109	99	92	109	99	93	79	96	100
1880–87,	98	100	79	95	102	67	75	88	151

Percentage Changes in Market Value.

YEARS.	Corn.	Wheat.	Rye.	Oats.	Barley.	Buckwheat.	Potatoes.	Hay.	Tobacco.
1862–70,	100	100	100	100	100	100	100	100	100
1871–79,	64	71	69	66	69	80	88	89	69
1880–87,	59	54	61	61	60	72	82	82	76

The above tables may be studied with interest, as helping to explain the causes which have produced such general depression in the agricultural community.

It will be seen that, so far as crop-production is concerned, there is little cause for alarm over diminished yield; for if we consider our five principal crops — corn, wheat, oats, potatoes, and hay, the aggregate value of which is 92 per cent of the total value of our leading farm crops — we shall find that these five crops had fallen off in their average yield but 1.6 per cent in the second period over what it was in the first period, and the average yield of the third period was within 8.8 per cent of what it was in the first; and this diminished yield is perhaps largely due to less careful cultivation, which the low prices of farm products seemed in many cases to excuse, if it did not justify.

But if we examine the table, we shall see that the average market values have greatly depreciated, the five crops already mentioned having fallen, during the second period, in their average market value to 75.6 per cent of what it was in the first period, and during the last period having dropped still lower, to an average of 67.6 per cent of what these crops sold for during the first period.

The average daily wages of farm laborers in thirty-six states for ten years have been as follows: Year 1879, wages 94 cents; year 1882, wages $1.07; year 1885, wages $1.05; year 1888, wages $1.06.

From the above it appears that the wages of farm laborers have remained nearly the same during the past ten years.

This remarkable shrinkage in the market values of agricultural products, while the cost of production remained practically constant, so far as the cost of farm labor goes, will alone account for the general complaint that farming has ceased to be profitable under existing conditions.

But in this connection it must not be forgotten that the productive power of manual labor upon the farm has been enormously increased during the past quarter of a century through the introduction upon the farm of labor-saving machinery of every description; and but for these appliances it would often appear impossible that the work of the farm at present could be accomplished.

While, therefore, the actual cost of manual labor remains practically the same, the results of such labor, aided by all these mechanical appliances, have been greatly increased, at the same time introducing a new item into the cost of production, viz., interest and wear and tear of all these implements of husbandry.

The following table gives in column first the average value of the leading farm crops of the state for the last twenty-six years according to the report of the department of agriculture.

The second column gives the number of bushels or pounds of each crop which could have been bought for $10.00, this being a convenient sum for comparison; and there is given, also, the number of pounds of ash or mineral matter, of phosphoric acid, potash, and nitrogen in these several quantities.

The estimate for milk is from the *American Agriculturist*, which gives 3.43 cents per quart as the average value to the producer of milk furnished New York City during the past twenty-one years:

	Average price.	Amount for $10.00.	Pounds ash.	Pounds nitrogen.	Pounds potash.	Pounds phosphoric acid.
Corn,	$0.816 per bus.	12.25 bus.	10.29	10.98	2.86	4.82
Wheat,	1.452 "	6.87 "	8.24	8.57	2.58	3.80
Rye,	.910 "	10.99 "	12.32	10.84	3.55	5.62
Oats,	.497 "	20.12 "	21.23	12.36	3.31	4.52
Barley,	.955 "	10.47 "	12.58	7.24	2.67	4.25
Buckwheat,	.749 "	13.35 "	8.97	9.23	2.07	4.37
Potatoes,	.569 "	17.58 "	43.26	3.38	26.35	7.92
Hay,	13.769 per ton.	1,452 pounds	83.49	24.46	22.79	4.34
Tobacco,	.126 "	79.37 "	12.86	2.14	4.61	.47
Milk,	.0343 per qt.	292 quarts.	4.40	4.40	1.07	1.88

The following table gives the market value of the several fertilizing constituents present in $10.00 worth of each of the leading crops:

	Nitrogen.	Potash.	Phosphoric acid.	Total.	Per cent of value of crop.
Corn,	2.09	.17	.39	$2 65	26.5
Wheat,	1.63	.16	.30	2 09	20.9
Rye,	2.06	.21	.45	2 72	27.2
Oats,	2.35	.20	.36	2 91	29.1
Barley,	1.38	.16	.34	1 88	18.8
Buckwheat,	1.75	.12	.35	2 22	22.2
Potatoes,	.64	1.58	.64	2 86	28.6
Hay,	4.65	1.37	.35	6 37	63.7
Tobacco,	.40	.28	.04	72	7.2
Milk,	.84	.06	.15	1 05	10 5

The practical lessons to be drawn from the above tables are very forcible, and cannot fail to carry conviction to any one who will carefully consider them. It appears that upon an average the cereals contain an amount of nitrogen, phosphoric acid, and potassium which, at the current market price for these materials, is worth almost exactly one-fourth the market value of the grain (24.1 per cent).

Potatoes contain somewhat more, 28.6 per cent of their average market value, while the hay crop contains nearly two-thirds (63.7 per cent) of its average market value. In other words, the farmer would have to pay for the potash, phosphoric acid, and nitrogen in $10.00 worth of hay $6.37.

It will be seen, also, that milk contains of these fertilizing constituents only 10.5 per cent of its value—less than one-half the value contained in the cereals, and less than one-sixth the value of these in the hay.

The practical conclusion is obvious: Increase the area and production of grass and hay, and feed it.

In view of the above facts, which cannot be controverted, I think I am safe in saying that during the past twenty-five years not one ton of hay out of a hundred has been sold by any farmer for a price at which he could afford to let it leave his farm.

In this connection there yet remains another all-important point, to which I beg leave to call your special attention. I spoke of increasing the fertility of our soils, and propose to show how this desirable result may be brought about.

Our experiments at Geneva have shown that even with growing animals not 6 per cent of the food consumed by them was retained, and in the case of four cows giving milk only 9¼ per cent of the food was utilized in the production of milk, so that it is safe to estimate that fully 90 per cent, upon an average, of all the fertilizing constituents of the food consumed by these animals was again returned, and if properly preserved may be used to maintain the productive capacity of the soil.

It was for the purpose of securing this invaluable product of the farm, as also in connection with the extended feeding experiments with the several breeds of cattle and swine, to provide the means by which the amount and value of this material could be accurately determined, that a method has been adopted by which it will appear to every one, even upon the most casual inspection, that every needed facility exists for the preservation of every pound and pint of manure.

Few, I think, even of our most intelligent farmers, fully appreciate the great importance of this matter.

In the case of eight animals, the aggregate amount daily of dry matter in the dung was 53.28 pounds. This contained, as the average of six of them, 2.025 per cent of nitrogen, or 1.08 pounds, which, at 19 cents per pound, was worth 20.49 cents; 1.75 per cent of phosphoric acid, or .93 pounds, which, at 8 cents per pound, was worth 7.46 cents; and .96 per cent of potash, or .51 pounds, which, at 6 cents a pound, was worth 3.07 cents; an aggregate for these three constituents of 31 cents, or $3\frac{7}{8}$ cents per day per cow.

There was also secured a daily aggregate of 108.7 pounds of urine from six of the animals, in which there was an average of 8.87 per cent of solids, 1.37 per cent of nitrogen, 1.337 per cent of potash, and a small quantity of phosphoric acid. This would give an aggregate average daily yield of 1.49 pounds of nitrogen, worth 28.31 cents; 1.453 pounds of potash, worth 8.72 cents, or aggregating daily 37 cents, or $6\frac{1}{8}$ cents for each animal. This, with the $3\frac{7}{8}$ cents already obtained, makes ten cents daily per animal. Now the market value of the daily rations fed seven of these animals was exactly $1.00, or 14.29 cents per cow, from which it is seen that the fertilizing constituents in the dung and urine equalled 70 per cent of the market value of the food fed.

The point which appears to be so clearly established by the above experiment is one of such great importance to our farmers that it will be the subject of more extended investigation in the future, for which we have excellent facilities; but at present it appears that the manure from fifty animals is worth yearly fully $1,834.00, even on as cheap a ration as 14.29 cents per day.

I hardly need to remind you, gentlemen, that the imperfect methods, even when any are adopted, for saving the most valuable portion are such that we may safely say that ninety-nine one-hundredths is wasted, and so careless are we of the remainder, that probably, upon an average, fully one-half of its fertilizing value is lost — leached away — before it is returned to the fields. But can any farmer who is keeping fifty head of cattle doubt that if he could afford annually to buy $1,500.00 worth of commercial fertilizers and apply them to his fields he would very speedily increase the productiveness of his lands? And yet, ten chances to one, this same person is allowing fully that value of fertilizing elements to go to waste.

Fifth. How may dairying be made more profitable? In my judgment, nothing will more speedily bring about this result than that our dairymen should conduct their business upon business principles. Go into any of the countless shops of this city and ask the proprietors if they know what their groceries, their dry goods, their hardware, of which they are selling millions of dollars worth yearly — ask these men if they know what these things cost them. Why, they would thin you either in jest, or recently escaped from an asylum for the insane. Know? of course they know.

And yet the dairymen of New York State, with nearly, if not quite, $400,000,000.00 of capital invested in their business — well, let them speak for themselves, for I might do them injustice. I recently sent out about 1,500 circulars into every section of the state, asking for information which every dairyman should have been able to give. I received some twenty-five responses, and these, as I of course expected, in many particulars imperfect. Let me read a letter which I received along with one of the replies, for it covers the whole ground:

"*Dr. Collier* — DEAR SIR: Enclosed I send you one of the New York dairy statistics, if it is not too late to be of any use. I had this filled out three months ago, but was waiting for one other blank to be filled, which I gave out. I have found one other man who will fill out one for me, and I will send that and another as soon as I get them, but I find on inquiry that there is not one man in a hundred of the average farmers that knows anything about what his cows eat, or how much it costs to keep them, nor anything about how much butter or milk his cows yield in the course of a year. In fact, they don't know anything about his cows, except that they feed them something and get some milk and butter. But I sincerely hope we may see a change in the management of cows for profit, and that the time will come when farmers will keep a record of their cows, and know when they get a profit for what they feed.

"I see by your last bulletin, No. 18, that you have commenced to get together a number of animals for the purpose of testing the dairy breeds of cattle, and as we are a good deal interested in the success of the undertaking, we hope to see you succeed.   Yours respectfully,

"————."

Now, gentlemen, tell me whether in this city, or in any city, or in any place on this whole round earth, there is to be found successful business conducted under the conditions stated by this correspondent? If it is not blasphemous, which I hardly question, to pray even for success in such a case, is it not at least supreme folly to hope to secure it?

And just here pardon me for a moment of fault-finding. In reference to one of our recent bulletins giving the results which thus far we have obtained in feeding the young cattle we have under experiment, the editor of the *Holstein-Friesian Register* was pleased to say that "this report is of more than ordinary interest to breeders of cattle," but he adds, evidently by way of a friendly criticism, that "this book of tables requires the most careful study, for at least a day, for the reader to begin to obtain an idea of its contents and teachings."

In reply, I would say, and I presume my friend the editor is present, why bless you, my dear man, do you not remember the case of the Irishman, who, after a prolonged absence, was revisiting the old country, and being shown the great changes and improvements which had taken place during his absence, when at last having had pointed out a new church just completed, he exclaimed, "Well, that beats the very divil!" when his companion replied: "Ah, Pat, me boy, that was the very intintion."

Here is a bulletin confessedly crammed with information of the greatest practical value to our dairymen, whose capital is invested in, and whose labor is given to, this industry; but for the dairyman to possess himself of this valuable information "it requires the most careful study for at least a day." Again I ask, is there any business which can be successfully conducted if but a day is given to the careful study of the fundamental principles which govern it? Think of the intense study and thought which, not for one day, but for every day in the year, is given by the business and professional men of this city to the details of their work. We hear much said about the necessity that more of brain and less of hand labor be put into the work of the farm, and yet a protest arises — friendly it is true, but none the less a protest — because the dairyman is called upon to devote two or three of these long winter evenings to a careful study of the principles of his business.

Think, too, of the effect upon our young men, who we hope to see devoting themselves to what Washington declared to be "the most noble, the most healthful, and the most useful occupation of man," if to them the impression is to be given that their lives are to be spent in a business demanding less of careful study and offering less reward for the highest exercise of their intellectual faculties than other fields of labor.

As for myself, after having spent many years of my life in intimate association with professional men, college professors, doctors of medicine, and scientists, with many warm friends among the legal profession, and even among the clergy, I can truthfully declare that I know of no profession, occupation, or business which demands for its intelligent conduct and which offers greater rewards to careful study than does agriculture in its several branches; none more attractive to a man of well-rounded symmetrical intellectual and physical development, *totus teres atque rotundus*.

Finally, to those of our dairymen who desire — and who of them does not? — to make this industry more profitable, I would suggest that they can learn anywhere in the country how not to do it, but they must disregard all such testimony, for it is not helpful to the solution of the problem. You all recall the case of the darkey judge down south in those days of reconstruction, who dismissed the criminal under arrest for stealing chickens, for although two witnesses swore positively to having seen him enter the coop and come out with the chickens, his clever attorney, also colored, called in a dozen witnesses who swore that they had never seen him near the coop; and this balance of testimony appeared to be greatly in favor of the culprit in the opinion of the judge.

Let us prefer, rather, the course of Napoleon I., who was as great in agriculture as in war, and who declared that "agriculture is the basis and strength of all national prosperity." When he proposed to build the famous Simplon road across the Alps, and was ridiculed for the visionary project, he is reported to have made diligent inquiry among the mountaineers, and found at least two who had been over, and he thereupon declared that where two had been, twenty could go, and where twenty could go, he could carry his army. As a matter of fact that famous road was built and over it Napoleon marched his army into the plains of Piedmont. Gentlemen, the dairy industry of to-day is confronted with no obstacles comparable with an Alpine range barring the way to success, and hundreds may be found who have surmounted all these obstacles and are to-day rejoicing in the fruits of their achievements. Where these have gone, who may not follow? What these have done, who may not accomplish? Would it not be better, instead of looking to legislatures and congress for relief from burdens which are largely self-imposed, to see what we ourselves may do to lift this burden from our shoulders? And we may by so doing be able to appreciate those words of the Roman poet: "*O, fortunatos nimium sua si bona norint, agricolas.*" Oh, too happy husbandmen, if only they were not ignorant of their blessings?

In conclusion, let me very briefly indicate the several points which I have sought to impress:

First. It is to science that agriculture is indebted for the wonderful advance she has made during the past half century; and those blessings are but an earnest of what science has yet in store, so soon as her methods become known and adopted.

Second. The experiment stations of the country are the pioneers blazing the way of advance along the lines which science shall indicate.

Third. The first duty of the dairyman is, by careful breeding and selection, to improve the quality of his cows and increase the quantity of their product.

Fourth. The character of food rations should be carefully studied as regards the quality and quantity of milk and the economy of its production.

Fifth. Produce and market your dairy products when they bring the best prices, and study the best methods by which their quality may be improved.

Sixth. Increase the fertility of your lands by carefully saving the manure, and increase the production and acreage of grass and hay, and feed it, selling only those products of the farm which contain fertilizing elements of least value.

Seventh. Remember that it is decrease in price, rather than of production, which largely causes the present depression, and that greater economy of production is the only apparent escape from the present condition of affairs.

Eighth. Conduct your business upon business principles. Keep an account of your fields and your herds.

Ninth. Study carefully the fundamental principles of your business, and be not satisfied with other than a practical understanding of the matter. Vague impressions are of no value.

Tenth. Carefully investigate the methods and practices of those who are most successful, for you have no time to waste upon those who fail, other than to learn by comparison the cause of their failure.

A MEMBER: I would like to ask the professor if he would kindly go on and tell us how he preserved the urine?

DR. COLLIER: Our way may not be the most economical, but the main thing was to show how great the saving was. I think the principle a good one, though the method may not be; but I have told the board of our station — I have told the legislature that if they would make the appropriation to provide the means, that it would pay its full cost every year. We are saving practically over $1,500 a year. I got the idea from a cattle-farm in Bohemia. They had a paved concrete platform, and on the edges of it were gutters, and at each corner of this platform were large reservoirs — cisterns — so that any rains that fell on the manure which was on this platform, or any leachings, would run into these cisterns, and while we were there we saw a man forcing this liquid up on the top of the manure so as to keep it from burning. Now that is practically what we have. Instead of the cisterns at the corners, we have actually a platform of cobblestones and grout and cement, the area of which is thirty-six by one hundred feet. It is about eight inches deep; that is, there is a flanging edge of four feet, so that it will hold about six inches of water. Within two inches of the overflow there are traps which allow any liquid, or rain-water, for that matter, to run into the reservoirs, which are built under the platform, built before the platform was built. Now, in connection with these three reservoirs — we have one at each end, and one in the middle, connected by vitrified tile — in the first one we have vitrified tile running up to a perfectly tight gutter behind our animals, and the floor of our pig-pens is slightly inclined, and under the partition separating two pens is a slot an inch and a half wide, and under this slot there is built in the cobblestone and cement a broad shallow trough that runs out and goes into a vitrified tile system, and connects with it, so that the washing of the pens and the liquid manure is all saved to us.

Mr. W. BROWN SMITH: Mr. President, if I may be allowed, I would like to ask the doctor a question. It may be a simple one, but the thought occurred to me when the doctor spoke of orchard grass in regard to corn. The question is this: Allowing the ground to be equally rich, and in the same condition, which of the four crops — orchard grass, timothy, clover, or corn — gives the largest amount of feeding value?

Dr. Collier: I won't pretend to answer the question, because I hate to guess; but I should think that the corn would do so. But the point that I wished to bring out was the great value of this ensilage, that many think is not of much value, and then, that it has a fair comparison even with orchard grass.

Mr. W. Brown Smith: Do you consider that equal to timothy or clover?

Dr. Collier: Well, I do not like to guess; and we haven't the comparison.

Mr. W. Brown Smith: You know what everybody else thinks, don't you?

Dr. Collier: I do not know. There has been a great deal of conflicting testimony about ensilage, and that is the reason why I introduced this. We are just at this present moment feeding some animals on timothy hay for the purpose of an exact experiment in regard to its relative value. I am sorry I cannot give that, but of course we have in one sense just begun.

Mr. Yeomans: I would like to ask the doctor one question. I would ask what method he has for preventing the poisonous gases of those cesspools into which his pipes run from the barn from escaping back into the barn for his cattle to breathe?

Dr. Collier: In the first place, there is absolutely no protection for that; but I think that if there was any trouble of that sort we should have recognized it. We hose out those falls quite often, and it is washed out. More than that, we have had three occasions to empty these cisterns; and then we have a wind-mill that is connected with one of these cisterns which is to pump the liquid from these reservoirs into a tank, from which we may load our cart and carry it to the fields, or draw it over by a hose and wet down this pile on the platform. We have really not yet tried it, to be perfectly frank, to such an extent as to know what the effect would be during the summer.

Mr. Yeomans: I have great fears it will be a question you will realize in future years. To explain: We rented a barn fixed on the same plan that you suggest; for some little time we supposed our cattle were doing finely, but one morning as we were turning out the cattle one cow dropped down dead without any apparent cause. The next night another dropped down dead in the same way, and on third day another one. By that time the people began to get alarmed, and on examination we found that the trouble probably came from the cesspools. The cattle were removed, the cesspool was abandoned and the pipes taken out, and the drops fixed to take up all the liquid, and we put in absorbents, and it was the last trouble we had, and the best scientists showed us that our trouble came from that cause.

Mr. E. A. POWELL: There is a difference in standing in a filthy place, and getting the odors from the cesspool.

DR. COLLIER: Do you think, Mr. Powell, there will be any trouble in putting an ordinary V trap to prevent that? We have, of course, the ventilators to these cisterns open at the top.

Mr. E. A. POWELL: It is a question whether you can have traps to work that way. It may possibly be done.

DR. COLLIER: We have several in our system of tile drains; we have several traps. If anything happens we can go from one end to the other of our tile drain, and from trap to trap, and examine it; and it is flushed out.

Mr. E. A. POWELL: If it is thoroughly ushed out, that is a protection for that.

DR. COLLIER: I should think that the V trap, with the liquid that runs through it, would prevent any fermentation taking place in it. There is another point: We have over these reservoirs at least a thirty inch square man-hole, and this pipe is a four inch glazed tile, and it goes at least, I should say, sixty to seventy-five feet before it reaches the cattle. The cisterns are ventilated by the man-hole at the top. It has a door which we could open if we choose. Then, our stables are well ventilated. We have several ventilating shafts; and, indeed, there is a standing order that they must be kept so that there is nothing at all offensive even to a man when he comes in there.

Mr. E. A. POWELL: I believe the poisonous vapors are not offensive.

DR. COLLIER: At any rate I am glad that Mr. Powell has called attention to that.

Mr. EDGAR HUIDEKOPER: I would like to ask one question. I think the speaker stated that he found in comparison of the corn ensilage with orchard grass, that the corn ensilage was deficient, in having too much water. I would like to ask how he makes up that deficiency. Another question that I would like to have answered, and that is whether he has tried oats as ensilage, and whether that would make up any deficiency in the foreign ration?

DR. COLLIER: I do not think oats would. That is, you mean as ensilage?

Mr. EDGAR HUIDEKOPER: As ensilage.

DR. COLLIER: You misunderstand that. There is not a very great difference between the orchard grass and the corn ensilage. I want to state it exactly as it was. There was always the same amount of the various kinds of feed in the ensilage as in the orchard grass, but the ratio is a little wider — more open with the corn than with the orchard grass, and the orchard grass is too wide anyway; but we corrected both by putting in bran, as the simplest method.

Mr. EDGAR HUIDEKOPER: Then would not oats ensilage help to correct that?

DR. COLLIER: I do not know what the composition of oats ensilage is. I do not think it would vary much from orchard grass. I do not know whether it would vary from corn. It depends upon it's analysis. The matter of the water in ensilage was, to explain, why with a greater percentage of it being digestible we did not get more digestible matter out of it than out of the same weight of orchard grass, and that was because there was more water in the ensilage than in the grass; but of the total dry matter of the ensilage, a larger percentage was digested than of the dry matter digested in the orchard grass.

Mr. C. E. RANDALL: The professor has compared orchard grass, which is not known to many. Orchard grass as cut green with cured ensilage in winter. When we feed ensilage in winter we cannot compare it with orchard grass to any advantage. We must compare it with what we feed in winter, which is hay; and there there is a disproportion. It is alarming to believe that we don't believe in ensilage, when we take two tons to an acre, and you figure how many tons of ensilage you can raise on that acre. On my farm I estimate the feeding value of one ton of ensilage, of one acre of ensilage, to be equal to the feeding value of at least six acres in hay. That is bringing it down to the way we feed. In other words, you can raise twenty tons of ensilage on good land, and it is somewhere between two and three tons of ensilage to a ton of hay in feeding value.

Mr. James Neilson moved that a vote of thanks be tendered to Dr. Collier for his important address, and the motion was put, and carried.

On motion, the meeting adjourned.

THOMAS B. WALES, *Secretary.*

MEETING OF THE BOARD OF OFFICERS

OF THE

HOLSTEIN-FRIESIAN ASSOCIATION OF AMERICA,

Held at the Fifth Avenue Hotel, New York, N. Y.,
Tuesday, March 18th, 1890.

The meeting was called to order by President Edgar Huidekoper at 3 P. M.

Present: Edgar Huidekoper, D. H. Burrell, W. Brown Smith, G. D. Wheeler, C. W. Horr, C. R. Payne, Martin L. Sweet, W. G. Powell, T. G. Yeomans, and Thomas B. Wales.

The following gentlemen were unanimously elected to membership:

ALEXANDER FORBES,	Eureka, California.
FRANK H. BURKE,	Menlo Park, California.
R. H. ALLEN,	Chatham, New Jersey.
F. A. POTH,	Philadelphia, Pennsylvania.
W. H. S. FOSTER,	Fostoria, Ohio.
GUY C. BARTON,	Omaha, Nebraska.
WILLARD S. MORSE,	Denver, Colorado.
WILLIAM H. BUSH,	Denver, Colorado.
A. S. GARRITSON,	Sioux City, Iowa.
FRANK STORRS,	White Plains, New York.
C. H. WARREN,	Verona, New York.
GEORGE B. REED,	New York, New York.

The application for membership of the Michigan Public School was referred to a committee composed of Messrs. Horr, Yeomans, Smith, Burrell, and Wales, as some doubt was entertained whether under our present charter such an institution could be admitted. The entire Board expressed a strong desire that the institution be accepted if it were possible. The Secretary was instructed to explain the matter to the Superintendent fully.

A communication was read from D. E. Smith, Esq., President of the Dominion Holstein-Friesian Association, asking if the Holstein-Friesian Association of America would establish a branch in Canada, and if so, upon what terms. A communication was also read from A. Gifford, Esq., Secretary of the same association, asking that the fees for the registy of bulls be reduced.

After careful consideration the Board decided that no branch of the Holstein-Friesian Association of America should be established in Canada, and the Secretary was requested to so advise the Dominion Holstein-Friesian Association.

The report of the Committee on the Bonds of the Treasurer, Secretary, and Superintendent of Advanced Registry was made by Chairman Watkin G. Powell, who stated said bonds had been approved.

On motion of C. W. Horr, it was voted that the President of the Association be custodian of the bonds of the Treasurer, Secretary, and Superintendent of the Advanced Registry.

On motion of Mr. C. W. Horr, the Secretary was instructed to authorize Mr. S. Burchard to secure a steer for the New York Experiment Station from the herd of William M. Singerly, of Philadelphia. Motion amended by W. Brown Smith giving Burchard authority to secure such steer from any herd at not over beef price. Motion passed as amended.

The request of Messrs. J. B. Dutcher & Son that five registered animals be registered under new names was granted, provided the animals were entitled to the names proposed, and on the payment of the fees called for by the by-laws of the Association.

The Board unanimously agreed to recommend to the Association that all fees for the registry and for the transfer of animals in the Herd-Book remain as now called for in the by-laws; also that the bounty for the slaughter and castration of bull calves remain the same as at present.

The Board fixed the salaries of the officers of the Association, for the ensuing year, the same as paid last year.

Adjourned to 8:30 A. M., March 19th, 1890.

THOMAS B. WALES,
Secretary.

ADJOURNED MEETING OF THE BOARD OF OFFICERS.

Held March 19th, 1890, at 8:30 A. M.

Present: Messrs. Huidekoper, Wheeler, Frye, Burrell, Horr, Smith, Sweet, Payne, Powell, Hoxie, and Wales.

Mr. F. L. Houghton was heard in relation to the work of the *Holstein-Friesian Register*.

On motion of C. W. Horr, after a careful consideration of the entire subject, it was voted that the Board unanimously recommend the Association to appropriate the sum of $1,250.00 to increase the circulation of the *Holstein-Friesian Register*.

The Board then adjourned.

THOMAS B. WALES,
Secretary.

ANNUAL MEETING OF THE BOARD OF OFFICERS

OF THE

HOLSTEIN-FRIESIAN ASSOCIATION OF AMERICA,

Held at the Fifth Avenue Hotel, New York, N. Y.,
March 19th, 1890.

The meeting was called to order by President D. H. Burrell.

Present: Messrs. G. D. Wheeler, John A. Frye, C. W. Horr, C. R. Payne, Martin L. Sweet, W. G. Powell, W. B. Smith, J. B. Dutcher, L. T. Yeomans, S. Hoxie, and Thomas B. Wales.

On motion of Mr. C. W. Horr, a committee of three was appointed by the chair to recommend to the Board, at an adjourned meeting, a list of special premiums to be offered by the Association for the year 1890.

The committee named was C. W. Horr, C. R. Payne, John A. Frye.

The chair appointed a committee composed of L. T. Yeomans, S. Hoxie, and W. G. Powell to report to the Board at an adjourned meeting a plan for expending the $2,000.00 appropriated by the Association for the benefit of the *Holstein-Friesian Register*.

On motion of Mr. S. Hoxie, duly seconded, the following persons were elected Inspectors of Advanced Registry and of Imported Cattle for the ensuing year:

O. P. CHAPMAN,	Wellington, Ohio.
S. BURCHARD,	Hamilton, New York.
S. N. WRIGHT,	Elgin, Illinois.
J. C. POOR,	North Andover, Massachusetts.
CAREY R. SMITH,	Santa Ana, California.
H. B. DAGGETT,	Hampton, Iowa.
J. R. BEUCHLER,	Leesburg, Virginia.
J. L. STONE,	Waverly, Pennsylvania.
A. R. STURTEVANT,	Springboro, Pennsylvania.
A. BRADLEY,	Lee, Massachusetts.
H. D. WARNER,	Lanesville, Connecticut.
W. A. ROWLEY,	Mt. Clemens, Michigan.
T. N. FIGUERS,	Spring Hill, Tennessee.
W. M. LIGGETT,	Benson, Minnesota.

Mr. Hoxie was authorized to name an inspector for Texas and adjoining states if necessary.

The committee appointed to examine the accounts of the Secretary reported through its chairman, Mr. J. B. Dutcher, that the accounts were found to be correct.

On motion, the report of the committee was accepted and the committee discharged.

The meeting then adjourned to meet at 7:30 P. M.

ADJOURNED MEETING OF THE BOARD OF OFFICERS.

The same members were present.

The Committee on the Appropriation for the *Holstein-Friesian Register* reported through its chairman, Mr. L. T. Yeomans, as follows:

"Your committee recommend the following, relative to the expenditure of the amount appropriated for subscriptions to the *Holstein-Friesian Register*:

"That each member of the Association be asked by circular-letter, to be issued by the Secretary, to forward to Mr. Houghton within sixty days the names of forty dairymen to whom the member wishes the *Register* sent for three months, and informed if such list is not received by Mr. Houghton within sixty days, names will be procured from other sources.

"*First.* Mr. Hougton shall furnish for three months two thousand five hundred copies of the *Register* to names from his private list of dairymen.

"*Second.* Two thousand five hundred copies for the next three months to names furnished to him by members of the Association in response to the circular of the Secretary; provided that if the number of two thousand five hundred names shall not have been received from the members of the Association, Mr. Houghton may make up such number from his private list of dairymen.

"*Third.* If not more than two thousand five hundred names have been received from members, the last preceding list shall be furnished for another period of three months, but names from members shall have preference over others.

"*Fourth.* Two thousand five hundred copies for the last three months to names to be furnished by Mr. D. H. Burrell and Mr. C. W. Horr, and any deficiency in this list may be made up from the private list of Mr. Houghton.

"The Association shall pay Mr. Houghton for each copy furnished for an entire year the sum of 80 cents. Mr. Houghton shall forward all letters and the lists to the Secretary, accompanied by a certificate of the number of copies furnished, and the Secretary shall give Mr. Houghton, at the end of each quarter, an order on the Treasurer of the Association for the amount due him.

"Mr. Houghton shall print and mail to each person to whom a copy is thus furnished a circular-note informing him that the *Holstein-Friesian Register* is furnished to him free with the compliments of the Holstein-Friesian Association. The expense of printing and mailing such notices shall not exceed $100.00, to be paid by the Association.

"Respectfully submitted,

"L. T. YEOMANS,
"S. HOXIE,
"W. G. POWELL, } *Committee.*"

On motion, the report was accepted.

The Committee of the Board on Special Premiums reported through its chairman, C. W. Horr, that in its judgment premiums should be offered as follows:

At each of the fairs below named the Holstein-Friesian Association of America will duplicate any premium won by a herd of registered Holstein-Friesian cattle offered by said fair, to the extent of $100.00 at each fair, provided a premium of not less than $50.00 is offered for herds of dairy breeds:

New England Fair, New York State Fair, Pennsylvania State Fair, Ohio State Fair, Michigan State Fair, Illinois State Fair, Minnesota State Fair, Iowa State Fair, California State Fair, St. Louis Exposition, Toronto Exposition. Also at the state fairs of the three other states owning the greatest number of Holstein-Friesian cattle not named above.

It was voted to adopt the report of the committee.

On motion of W. G. Powell, it was voted that when the Board adjourn it be to meet at Syracuse, New York, at 2 o'clock P. M. on the day previous to the meeting of the Association, and at such place in the city of Syracuse as may be named by the Secretary.

The committee appointed to examine the accounts of the Treasurer and the Superintendent of Advanced Registry reported through its chairman, C. E. Rumsey, that the accounts had been found correct.

It was voted that the report of the committee be accepted and the committee discharged.

The Committee on Bonds of the Treasurer, Secretary, and Superintendent of Advanced Registry reported through its chairman, W. B Powell, that the bonds furnished were found to be satisfactory, and recommended that the said bonds be placed with the President of the Association, as per vote of the Association.

The report of the committee was accepted and the committee discharged.

www.ingramcontent.com/pod-product-compliance
Lightning Source LLC
Chambersburg PA
CBHW020535300426
44111CB00008B/669